UNFLINCHING ZEAL

The Air Battles over France and Britain, May–October 1940

ROBIN HIGHAM

NAVAL INSTITUTE PRESS
ANNAPOLIS, MARYLAND

Naval Institute Press
291 Wood Road
Annapolis, MD 21402

Library of Congress Cataloging-in-Publication Data
Higham, Robin D. S.
  Unflinching zeal : the air battles over France and Britain, May–October 1940 / Robin Higham.
    p. cm.
  Includes bibliographical references and index.
    ISBN 978-1-61251-111-5 (hbk. : alk. paper) — ISBN 978-1-61251-112-2 (e-book) 1. World War, 1939–1945—Aerial operations, French. 2. Combat sustainability (Military science) 3. World War, 1939–1945—Campaigns—France. 4. Air power—France—History—20th century. 5. France. Armée de l'air—History—World War, 1939–1945. 6. Britain, Battle of, Great Britain, 1940. 7. Great Britain. Royal Air Force—History—World War, 1939–1945. 8. Germany. Luftwaffe—History—World War, 1939–1945. 9. World War, 1939–1945—Aerial operations, British. 10. World War, 1939–1945—Aerial operations, German. I. Title.
  D788.H55 2012
  940.54'4—dc23
                                                                              2012027965

♾ This paper meets the requirements of ANSI/NISO z39.48-1992 (Permanence of Paper).
Printed in the United States of America.
20 19 18 17 16 15 14 13 12   9 8 7 6 5 4 3 2 1
First printing

CONTENTS

TABLES AND ILLUSTRATIONS

Tables

Chapter 5

Chapter 6

Illustrations

ACRONYMS AND ABBREVIATIONS

AA	antiaircraft (Br.); for French, *see* DCA
AALMG	antiaircraft light machine guns (Br.)
AASF	Advanced Air Striking Force (Br.)
AC	Air Component; Army Cooperation (Br.)
ACBEF	Air Component of the British Expeditionary Force (Br.)
ACM	Air Chief Marshal (Br.)
ADGB	Air Defence of Great Britain
AHB	Air Historical Branch (Br.)
AIR	Air Ministry and RAF Records (Br.)
AOC	air officer commanding (Br.)
AOC-in-C	air officer commanding-in-chief (Br.)
AP	air publication (Br.)
ARP	air raid precautions (Br.)
A/SR	air/sea rescue service (Br.)
ASU	aircraft storage unit (Br.)
ATA	air transport auxiliary (Br.)
AVM	air vice marshal
BAFF	British Air Forces France, 1940
BCR	bombardement, combate et reconnaissance, bomber-combat-reconnaissance aircraft (Fr.)
BEF	British Expeditionary Force
BFI or BFW	Bayerische Flugzeugwerke; Bavarian Aircraft Works (Ger.)
BSA	Birmingham Small Arms (Br.)
C_3	command, control, and communications (Br.)
CAB	Cabinet (Br.)
CAS	chief of the Air Staff (Br.)
CD	confidential document (Br.)

CGSAF chef d'état majeur de l'Armée de l'Air; chief of the general staff air force (Fr.)

CIGS chief of the Imperial General Staff (Br.)

COS Chief of Staff (Br.); General der Stab (Ger.)

CQG grand quartier general; army field HQ (Fr.)

CRAS Centre de Réception des Avions de Series; Reception Center(s) for Production Aircraft (Fr.)

CRO Civilian Repair Organization (Br.)

DAT Défense Aérienne du Territoire; air defense of the territory (Fr.)

DCA *défense contre avions*; defense against aircraft (Fr.)

FAF Armée de l'Air; French air force (Fr.)

FFAF Forces libres français aérienne; Free-French air force (Fr.)

FLIVOS Fliegerverbindungsoffiziere; German air force liaison officer

FTAA Forces Terrestres Anti-Aerienne (Fr.)

GAF Luftwaffe; German air force

GAO Groupe Autonome d'Observation, Groupe Aérien d'Observation; air observation group (Fr.)

GB Groupement, Bombardement bomber group (Fr.)

GC *groupe chausseur*; fighter group(s) (Fr.)

GOC General Officer Commanding, Army (Br.)

GQG Grand Quartier Général; army field HQ (Fr.)

GQGA Grand Quartier Général Aérien; general headquarters of the Armée de l'Air in wartime (Fr.)

GSAF état major de l'Armée de l'Air; general staff air force (Fr.)

HDAF Home Defence Air Force (Br.)

HQ headquarters

IE initial establishment; number of aircraft Air Staff determined a unit would need (Br.)

JG *Jagdegeschwader*; fighter wing (Ger.)

KG Kampfgeschwader 100; Pathfinder force (Ger.)

kph kilometer per hour

LADA London Air Defence Area

LOC lines of communication

LQMG Luftquartiermeister General; Luftwaffe quartermaster general (Ger.)

MAC   Manufacture d'Armes de Châtellerault; French air force arsenal

Met'   meteorology, meteorological

MRAF   marshal of the Royal Air Force

MT   motor transport (Br.)

NCO   noncommissioned officer (Br., Ger.); *sous-officier* (Fr.)

OCA   offensive counterair (Br.)

OKH   Oberkommando des Heeres; high command of the army (Ger.)

OKW   Oberkommando der Wehrmacht; high command of the armed forces (Ger.)

ORB   Operations Record Book (Br.)

OTU   *Jagdlfliegerschuler*; operational training unit (Ger.)

OTU   operational training unit (Br.)

POL   petrol (gasoline), oil, lubricants (Br.) (Fr.)

PRO   Public Record Office, now The National Archives (Br.)

PRU   photo-reconnaissance unit (Br.)

PTT   Postes, Télegraphes et Téléphones; Public Administration of Postal and Telecommunication Services (Fr.)

PV   private venture (Br.)

QMG   Quartermaster General (Br.)

RAE   Royal Aircraft Establishment (Br.)

RAeS   Royal Aeronautical Society (Br.)

RAF   Royal Air Force (Br.)

RAFVR   Royal Air Force Volunteer Reserve (Br.)

RLM   Reichsluftministerium; national air ministry (Ger.)

RNAF   Royal Netherlands Air Force

R&O   reconnaissance and observation (Br.)

rpg   rounds per gun

rpm   rounds per minute, revolutions per minute

RSU   repair and salvage unit (Br.)

R/T   radio telephone (Br.)

SASO   senior air staff officer (Br.)

SD   secret document [e.g., *SD 98*] (Br.)

SHAA   Service Historique de l'Armée de l'Air; air force historical service (Fr.)

Sigint   signals intelligence (Br.)

TAF [TAC]   Tactical Air Force (Br.)

T-Amt   Technisches-Amt; technical directorate (Ger.)

TO   Technisches Amt; technical office (Ger.)

UAV   unmanned air vehicle

UHF   ultrahigh frequency (Br.)

W/T   wireless/transmission

ZI   Zone Interieur; zone of the interior (Fr.)

ZOAA   Zone d'Opérations les Alpes; air zone of operations Alps (Fr.)

ZOAC   Zone d'Opérations Central; air zone of operations central (Fr.)

ZOAE   Zone d'Opérations Est; air zone of operations east (Fr.)

ZOAN   Zone d'Opérations Nord; air zone of operations north (Fr.)

ZOAS   Zone d'Opérations Sud; air zone of operations south (Fr.)

ZOAW   Zone d'Opérations Ouest; air zone of operations west (Fr.)

ZONE   Zone d'Opérations Nord-Est; air zone of operations northeast (Fr.)

PREFACE

The Battle of France opened on 10 May 1940. The Allies—France, Britain, the Netherlands, and Belgium—kept to French Army General Maurice Gamelin's plan to fight forward and not in France, and thus they surged toward the Dyle River in Belgium. As they moved eastward out of their prepared positions, the Germans struck through the Ardennes region and seized the crossing of the Meuse at Sedan in France. The Luftwaffe (German air force) gained air superiority and let the Panzers loose to reach the English Channel and surround the Franco-British forces in the northeast Dunkirk pocket. The declining events led finally to the Franco-German armistice, which went into effect on 24 June, after the British had earlier evacuated from Dunkirk.

Unflinching Zeal originated as a stand-alone sequel to a previous book, *Two Roads to War: The French and British Air Arms from Versailles to Dunkirk*, a comparative study of the growth of French and British airpower up to the summer of that year. This current work evolved from my curiosity as to whether or not the Armée de l'Air (French air force) of 1940, given all the handicaps under which it had come into being and developed, was capable of destroying the 1,000 Luftwaffe aircraft it claimed. To unravel that query I applied knowledge of the Royal Air Force in the Battle of Britain, and also of the Luftwaffe in the campaigns of 1940, and I initially came to the conclusion that in reality the French claim could not have been far more than 232 Luftwaffe aircraft destroyed.

Then, during the months in which my manuscript sat untouched as I worked on *Two Roads*, I had obtained access to Paul Martin's 1990 work, *Invisible Vainquers,* and Peter Cornwell's 2008 *Battle of France Then and Now.*[1] Both authors provided carefully researched statistics that gave the Armée de l'Air credit for every aircraft brought down, and Cornwell mentioned how well the Armée de l'Air appeared to have held up. Tabulating from Martin's count of 400 and Cornwell's tally of 369, I used the average of 384. From that I reached two important conclusions: (1) that my own estimate of 232 was too low, and (2) that the *chasseur* more than doubled the sorties-to-kill ratio of the RAF and Luftwaffe: 36.5 compared with 15.5 of the French.

The Armée de l'Air, in spite of all the odds and in spite of ultimate defeat, did succeed in shooting down about 384 enemy aircraft in the forty-two-day Battle of France. If the sortie-to-kill ratios are valid, this then reflects the experience of my estimated average 750-hour *chasseur* (fighter pilots) versus the much fewer, 150-some hours, of newly fledged RAF fliers who joined a squadron. And yet, granting that all of the above is true—and *despite* the fact that all of the above may be true—the June 1940 Battle of France was not a success. In the final analysis the Germans won because the French Armée de Terre was defeated. Conclusions drawn out of the historical record indicate that the Armée de l'Air Haut Commandement (High Command) felt compelled to substantiate and elaborate the role—creating perhaps a "myth"—of the Armée de l'Air in order to deflect the French army accusations of Armée de l'Air blame for the overall debacle. This elaboration had aimed to preserve the morale of the Armée de l'Air, which was by then part of the Vichy regime, and shift the culpability for its defeat onto armée and civilian political shoulders.

Unflinching Zeal explores a number of themes of the two major air campaigns of 10 May–31 October 1940, the Battle of France and the Battle of Britain:

1. Research and development

2. The doctrine and tactics employed

3. The C3—Command, Control, and Communications—systems, and the personalities of the commanders and their experience

4. The logistical systems and their effectiveness, including salvage and repair

5. The training and skill, as well as the experience, of the pilots

6. The equipment the pilots had to use

7. Accident rates and causes

8. The veracity of claims

9. Conclusions and lessons to be drawn from the campaign

With regard to the air Battle of France, the intent herein is to show that despite certain statistical positives, the conflict was lost because it was chaotic, ad hoc, and ill-directed. As a consequence of lack of doctrine and poor preparations in aircraft development, production, testing, and delivery the Armée de l'Air was manned in many cases by a poorly trained insufficient coterie of professional pilots (despite those with 750 or more flight hours logged) supported by far too small numbers of quickly fatigued ground crew, with inadequate replacements available. Critical as well to the situation were the French failures post–World War I to foresee a different modern war and to establish the role of the Armée de l'Air in grand strategy, and then to obtain the funds and industrial facilities to enable the Armée de l'Air to fulfill that assignment. Post–World War I, the settled French grand strategy for a potential new war was focused on maintaining a defensive position for several years to gain time to mobilize fully France's own and French allies' resources while exhausting the enemy's. The end result was an air force that even with British aid could not meet the challenge of the German Luftwaffe. The Armée de l'Air, on the whole, was an aviation force whose claims were patently unrealistic.

The assertion that the Armée de l'Air was undefeated in the Battle of France was generated in July 1940 by the French Armée de l'Air Haut Commandement and bolstered by the creation of aces and the propaganda that the small force of *chasseur aérienne* (fighters), the *défense contre avions* (antiaircraft [DCA]), and the Royal Air Force together had destroyed those purported nearly one thousand German planes. In the fluid, unstable conditions of May 1940 France, victory claims were converted by Intelligence into assessments of enemy losses and strengths. It is important for the reader to remember that in air actions a rule of thumb is that if claims are divided by three or perhaps five, the result equals about what the opponent actually admits he lost. As in the case of the RAF at that time, when carefully investigated battlefield claims proved to be five times reality—only 19 percent being substantiated. General Lucien Robineau, former chef of the Service Historique de l'Armée de l'Air (air force historical service [SHAA]), has noted in a personal communication of 20 December 2008.[2]

> The practice was, not always but often, to count one victory for every flight member who had participated in the shooting down of one enemy aircraft. As a consequence, the number of victories could not match the actual number of aircraft shot down. This is the reason why one can find in some papers (sometimes hastily established following June 1940*) numbers ranging from 800 to over 1000.

However, General Robineau acknowledges that having met several of the French World War II aces and recorded their testimonies at the SHAA, he believes some of them were very "moderate and reliable in their memories." The ultimate "twisting" of the figures, then, must rest with the Haut Commandement itself.

---

*One of them (of July), bearing the signature of Chef d'état majeur de l'Armée de l'Air Mendigal by Vuillemin's order, has an annex with a false addition.

Air war is for the historian not so much the clash, success, or failure of small forces—especially in those days, as Marshal of the Royal Air Force (MRAF) Lord Tedder has noted, before the big battalions—as it is the discovering of forces and patterns having their roots in the past. Victory in 1940 could be achieved in forty-six days, in fact, in France in May in four days—or, paradoxically, a stalemate could occur within sixty-six, as in the Battle of Britain. The Germans gained air superiority in the first four days in France, 10–14 May 1940. The Armée de l'Air fought on, but the battle was lost on the ground by the Armée de Terre, which had prepared for a 1918-style trench war and was flummoxed by the German blitzkrieg. The fundamental question remains: *Why was there a French failure?* The answers to that are in *Two Roads to War.*

One of the interesting statistics that emerges from this story is that the Luftwaffe Quartermaster General issued more new aircraft during the campaign in the west than the Allies claimed to have destroyed. This discrepancy is explained by the German blitzkrieg philosophy of win now, salvage and repair later, and by the damage caused by rough French landing grounds. The German "lightning war" combined motorization of all weapons, with a close-support Luftwaffe and radio communications, but added to this is a dearth of information on Luftwaffe salvage operations. Some 22 percent of German aircraft production was in fact repaired machines. So without such a recovery service, aircraft production was insufficient.[3]

As this study shows, published numbers do not agree, and thus as noted I have chosen those that seem to me to be the most accurate. I hope readers will forgive me if the figures do not coincide with their beliefs or remembrances. The tables and illustrations herein are meant strongly to relate to the narrative in order to help explain the patterns of the air battles, to stress the logistics, and especially—in relationship to the Armée de l'Air—to show how it lacked the focus and the sinews for modern war. (In an attempt at consistency, I have, as noted above, chosen the figure of 384 Armée de l'Air victories. The figures presented on both the Royal Air Force and the Luftwaffe, as well as the text herein, emphasize the need for at least five years of preparation for an industrial war with its factories, testing and refinement, depots, transportation system, a field recovery, and a repair system. But what the tables and figures cannot quantify is leadership, which historian Mark Parillo and I have called "The Management Factor." That has to include perspicacity and the power to prod the partnership to the viable conclusion. In addition, the illustrations herein confirm that not only did wastage and consumption need to be balanced by men and matériel in order to keep the first line intact, but also that record keeping—especially of one's own strengths—was as important as the Intelligence of the enemy's.

Essentially, then, in the end, rather than an indictment of the French air arm, this work intends to be a comparative view of the three major European air forces of 1940—the British Royal Air Force (RAF), the German Luftwaffe (GAF), and the French Armée de l'Air (FAF)—and their national milieus. The paradox remains of the overall French defeat amidst the statistical successes of the Armée de l'Air, and perhaps it indeed can be concluded that the Armée de l'Air was as its Commanding General Joseph Vuillemin had hoped and maintained in 1940—undefeated.

It is a matter for historians to review.

—Robin Higham

ACKNOWLEDGMENTS

I am grateful to the following colleagues who agreed to read the initial draft of this manuscript: Ralph Titus, Mark Parillo, Steve Harris, James S. Corum, Brigadier General Michael Clemensen, Air Vice Marshal Peter J. Dye, Brian R. Sullivan, Colonel A. C. Cain, Oberst Manfred Kehrig, Dr. Horst Boog, and General Lucien Robineau. I very much appreciate the time they gave me and their comments.

My appreciation as well to my researchers, Jonathan Small and Casey Zimmerman, whose accounting skills spotted my errors, and Dr. Kevin Jones; to Marolyn Caldwell, who committed my original handwritten manuscript to type; and especially to Carol Williams for forty years of collaboration.

INTRODUCTION

The Armée de l'Air of the Third Republic was limited in resources after 24 June 1940 and soon became the Armée de l'Air de Vichy until November 1942 when the Allied invasion of North Africa caused the Germans to take control of Unoccupied France governed by Marshal Pétain.

The saying is that there are lies, damned lies, and statistics. In this work, for a variety of reasons—date, source, and so forth—the numbers do not always agree. That is part of the point herein. The comparison of the British, French, and German air forces from 10 May to 31 October 1940 provides insights into how wars are lost and won, as well as perceptions of the human frailties and beliefs that affect the equation. All of the themes noted below applied in varying degrees to each of the three principal air forces studied here. How each managed these issues determined the outcomes. The historian's challenge is to sift through exaggerated claims and superficial analysis to a truthful account and in the end to provide a meaningful evaluation of the "whys" and other relevant factors.

The air battles of 1940 were the first true European clashes of independent air arms and the first real test of the theories and doctrines that had evolved in the interwar years, influenced by the Technological Revolution. Factors affecting the two grand-strategic campaigns of 1940—which in reality were one— were political, diplomatic, military, economic, technical and scientific, medical, social, and ideological. Involved as well were the qualities of leadership.

The Germans and the British were critical years ahead in design, technology, testing, and manufacture, which gave them an edge that the French Armée de l'Air did not possess. Of these three principal air forces involved, the new German Luftwaffe had the advantage in maturity of thought, staffing, organization, and technology, in addition to—above all—a clear purpose, to reestablish Germany as the Great Power in Europe. The Luftwaffe of 1935 was to be the handmaiden of the Wehrmacht, though at first consideration also was given to it becoming a grand-strategic bomber force. By 1940 its role, as demonstrated in Poland in September 1939, was evident as a support for the German army's blitzkrieg once the Luftwaffe had established air superiority. The Luftwaffe's sole purpose was to help win a short war.[1]

The British Royal Air Force, however, had perversely for internal political reasons—national, aeronautical, and economic—abandoned the lessons of the World War I, 1914–1918. The RAF had founded its Staff College at Andover in 1923 and sent some of its brighter World War I officers there. But they were derailed by the 1923 doctrine that the Home Defence Air Force (HDAF) was primarily a bomber deterrent, and this was not challenged. The Air Staff, moreover, became very set in its ways and thus except on the defensive fighter side never tested its preconceptions against realities.

A second war twenty years after a first is too soon. The senior officers of the first—at least those above the rank of colonel—in the victorious force concluded they knew how to fight a war. And maybe some of them still did, if yet on active duty, though they perhaps suffered the deadening pomposity of experience. Yet if the two decades that passed between the wars had seen a technological revolution, the senior officers might not have been able to handle the changes unless they would have had Operational Commands during those critical twenty years.

As it was, the RAF forsook the tactical lessons of army cooperation and instead grasped the abandoned nettle of grand-strategic bombing in order to create a role for itself as the HDAF. Two-thirds of the fifty-two squadrons of that force were to be bombers, which—as Prime Minister Stanley Baldwin said in 1932 of the French—would always "get through." The carefully constructed London Air Defence Area (LADA) of 1918 was at the least a definite step down, but it did have a role to play to protect Britain against the "air menace," and thus was incorporated in the new 1925 Air Defence of Great Britain, the ADGB Command under a single air officer commanding-in-chief (AOC-in-C). The Tactical Air Force (TAF) at Home had roles and doctrine, even if upside down, but the bomber offensive was to prove impotent until 1944. The two halves of the Air Ministry failed to see the mirror effect of defensive fighter versus attacking bomber.

The French Armée de l'Air, which following 1918 was a claimant to the title of the world's largest air arm, drifted during the interwar years, as did the Armée de Terre. The Armée de l'Air until 1928 did not have an Air Ministry, such as the RAF had gained in 1918, and did not come into being as an independent force until 1933. Yet even then its organization was determined by Parlement and Parisian politics and not by grand strategy. From 1933 to 1940 the Armée de l'Air debated which of its potential roles should get priority—the grand-strategic air offensive of an independent force; the Défense Aérienne du Territoire (air defense of the territory [DAT]), that is, Metropolitan France; or *aviation d'assaut* (army cooperation), namely, reconnaissance and observation. The problem at that time was not so much the want of funds (credits), until 1938, as it was the inability to make policy decisions regarding technical maté-riel and personnel demands in order to be able to man the new Armée de l'Air. All of this was held back by politics and personalities.

Britain, Germany, and France were the three principal European powers in the 1930s. Each would arrive on the battlefields of 1939 with different needs due to their geographical locations, economic requisites, and defense perspec-tives. Isolationist, insular, imperial Britain suffered from a stable but not very imaginative government, as well as from the losses of men and matériel during World War I and a lingering depression that deepened in the 1930s. However, it did have the fiscal sense to abandon the gold standard and to support the Royal Navy until 1934 as the first line of defense of the Empire. But after World War I Britain wanted no more "Continental involvements" and was willing to see the 1919 Peace of Versailles modified, as with the Anglo-German Naval Agreement of 1935. And although Britain had seen severe unemployment in the 1920s, the challenge had been met by the formation of the National Government and by the recovery that in 1934 was stimulated by rearmament. Moreover, the nature of British society was much more deferential to authority than that in France; it was stoic, less confrontational, and accepting of planning and implementation.

In contrast to Britain, Germany had borne the shame of defeat in 1918 and of the Weimar government until 1933. The continental Germans after 1919 did not believe that they were a Great Power, but when Hitler gained author-ity the country determined to manifest itself as such once again. Under Hitler, the Third Reich had revived nationalism and suppressed dissent. Hitler and the National Socialist German Workers (Nazi) Party determined to abolish the 1919 Versailles *Diktat* and to reestablish the power and prestige of the Third Reich. The Treaty of Versailles was supposed to eliminate Germany as a threat to French security, but it had not, for the United States did not ratify it and the British were inclined to agree with the Germans that the *Diktat* was harsh. Thus Hitler set about acquiring the needed raw materials and resources and the sin-ews of power and control, as well as dismantling the French bloc, the Little Entente in Eastern Europe—Poland, Czechoslovakia, Romania, and Yugoslavia. At the same time, rearmament was begun with the advantage that during the

Weimar Republic the Germans had engaged in intellectual approaches to modern war, including the secret design of aircraft. In 1935 Hermann Goering unveiled the new Luftwaffe, already quickly overtaking Britain and France in first-line strength—those aircraft in Regular units that were ready to go.

Germany had the population, the administrative understanding, and the military, industrial, and social organization to manage the needed new warfare, as well as the blitzkrieg philosophy and the Technological Revolution. "Guns before butter" was a meaningful slogan, which together with the swastika symbolized purpose. The Germans were willing to finance armament rather than social needs, and they had the psychological edge and a grand strategy suiting their means to their ends. Although Britain's island air base left the nation with the vast metropolitan area of London likely vulnerable to the "air menace," Germany had a concern as well in its penetrable land frontiers all around. And so, as Germany had done historically, it developed its Wehrmacht and with it the Luftwaffe as a secondary partner in tactical warfare. The 1918 World War I defeat had largely rid the German military mentality of that war's ideas and imbued it with a realization that for many reasons the next war had to be short and decisive—a view much appreciated by Hitler. In 1940 the Germans carried on their historical patterns of quick wars of annihilation in defense of the Third Reich, as Robert Citino notes in *The German Way of War*, a lesson the French and British did not comprehend.[2]

The Germans had the advantage for the Luftwaffe of the 1936–1939 war in Spain, and the Polish campaign of September 1939 for the whole of the Wehrmacht. Above these two experiences was the German insistence that commanders all up the line report the bad as well as the good about their units so that Headquarters could institute training programs to correct the deficiencies and provide intense physical and mental stressing needed for war. These corrective activities continued into May 1940. Neither the French nor the British, however, made such use of the lessons of the brief 1939 Polish campaign.

At this same time, the other European powers were the isolated Soviet Union and Italy. The former had the world's most powerful air force in 1934 and once had kept close sub-rosa ties with the Germans, though that was stopped by Hitler. Italy, ruled by Mussolini who had seized power in 1922, was both a friend and rival to the French until 1935 when Mussolini's ambitions in Ethiopia and Italian North Africa became a threat. And while the USSR had held potential as a French ally, as during 1894–1917, anti-Socialist and anti-Communist ideologies in French domestic politics of the 1930s prohibited it.

It is clear that British, French, and German air forces in advance of 1940 needed to have engaged in realistic exercises, preparation for the war to come, and careful examination of what Intelligence did and did not reveal, as well as careful assessment of their assumptions regarding the courses of the next conflict. And yet, despite being a continental power having a long held concern for territorial frontiers, the Germans nevertheless were unprepared mentally as much as physically for a cross-Channel war. Moreover, their way of war, those short victorious campaigns (barring World War I), disregarded logistics and assumed that the campaign would end before supplies ran out. Though they were able to build the Luftwaffe with planes and aircrew and move it to new bases, they were not ready to fight a determined British foe that was protected by the English Channel and with sufficient air resources to outlast them. As in the 1914–1918 war, the Royal Air Force did not have to achieve a traditional victory; it only had to hold or parry.[3]

In contrast to the Germans, the British after centuries of conflict eschewed a fresh involvement. They remembered World War I with horror, despite having benefited from it both in terms of defense and stature. Yet they had been sufficiently alarmed by the Japanese aggression against China from 1931 to abandon Disarmament and prepare to rearm. For Britain, the greatest vulnerability was the seaborne trade upon which her life depended, but with the primary focus on the potential German air menace and London being the world's largest target, Britain's center of concern turned to air defense, with the Royal Navy and sea trade secondary.

The Royal Air Force had long been sanctified by the Air Force Act of 1917 and in 1923 had been given the specific task of Home Air Defence, as compared with the Armée de l'Air and the Luftwaffe, which were creations of the early 1930s. And while the Armée de l'Air focused its energy on its relationship to the Armée de Terre and the Luftwaffe upon support of the Wehrmacht, the Royal Air Force in its role of Home defense was in a singular position to conceive of grand-strategic bombing. Nevertheless the methodical Germans still were able to develop cutting-edge air weapons, though from the French emerged a less cohesive, less up-to-date, and less reliable force. The British developed the lifesaving fighters followed by the war-winning tactical and grand-strategic air forces. In sum, in 1940 the contrasting three air arms proved the importance of sustainability and foresight—planning, training, production, logistics, and reserves.

As compared with the Third Reich, France lacked the population and, after 1929, the determined leaders with a viable and believable grand strategy. In addition, the French lived with the myth of Napoleonic genius for offensive war and large casualties at a time when France was no longer a Great Power nor had the means to counter a blitzkrieg. She was a continental nation. The Armée de Terre was for economic reasons made into a cadre force behind the Maginot Line then being built to protect the German (but not the Belgian) frontier on the east. Complicating as well was that French conscription had been cut to one year in 1930, political instability had led in early 1934 to the verge of another revolution, and the country had stayed on the gold standard until 1936.

The poor but valiant showing of the Armée de l'Air in the Battle of France was related to the country's social-economic-political fissures. Workers on the Left were divided between the Communists and the Socialists—mostly industrial workers, the large agricultural sector, the *petit bourgeoisie* (the conventional French lower middle class), and the *patronats* (the wealthy French industrial class), who controlled a large part of French wealth. With mobilization, the *patronats* were secure enough to be divided. Both they and the government wanted to keep business and the workers as usual, and both had their eyes on the postwar world. War brought profit and benefits to the heavy (steel, coal) industries and those with government contracts—the "sheltered." But small businessmen were shut out of rearmament as they lacked capital and other resources.

Fierce struggles over labor and raw materials erupted in France. Poaching of workers by the better-payers, such as the aircraft industry, drew complaints. The self-interested views of many *patronats* made them hostile to the government's wartime controls, though not to the war itself. The *patronats* were reluctant to enter the war economy, much more than their equals in other countries. The French minister of Armaments in 1939–1940, Raoul Dautry, was a graduate of the École Polytechnique, but in historian Richard Vinen's opinion was too unbalanced and soft to solve the problems of mobilizing the French economy. War raised the specter of inflation, and that alarmed the *rentiers,* those on fixed incomes. Vinen concluded that heavy industry's acceptance of the devaluation of 1936 was a sign of a disintegrating social alliance.[4]

France had an empire from which she expected to draw colonial troops, but to which otherwise she paid little attention, in spite of occasional wars therein. Most importantly, French grand strategy hinged upon the Little Entente and upon another 1918-style methodical war. France's aviation industry by 1934 was backward, and the aircraft designs behind those of her likely opponent. It was true that by 1940 the nation had the best tanks in the world, but France had neither the doctrine nor the air arm and wireless net to go with them.

Over and beyond the doctrinal weakness of an unimaginative grand strategy was the flabby rotational nature of the French political leadership, on top of the roiling social divisions. As a result, whereas Germany began to rearm in 1933 and Britain in 1934 with its shift to the Royal Air Force as the prime defender, France only began a troubled rearmament in 1936 when the arms and aircraft industries were nationalized. And whereas Germany and Britain expanded both the matériel and manpower of their air arms, the Armée de l'Air stood pat. In 1939 France was a self-styled Great Power, still a peasant economy beginning to be ruled by small-town bourgeoisie opposed by the Bank of France and dominated by the armée and the memory of World War I casualties. Perhaps, too, it can be argued that the nation began the Maginot Line from the wrong end, for France's essential industry was in the northeast, and that for centuries had been the traditional invasion route. In sum, the Armée de l'Air of 1933 was an immature military force created amidst the birth of the Technological Revolution without either sufficient credits or the expertise to manage its impact.

The Origins of Dysfunction

The root cause of the ultimate failure of the Armée de l'Air during May–June 1940 was the descent of France to its lowest point as a Great Power and the very basic nature of the French culture. There had been too much talk and too few decisions since the French leaders of 1918, such as Clemenceau, Poincaré, and Foch, had faded away. In addition, the Armée de l'Air had helped engineer its own defeat by choosing to disagree both within itself and with the armée on doctrine while at the same time hazily attempting to create an élite body. Unfortunately such a military force at the time of the Technological Revolution required a substantial infrastructure, including communications as well as equipment superior to that of any potential enemy, and the ability to outlast such enemies in war. And it required, above all, money (credits).

Regrettably—*malheureusemen*—the état majeur de l'Armée de l'Air (French General Staff Air Force [GSAF]), created an inferior product. And yet, the Armée de l'Air, as it faced defeat in June 1940, also began to have visions of resurrection. Its leaders could look back in French history to the post-Napoleonic period, to the recovery in 1871, and to examples from other countries such as Austria-Hungary and Germany in 1918. Today we now also can cite the governments in exile of World War II—the Netherlands, Belgium, Poland, Norway, Greece, Italy in 1943, and that of de Gaulle. How the French leadership of 1940 answered the institutional, doctrinal, physical, matériel, manpower, and esprit de corps questions has been noted by Mme. Dr. Claude d'Abzac-Epézy in her excellent *L'Armée de l'Air de Vichy, 1940–1944* (Vincennes: SHAA, 1997) and thus need not concern us here.

France had gone to war in 1939 for a variety of reasons, one of which was an overconfident mis-estimate of its grand strategy and resources, and a failure to realize that the German solution to the stalemate of 1914–1918 was not another "*sitzkrieg*"—a "sitting"/trench war—but in fact a blitzkrieg. From 10 May 1940 the French ship of state was wrapped in a *Titanic* cocoon, heading through the fog of war on a predetermined course straight into the iceberg. Over the past thirty years, French official historians have sought the truth, yet they still have not defrocked the gallant aces and their fellow airmen and mechanics of the long-established paradoxical story that the Armée de l'Air fought hard and well against the superior German Luftwaffe, inflicted heavy losses, and emerged undefeated.

The empirical approach herein endeavors to show that the facts in the case of the Armée de l'Air are unreliable. Though not wanting to challenge the hopeless gallantry of that organization in the short six weeks of early summer 1940, the search for the truth does require a close examination of the available evidence to reach a reliable conclusion. What GSAF General Joseph Vuillemin and company had engaged in from mid-1940 was a campaign of disinformation that made the Armée de l'Air appear much more successful and heroic than it actually was. In a way, this propaganda—predicated upon an undercurrent of belief that the war was, in fact, for the Armée de l'Air a "lost cause"—was symbolic of the nadir to which France had slid by 1940, due to a small coterie of influential beings in Paris, led by Army General Maurice Gamelin.

Initially this volume started out to show that the Armée de l'Air in the Battle of France did not destroy 1,000 or even 782 Luftwaffe machines, but rather a much more modest number. Those figures, however, became eclipsed by the realization that the 1,000 or 782 claimed—whichever—were part of the undefeated "myth" that General Vuillemin and others began to perpetuate as soon as the fighting stopped on 24 June 1940.[5]

Delving into the evidence of the Battle of France and of the Armée de l'Air allows a more balanced assessment of a fighting élite, primarily the *chasseur*, who apparently acquitted themselves much better than we have a right to have expected. In the critical years of 1934–1940 the civilian logistic infrastructure was equally vital, and that depended upon a viable interface between the politicians (cabinets and ministers), the airmen in the ministries and in command, and the aircraft industry. The complexity of the necessary structure is best gauged from the accompanying diagrams herein, "The Invisible Infrastructure—The Bamboo Basket, Britain 1939–1945" and "The Invisible Infrastructure—The Bamboo Basket, France 1940" (Figures 1 and 2). The top of the basket indicates that a country, state, or nation has to provide leadership and approval or acquiescence to a grand strategy or overall policy. The military then has to translate that into doctrine and, once that is in hand, into hardware and trained personnel, in addition to a viable system of bases, logistics, mainte-nance, and salvage and repair. An important element of all these deliberations and calculations is a sense of time and urgency, and a power's perception of its place or space in the world, as well as others' conception of it. Success or vic-tory requires various levels of authority, from dictatorship to consensus and cohesion. Input has had to go upward from the military and the technicians to the politicians, then down the civil side through industry to provide supplies and down the air side to produce the trained manpower to make a viable force.

For the whole to be effective and efficient, a start has had to be made with viable assumptions in a time of "uncertainty," as Imlay and Toft have noted.[6] By the end of 1930, that required a lead time of almost a decade, providing of course that money, matériel, and management were available. Moreover, among the uncertainties were factors such as the production rates, consump-tion, and wastage rates, the needs of training, operational serviceability, and the ability either to find and hit an enemy target or to launch fighters to defend vital points. In calculating consumption and wastage rates, salvage and repair of both accidents and combat had to be estimated and recovery or salvage and rebuild facilities organized.

The vital ingredients in this mix that make up the Bamboo Basket are a broadly focused general staff and not only Intelligence but its appreciation and dissemination. An examination then of the air battles of 1940 involves much more than estimating whether or not each air force achieved its objectives, whether or not its claims were realistic, and how resilient it was in the face of battle.[7]

The Outcomes of Dysfunction

In 1937 Brigadier General Jean Hébrard stated, "The establishment of doctrine and all that stems from it—equipment programmes, manufacture, tests, use of funds, organization, industrial mobilization, tactical and strategic deployment—emerges therefore as essential and will condition future successes or failures."[8]

In spite of available Intelligence, the Armée de l'Air had prepared itself mentally and physically for a 1918 static war rather than a 1940 modern mobile war, a blitzkrieg.[9] In addition, the nearly 1.5 million dead of the 1914–1918 war and the fear of another such slaughter had been a pall over France in the inter-war years. In a sense, then, the undefeated "myth" was propagated by people who were anxious after 24 June 1940 to deflect the armée criticisms and who were not prepared to admit their culpability in part for the defeat of France, which still in the 1930s had been but an artificial great power.[10]

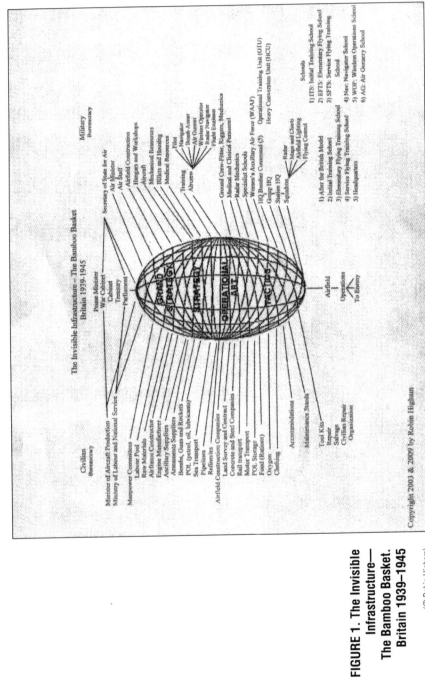

FIGURE 1. The Invisible Infrastructure—The Bamboo Basket. Britain 1939–1945

(© Robin Higham)

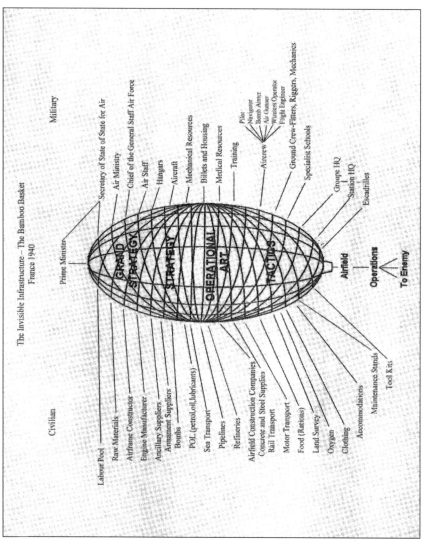

The Invisible Infrastructure – The Bamboo Basket
France 1940

Military

Civilian

Prime Minister

Secretary of State of State for Air
Air Ministry
Chief of the General Staff Air Force
Air Staff
Hangars
Aircraft
Mechanical Resources
Billets and Housing
Medical Resources
Training

Pilot
Navigator
Bomb Aimer
Air Gunner
Wireless Operator
Flight Engineer

Aircrew

Ground Crew–Fitters, Riggers, Mechanics

Specialist Schools

Groupe HQ
Station HQ
Escadrilles

GRAND STRATEGY
STRATEGY
OPERATIONAL ART
TACTICS

Airfield
Operations
To Enemy

Labour Pool
Raw Materials
Airframe Constructor
Engine Manufacturer
Ancillary Suppliers
Armament Suppliers
Bombs
POL (petrol,oil,lubricants)
Sea Transport
Pipelines
Refineries
Airfield Construction Companies
Concrete and Steel Supplies
Rail Transport
Motor Transport
Food (Rations)
Land Survey
Oxygen
Clothing
Accommodations
Maintenance Stands
Tool Kits

FIGURE 2. The Invisible
Infrastructure—
The Bamboo Basket.
France 1940

(© Robin Higham)

René La Chambre had been a junior minister of war before being appointed to the French Air Ministry offices on Boulevard Victor. He knew nothing about aviation and found the Ministère de l'Air (Air Ministry) in a lamentable state, but did not know enough to reorganize it. General Joseph Vuillemin, a World War I bomber pilot and noted North African explorer-flier, was a political appointment to the position of CGSAF[11] in order to restore morale in the Armée de l'Air. He was not a technical expert, nor was he versed in the ways of Paris. Vuillemin's July 1940 approach was more than paradoxical. While on the one hand he proclaimed the plethora of modern aircraft on charge on 24 June 1940, on the other he said that throughout the battle their serviceability (*disponible*) rate was only 30 percent.[12] Moreover he ignored the organizational and structural weaknesses of his force—the shortages of pilots and mechanics, especially of specialists, the lack of radios, and many aircraft on charge unfinished and thus not *bon de guerre* (operationally war ready). In other words, of the C_3—Command, Control, and Communications—the Armée de l'Air was deficient in all three, including an established doctrine to guide procurement and deployment. The nation needed a streamlined procurement process, for as Air Vice Marshal (AVM) Peter Dye has noted, "increasing production was not matched by increasing deliveries."[13]

Interestingly what happened in Paris in the 1930s was not a unique military/political experience. Much earlier, in 1861 in Washington, D.C., at the outset of the War Between the States, senior officers in the U.S. Navy Department had failed to use the knowledge and experience available to formulate well-considered plans for the blockade of the rebellious South—another mis-estimate of strategy and resources. Nor were comprehensive instructions to the Union Fleet drafted, which then should have been modified as reports came in.[14] And the same could be said of the British Army in 1905 and the Red army in 1939–1940. Mark Hinchcliffe notes that Colonel Richard Szafranski (USAF) has argued that the force command should be related to the objective. Centralized control and decentralized execution are necessary, as in World War II. But the practice must not lead to overload at the command level.[15]

The Armée de l'Air from the end of June 1940 was split between the remnant 42,000 personnel of the post-1933 force in Unoccupied Vichy France and the Free-French Air Force (Forces libres français aérienne, FFAF) in Britain under General Charles de Gaulle in London. While the former was equipped with a limited number of pre-May 1940 types and airmen, the latter manned largely British-manufactured aircraft. There was a rump Armée de l'Air in North Africa and Indochina, which after the Allied invasion of November 1942 joined the FFAF.

In France in July 1940, General Vuillemin and his successor, the new Vichy chef of the état majeur de l'Armée de l'Air (General Staff Air Force [CGSAF]), General Jean Mendigal, wished to substantiate that the élite of the Armée de l'Air had not been beaten, that they were men of honor let down by the politicians and the armée, and that the Communists especially were the evil enemy. Vuillemin, however, was not able officially to push the "lost-cause" belief because he was summarily retired due to age in October 1940 under a new Vichy law. According to d'Abzac-Epézy, the Armée de l'Air de Vichy of later 1940 had 80,000 personnel allowed by the Germans.[16] In May 1940 the total had been 97,000 and not the 177,000 bruited about, a number that apparently enabled Mendigal and Vuillemin to claim to have saved the Armée de l'Air personnel from appearing defeated. They did less well as to aircraft, yet even so these were more modern machines than in September 1939.

The parallels between the American South in 1865 and Germany from 1918 are much to be pondered in the story of warfare. The "lost-cause" proponents and the Union victors both created the folklore of war that concentrated on bravery in battle and did not mention the shame of defeat. The South was unable to mobilize scarce resources of industry and to trade space for time against inevitable defeat due to lack of manpower, grand strategy, and political will, as well as declining faith in the currency and the cause. And the Union physically made it plain that the South was losing and in the end enforced unconditional surrender. Was the mythology, then, of Robert E. Lee created by the southern nobility as a social phenomenon to enable them to keep their place and their honor and self-esteem, and to justify the cost of the war in wealth and human lives?[17] The answer will lie in another work.

In the German case of World War I, the failure of the Allies to occupy more of the Rhineland, the return of Alsace-Lorraine to France, and the move of the Reich government to Weimar, in contrast to the return to legitimacy of the Vienna settlement of 1815, allowed the generals to claim they had not been defeated but had been stabbed in the back by the weak civilian government and the Communists. In 1945 the Allies made it plain that Germany was beaten, conquered, and divided.

Suffice it to say that with France, political and diplomatic, economic and technical, and social and ideological reasons, as well as flaws in the culture, were responsible for what happened to the Armée de l'Air in 1940. During World War I the French Third Republic had seen the evolution of the power of Parlement. The aviation committees had grown to take a controlling role, not merely in budgeting, but also over the air ministers' actions. Owing to the short tenure of cabinet members, they could rarely get a program through and were constantly badgered by the Chambre des Députés (Chamber of Deputies) and the Comité d'Aviation de la Sénat (Senate Aviation Committees). Moreover, the air arm had been part of the armée until in 1928, when it was split off administratively under a separate Air Ministry.

Yet it was not until 1933 that the new young Air Minister, Pierre Cot, decreed that the Armée de l'Air would be a separate organization. This was confirmed by Parlement in the Law of July 1934, though not without altering Cot's vision. The result was that the command structure was changed in 1933, 1934, 1936, and 1938. At the same time, the matter of doctrine was bitterly debated between the proponents of the Armée de Terre's need for close support and reconnaissance and the airmen's desire for an independent bombing force, while the third leg of the tripod, the Défense Aérienne du Territoire (DAT), came in last. This dispute had not been clearly resolved by 1940, certainly not in time to create an air force and a DAT.

Related to this, of course, was the matter of both the types and the numbers of aircraft. The 1934 solution—in part to modernize the artisanal (handcrafted) aircraft industry on the eve of the Technological Revolution—was an order for 1,010 of existing types, mostly bomber-combat-reconnaissance (BCR) aircraft, a development that was complicated by the leftist Popular Front's nationalization of aircraft production in the wake of its 1936 election victory.[18]

Politically the whole was clouded because of the convoluted and overlapping structure of national defense in which the Armée de Terre's (French army) General Gamelin was the principal player until 19 May 1940. As a result, the Armée de l'Air was gradually subordinated again to Army Command and its assets spread across the industrial Northeast (former Western) Front. Gamelin's strategy, a derivative of the Gallic ground strategy in whose making he had played a part, was wrong. His thrust forward to parry a German attack assumed a repeat of 1914, and he failed to consider the passage of the Ardennes. As a result, his military created a weak-hinge gap into which General Heinz Guderian's Panzer Group charged ahead to the sea, isolating the Anglo-French armies and forcing the evacuation at Dunkirk.

In this new mobile war, the Allied Air Forces were quickly moved off their airfields into the refugee-packed roads and rapidly separated from their administrative coils. Moreover the RAF at least did not have the motor transport (MT) to allow it to move, and thus in less than ten days had to be withdrawn to England. In the meantime, France had tried to create an Eastern Bloc of countries (Poland, Czechoslovakia, Romania, and Yugoslavia) to safeguard itself against a resurgent Germany. But that Little Entente was subject to the nature of geography, especially an Italy turned hostile, and later Hitler's annexation—Anschluss—of Austria, ultimately leading to the dismantling of Czechoslovakia at Munich in 1938 and after. France had also tried to maintain the 1914–1918 alliances against the backdrop of the League of Nations and Disarmament after World War I and the isolationism of Great Britain. And it was then that while France thought in terms of another continental war taking up where it had left off in 1918, Britain moved steadily away from a continental commitment to defense against a massive air attack, first from France and, then, after 1933 from Germany.

While Paris argued about the roles of airpower, the Royal Air Force studied doctrine, and London from 1923 favored a Home Defence Air Force of two-thirds bombers and one-third fighters. Britain worked steadily to refine its 1918 system of air defense so that when radar and R/T (radio telephone) became practicable in the late 1930s, they could be grafted onto a perfected system. In contrast, in 1939 France had neither a DAT Command with antiaircraft apparatus, nor radar. In addition French diplomatic and military efforts were further stymied in 1936 when Belgium reverted to neutrality, leaving France without the envisaged Maginot Line of fortifications extended to cover her industrial northeast. In these circumstances, Paris opened talks with London, seeking to "borrow" RAF Fighter Command to protect French industrial centers. At a time when other countries in Europe and America were expanding their aircrew and ground crew training to produce wartime reserves, the Armée de l'Air Haut Commandement (high command) was not. French expansion was only belatedly begun in late 1939 after the war had started, with the results not due until at the earliest mid-1940.

Added to all of this was the problem of credits. French finance, wedded to the gold standard, was not attuned to the demands of modern war. The Armée de Terre and the Maginot Line absorbed the majority of the funds voted, and thus it was not until 1938 that at last credits began to flow to the Armée de l'Air. By then, however, the aircraft industry was falling two years behind both the Luftwaffe and the Royal Air Force in the design, development, testing, and in-service dates of cutting-edge, frontline machines and in creating the ancillary industry, the logistics, and the number of mechanics to support them. And social and psychological problems also arose in the country. The tough old guard of politicians who had won the war in 1918 had retired by 1930, leaving only the ageing marshals of France as leaders. The new bourgeoisie ministers and members of Parlement were provincials. Moreover, they characteristically thought that merely to talk about a difficulty was to produce a real solution.[19] Out of this atmosphere then arose the need in 1940, as perceived by the postwar leadership of the Armée de l'Air, to create the protective construct of an undefeated air force with its aces.

The Realities amidst Dysfunction

Three ministers "made" the Armée de l'Air: Pierre Cot, who tried to modernize the industry but could not get investments; General Victor Denain, Chief of Staff to Air Minister Pierre Cot and then himself minister, who foresaw war in 1935 and ordered precipitately from an unready aviation industry; and Guy La Chambre, about 90 percent of whose plan was realized by May 1940, but who insisted on deliveries even though many were unfit for war.

To obtain its independence in 1933 the French Armée de l'Air had to agree that the armée would operate the observation squadrons at division, corps, and required levels. This could have been efficient in an offensive strategy, but in a defensive one was fatal, for in 1940 the Armée had a 1918 offensive strategy for a defensive war. In recent years two volumes have explored why societies or cultures (and an Armée de l'Air is one of the latter) are defeated and collapse. Wolfgang Schivelbusch in *The Culture of Defeat*[20] examines the American South, France, and Germany. He notes that the losers' first reaction to defeat is surprise, dismay, disbelief, and the search for scapegoats; then they begin to examine history to find reasons for their failure: how did they go astray and what is their national destiny—old ideas reclothed. There is, as well, the tendency to turn military reverses into spiritual triumphs, and at the same time in the hysteria of defeat this is martyrdom.

Jared Diamond's *Collapse—How Societies Choose to Fail or Succeed* takes a sweeping global view that rests largely on societies on the periphery and in isolation, but then he draws lessons from that evidence: failure to anticipate, failure to perceive, national bad behavior, disastrous values, other irrational failures, unsuccessful solutions, and hope.[21] These lessons apply both to French government as a whole in the interwar years and to the Armée de l'Air. The mea non culpa of July 1940 was part of a universally observable pattern. To the two titles above also must be added the Robin Higham and Stephen J. Harris volume, *Why Air Forces Fail: The Anatomy of Defeat*, which provides case studies of numerous air arms of the mid-twentieth century and why they fell.

In 1940 the French were unready mentally and physically; the Royal Air Force was just ahead enough because of history, insularity, and planning to be able to parry and hold. General Lucien Robineau, former chef, Services Historique de l'Armée de l'Air, noted in his 20 December 2008 comments to the author regarding this manuscript that in 1938 General Gamelin had said that France could very well fight a war without aviation, and in July 1939 had stated that the air force would not have the importance in war that the strategists were predicting. After the fighting stopped, of course, everyone wanted to blame the Armée de l'Air, and thus it countered by exaggerating its claims in its attempt to state it had fought well.

We can understand the mindset of the French high command at this time if we look back to the days following World War I. Out of its 39 million population in 1914 France had suffered more than 1 million killed, another million crippled, 700,000 widows, and 700,000 spinsters doomed to a long single life. Some 2,000 villages and small towns had been destroyed, with 800,000 houses in ashes. That legacy made no one in France anxious to go to war again, and thus official policy became pacific and military strategy defensive; and as for aviation, there were to be no bombers and no offensive air action, even after the end of the Phoney War, that period after the invasion of Poland in 1939 when nothing more seemed to happen—what after 1940 was called the *sitzkrieg*. With their invasion of France, the Germans had used the symbolic 1919 figure given them at Versailles of 100,000 men to be allotted for the Wehrmacht (German army), but no air force. Later, however, the Vichy government was allowed an Armée de l'Air after the British had attacked the French Royale (navy) at Mers el-Kebir in North Africa demanding surrender of the French ships in order to prevent the Germans from taking them.

Apparently after the June 1940 Franco-German armistice, according to General Robineau, 700 Luftwaffe POW aircrew were handed back to the victors.[22] The Battle of France, which the Gauls lost, and the Battle of Britain, which the British "won," were the two significant battles of the summer of 1940. The Germans won the first campaign in three days and lost the second in sixty-six. Although the Royal Air Force had been defeated in the campaign of May–June 1940, it retired to its island aerodrome where it recuperated. And the Luftwaffe, which was seen to have won handily in France, thought it could beat Britain, but the tactical Luftwaffe was cast in a grand-strategic role for which it was not designed, and its Intelligence was faulty. Moreover, its philosophy that centered on a short war failed to consider the need for salvage and repair and the fact that 22 percent of its "new" aircraft were rebuilds. Thus the Luftwaffe not only lost the Battle of Britain, but because of this deficit went into the Soviet Union under-equipped for the tactical task assigned.

The two air campaigns of 1940 put the focus on the leaders—political and military—and on the pilots and other young aircrew, to the neglect of the essential nature of ground crew, logistics, and technical support. In addition, the Intelligence assessments in the air battles of the summer of 1940 were faulty. They were based upon debriefing of excited youthful survivors of a few minutes of swirling, confused air action, an interrogation process handled by untrained, newly commissioned officers or reservists. These reports were then analyzed at Headquarters by persons also with little experience or even "rules of thumb," and we now know that only 19 to 20 percent of the claims of enemy aircraft shot down were valid. On the other hand, the losses of one's own side were real, except that 35 to 45 percent of aircraft shot down or force-landed in one's own territory were repairable. These two factors had a subtle, if unrecognized, effect upon assessed strength.

Interestingly the German Condor Legion in Spain had learned the need for mobility, and Luftwaffe (later General) Adolph Galland had his whole squadron mounted on special trains for ease of movement, whereas the Allies' operational logistics was still based upon a static front conception. The Allies failed to comprehend the German mobility, the blitzkrieg philosophy (they saw no lessons in Poland), not realizing its acute danger. Coupled to this was the successful German emphasis upon junior officers taking the initiative, in contrast to the French insistence that decisions could only be taken at the highest levels. German "Lightning war" was met by French bureaucracy. It then is not surprising that the Allies were defeated in the Battle of France.

The French *chasseur aérienne*—the fighters—found themselves flying armée support down low. But they had practiced this little against the Armée de Terre, so that the assumptions gathered had been erroneous. The Armée de Terre ground forces merely *talked* antiaircraft defense, whereas the German army—the Wehrmacht—had learned the lessons of 1918 strafing by the Allies and thus had developed flak, the quad 20-mm guns for low-level and the favored 88-mm for high, which they had used in Spain and Poland. The Wehrmacht were better armed and fully aware that the enemy in the air would attack forces on the march or holding. Thus the German flak was plentiful, well aimed, and potent as the British RAF Battles and Blenheims and the French Armée de l'Air machines discovered, to their cost.

In addition, the importance of Command, Control, and—above all—Communications combined to make the Luftwaffe Command more effective. While the Luftwaffe fighters under Adolf Galland had a forward observer to guide them, as well as overall a rapid system for requests from the Wehrmacht and response from the Luftwaffe, and the British had their radar sector-control system at Home, the French had nothing. In a war in which minutes counted, the Gallic system worked like cold, thick treacle. Yet, in a June 2004 assessment, after noting the shortcomings of the Armée de l'Air, General Lucien Robineau concluded that it could hardly have done better due to its shortages of manpower. It had only 54.8 percent of its supposed 177,000 total.

Foresight is certainly an essential mental activity for a commander and his staff. At the national defense level foresight has to include knowledge of the diplomatic, military, political, economic, scientific, technological, medical, and social factors, as well as the religious and ideological aspects. Hitler and the British were conscious that all the above were included in grand strategy. But their perceptions were conditioned by history and memory. Neither side envisioned the coinciding effects of blitzkrieg—the clogging of the roads with refugees, which hampered the Anglo-French defense more than the conquerors in May–June 1940.

Both sides needed broadly trained staff who were not afraid to challenge their superiors' wishes and to use their experience and education to predict the future. Though the Europeans drew their officers from institutions of higher education, these men lacked knowledge of technology and logistics, as well as of what in their day could be described as "global" patterns and events. The British had trained their better future generals of World War II at Woolwich in artillery and engineering, much as the Germans of the landed class had been trained.

One of the lessons of history has been that the next war would not be like the one before. But the French expected the next war to be like the previous one. War may hang in the balance as to whether or not both sides are equally prepared, both to their own circumstances and to parry and hold the opponent's innovations. In the years 1937–1940 all air forces suffered the consequences of the Technological Revolution, and the lack of understanding among both politicians and senior officers of the causes and of the learning curve. From procurement plans to generalized readiness required several years, not months, as had been experienced earlier. The whole process was new and full of uncharted precedents. And yet the past indeed could not be totally discounted, but rather, as Shakespeare noted in *The Tempest*, must still be considered prologue.

Conclusion

In October 1977 I wrote down five questions that I would have asked in 1945 about the Battle of Britain and seven I would ask then, in 1977. Today, in 2009, I would suggest that these twelve questions can be posed when considering both air campaigns of 1940.

In 1945 I queried:

- Who won the Battle?
- Where does the conflict fit in the history of World War II?
- Was it a contest of personalities?
- Was it a propaganda struggle between nations and between services?
- How important was defensive technology?

Subsequently, in 1977 I asked:

- Why did the Germans lose the battle?
- Why was it a decisive contest?
- Was it a victory for airpower?
- How did it compare with the 1939 Polish and later 1940 blitzkriegs?
- Why did the Luftwaffe lose the Battle of Germany, 1944–1945?
- How does battle history of this sort compare in difficulty with that of Pearl Harbor, and why?
- What did the Battle of Britain do for Marshal of the Royal Air Force (MRAF) Lord Hugh Trenchard's reputation?

Of the three major air forces engaged in the battles of 1940, only the Germans, with their experience in Spain, had leadership, doctrine, and tactics both with fighters and for army cooperation. The British had doctrine and leadership, but faulty RAF strategy and fighter tactics. The French had neither leadership nor doctrine. Yet the Battle of Britain was not the Germans' sort of battle.

In what follows, to provide a control I have used two different "comparable" overlapping forty-three-day periods of the Battle of Britain in order to judge the Battle of France: 10 July to 23 August 1940 and 12 August to 23 September. The first (10 July–31 August) of forty-two days and the second (12 August–23 September) of forty-three days.

PART 1
THE AIR FORCES

CHAPTER 1

THE ARMÉE DE L'AIR

The Battle of France lasted forty-six days, from 10 May–24 June.

Introduction

For France, then a declining Great Power, 1940 made the nation face the realities of war—not a 1918-style static conflict, but a modern mobile one. Essentially when in 1938 the Armée de l'Air (FAF) was ordered to synchronize doctrine with national policy and to create an air defense force and one for armée cooperation, it dragged its feet, still failing to grasp the new tempo of war. The Armèe de l'Air was focused on an air war and not on a combined-arms conflict. And that, wrote Faris Kirkland, was really where the Battle of France was lost.[1]

Unfortunately the unresolved arguments about air doctrine, and in consequence the late development of modern aircraft types and of trained airmen for both air and ground work, were delayed. As a result, instead of a defensive Armée de l'Air fighter force—*chasse*—of more than 5,200 aircraft and 738 pilots, *le belle France* had but 632 to 637 fighter planes in 31 *escadrilles*, of which 372 were serviceable, and only 348 *chasse* pilots to face a Luftwaffe armada of 3,500 machines.[2] Moreover, the French Armée de l'Air Haut Commandement (air force high command) was impotent for self-inflicted reasons.

The myth of the number of Luftwaffe (German air force [GAF])shot down by the Armée de l'Air in the Battle of France of 10 May–24 June 1940 began as early as 29 July 1940 when General Jean Mendigal, chief of staff of the then–Vichy-controlled Armée de l'Air, and General Joseph Vuillemin, inspector general, stated that the Germans had lost 775 aircraft shot down by the *chasseur* and 204 by the French *defense contre avions* (antiaircraft [DCA])—a total of 979.[3] General Vuillemin's calculation of 30 percent "available" aircraft—*disponible*—for the Armée de l'Air between 10 May and 24 June 1940 is probably about correct considering mobility and shortage of mechanics, in addition to the chaos in the logistics system and in aircraft manufacturing. Yet, on 10 May the available rate was said by the French Armée de l'Air actually to be 68 percent.[4] In March 1939 Vuillemin had said that sixty new aircraft per month would be sufficient for the needs of the Armée de l'Air; when he received 335, he stockpiled them instead of creating new flying units, as he lacked personnel.

The embarrassment of defeat by the Germans in 1940 was followed by the Riom "trial" (procès) of 19 February 1942–21 May 1943, the Vichy regime's failed witch hunt to prove that the loss should be attributed to the Third Republic leaders prior to 1940's Franco-German armistice.[5] In that process René La Chambre, the Ministre de l'Air (air minister), had tried to blame the prewar état majeur (air staff) for the failures of the Armée de l'Air, but General Vuillemin, La Chambre's then–chief of the General Staff Air Force (CGSAF) and later commandement en chef (commander in chief) of the Armée de l'Air, would have none of it. Vuillemin pointed out that La Chambre himself had been in on the decision-making, in which he was the superior authority.

At Riom, Vuillemin challenged La Chambre's description of how a French aircraft type was conceived and given birth. The process focused on the technical aspects in conjunction with the designers, but the General Staff Air Force (GSAF) made recommendations *after* the prototype stage, followed by the Conseil Supérieur de l'Air (Supreme Air Council), presided over by the minister, then giving approval. In contrast, according to *Combat and Command*, by Marshal of the Royal Air Force Lord Sholto Douglas (who as an air vice marshal was the then–assistant chief of the Air Staff in London), the British Air Member for Supply and Research passed the Air Council's wishes to the director of Operational Requirements, and he was then responsible for the specifications and equipment of all the aircraft in service.[6]

The Haut Commandement of the French Armée de l'Air was, in fact, responsible for fateful choices made in the 1930s as to the design and ordering of aircraft and also for the decision not to train the necessary pilots and mechanics. During the 1930s the Haut Commandement sought a doctrine that would provide air cover for the armée, which was largely composed of cadres—nuclei of trained soldiers—to be mobilized on a no longer applicable 1918 schedule. Furthermore, under the Law of 1934, only 16 of 134 *escadrilles* were to be controlled by the état majeur as a Douhetian strategic-bombing force. The French military did not see the German blitzkrieg (*attaque brusque*) as a serious threat and, at the same time, airmen sought autonomy for their air arm and their role, with bombers as the symbolic guarantee of that.

So the doctrinal quarrels over the role of the Armée de l'Air after 1933 saw first the abortive bomber-combat-reconnaissance (BCR) multipurpose machine developed and then the evolution from that (or reversion) to World War I thinking again of short-range protection for reconnaissance and observation machines, a role that single-seater fighters could fulfill. When war came, France had but a handful of bombers and they quickly were forced to operate only at night.

In the debates of 1936–1937 Ministre de l'Air Pierre Cot's Chief of Cabinet, Lieutenant General Jean-Henri Jauneaud, had pointed out that institutional independence was not the same as operational autonomy, for what the airmen opposed was being tied to the dangerous role of armée cooperation or support. Jauneaud wished to prepare the Armée de l'Air to meet a surprise attack that was likely to start any future war, so that the FAF would always have to be ready to counter-attack while also covering military mobilization. Jauneaud saw the role of the FAF in offensive Napoleonic terms in his instructions of April 1937. The Armée de l'Air's organization was tailored to this concept of a grand-strategic doctrine of two corps, one fighter and one bomber, in spite of the fact that the Ministère de l'Air (Air Ministry) Deuxième Bureau (French military intelligence agency) Intelligence assessments of the Luftwaffe were on target—the Luftwaffe was not nearly as strong as Goering boasted.

Yet others also shared the blame for the French defeat. Parlement did not vote the needed funding for the air arm until too late to produce tangible results before 1941–1942. By comparison, these French credits voted were less than half the Royal Air Force budget, even allowing for France's smaller population but greater area and longer frontiers. In addition, neither Ministre de l'Air La Chambre nor General Vuillemin in 1938 had cared for the better chef d'état majeur (chief of staff) candidate, General Jauneaud, and thus got rid of him. At the Munich meeting in late September 1938 between Hitler, Chamberlain, Mussolini, and Daladier, the obvious French aviation weakness determined Prime Minister Daladier's stance to avoid war and allow Germany to annex Czechoslovakia's German-populated Sudetenland at its border.

Thus a valid question is: Did Vuillemin, like armée General Maurice Gamelin, suffer from what Robert Pois and Philip Langer in their psychohistorical analysis call dysfunctional personal rigidity?[7] Vuillemin was clearly not the right man for the job. It seems evident that the capacity of the two French leaders to deal with the military tasks at hand in 1940 became severely constrained. It is doubtful that either fully appreciated the changes in the nature of war as it once had known it. Yet it is also true that analysis of their past achievements might not have predicted their failure in 1940. But then humans are inconsistent, especially when decision-making involves risk-taking, and when things go wrong they often fault their subordinates—or the politicians.

The defeated uphold the bravery of their opponents and bemoan the fact that they were overwhelmed by enemy numbers. This avoids a probing analysis of the overall causes of a failure and of the factors that lie outside of a narrow historical interpretation. The point is relevant to France in 1940. In the case of the Armée de l'Air, the opprobrium associated with Vichy during 1940–1944 has distorted and obscured the desperate elements of success that had existed with the FAF in May and June 1940. One of the end results of defeat is a series of efforts to place the blame, to excuse failures, and to rebuild an image. Failures thus may be artfully cloaked as success in order to preserve honor, rebuild morale, and lay the foundations of fire for a later rising phoenix.

Such activities essentially avoid and prevent serious analysis, and instead propagate myths. Out of touch with down-to-earth realities, unwilling to accept fact, the upper leadership pretends disaster never happened, as both Wolfgang Schivelbusch and Jared Diamond note.[8] In evaluating defeats, then, and their aftermath, these questions might be asked: Did the defeated military, as much as failed corporate leaders, not see that their strategy and tactics had brought on the downfall? Did they refuse to review these prior to disaster? Did they suppress those who might have questioned policy or procedure?

Patrick Facon, Director of Research at the Service Historique de l'Armée de l'Air (SHAA), in 1997 attempted to cleanse French history of these myths in his *Armée de l'Air dans la Tourmente*.[9]

The ignominious and sudden fall of France in forty-six days in 1940 shamed the country and embarrassed some Gauls, much as they still do not want to acknowledge this in 2011. France had reached a nadir both politically and socially. People had lost faith in the leadership of Paris. Armée de Terre (French army) reserves were ill-trained, ill-equipped, and ill-led, and as soon as they could, many deserted and returned home. In the 1940 Battle of France the Armée de Terre had 123,000 killed and 1,845,000 taken as POWs, many after General Henri-Philippe Pétain announced armistice talks with the Germans. The Armée de l'Air, however, was more élitist at all levels and *escadrilles* more homogeneous. Although there was desertion, some of it was from units left behind that had disintegrated. On the whole, during and after the May–June campaign most of the FAF retreated to southern France and North Africa more or less intact *sans* casualties.

In most armed forces, a strange dichotomy has developed between those with faith in the invulnerability of their own weapon and therefore a lack of need to consider protection against an enemy determined to destroy it and the opponents bent on just that. Thus the problem for the Allied Air Forces became acutely, after 10 May, how to deal with swarms of GAF escorts that made it hard to get at the bombers. That question was exacerbated by the speed of modern bombers and by old-fashioned legacies of the need for defensive fighters to fly in tight formations in order to bring enough firepower to bear to be lethal. Those tactics were based upon the two- to-four-gun fighter with guns only firing in the 600 rounds per minute range. Even the FAF fighters were able to throw more weight than that. But the real reason to abandon formation tactics (and later AVM Trafford Leigh-Mallory's "Big Wing") was that the eight-gun Hurricanes and Spitfires with their 1,200-rpm rate of fire were in themselves lethal with a two-second burst, provided their pilots were trained to aim effectively and had incendiary ammunition.[10]

After the June 1940 Franco-German armistice—not a *capitulation*, but a Versailles-style *Diktat*—the Armée de l'Air of Vichy was still commanded by the same group led by General Vuillemin, and would be until his retirement in October 1940. Up to late 1942 with the Allied invasion of North Africa, the FAF's problem was the effort to reestablish an élite force while still being ruled by the aged Marshal Pétain as head of the government of Unoccupied France. The Riom *procès* then brought it all to a crisis point, as the military in the end embarrassed the politicians. Hence, General Vuillemin needed to establish heroes and the fact that despite evident defeat the FAF nevertheless had been successful, and that it had, he averred, at the very least inflicted heavy casualties upon the enemy in spite of great odds and many wants. Thus he created a paradox.

General Vuillemin actually had predicted since 15 January 1938 that in a war with Germany the Armée de l'Air would collapse in two weeks. He had repeated that foreboding in September 1938 as Prime Minister Édouard Daladier signed the Munich accords. However, he apparently chose not to deal with or resolve these weaknesses in the air arm, ignoring the realities of modern mobile warfare, especially the performance competitiveness in the air of both machines and men. In addition, he apparently ignored the depth to which replacement of wastage and consumption had to be prepared and available on the opening day of a war, in this case 10 May 1940, together with a sustainability system.[11]

However, the Germans had analyzed the lessons of World War I, including the observation that unescorted bombers such as Zeppelins and later Gothas had to take into account the defenses, which included fighters. Ironically, the British derived two paradoxical lessons: one from the fighter and air-defense authorities that believed the attacker could be mastered, and one from the counterstrike-deterrent bomber policy-makers that believed the bomber would always get through. But in the Armée de l'Air, as Lieutenant Colonel A.

C. Cain noted, from 1933 to 1939 there was a lack of proficiency generally as revealed especially in maneuvers.[12]

H. R. "Dizzy" Allen, a Battle of Britain squadron leader, argued in 1974 that the 1940 campaign was not well fought; he detailed mistakes by the Air Staff as to armament and tactics, as well as the faulty insistence on sticking to the .303 caliber with its four-ounce bullet versus the American Colt .50 caliber with its four times more lethal round having twice the range. Allen also noted that RAF gunnery was pitiful, with the result that thousands of bullets were wasted before an enemy aircraft was brought down.[13] And though Armée de l'Air pilots may have had more hours, there is no proof they were better pilots or marksmen in spite of their claims.

Confirmation of these criticisms is to be found in the report of the secret Vichy Commission G. This body was under Colonel Jean Carayon and four others who were hidden in the archives at Toulouse where they studied the past, modern war, and the implications for the future at a time—1942—when it began to seem like the Allied camp would win. The commission examined the defeat of 1940. It criticized the lack of a national air program that left each armée seeing only its own battlefield, while aviation was the indispensable arm. It found that the FAF was inferior in quality and quantity to the enemy, concluding that was the fundamental cause of the defeat of 1940. In September 1939 the French aircraft industry was far behind the British and Germans, especially regarding bombers. Moreover the French suffered in 1940 from the extreme complexity and inefficiency of the chain of command as well as operational deficiencies. There were far too many echelons of command and these were confusing to the participants. At the time, the Armée de l'Air was seeking suitable solutions to the exigencies of combat and the ability to intervene quickly in the ground war. Furthermore, the commission noted that cooperation in modern war was not incompatible with independence. In addition, what was needed was a corps of armored aircraft to work with tanks, while bombers should also be employed in the attack, as were the Stuka and other antitank aircraft. The commission also called for airborne troops as well as aviation at sea to seize command of the air there.

Commission G further stated that in the Battle of 1940 the FAF had not been able to apply its doctrine because its matériel was lacking in quantity and quality and so was effective in neither army cooperation nor in the air. The 1934 strategy could still be a model for the future, but the Haut Commandement needed to be restructured in a simplified form à la the Law of 1934, so as to adapt peacetime organization to war. Doctrine had to be harmonized with the new tactics of modern war, including the use of the airborne and transports.

In reconstituting the new FAF, the human was just as important as the matériel, according to the commission. France's preparation had been wrong, and that had prevented her taking the initiative. Mobilization had become synonymous with imminent war. Commission G saw three important periods before a conflict: (1) *la periode normal*; (2) *la period de preparation intensive*; (3) *la mobilization general*. These stages were needed for the creation of a solid new air force that would think about air warfare. In addition, the FAF needed a new esprit de corps, which meant a break with the France of the past. After the defeat, the gap had widened between the armée, bred on the exploits of World War I, and civil society, which had discovered the falseness of all in which it had believed. And last, the Commission G blamed the aircraft industry for France's technological inferiority, which could not be recovered by purchases from the United States.

General Lucien Robineau, sometime chef de SHAA, in a private e-mail to the author (19 January 2000), sent a copy of his article "L'Armée de l'Air dans la Guerre 1939–1945," which appeared in the journal *Carnet de la sabretache: Revue militaire rétrospective* (1999). Robineau notes that what happened to France in June 1940 was a "Byzantine question." The armistice allowed the FAF to survive, though the majority of the reservists that had been mobilized returned home or decided to join the Forces libres français aérienne (Free-French air force [FFAF]).[14] The causes of the defeat, according to Robineau, originated from before World War I when the French état majeur (general staff) showed an interest in the new third dimension of war. In November 1914 General Joffre had laid down the tasks of the *escadrilles* as observation, reconnaissance, and the destruction in the air of enemy machines. The GSAF failed to set forth a doctrine, however, and the unprepared industry produced only slowly, rising from forty aircraft at the end of 1938 to five hundred in May 1940, when at last it equaled its British and German rivals, though still not *bon de guerre*—ready for war.

The FAF was outclassed in modern aircraft and on 10 May had too few and largely untrained bomber units. The air forces were divided between those of cooperation and those reserved, the bulk being assigned to the armée. The Haut Commandement had no counterforce at its disposal. Its power was dispersed in penny packets due to lack of intellectual preparation. As a result it lost nearly 900 aircraft, mostly to intense flak, without seriously damaging the potential of the Luftwaffe and fire support. By 1916 experience had shown the need to obtain air superiority and the offensive actions of many airplanes, as seen in the Duval Division of 1918 of roughly 1,000 aircraft, culminating in the American Billy Mitchell's 1,500 planes at St. Mihiel.

The figure of 900 in 1940 had been the earlier one.

In 1990 Paul Martin gave the FAF loss from 10 May–24 June 1940 as 647 aircraft to the GAF's 664 in combat, plus 75 French and 430 in accidents.[15] In contrast the Armée de l'Air from 3 September 1939 to 9 May 1940 lost 72 in action. Peter Cornwell, in *The Battle of France Then and Now*, tallied the FAF loss then at 1,403, to which has to be added 286 in the Phoney War for a grand total from all causes of 1,689.[16] For the same 3 September 1939 to 9 May 1940 the write-offs were 189, followed by 1,067.[17] In the Luftwaffe case, the attrition was 5,050 up to 9 May 1940 and 1,814 thereafter.[18]

The RAF total for 3 September 1939–9 May 1940 was 189, plus 1,067 for 10 May–23 June 1940, for a grand total of 1,256. The Luftwaffe lost 151 and 354, or 505 before 9 May, followed by 1,476 in May, plus 338 in June, for a total of 2,319. In contrast, at the 1918 Armistice between the victorious Allies and Germany, French military aviation had roughly 12,000 machines in 300 *escadrilles* in the schools and in reserve.

But the emphasis upon individual combats and aerial victories produced an undesirable effect; it concealed to 1939 the need for an air force organization conforming to the needs of rapid movement of modern war. The Haut Commandement had two fixed ideas: that airpower was to be used for observation, and a confused concept that air superiority meant using fighters in direct protection of observation machines and to cover the armée on the ground—a vision reinforced by colonial operations where there was no aerial opposition. After the 1928–1934 interval, the Armée de l'Air made additional demands upon a limited budget.

The concentration of the air circumstances at the time explain the defeat of 1940. The Armée de l'Air saw its role as attacking the enemy's economic and industrial resources, airfields, and the battlefield. But French politics was pacifist and supported the grand strategy defensive. The first comprehensive rearmament plan dated only from March 1938 and of necessity concentrated on production of existing types as opposed to prototypes.[19] Furthermore the German advance into France was well supplied with fuel and ammunition and still had at least 50 percent of its tanks in running order on 20 May; most actually had not been destroyed. Those left en route only needed first- or second-line repairs.

Preparation for War

After his August 1938 visit to Germany, General Vuillemin had predicted that the FAF would lose 40 percent of its effective strength in the first month of a war and 64 percent in the second. To Prime Minister Daladier's surprise, Ministre de l'Air La Chambre supported this pessimistic view of France's impotence. Daladier felt the heavy weight of the Luftwaffe, and La Chambre and Daladier were both prisoners of the French defensive grand strategy and of the desire for a British alliance. Gradually agreement was reached for a twenty-squadron British Advanced Air Striking Force (AASF) of 240 bombers to move to France on the outbreak of war. However, in the spring of 1939 the British still refused to commit Fighter Command to the defense of France, despite the French plea that their own *chausseurs* were too few to cover the mobilization of the armée and to defend vital targets. Concurrently British thought was dominated by fear of a massive German air attack against London, a view still held in June 1940; but London did agree to send four fighter squadrons to France as part of the Air Component of the British Expeditionary Force.

General Gamelin was disappointed by this, for he wanted a complete British bomber force sent to France to attack Germany while the Armée de l'Air would be entirely devoted to the ground-cooperation role. Closer relations came in the spring of 1939 at the time Prague fell to the Germans, but the Royal Air Force Fighter Command was to remain firmly in Britain. This was another disappointment for Gamelin, who again noted that the French *chasse* were too few to protect the assembly of the ground forces and the vital centers in France.

At the Council on National Defense meeting on 23 August 1939, while General Gamelin was optimistic about the outcome of a war, General Vuillemin—like Admiral "Jacky" Fisher at the Cabinet meeting in London on the Dardenelles in 1915—remained silent; he was never asked to speak, as La Chambre spoke for him saying the FAF was not in as negative a condition as a year earlier. In addition the Inspector-génèral of the Armée de l'Air, General Georges Aubé, never mentioned the "immense insufficiencies" of the DCA—the antiaircraft—a deficiency that would allow French cities to be bombed. Following the Council meeting, General Vuillemin and his chef d'état majeur, General Mendigal, drafted a letter of advice to Prime Minister Daladier because he had a professional sense of his duty to his country. Vuillemin, the "Chief," was a brave man of action, a legend, though lacking in political savoir faire and audacity; he was not a risk taker.

In late 1939 General Vuillemin seemed to change his view of the coming war, seeing the British commitment as strengthening French political will against Germany; then, too, there was London's willingness to use RAF bombers more widely in the continental war. Vuillemin believed also that the fruits of French rearmament were becoming visible. However, after the June 1940 Franco-German armistice, General Gamelin, the overall commander in chief to 19 May, and Alphonse-Joseph Georges, the Commandement en chef (general in chief), Zone d'Opérations Nord-Est (air zone of operations northeast [ZONE]), blamed the critical loss of the Meuse crossings on the inferiority of French aviation. General Georges added that the prewar failure to integrate the armée and air staffs (état majeur) was a mistake, though Britain and the RAF were also to blame for the loss.

By the Battle of Britain in the summer and fall of 1940, when the Luftwaffe sought to decimate the Royal Air Force, RAF Fighter Command had fifty-five squadrons with an initial establishment—the number of aircraft the Air Staff had determined they would need—of 16 aircraft plus 2 spares each, for a total of 990. With France's physical area approximately 2.25 times that of Great Britain, France should have had 124 *escadrilles chasse* of eighteen planes each, or 186 *escadrilles* of 12 planes for a total of 2,232 aircraft. Britain's Air Chief Marshal Sir Hugh Dowding of Fighter Command's fifty-five squadrons had an initial establishment of twenty-six pilots for a total of 1,430. Extrapolating once again, this means that the 124 Armée de l'Air *chasseur* at twenty-six pilots each should have had a total of 3,224, not the nominal 637 of 10 May 1940.[20]

Using the 1936 British *SD 98* rates on wastage and consumption, the Armée de l'Air's *chasse* twelve-aircraft *escadrilles,* with an initial serviceability of 68 percent of twelve machines, needed an eighteen initial establishment (IE) for maximum effort. At 50 percent serviceability they needed to keep twenty-four machines on the airfield, and at 30 percent (the latter being French General Vuillemin's claimed rate) forty aircraft.[21]

In other words, the fighting squadrons needed a steady supply of replacement aircraft just to sustain operations without allowance for aircraft shot down, damaged, or missing, or for replacement of pilots whose fitness would have declined rapidly after three days of intensive operations.[22]

Yet despite what appear to be inadequate numbers of aircraft and pilots for the Armée de l'Air, nevertheless all ground attacks on the enemy and especially the destruction of enemy air arm were to be an FAF responsibility. Ministre de l'Air Pierre Cot and his Chef de Cabinet Lieutenant General Jauneaud had created the necessary air force *on paper* with a strategic unity of heavy bombers and fighters, a plan that had been promulgated in September and October 1936. It was later opposed by General Vuillemin on behalf of cooperation (support) aviation and by General Philippe Féquant, then chief of the état majeur de l'Armée de l'Air, as being contrary to the Law of 1934. Critics within the Air Ministry were also opposed, and when in February 1937 Cot proposed to the Comité Permanente de la Défense Nationale (permanent committee of national defense) to expand the FAF by Plans III and IV, the proposals were blocked by the armée, and especially by Marshal Pétain. It was General Jauneaud's later opinion that if funded and provided with suitable aircraft, these plans might have saved France in 1939. With Plans III and IV rejected, in the "*deuxième semester*" (the second half) of 1937 the emphasis, as in Britain, was placed upon fighters. Yet at the same time Cot recognized that the Armée de l'Air would have to be closely involved with the Armée de Terre, which meant also light bombers and ground-attack (assault) machines. Both La Chambre and Vuillemin were critical.

However, the FAF and the armée misunderstood. Earlier, in 1935, Colonel Amedeo Mecozzi of Italy's Regia Aeronautica had begun to confirm that assault aviation was simply another form of cooperation, and that caused airmen to fear being placed again under the armée.[23] The success of the Germans and Italians in the Spanish Civil War that began in 1936, and on into 1939, exacerbated arguments in Paris where the armée was not sympathetic to aviation.

The Spanish Civil War had caused the FAF to rethink its own theory, based upon numerous published reports on the air war in the Iberian Peninsula, for General Maginel assessed the Guadalajara Campaign as a textbook case of air-ground cooperation. Pierre Cot, the World War I cavalry officer and Ministre de l'Air from 1933–1934 and 1936–1938, tried to change French air force doctrine and organization to focus it not on the defensive but on the offensive, with production of bombers rather than defensive fighters for the new national air organization—as opposed to regional—subordinate to Commandement d'Armée (army command). Cot's interest in aviation had stemmed from the 1931 Aeropostale affair, when the Chambre des Députés (Chamber of Deputies) would not renew the company's government subsidy amidst its plunge to bankruptcy. The result was a run on three Paris banks that had large investments in Aeropostale. Cot subsequently had received his civilian pilot wings in 1933.

A special issue of the *Revue d'Histoire de la Deuxieme Guerre Mondiale* (January 1969), devoted to aviation from 1919 to 1946, saw authors placing the debate on three themes: (1) the supposed numerical and qualitative inferiority of the Armée de l'Air in May–June 1940, (2) the Haut Commandement deployment of its air assets, and (3) the state of aerial rearmament before the war.[24] It was pointed out that after the 1938 Anschluss, Germany had 82 million people to France's 42 million and Britain's 50 million, with the Allies having the combined advantage.

At the Riom *procès* in 1942 the Armée Haut Commandement led by Gamelin blamed the Armée de l'Air for the failure at the Meuse.[25] The generals claimed it had occurred because they did not control the air arm, but they neglected to note their own failure to develop tanks, antitank guns, and DCA, as well as a counter-blitzkrieg doctrine. Vuillemin replied that the FAF's maté-riel was not modern, the replacements were making delayed entry into service, and that the FAF was wrongly employed without any hope of concentration. Moreover, the FAF had had to expand its resources to make up for deficiencies on the ground. Much of the Armée de l'Air's troubles, Vuillemin claimed, came from too little, too late. The air arm could not make up for the domination in defense of the armée's traditional infantry-artillery cooperation.

As to matériel, at Riom the chef de l'Entrepôt de Armée de l'Air 301, the reception center, maintained that he had supplied from 1 September 1939 to 25 June 1940 all the aircraft that the GSAF had demanded—1,732 to the units and 1,684 to the training schools—and that on 25 July 1940 there were 4,268 in Vichy (Unoccupied) France, of which 1,730 were first line, plus another 1,800 in North Africa, of which 800 were first line. Cot argued that the FAF could have maintained 1,649 aircraft in the field if the Haut Commandement had so wished. (But for these the FAF did not have air, nor ground, crews.) And to these could have been added the RAF's 1,875 machines *"bon de guerre."* Cot averred that not until 1972 did the Service Historique de l'Armée de l'Air (SHAA) stop falsifying the GAF totals so as to make it appear the GAF supe-riority was 3:1.[26]

General Vuillemin had claimed, in spite of the accurate estimates of the Deuxième Bureau Intelligence, that the Luftwaffe had 9,000 planes (a bit less than the erroneous British Air Ministry estimates in London of 14,000).[27] Cot stressed in 1971 that if the Allies had put their air forces together, they would have been roughly at par with the Germans—3,600 to 3,356, but the GSAF in Paris had failed to prepare for modern war. The key fault came in May–June 1940 in the failure to make up for losses with modern aircraft *bon de guerre* at the front. Yet Allied aircraft production in September 1939 exceeded that of the Germans by 3,122 to 1,684.

However, not only does this not square with the facts, but also Cot over-looked training time, plus the transition hours for pilots going on to new types together with the severe maintenance shortages that led to *indisponibles*, and the lack of a ferry system to bring new machines forward. In other words the Armée de l'Air lacked sustainability. Cot faults the Haut Commandement for not employing all of the 4,554 modern aircraft on charge—that is, on a unit's records—rather than only the 1,558 plus 91 reserves available on 10 May. One result of this charging system was that Paris carelessly thought it had many more modern aircraft than it really did as the majority were unusable. Only 20 of the new French Dewoitine 520 fighters reached the front, while at least 120 were at depots not *bon de guerre*.[28]

Yet Cot overlooks the strange Gallic system whereby aircraft far from *bon de guerre* were on charge. That lacuna was due, he says, to poor organization (but which he had overseen to 1938). And then there was the failure to employ the available assets. The answer is because the GSAF failed to create a modern Armée de l'Air with bomber units. In fairness, Cot had tried in 1936–1938 to develop one, but his successor La Chambre dismantled it, and that destroyed the work begun in 1933. In the end, Cot said it was a grand-strategic, strategic, and intellectual failure—an immense line from Norway to the Mediterranean to oppose the concentrated Luftflotten 2 and 3 (air fleets). And the FAF and the RAF had neglected the tactical lessons of Spain and Poland.[29] Cot concluded that the defeat of 1940 came from assigning the air assets to 1918 roles, a lack of assault aircraft, wasteful consumption of aircrew in continuous action (à la the RAF in 1918), and a failure to recruit enough personnel.

This was why the Armée de l'Air was better equipped on 25 June 1940 than in September 1939. Still, at the Franco-German armistice, on 24 June 1940, the Allies needed 1,800 replacement machines to the German 1,700. The results of the battle showed, Cot said, that in both matériel and training the Armée de l'Air was not as bad as claimed.[30]

The new French air doctrine advocated the seizure of air superiority and denial of the sky to the enemy. Cot argued also for army cooperation and for the centralization of air defense. In early 1938, however, his efforts and ideas were repudiated by the new Ministre de l'Air, Guy La Chambre, a former undersecretary of war, and the lessons of Spain ignored. Cot had gained his ideas from General Denain and then from General Féquant. La Chambre took his from Vuillemin. All had to respect the wishes of the ministers of national defense.

The French Ministère de l'Air Plan V had put the emphasis on bombers, but the industry could not produce them and thus observation machines and fighters had been built instead. Out of the 864 planes in Plan V, 144 U.S. dive-bombers had been ordered, but the Armée de l'Air was not interested in them and in late 1939 they were given to La Royale, the French navy. The état majeur had put fighters first and wanted perfection, wrote Patrick Facon, but that is not what they ordered, as the text herein shows that follow on the MS-406, Bloch 151/152, and D-520. The lack of assault aviation in May–June 1940 would not have made any difference, Facon noted, in spite of La Chambre saying it would have.[31] In the view of our contemporary Brigadier General Michael Clemessen of the Danish army, who had had twelve years' experience in the education of staff officers, the GSAF was part of a de-professionalized military in which the staff carried responsibilities that should have been the duties of other more qualified officers, and for this faulty system the GSAF had to share the blame.[32]

As to the case of the antiaircraft potential, time was lost both regarding Command arrangements and technically from 1931, and that could not be regained. Under the Law of 11 July 1938 the Ministère de l'Air was placed in charge of the Défense Aérienne du Territoire (DAT), but the Ministère de la Guerre (war ministry) obtained the antiaircraft protection of the armée. While the law made the air commander the controller of all aviation for defense, in fact he commanded only that in the Zone d'Interiuer (zone of the interior [ZI]), leaving the armée the battlefield and the Royale the coastal waters. Once again, in historian Facon's view, service rivalries stymied a necessary rationalization and led to a wasteful distribution of financial resources and material means. Political and fiscal weakness prevented taking the drastic steps necessary.

This approach to DCA was vigorously opposed in the état majeur and in the Ministère de la Guerre, as well as in the Permanent Council for National Defense, as unbalanced and dangerous, and thus Ministre de l'Air Cot's expansion Plans III and IV had been blocked and delay ensued. At the same time, Cot saw that the ground battle would need light bombers and assault aircraft to attack enemy shock troops. The question of how to employ air assets that were constantly modernizing added confusion to the issues, and the infrastructure needed to support them was ignored.

Unfortunately in September 1939 the reorganization of the Armée de l'Air for war and the question of who would control it were still unclear, as was concentration or distribution of the air assets. While other air forces had specific—if sometimes misguided—doctrines, the Armée de l'Air was still in 1940 trying to clarify its roles: deterrent bombing force, air defense of the metropolitan territories, or army cooperation (reconnaissance and observation). Even its command structure had not been settled since Pierre Cot's 1933 decree creating an independent air arm. Command and control was in May 1940 still vague and communications lacked the wireless net needed for proper management. On top of that, the chain of command was far too rigid and slow for modern battle—targets were long gone before authority to strike them arrived.

Unlike other air forces in the world—the U.S. Navy, the Royal Air Force, the Luftwaffe, and the Soviet—the Armée de l'Air in the 1930s had decided not to expand its personnel, keeping instead a small élite force of pilots, aircrew, and mechanics. As a result, when expansion became a necessity, the FAF could not man or maintain the complex new types coming off the production lines nor a suitable training infrastructure. It is of interest to note the apparent lack of such when compared with, for example, the record of the Finnish air force.

In 1938 when French army General Gamelin, who oversaw defense, had claimed that France could defend itself perfectly well without aircraft, the

Comité Permanente de la Défense Nationale (national defense committee) did not challenge him as it was not interested in aviation. When Premier Daladier had asked on 23 August 1939 if France was ready for war, General Gamelin was optimistic—he thought the Poles could hold out until the spring of 1940. And at the time, Daladier believed that French production of fighters had caught up with the combined German-Italian force—though in reality fighters accepted by the Armée de l'Air were a far cry both in terms of war readiness and operationally ready aircrew. Added to that, another part of the problem, in historian Facon's view, was that General Vuillemin had all the assets of a fighting leader but none of a chief of staff.[33]

Looking back at the Armée de l'Air and its *chausseurs* in 1940, it must be said that the inadequacies in numbers, technical development, and personnel had deep causes. In part, the deficiencies were rooted in the domination of the army in French defense, even after the Armée de l'Air came into being in 1933. Though the Ministère de l'Air had been created in 1928 and Albert Caquot, the World War I engineer, had been brought back in to help France regain her technical preeminence in the air world, the prototypes he sponsored were still of the 1918 line and of little use at the dawn of the Technological Revolution.

That radical change in aeronautics, unfortunately, coincided with the rise of the radicals in politics, which led to the decision of the Popular Front government of 1936–1938 to nationalize the aircraft industry. Confusion resulted, as well as delays in design, approval of prototypes, and production, in addition to a lack of funding. This confusion and delay could be blamed on the army because General Gamelin had refused to allow airmen any rein, while not understanding the process of modern aviation progress, rapid as it was when compared with 1918. But the Parlement also shared the criticism because its committees did not push for funds, being far more interested in the politics that caused short-lived Cabinets and discontinuous policies.

Significant as well was that while the état majeur de l'Armée de l'Air (French Air Force General Staff) argued about doctrine, they failed to undertake a rigorous examination of the trends emerging in Germany, in Spain, and across the Channel, where the RAF since 1918 had been examining many of the future issues in both the light of the past and for the future, unhampered by a dominant armée, but aided by continuities in power. Foresight and finance were essential. France, unfortunately, lacked both of those, together with continuity of direction and the will and vision to create a viable defense in spite of the costs of the 1914–1918 war.

That the Armée de l'Air was not prepared for war is to be seen not only in the inefficient and misleading delivery of aircraft to its depots and its lethargic preparation of them to be war ready, but also in the fact that after 3 September 1939 the training establishments in North Africa were shut down during the Phoney War and the attitude in Metropolitan France was that trainees should enjoy themselves and worry about learning new skills later. Then, too, there was the mishandling of the Polish and Czech volunteers, many of whom had their pilots' brevets (wings), but who were shoved off to nonflying positions or retrained as gunners. The Air Force General Staff also failed in its duty when it opted not to develop an enlarged training organization to meet the need for both aircrew and ground crew to man the new machines being produced under the fresh plans. In spite of starting training in September 1939, the FAF schools turned out no pilots who flew in combat before the Franco-German armistice. On 10 May 1940 the Armée de l'Air was short of pilots and had only 22 percent of the balloon technician specialists it needed.[34] Mechanics in general were only 66 percent of need. Noncommissioned (NCO) pilots were only 70.8 percent of establishment.[35]

French Fighter Aircraft

During the 249-day Phoney War, from 3 September 1939 to 10 May 1940, the Armée de l'Air flew 9,500 fighter sorties (32.3 per day) and 2,000 reconnaissance flights for a loss of 174 (or 1.5 percent) as against Luftwaffe losses of 74 to 77. By May 1940 the fighter *groupes* each had twenty-six planes. Of the 637 fighters based in metropolitan France, 570 were single-seaters. Some thirty-five of the forty-six Groupement d'Air Observation had the new twin-engined Potez 63-11s. Because the Battle of France was all about aerial combat, and because the Armée de l'Air made great claims of victories, an examination of its equipment and firepower is required. The following information is taken from the two volumes by Dominique Breffort and André Joineau, *French Aircraft from 1939 to 1942*.[36]

French fighter aircraft were at least a year behind those of the Royal Air Force and three years behind the Luftwaffe. The design process was slow, but no slower than for the others. Prototypes were not always successful, or perhaps the Ministère de l' Air expected perfection. In France the procurement system was chaotic and lacking in controls and responsibility. The GSAF decided what it wanted, then drafted specifications, which after approval by the minister were sent to select manufacturers. After nationalization in 1936, these manufacturers were really design offices. The companies then went to work and submitted prototypes, one or more of which was then selected for a preproduction order. These aircraft were then delivered to the reception center, taken on Armée de l'Air charge, and the manufacturer paid. However, the machines probably lacked propellers, engines, and radios, which were belatedly supplied by contractors, and the machines then went slowly to have armament fitted. Eventually the plane was flown briefly by a service test pilot who might or might not be able to declare it ready to be issued to a service or frontline unit. Of the aircraft produced, about a third never left the depots, or were delivered to *escadrilles* still unfit for operations.

The acquisition process early on discharged the manufacturers, while the arsenals then had to deal with the lethargy of subcontractors and consequent shortages of equipment from propellers to armament to radios. According to the British Air Ministry, *Battle of France,* Appendix E, regarding the Armée de l'Air, on 6 May the Bloch *escadrilles* had twenty to twenty-five aircraft each, the Morane 406 eighteen to thirty-eight, and the Curtiss Hawks twenty-eight to thirty.[37]

The Morane-Saulnier MS-406

Taking the story of each type in the *chasseur* arsenal, a start must be made with the Morane-Saulnier MS-406, the most numerous type, with 179 on the books of the thirteen *groupes chausseurs* (GC) sent to the front, but they were only effective when in the hands of very good pilots. Like the engines of the day, the aircraft suffered from flaws not corrected in peacetime: the cowling flew off in a tight turn, the weapons and radio were defective, and the fragile tail skid did not stand up to rough airfield conditions. (RAF aircraft suffered some of the same problems, but they were dealt with as urgent.) The MS-406's Hispano-Suiza engine was underpowered, fragile, and a maintenance hog. It proved unable to stand the fighter routine of an hour at full throttle. The British Rolls-Royce Merlin engines also had teething problems, but the company was concerned about its reputation and had the talent to fix them. Moreover, in World War I, Rolls-Royce had established the practice of attaching factory representatives to units in the field in order to get feedback to the factory from trained personnel they could trust. RAF tests required 150 continuous hours at full throttle.

The MS-406 was the only FAF plane of which nearly 1,000 had been produced by the end of 1939. Conceived as the 1934 C-1 based upon 1932 armament requirements, this program's specifications were revised in November 1935 to have a top speed of 280 mph and a service ceiling of 37,900 feet, an airframe not to exceed 5,500 pounds, and an 800–1,000-hp engine. The prototype first flew at Villacoublay on 8 August 1936 and underwent a yearlong trial at the end of which only minor modifications were made (evidently the aircraft was never "wrung out," as defects remained). In spite of a French reputation for engineering, the failure to test the MS-406 apparently was typical of what ailed the Armée de l'Air. Though in May 1940 the fighter was coming to the end of its service, it was not a well-honed weapon. In part this was because the whole FAF procurement system was lax, and in part because the aged *chasseur* pilots were afraid of the new high-speed monoplanes, a phenomenon seen in other air forces during the transition from open cockpit, fixed-undercarriage biplanes to the new enclosed cockpit, retractable-undercarriage monoplanes. Engines, too, were unreliable because there were too few older and experienced mechanics to get the "bugs" out. Nor did the rigid air hierarchy with its solid top encourage the posting of information up the chain of command to those who were clearly not interested in technology.[38]

The MS-406 was slow, climbed poorly, had an ineffective, drag-inducing cooling system, a propeller that did not function properly, and was limited to 31,000 feet. The cannon was kept warm over the motor, but the shells tended to explode prematurely on leaving the aircraft. The wing-mounted machine guns were defective, with a drum of 300 rounds, causing a drag-inducing bulge under the wings—a lack of finesse in a machine that needed it. In addition, these guns dispersed rather than concentrated their fire, and the rearview mirror oscillated. One day a pilot aimed at a village and hit nothing. And during the cold nights of 1939–1940 the engines were hard to start and used several bottles of compressed air, thus delaying takeoff. One wonders how such an ineffective system could have been accepted by the responsible technical and military parties.

The MS-406 was ordered as a preproduction batch in March 1937, with a production order in November. With the tense international situation and the deplorable position of the FAF fighters, the advantage of the nonproprietary national aircraft factories was that mass production could be dispersed over several sites. However, production was slow because the industry had barely shifted to all-metal construction and because the Morane-Saulnier design required 16,000 hours to assemble—more than double the labor needed for the German Messerschmitt or the French Dewoitine D-520. MS-406 production did rise up to mid-1938, but a shortage of Hispano-Suiza engines then held up deliveries. The result was that when war broke out on 3 September 1939 only 572 MS-406s were war ready, as opposed to an expected 955. By the 24 June 1940 Franco-German armistice, the Centre de Réception des Avions de Series (CRAS), which received production aircraft, had taken only slightly more than 1,000 on charge, of which 932 had been built in 1939 alone. On 10 May the MS-406 equipped twelve of the twenty-two *groupes chasseur* in France and those in the colonies with more than 250 aircraft in service, plus those in training schools and the DAT in Metropolitan France.

The MS-406 had an all-up weight of 5,588 pounds, an 860-hp Hispano-Suiza engine, a 20-mm cannon, two 7.5-mm MAC 34 M39 machine guns, and a Chaunier three-blade propeller giving it a top speed of 306 mph. It had a better performance than the RAF's last biplane fighter, the 840-hp Gloster Gladiator, which with an all-up weight of 4,750 pounds could only do 253 mph, though the Gladiator—both the French and the British—had four machine guns. Just before the war, a cockpit roll bar was added and the aircraft received an improved landing gear. The MS-406 had sixty rounds for its 20-mm cannon and either 300 or 675 rounds per gun (rpg) for its two machine guns. In spite of the 20-mm cannon, the aircraft could not effectively attack tight enemy formations with their defensive crossfire even if it could catch the German bombers.

Almost half of all Armée de l'Air pilots lost between 10 May and 24 June were killed in MS-406s, and at an increasing rate when employed in ground attacks against Wehrmacht columns defended by quad 20-mm flak guns. All in all, about 387 MS-406s had been lost by 24 June, including 150 in combat and those machines abandoned during the withdrawal to the south when *escadrilles* changed airfields daily. The MS-406 *escadrilles* claimed 190 enemy shot down and 90 probables, or 1.9 enemies for every MS-406 lost—not a very efficient score against enemy bombers as well, given the Morane's difficulties with Me-109s in the air and enemy flak in the ground-attack role.

The Bloch 151/152

The second most-produced French fighter was the Bloch 151/152. The original design to the 1934 specification was the MB-150, the prototype of which on 17 July 1936 was unable to get off the ground on its maiden flight. It was not an auspicious beginning and thus it was shelved. In September 1937 the Ministère de l'Air revised the specification and Bloch entered the competition again. A prototype was ordered in January 1938 followed in April by a preproduction order of twenty-five. However, the aircraft was not easy to mass-produce, and thus the design was reworked. The new machine suffered from engine overheating due to the tight cowling, making it still unacceptable and unable to meet the specifications. By April 1939 only four MB-151s had been delivered, but by May 1940 production had reached twenty-two per month, still with cooling problems, as well as with propeller concerns. The production order for 488 was then divided into two parts: the MB-151 with 920 hp, and the MB-152 with 1,020 hp. Nevertheless of the 120 delivered by September 1939, 95 did not have propellers. Only Groupe Chasseur 1/1 had MB-152s in July 1939, but it was not operational and thus the unit was switched to the new Dewoitine D-520.

By late 1939 four *groupes* had MBs, but their pilots were only lukewarm about the machine, especially its instability in a dive. During 10–31 May 1940 more than 144 MB-152s were in service, with another 84 more supplied to units between 1 and 6 June. All told, by 24 June the FAF had received 632 MB-151s and MB-152s, with 80 lost. Because the MBs had insufficient range (337 miles) to reach North Africa, they remained in France after the armistice. Fitted with a license-built American Wright engine, which proved to be thoroughly unreliable, they were not prized steeds. They were overweight at 6,380 pounds and could barely do 306 mph. The MB-151s were under-armed with four MAC34 machine guns of 300 rpg and a rate of fire of only 550 rounds per minute (rpm), giving 32 seconds of firepower, with 8.4-oz bullets for a throw weight (impact) of 249 pounds or 2,149,120 foot-pounds (the amount of energy needed to move one pound a distance of one foot). The MB-152s had two MAC30s and two 20-mm cannon with 60 rpg and a rate of fire of 500 to 750 rpm.

In contrast to the MBs, the British Hawker Hurricane, which had entered service in 1937, was essentially a monoplane version of the successful Hawker Fury line. It weighed 6,600 pounds, could do 316 mph at 17,000 feet with its 1,050-hp Rolls-Royce Merlin engine, could climb to 15,000 feet in 6.3 minutes, and had a range of 460 miles. The companion Supermarine Spitfire had the same Merlin engine, but weighed only 5,784 pounds, had a maximum speed of 355 mph at 19,000 feet, and had a time to climb of 6.3 minutes to 15,000 feet and 10 minutes to 20,000 feet.[39] Both were armed with eight Browning .303s.

The Arsenal VG-33

The Arsenal VG-33 fighter and variants had been started in 1937 as replacements for the MS-406, but only one had reached the Armée de l'Air by April 1940. The VG-33 had an 860-hp engine and could do 344 mph when test-flown in the spring of 1938; the VG-39, with a 1,280-hp Hispano-Suiza engine, touched 393 mph. But French engine makers could not keep up the rhythm of production, so that this promising line of fighters never entered service. Apart from the Arsenal design of the VG-33 and variants, which did not enter production before the armistice, the best Armée de l'Air fighter was the Dewoitine D-520, a private venture.

The Dewoitine 520

When the French aircraft industry was nationalized in 1936, the design offices remained in private hands and had remuneration paid them in compensation for the state taking over their factories. Emile Dewoitine then took his team to Toulouse in partnership with Mark Birgit of Hispano-Suiza. By that time Dewoitine had had a very wide experience in the Romanian, Russian, and French aircraft industries. His second truly modern design was accepted by the GSAF on 12 January 1937.

The GSAF's new 1936 specification had called for a monoplane capable of 312 mph at 43,500 feet (13,200 meters), armed with either a cannon and two machine guns or two 20-mm cannon. Built around Birgit's new Hispano-Suiza 12Y12 engine, the monoplane was quickly modified to get 325 mph and was accepted on 12 February 1937. Delay then followed because the factory was nationalized in March and subcontractors had to be arranged. Three prototypes thus were not ordered until April 1938, and the first did not fly until 2 October. A forced landing in November caused a further impediment, and the second prototype did not fly until late January 1939, the third not until 5 May. With Dewoitine's rivals falling by the wayside, 200 machines were ordered in March 1939 for delivery by the end of the year, and a further purchase of 510 followed. Under Plan V, approved in June, another 200 were added.

The French *Aero Journal* has published a series on both Armée de l'Air *groupes* and on their aircraft. Issue No. 40 carries a long article on the cannon-armed, fixed-undercarriage, open-cockpit Dewoitine D-500/D-510, the first modern French fighter. [40] It entered service in March 1935, only six months ahead of the Me-109B, yet already by then there was a great gap between the two. Emile Dewoitine and his staff had been in exile in Romania when recalled by Albert Caquot in 1929 to assist in "the policy of prototypes." The earlier D-500 series were radical in that they had a 20-mm cannon firing through the propeller hub of the 690–760-hp Hispano-Suiza engine. Including 47 for export, 383 were produced between 1932 and 1937. *Escadrilles* with the D-510 were still being converted to either the MB-151 or the Dewoitine 520 as late as May 1940. [41] On 10 May, only one *groupe* had the dream machine, the Dewoitine D-520.

The first production aircraft with a 945-hp supercharged engine had its initial flight on 31 October 1939, but further manufacture was held up by engine overheating and by inoperable armament, delaying until January 1940 the test models sent to the evaluation center at Villacoublay. An experimental squadron, as was usual, then formed to work out any complications. The D-520 was not declared *bon de guerre* until 1 April, by which time 139 had been built, but only 75 were with the Armée de l'Air. In all, 2,200 were ordered by 14 April 1940, and by 22 June 361 had been delivered; 221 were in combat with VF1+1, and 99 had been lost in action or written off.

In service the D-520's 330-mph top speed compared favorably with the Me-109E's 342 mph, and its time-to-climb to 15,000 feet equaled the 6.3 minutes of the Spitfire. The D-520's single 60-round 20-mm cannon and two 7.5-mm machine guns gave it a throw weight of 3,467,500 foot-pounds. The D-520 was racy, hard to handle, delicate on the controls, and underpowered versus the German Messerschmitt Me-109 except at altitude; but it was excellent in a dive. British test pilot Eric Brown, author of *Testing for Combat*, had flown 487 basic types at the time his book was published in 1994, and he did not rank the D-520 very well at all.[42] The impression left was that it was never wrung out in testing, time of course being a factor. The aircraft had a variety of vices, including sudden stalls under G, turning into vicious—even inverted—spins during which it lost ten thousand feet. And while very maneuverable, it snaked in turbulence, as in another's slipstream, making it an unsuitable platform for its weak armament. The D-520 was no match for the Me-109E; it was tricky to land and ground-looped easily for lack of rudder control in the three-point position.[43]

On 10 May only GC I/3 had turned in its MS-406s and was operational with the D-520, which represented only an eighth of the *chausseurs*. Two more *escadrilles*, GC II/3—which took thirty-thee machines to the northern front on 20 May—and II/7, slowly converted in April and May and were *bon de guerre* on 13 May, but were withdrawn to North Africa after 10 June. By the end of May GC II/5 had been converted, followed in early June by GC II/6. On 9 June this *groupe* reached the front, but a few days later left Nonancourt for North Africa, because the Haut Commandement had opted to send as many as possible of the latest FAF fighter out of reach of the Germans. GC II/7 only received its D-520s in late April 1940; it entered the fray on 1 June and obtained its first kills on 15 June and then was evacuated to North Africa. GC III/6 was the last unit to convert from the MS-406 beginning 2 June and to see action. It fell back on Luc en Provence to begin training, saw action against the Italian Regia Aeronautica on 13 June, and left for North Africa on 20 June. Still then being in the conversion stage, GC III/6 had twenty-one D-520s at the time of the Franco-German armistice.

Overall, the 5 D-520 *groupes* fought only from 13 May to 10 June and then 175 went to North Africa from 18–25 June. The D-520 *groupes* were limited by the armistice to 4, while the 4 remaining units were sent to the Levant with a total of sixty-three machines of which they lost thirty-seven in the one-month campaign against the British attack on Syria in July 1941. Another source says GCIII/6 lost twenty aircraft and five pilots for twenty-one kills and four probables in thirty days.[44]

The Curtiss 75/P-36

The tardiness of French aircraft production caused Minister La Chambre, with Premier Daladier's approval, to order more than five thousand American engines, as well as one hundred Curtiss Model 75A export fighters. This 5,880-pound machine could do 322 mph maximum, with a ceiling of 32,350 feet and a range of 650 miles.[45] The original FAF H-75A Hawk was equipped with an unsatisfactory French-built Wright engine of the type supplied to France. Production models as delivered had either improved Wright or Pratt & Whitney motors. Designed in 1935 for the competition to replace the Boeing P-26A, the "Peashooter," the H-75 competed against the Seversky P-35, which won. Nevertheless the U.S. Army Air Corps ordered three prototypes in July 1936, and a year later purchased two hundred Curtiss P-36s (the USAAC designation), and those began to be delivered in April 1938.

The original 675-hp engine of the P-36A Hawk was succeeded by a 1,050 hp in the P-36B and a 1,200 hp in the P-36C. In the meantime, lengthy negotiations with France due to rising costs resulted finally in May 1938 in an order for one thousand H-75A (P-36B) with 1,050-hp engines. Built in France, they were armed with four 7.5-mm Browning machine guns, also made in France, and had a throw weight of 2,149,120 foot-pounds per minute. After Munich the armament was increased to six guns with a throw weight of 3,223,680 foot-pounds, and in 1939 another one hundred H-75s were ordered. By September 1939 all two hundred had been taken on charge by the FAF, the first having gone to *escadrilles* in March and April 1939.

After the outbreak of war, a new French purchasing mission managed to overcome the difficulties created by the isolationist Neutrality Act of 1936, which had initially restricted U.S. loans and trade with belligerents or those involved in civil strife but in 1939 allowed sales on what was often termed a "cash and carry basis." A further 531 H-75s were ordered, together with a license to manufacture 1,000 engines and propellers in France. The H-75s, with 1,200-hp engines, only began to reach France just before 24 June 1940, and dozens were still at sea, sunk, or on the French aircraft carrier *Béarn* in Antigua. In addition the H-75s needed new cowlings for better cooling. In fact when France fell, the French orders, taken over by the British as the Mohawk, were shipped to the Middle East where engine problems grounded them.[46]

The Hawk 75 was a comfortable machine, but lacked power and speed compared with the Me-109 and had a weak four-gun armament and inadequately protected fuel tanks. Approaching obsolescence in 1940, in the hands of dedicated pilots it did well; it had superior maneuverability as compared with the Me-109 and could absorb punishment. In the Phoney War, from

September 1939 to April 1940, Hawk pilots had claimed forty-two enemy aircraft and twenty-two probables for a loss of five pilots and eighteen aircraft. In the ensuing Battle of France, Hawk *escadrilles* claimed 233 kills confirmed and 84 probables (possibly 100 all told) for a loss of 30 pilots in combat and accidents and about 100 H-75s lost in combat, destroyed on the ground, and in accidents—in all, about 33 percent of those delivered.

Interestingly during 1939–1940 the Finns fought the Red air force, which had bloodied itself at Nomohan in 1937 against the Japanese and in Spain, yet the Finns did very well flying the contemporary to the Curtiss Hawk 75, the Brewster F2A Buffalo. They studied the aircraft's assets and deficits and its armament, and they honed their skills in it. The Finns ordered fifty-four F2As and lost eleven in accidents from 1940–1948, or only slightly more than one per year. The initial forty-four had arrived in Finland just before the Soviet-Finnish armistice of 21 March 1940, and they next went into action in June 1941, allied with the Luftwaffe.[47]

The Finns worked hard with their Brewster Buffaloes and practiced gunnery using the Spanish Civil War "finger-four" fighting formation. They examined their mounts carefully to determine their limitations; they recognized they had restricted ammunition and therefore had to shoot well. Many of their pilots were NCOs, as in the Armée de l'Air, but the Finns were encouraged to use both their initiative and their radios and signal Intelligence.[48]

Interestingly, similar to the French of the 1930s would be the Imperial Japanese Navy Air Force years later after the losses at Coral Sea and at Midway in 1942 because it had suffered so few casualties in China that it only trained one hundred replacement pilots annually. But unlike the French situation, for the Japanese the war was not over. The Imperial Japanese Army learned about modern war at Nomohan in 1939, but each Commandement d'Armée was an entity unto itself and thus not all the lessons were applied that could have been. And the French air force was built up in a less-than-rigorous manner.

The Potez 630, 631, 633

Except for the D-520, all the fighters reaching the Armée de l'Air before 24 June 1940 were behind the power curve, lacking top speeds equal to the Luftwaffe's Me-109E. The twin-engine fighter leaders, the Potez 630, 631, and 633, were withdrawn at the beginning of the war due to engine troubles, inadequate performance, suicidal and fatal tendencies, and weak armament and armor. In May 1940 the Potez 633 saw action for two days, with six machines lost "for a variety of reasons," and so was withdrawn. The two Potez 637 *escadrilles* lost all their establishment of machines in fourteen days. The Potez aircraft had entered service in 1938, never was refined, and thus was being phased out during 1940–1942. However, according to loss tables, the 63.11 saw much service.

The Personnel and Their Machines

In January 1940 the French armed forces had 2.7 million men, including in theory—"on the books"—187,400 airmen. Those were the budgeted figures. The effectives—on active service—were but 8,695 officers, 28,110 NCOs, and 117,016 men, both active and reserves, totaling 153,821. The budgeted figure was 187,400 and the total effectives by June 1940 were again 153,821, but as of 10 May 1940 only 97,123 were on active service, or 63.1 percent of the effectives, leaving a large shortage. Of these, only 3,334 were commissioned and noncommissioned pilots in October 1939 in the whole Armée de l'Air. Of the discrepancy between the "paper strength," the 153,821 that the Armée de l'Air thought it had in June 1940, and the 97,123 effectives actually on duty (aux armées), most of that would have been reserves on the books who had been called up on mobilization and then subsequently returned to industry. This was an example of lack of prewar manpower planning. This also meant that the real shortage, at least of each category, was closer to 40 percent rather than the 20 percent the French noted.[49] French accounting apparently leaves something to be desired.

Ministre de l'Air Cot in 1936 had tried to democratize the FAF, but when in 1938 La Chambre succeeded him, he reverted to an "aristocratic" recruitment from the upper class. However, his personnel schedule under Plan V would not make newly recruited aircrew available until March 1941. Fresh recruits had changed the officer "pyramid" dramatically in 1940, and the blockage by age was brutally pushed aside by the war. But the defeat did not allow the rejuvenation of the Armée de l'Air to take place. The changes of Plan V and Va to VI, resulted in 1,200 pilots detailed as instructors needing 3,760 aircraft. In spite of 1,028 sous-lieutenants being added to the FAF in January 1940, on 10 May the air force was dramatically short of qualified pilots because the GSAF planners badly miscalculated the time needed to build, equip, and man training establishments.

The end result of this was that the 1938–1939 aircrew were not starting to reach units until June 1940. Yet on 18 April General René Bouscat, commandant of Zone d'Opérations Est (air zone of operations east [ZOAE]), had said that he had a personnel credit on his hands. Immediately, then, after the calamity of 1940, the Armée de l'Air started to absolve itself of responsibility. It was Commission G of the Vichy Air Force that concluded that the FAF had required 500,000 personnel and 7,500 machines, but that it had only 166,000 officers and men (another different total!) and 4,398 machines.[50]

At the same time, General Vuillemin proclaimed that the FAF had more modern machines in July 1940 than it had had in September 1939, but this was true only on a purely numerical basis. What the general did not say was that these recently produced aircraft were "on charge"—"in the process"—but not ready for war. The truth was that the machines had been delivered to an FAF acceptance center and placed on charge so that the manufacturer could then be paid. However, these aircraft lacked propellers, engines, armament, and radios; and until they were supplied and installed and the aircraft tested, they were not ready for issue to operational units and for combat. Even then, of the thirty-two machines delivered daily to frontline *escadrilles* from 30 May to 10 June 1940 (352 all told), only 68 percent (239) were usable. Thus the net loss of the armée in the battle was 1,404 of all types in combat and other causes, in accidents, with 20.5 percent damaged but repairable and 9.7 percent abandoned. The total combat losses of the *chasseur* was 332, of the bombers 165, and of the reconnaissance and observation (R&O) 150.[51]

The proportion of the losses was *chasseur* 51.3 percent, bombers 25.5 percent, and R&O 23 percent. On that basis the 332 *chasseur* would have been replaced by 181. Assuming 68 percent serviceability, the *chasseur* might have had only 327 by 31 May, and at 30 percent only 144 *bon de guerre*.[52] As Christienne and Lissarrague noted, the serviceability on 10 May was 67 percent. Of the 2,176 aircraft in Metropolitan France at the front, only 1,368 of these were first-line; 717 of the 2,176 were "unavailable"—*indisponible*, some 33 percent.[53] Essentially, then, General Vuillemin had correctly claimed that the *indisponible* totaled 30 percent, a reflection of the shortage of mechanics and an inadequate supply system.[54]

Unfortunately neither Paul Martin nor Peter Cornwell have produced daily-states lists such as the British in London kept for the RAF to know its strength, and thus the *bon de guerre* on 30 May has to be a "guesstimate." Martin gives the totals for machines lost in accidents from 3 September 1939 to 24 June 1940 as 46 *chasseur*, 57 bombers, and 40 reconnaissance and observation, for a total of 143.[55] But many more were damaged and therefore unserviceable, awaiting repair. Table 1 in this volume indicates at 68 percent compounded serviceability only 151 aircraft on 31 May, and zero at 30 percent. The other way to approach the subject is to use Martin's graph of losses (opposite page 237), and his table (pages 460–461). The Armée de l'Air had lost 344 aircraft, 10 to 30 May. The Luftwaffe had lost 355, which at the FAF 15.5 sorties per enemy aircraft brought down (not counting DCA kills separately) meant the armée flew 5,502 sorties in twenty-two days, or a daily average of 250.

TABLE 1. Estimated Daily States of Armée de l'Air *Chasse* Serviceability*

DATE	A: 100 PERCENT	B: 68 PERCENT	C: 30 PERCENT
10 May 1940	637	433	191
11 May	607	413	182
12 May	580	394	174
13 May [bad weather]			
14 May [hazy but full of action]	523	355	157
15 May	485	330	146
16 May	466	317	140
17 May	437	297	131
18 May	409	278	123
19 May	381	259	114
20 May	352	239	106
21 May	323	220	97
22 May [bad weather]			
23 May [bad weather]			
24 May	238	162	71
25 May	209	142	63
26 May [driving rain]			
27 May [good cloud cover]	152	103	46
28 May [heavy rain]	124	84	37
29 May [partly cloudy, low]	95	65	29
30 May [bad weather, but some operations]			
31 May [weather terrible]	38	26	11
1 June	10	7	3
2 June			
3 June			
4 June			
5 June			
6 June			
7 June [early fog]			
8 June			

* Figures herein (rounded) were based on 637 fighters available on 10 May and were calculated therefrom. These *theoretical* figures were derived as follows: Column A, starting with 637 *chasse* at 100 percent *disponible* and reduced daily by an average 28.5 losses less 14 daily replacements (or 14.5 net). Column B is 68 percent of Column A. Column C is 30 percent of Column A. Actually the *chasse* available was on a declining curve from 100 percent to 30.

Of the 852 planes accepted by the Armée de l'Air from 10 May to 5 June, 273 (32 percent) had to be held at depots because they were not *bon de guerre*.[56] After the battle, on 20 July the strength of the FAF was about 5,250 of all types on charge or in depots—the same as on 10 May, but of more modern types, and in late June as noted in d'Abzac-Epézy.[57]

In the opinion of 1940 veteran pilot Pierre Boillot who later became a general, the old peacetime hands were well trained, but those new, younger, and prewar had little training. They wanted *la gloire* and, often typical of the young, did not listen to what the older pilots could tell them. They even failed to study enemy aircraft silhouettes. In addition, ground personnel were not trained mechanics as in other air forces, but were artisanal workers. Still, in 1993 Boillot believed the Armée de l'Air had destroyed some nine hundred enemy aircraft.[58]

How was this then accomplished? Evidently, this success was attained via the enthusiasm and high morale of the *chausseurs* (the old *élan*). But Boillot also noted that French aircraft were under-engineered. They lacked optics and test-flying, and only belatedly, in May 1940, was there work in train on electric control of propellers and on electro-pneumatic firing of guns. Boillot's complaint was that among other defects, the two 7.5-mm machine guns in the wings of the MS-406 were not harmonized so that the bullets converged ahead at the aiming point. The Ministère de l' Air and GSAF hierarchy were filled with preconceived ideas that prevented careful reading of the evidence. The MS-406 alone needed many modifications; but on 10 May it was still in a pristine state.[59]

In 1939, Chef d'état majeur de l'Armée de l'Air (General Staff Air Force) Vuillemin complained that he had only 1,000 modern training planes but needed 3,760 to train 1,800 new pilots and 3,200 fresh observers. What he actually had were 2,700 obsolete combat machines. An upgraded program did not start until March 1940—too late to have results. Earlier, in 1936, Ministre de l'Air Pierre Cot had shifted units in order to create a grand-strategic bomber force, but in1938 his successor, La Chambre, reversed that to strengthen the *chasseur*. Time, however, told against La Chambre, for his ninety-nine-*escadrilles* scheme with 100 percent reserves had only reached 67 by 1 May 1940, and only 27 of these were available for the Battle of France.[60]

Sustaining and maintaining both FAF *escadrilles* and Royal Air Force fighter squadrons proved difficult. And the nondevelopment of the higher-horsepower Hispano-Suiza engine is a mystery. Herschel Smith notes: "Politics and ideology led to strange things in pre-war France, and it must be in these areas that the explanation is to be found." Only in 1951 was a 2,500-hp Hispano-Suiza developed and then only to sell to countries that needed replacements for World War II engines.[61]

Matériel and Personnel

In France the Hispano-Suiza W engine had evolved into the W-18 of 1,125 hp and was the world's most powerful production engine in 1934 when Hispano-Suiza introduced the 12X and 12Y series. The X had just under 700 hp while the Y was just under 1,000 hp. Three H-S designs were widely licensed, and the Soviets developed the 12Y to 1,600 hp. But French production was so chaotic that the Armée de l'Air had to buy engines from Skoda of Czechoslovakia in 1939. A 1,300-hp H-S version was only in test in 1940. At the time, 1,100 hp was the minimum for wartime service. Lack of horsepower caused the FAF to reduce fighter armament to four MAC .30 7.5-mm machine guns or one slow-firing 20-mm cannon.

While the French were able to manufacture engines, they lacked a rigorous testing protocol. As a result, as the Schneider Cup races had shown, they failed to produce the necessary powerful engines that were at the heart of a successful fighter. Engines were slower to perfect than fighter designs, and the 1930s were a time of rapid change. Britain's cost-plus-10-percent development contracts that led to the permanent acquisition of the Schneider Trophy gave the RAF the edge in the Rolls-Royce Merlin while Bristol's licensing agreements produced the income that allowed that company to produce radial engines to rival Rolls-Royce's in-lines.

The reconnaissance version, the Potez 63-11 aircraft, had deficiencies the crew had to make up, but as an indication of French production problems, original deliveries in 1939 were delayed by a shortage of Ratier propellers with only 150 per month coming off production lines. Nevertheless 800 Potez were in service on 10 May 1940, though 147 were still fitted with two-bladed wooden airscrews. The Potez 63-11 were assigned to general-observation *escadrilles* and suffered heavily on operations. But 70 percent were not war-ready due to shortage of spares, and a number were destroyed on the ground on the first day of the 10 May blitzkrieg. Frequent movements also hurt serviceability; for instance, Groupe Autonome d'Observation (self-assigning observation squadron [GAO]) 510 lost 12 aircraft on the ground and moved fourteen times between 10 May and 24 June. From 5 June the squadrons changed bases daily due to German motorized units threatening them.

Lack of R/T (radio-telephone) equipment meant that Armée de l'Air pilots could not be directed from the ground and that when airborne they had to use hand signals, which were not very visible from enclosed cockpits. Moreover they could not warn each other of enemy fighter attacks, normally from above and out of the sun, and so were increasingly vulnerable. Often, therefore, jumped by Me-109s, they had to fight for their lives and could not concentrate on shooting down Heinkel 111s and other German bomber aircraft. In addition, vacuum-tube radios were easily put out of action by rough handling such as taxiing, takeoff, and landing on unimproved fields. Added to that, the Armée de l'Air was short of electrical (let alone radio) specialist technicians to service and repair what they had. Then, too, as the infamous German raid on Paris demonstrated on 3 June 1940, the French were naïve in telecommunications—attempting to broadcast warnings from their aircraft shadowing the enemy bombers via the Eiffel Tower. And these the enemy jammed. During that same attack the Poles and Czechs manning the Bloch 151/152s were surprised on the ground or badly mauled in the air.[62]

Technical Conclusions

It is obvious that in the 1930s the basic weakness of French aircraft was in aerodynamics and engines, especially the lack of horsepower and reliability, as well as the mass production of all-metal machines.[63] Mobilization had greatly affected the industry, as skilled men were called up, so that in late 1939 half the workforce was made up of inexperienced women. In addition, orders relating to retaining specialists only reached the industry on 1 September 1939, and it had not been anticipated that the fresh rules would need to apply to the many new firms ancillary to the industry. Because many FAF mechanics were in the reserves, their call-up affected serviceability and morale. And this, coupled with the grouping of the munitions industry under a Ministère de l'Armement (ministry of armaments) was disruptive of the 1936 nationalization and its aftermath and led to a priorities dispute. However, though this was resolved, difficulties remained at the depots where armament was fitted. But the biggest problem of all was the redefinition of the industry's objectives in both the short and long term, 750 machines per month or possibly 1,500. The decision to double production led to management stress, financial problems, and difficulties in recruiting labor and in finding suitable factory locations. It also placed the état majeur (air staff) in a bind as it had not planned personnel increases before the spring of 1941, especially for aircrew. There was also the gap in the delivery process between when aircraft left the factory and when they were certified ready for war.

On top of this, there were few aircrew to test, deliver, and man the new machines. According to General Charles Christienne, former chef de SHAA, the only modern French fighters were the nascent D-520, equal to the Hurricane but not to the Spitfire, and the Arsenal VG-33.[64] The matter of the number of aircraft produced versus those accepted can be illustrated by a few sample figures for fighters: on 1 November 1939, only 35.2 percent (1,580) of the 4,482 produced were delivered to units; in March 1940, only 38.42 percent (765) of 1,991 produced were delivered to units in Metropolitan France. In theory the remainder should have been in ready reserves. Both at home and overseas, the *escadrilles* had but 45 percent of the fighters produced.[65] Equally important, the Armèe de l'Air had no clear idea of its requirements because it had not settled its doctrine.[66]

In sum, French aircraft production only began to accelerate in late 1938 with modern types. But production in 1939 still faced problems, especially in aeroengines, and thus 5,229 modern engines had to be imported from the United States as French deliveries were insufficient and too low in horsepower,[67] and propellers, in short supply right up to the Franco-German armistice, had to be ordered from the United States. While armaments were supplied by the Ministère de la Guerre (ministry of war), they were fitted at the FAF Chateaudun depot and were the cause of many delays. When war came, having the state guarantee contracts both hampered and helped due to the need to work out financial and administrative procedures.[68]

In September 1939 the FAF had 1,400 aircraft, of which 500 were modern, rather than the 1,730 it should have had under Plan IV. The FAF was just beginning to recover from its low point. Of the *chasseur*, nineteen of twenty-three *groupes* had modern aircraft. On 14 September Plan V was approved for 3,200 first-line planes, plus 6,500 reserves to be delivered by 1 April 1940—an entirely unrealistic date. By then, only 2,138 of 2,960 fighters and 280 of the 1,940 bombers on order had been taken on charge. Plan V *bis* of February 1940 was never touched and was replaced in April by Plan VI, which was to have been completed by April 1941 when there would have been 1,770 *chasseur* in fifty single-engined *groupes*. By June, 4,400 aircraft had been built, more than 2,000 just in 1940.[69]

The dearth of serviceable, operational aircraft was due to bottlenecks in the supply line caused by a shortage of aircrew. All wartime formation flying at low altitude met effective flak and the aircraft were either shot down or so badly riddled they had to be written off. When the blitzkrieg broke through along the Meuse, French airfields were overrun and aircraft awaiting repair were lost. And from mid-May the situation was fluid.

Only aircraft production was beyond the control of the état majeur. That work was satisfactory, but the charge system created a hole. Moreover the état majeur neglected a streamlined command structure,[70] dedicated communications, tools and spares to keep maintenance and repair efficient, training facilities, and graded airfields. New aircraft were deliberately kept from being *bon de guerre* by not fitting them with radios and guns. Even so machines ready for war were stashed all across Metropolitan France. As in Britain when squadrons exchanged obsolete for modern aircraft, they were out of the line while both air and ground crew learned how to operate and care for the new steeds. On the ground, shortage of fliers placed the FAF at a 1:3 deficit to the Luftwaffe and because of 0.9 daily sorties in the air versus the GAF's 4.0, at a 1:12 disadvantage. By early June the FAF was impotent to deliver a counter-strike to the exhausted GAF, partly because its élite had been ordered to North Africa.

But before we can apply these deficits to the Armèe de l'Air claim, the status of the *chasseur* force has to be pondered. Given the fluid nature of the Battle of France and the fact that air assets had been parceled out to division commanders, the FAF could not fight for air superiority as its ancestor had over Verdun and later in the Duval Division.[71] Thus it is not unreasonable to assume that the serviceability and the effectiveness of the FAF declined dramatically in the six weeks of action.

With an order of battle initial establishment of 632/637 fighters in thirty-one *escadrilles* of 12 aircraft each (372 machines), on 10 May and in spite of new or replacement aircraft, the FAF fighter force was impotent.[72] The possible effectiveness of that organization, tied as it was to the armée, was seriously lessened by a very limited knowledge of radar and lack of its application, and even more importantly by its almost complete lack of a control system. This is surprising since the 1934 and 1935 maneuvers especially stressed early warning and communications and reduced the warning time from 6.5 minutes to 1.5—which the FAF could not meet.[73] In general, critics of the maneuvers of the 1930s noted that the participants were ill-prepared and that lessons that should have been drawn were not. There were no sector stations, no fighter controllers, and all orders had to pass by public telephone lines after the enemy had been reported by the same means. Even priority messages were delayed, not by minutes but by hours.[74]

Of the 910 *chasseur* on charge on 1 June 1940, only 338 were serviceable (37 percent), with the other 572 (63 percent) *indisponible*. Yet the FAF claimed to have shot down 733 enemy aircraft out of a total of 930 by the FAF, DCA, and the RAF. Using the rule of thumb that claims are three to five times reality, these real figures should be 195 to 310. The German admitted loss was 534.

On 10 May, the FAF flew the greatest possible number of sorties at the rate of 0.9, or 304. At the RAF and German rate of 36.5 aircraft sorties per aircraft shot down, the French *chasseur* could only have killed 8.33 Luftwaffe machines on 10 May (304 ÷ 36.5 = 8.33). Put another way, for 10 May–24 June, it would have taken the Armée de l'Air 26,754 sorties to bring down 733 German aircraft (36.5 x 733 = 26,754). To bring down one-third of the 733 (or 244), 8,966 sorties would be required; or, to bring down one-fifth, 5,351 sorties. If, on the other hand, we use Paul Martin's 15.5 sorties per kill, then on 10 May, 417 sorties would have netted 27 GAF machines. To bring down the 384 amended claims accepted by Martin and Cornwell would have needed, from 10 May–24 June, 5,952 sorties.

In the meantime the DCA of the Défense Aérienne du Territoire (DAT) claimed 120 on 10 May–24 June, with 27 to 28 on 10 May, declining to 2 on 15 May, rising to 8 on 20 May, and thereafter dying away by 22 May as the gun sites were overrun. Altogether the French claimed 853 Germans downed by the FAF and DCA (though reduced by Martin to 575), to which the RAF added 258 for 10–20 May; the French then enjoyed a bit of a lull until 1–10 June, when heavily engaged again, but after 10 June, only sporadically in action.[75]

The factors relevant to the explanation of the defeat of the FAF in forty-six days in May–June 1940 are fatigue of both air and ground crew and the lackadaisical training apparatus. Of the forty-six days, 10 May–24 June, of the Battle of France, more than eight were unflyable (nonoperational) days, and to these must be added the fourteen days from 10–24 June when few *chasse* flew—a total of twenty-two days out of forty-six (47.8 percent of the time) when there was little or no flying. There were only twenty days for action. (See Paul Martin's graph in *Invisibles Vainqueurs*, 236.) The FAF also was vulnerable because it had not started to develop its DCA until 1938, which was too late.

Though morale in the *escadrilles* was high at first, fatigue and irreplaceable casualties quickly took their toll. To gauge by the end results in terms of 15.5 sorties per kill of an enemy aircraft, the Armée de l'Air was a skilled élite *chasseur* force until after 10 June. Of the officer aircrew in 1939, d'Abzac-Epézy noted in 1997 that there were 30 generals, 59 colonels, 130 lieutenant colonels, 339 commanders, 634 captains, 423 lieutenants, and 309 *sous*-lieutenants, for a total of 1,924.[76] Of these, 124 were 50 to 54 years of age; 350 were 45 to 49; 247 were 40 to 44; approximately 424 were 35 to 39; 381 were 30 to 34; 358 were 25 to 29; and only 40 were 20 to 24. Of these only 796 (41 percent) were qualified fighter pilots. Of the 339 in the rank of commandant, only 4 had attended a special aviation school. Of the 634 captains, 58 percent had been at St. Cyr or the Polytechnique, but 23 had attended the École de l'Air; and of the whole group, only 20 percent had an aeronautical specialty, their promotion being blocked by the former armée officers above them in age—all of which contributed to maintaining a service of *appareils périnés* (obsolete, unrepairable machines). In 1940 no captains had attended the École de l'Air, only older lieutenants. Of the first three classes, 206 flew combat in 1940 mostly in *chasseur* and a few bombers. In contrast, the Luftwaffe, recruited *ab initio*, was full of young specialized officers.[77]

The difference in the ages of the pilots is that d'Abzac-Epézy's numbers were officers while Porret and Thevenet, in their work on the aces, also included NCOs, who were generally more recently joined and younger.[78] Almost half of the *chasseur* were under the command of General Marcel Tétu and committed to armée cooperation. In the end, of this small pool of *chausseurs* more than 500 were out of action between 3 September 1939 and 20 June 1940. In other words, the Armée de l'Air lost 63 percent of its 796 pilots of whom 464 or 58 percent were 45 or older. The young lacked experience and the old lacked stamina, if indeed they flew at all. More cohesion was to be doubted in units so top-heavy with officers above the rank of captain. Still the Armée de l'Air fought, as d'Abzac-Epézy agrees, to defend its honor.

In this vein, analysis of the RAF Fighter Command's personnel shows a high proportion aged 18 to 24 and 25 to 29 versus FAF's 40 pilots under 24 and 358 aged 25 to 29.[79] The study by Porret and Thevenet shows that there were many young FAF NCO pilots, but, as in the RAF, these were not counted. This meant that the *chasseur* probably had many more than the 632 pilots stated. (Nowhere is a total for pilots in the *chasseur* given for 10 May 1940, but 637 is close. Christienne and Lissarrague note that the FAF had "only 637 fighters at its disposal.").[80] Of the 637, only 46.5 percent were modern, with another 237 in the interior or colonies, of which 43 percent were modern. The question of which aircraft were considered *anciens* and which *modern* was settled by types.[81] Buffotot and Ogier, then, counted only those at the front in France.[82] Of the 2,176 aircraft in the first line, 1,368 were *"aux armées,"* and 717 were *indisponible*, or 33 percent (many being new and not yet ready). Only 17.6 percent of the 2,176 were bombers.[83] Claude d'Abzac-Epézy notes that the strength of the *chasseur* had been reduced in the spring of 1940 by the withdrawal of 1,200 pilots to be instructors; she also indicates that the establishment was 637.[84]

As to losses in the six weeks of war, the FAF admitted 471 shot down, 231 bombed, and 254 in accidents, or in total 956—70 percent of the first-line strength on 10 May 1940 of 1,356 (Table 2). On the other hand, during the period 10 May to 10 June, reinforcements of 1,024[85] were sent up. According to Buffotot and Ogier, 599 *chasse* were delivered, 58 percent of the 1,024, but many still were at the depots. The *disponibles* thus were but a fraction of the total, for industry and arsenals were incapable of meeting the rhythms of war. On 5 June, Buffotot and Ogier note that 852 were to have been delivered to units, but only 581 were received, and 271 were still not finished or on FAF charge, and some

TABLE 2. Comparative Aircrew Losses in the Battle of France

AIR FORCE	FIGHTERS
Armée de l'Air	956
Royal Air Force	1,208
Luftwaffe	454

TABLE 3. Daily Replacement of *Chasseur* and All Other Aircraft to Units

DATE	CHASSEUR (FIGHTER) AIRCRAFT	ALL OTHER AIRCRAFT	DATE	CHASSEUR (FIGHTER) AIRCRAFT	ALL OTHER AIRCRAFT
10 May	11	19	25 May	18	37
11 May	11	19	26 May	8	28
12 May	11	19	27 May	8	28
13 May	11	19	28 May	14	25
14 May	7	13	29 May	14	25
15 May	12	15	30 May	14	28
16 May	41	56	31 May	8	24
17 May	3	7	1 June	8	26
18 May	3	16	2 June	6	9
19 May	18	18	3 June	10	11
20 May	32	32	4 June	10	11
21 May	0	0	5 June	10	11
22 May	25	32	6 June	10	11
23 May	13	29	Total	349	597
24 May	13	29	**Total All Aircraft:**		**946***

Source: P. Buffotot and J. Ogier, "L'Armée de l'Air française pendant la bataille de France, 10 mai a l'Armistice: Essai de Bilan numerique d'une bataille aerienne," *Revue Historique des Armées,* 3 (1975): 88–117; reprinted in *Recueil d'Articles et Études (1974-1975)* (Vincennes: SHAA, 1977): 197–226.

*Only 30 percent serviceable = 284.

had been sent to units in the interior.[86] Replenishment/replacement aircraft then ceased to be delivered to operational units. Buffotot and Ogier document that earlier, on 1 June, of the 989 *chasse* only 363 were *disponible*, and of the 910 *aux armées* (allocated to the air armies) only 338 were *disponible*—leaving 572 *indisponible* (unserviceable, unavailable). All told, 71 percent of the FAF *aux armées* aircraft were unserviceable—60 percent of the bombers and 86 percent of the observation machines[87] (Table 3).

The Armée de L'Air's Tally

A number of calculations are necessary to reach the Armée de l'Air tally. First the FAF fighter force, the *chasse*, had 632–637 aircraft and 348 pilots on 10 May, and 1,084 machines early in June. In theory, this meant that the *chasse* should have been shooting down more Germans by June. However, several factors mitigate against this conclusion.

According to the official French historian Claude d'Abzac-Epézy,[88] on 10 May the Armée de l'Air had 5,250 aircraft in both Metropolitan France and in North Africa. In the Battle of France, the FAF consumed and wasted 1,033 machines destroyed and 77 (damaged), of which 511 (49.46 %) were destroyed in the air and 231 on the ground, 742 (or 72 percent) were destroyed by enemy action and 291 in accidents. (In this volume, Table 24, with data from *Abteilung* VI [Luftwaffe intelligence department], and Table 50, from my estimates, do not agree.)

On 10 May the *chasse* force had perhaps 632–637 aircraft to face 1,700 German fighters and 348 pilots against the GAF's 16,000–20,000 who were fully trained and operational. The total aircrew pool of 1,804 qualified officers and airmen in 1938 had increased only 7.5 percent to 1,939 in 1939. By 1940, units were desperate for personnel to bring them up to full strength. Although 850 reservists were mobilized, there remained a 9 percent shortage of flying officers and a 31 percent deficiency of NCO aircrew. This gave a total of 2,787 commissioned officers on 10 May, but only 58 percent (1,616) were qualified fliers. However, there were 2,897 qualified NCOs. The combined 4,513 could only man 1,675 airplanes.

Personnel had been limited for career concerns. And while the 132 *escadrilles* of 1926 had risen to 199 by 1939, a 66 percent increase, the number of generals had increased 471 percent, the colonels 392, lieutenant-colonels 311, and majors 183 percent. By 1940 the FAF had one general for every 27 first-line machines. The average age of officer fliers in 1937 was 36.5 years. Starting in 1936 the Ministère de l'Air retired 400 officers (in another military purge, although not as violent as in the USSR), who were replaced by commissioned NCOs. By 1939 the average age had dropped to 35.9 years. The former NCOs would serve fifteen to twenty years, but would not rise above captain and so would be no career threat to the new academy graduates just coming onto active service in 1937. To judge by Daniel Porret and Frank Thevenet, *Les As de la Guerre 1939–1945*, a fair proportion of FAF *chasse* pilots were NCOs and under the average age of twenty-four years. Was—and is—the difficulty in the Armée de l'Air that *sous-officiers* were not counted, thus magnifying the work of officer pilots?

Another operational factor that doomed the FAF was fuel exhaustion. It was noted that RAF Hurricanes in France frequently were forced to land for lack of fuel, and no doubt some of the 174 left behind were such.[89] The Hurricane I used 71 gallons of fuel per sortie, according to *SD 98* tables.[90] The

Bloch 151/152 had a very short range and so it is reasonable to assume that some of their losses especially came from fuel starvation and an inability to refuel and recover such aircraft even if they had made a safe landing and were undamaged. Historian Marc Bloch, an armée fuel-supply officer at this time, noted that after 10 May the French quickly began to burn their fuel dumps, depots, and transports.[91]

During the Somme counterattack more aircraft (60 percent fighters) were delivered, but by 10 June the *chasse* had lost 504, which still gave it a total of 1,084. The arrival of replacements was erratic, though the average was 13 daily. During 10–15 May the number varied from a high of 32 to a low of 4, and in early June was about 10 daily.[92] With the ability only to mount sorties based upon serviceable and available aircraft, the Armée de l'Air was merely capable of sending up 368 sorties on 10 May. Soon, with very fatigued pilots (few officers under forty years of age), only 150 went up on 15 May, and none on 1 June. This means that on those days the maximum number of confirmed (postwar) claims could not have exceeded eleven, four, and zero (Tables 4–7).

TABLE 4. Enemy Aircraft Credits Claimed by the FAF Aces

AIRCRAFT	DEFINITE	PROBABLE	TOTAL
He-111	173	19	192
Ju-88	23	8	31
Me-109	96	29	125
Do-17	100	19	119
Do-215	22	9	31
Hs-126	125	7	132
Ju-87	20	6	26
Me-110	28	8	36
Hs-124	1	—	1
Ju-86	4	—	4
Ju-52	2	—	2
Fiat BR-20	2	—	2
Fiat CR 42	5	—	5
Do-15		2	2
Unknown	2	—	2
Total	**603**	**107**	**710**

Source: Daniel Porret and Frank Thevenet, *Les As de la guerre 1939–1945*, 2 vols. (Vincennes: SHAA, 1991).

TABLE 5. Armée de l'Air Losses, September 1939–25 June 1940[a]

LOSSES BY UNIT, DATE	IN THE AIR		ON THE GROUND		IN ACCIDENTS		TOTAL	
	Destroyed	Damaged	Destroyed	Damaged	Destroyed	Damaged	Destroyed	Damaged
Chasse, Sept. 1939–25 June 1940	300	25	136	—	201	139	637	164
Chasse, May–June 1940	276	16	136	—	137	9	549	25
Bombardment, Sept.1939–25 June 1940	128	7	44	—	109	68	281	75
Bombardment, May–June 1940	122	6	44	—	87	17	253	23
Reconnaissance, Sept. 1939–25 June 1940	107	22	51	—	103	126	261	148
Reconnaissance, May–June 1940	73	18	51	—	30	11	154	29
Total, Sept. 1939–25 June 1940	**535**	**54**	**231**	**—**	**413**	**333**	**1,179**	**387**
Total, May–June 1940	**471**	**40**	**231**	**—**	**254**	**37**	**956[b]**	**77**

[a] From Claude d'Abzac-Epézy, L'Armée de l'Air de Vichy, 1940–1944 (Vincennes: SHAA, 1997), 55.

[b] Total destroyed and damaged, May–June 1940: 1,033.

TABLE 6. Assessments of Armée de l'Air Aircraft Losses by Various Authorities, 10 May–24 June 1940

AUTHORITY	COMBAT LOSSES	BOMBING LOSSES	ACCIDENT LOSSES	TOTAL
Vuillemin	413	234	245	**892**
Mendigal	320	240	235	**795**
Pierre Cot	306	?	?	**757**
Archives, GQGA*	410	232	730	**1,372**

Source: Patrick Facon, "Les mille victories de l'Armée de l'Air en 1939–1940: Autopsie d'un mythe," *Review Historique des Armées* 4 (1997): 83.

*General headquarters of the air force.

Armament and Production

A further reason to disbelieve the Armée de l'Air claims as to numbers of German aircraft destroyed in combat is the matter of lethality, as noted earlier. The combined weight of fire of the Me-109Es armed with two 7.9-mm machine guns and two wing-mounted 20-mm cannon was 9.7 pounds every two seconds.[93] The .303 bullet weighed 174 grains, and at 1,100 rounds per minute the eight machine guns in British fighters delivered 2,200 pounds per minute (36.6 pounds per second) as compared with the 148-grain 7.62-mm French machine gun at 500 rpm[94] from four guns delivering only 700 pounds. In other words the French lethality was only one-third that of the British. The Germans hit with less weight but fired 120 x 20-mm rounds per minute with much greater damaging power. All these figures have to be prorated to fifteen seconds of firepower in two-second bursts.

FAF fighters with four guns could not, according to RAF studies by S/Ldr Ralph Sorley, shoot down an enemy aircraft because they could not deliver the necessary lethal burst within the one-two seconds of opportunity.[95] This assumed that pilots were well enough trained to aim and fire a killing burst in two seconds, though in reality S/Ldr. H. R. "Dizzy" Allen, RAF, a 1940 Spitfire squadron commander, claimed that most pilots were poor shots.[96]

A comparison of the throw weight—the impact of the guns fitted on the aircraft—indicates the Armée de l'Air's disadvantage in firepower, measured in foot-pounds per minute (Table 8).[97] Each of the British Hurricane's eight Browning .303 machine guns had a belt of 300 rounds of 9.6 ounces each, weighing 180 pounds, which allowed a total of fifteen seconds in bursts.[98] The weight of all eight guns in a Spitfire or Hurricane was 195 pounds and the

TABLE 7. Killed and Wounded Regular Officers and Reservists, Armèe de l' Air, 10 May–24 June 1940

MAY			JUNE		
Date	Total killed	Total wounded	Date	Total killed	total wounded
10	6	8	1	—	—
11	6	5	2	13	12
12	—	—	3	—	—
13	9	12	4	0	6
14	7	5	5	11	16
15	7	5	6	6	5
16	2	13	7	9	7
17	1	8	8	—	—
18	—	—	9	0	5
19	5	2	10	2 ?	6
20	3	9	11	5	6
21	13	—	12	4	5
22	4	1	13	7	2
23	—	8	14	—	—
24	1	9	15	—	—
25	—	—	16	2	3
26	—	—	17	4	6
27	—	—	18	1	2
28	—	2	19	3	4
29	0	2	20	0	8
30	4	9	21	0	2
31	—	—	22	—	—
			23	1	2
			24	0	1
Total May	55*	98	Total June	66*	98

Total Killed and Wounded, May–June: 317

Source: Patrice Buffotot and J. Ogier, "L'Armée de l'Air: Le française dans la campaigne de France, 10 mai–25 juin 1940. Essai de bilan numerique d'une bataille," *Revue Historique des Armées* 3 (1975): 88–117; reprinted in *Recueil d'Articles et Études (1974–1975)* (Vincennes: SHAA, 1977): 197–226.

* These are Buffotot's and Ogier's figures; the actual numbers should both be 68 (total killed May, total killed June).

Note: Adding up the total FAF killed in May and June 1940 (55 + 66 = 121) and the total wounded (98 + 98 = 196) and considering those two (121 + 196 = 317), it must be concluded that only a small Armée de l'Air *chasse* was engaged even though casualties amounted to 49.7 percent (317 ÷ 637) not counting POWs, as compared to the RAF's 28.7 percent (537 ÷ 1,873) in twice as long in a less intense campaign but with more novices.

weight of the ammunition 1,440 pounds for 2,400 rounds. The weight of five rounds per second from eight guns was 4 pounds.[99] In terms of lethality, the German Me-109E had only 57.2 percent of that of the Hurricane, the MS-406 only 45.4 percent, and the Curtiss Hawk only 28.6 percent—or in terms of opponents to the Me-109, the Hurricane had a 175 percent advantage, while the MS-406 was at a 79.3 percent disadvantage and the Curtiss Hawk 75 at a 50 percent disadvantage (Table 8). These figures and my interpretation/interpolation apparently make plain to me originally the fact that the Armée de l'Air *chasseur* could not possibly have destroyed much more than one-third of the enemy aircraft claimed.

In 1918 the RAF began to realize that the newer aircraft would need to be "killed" by the heavier .50-caliber machine gun as rifle caliber (.303 inch) could not penetrate armor. Study continued until 1929 when the army's dominance of gun design caused the subject of the .50 caliber to be dropped.[100] Both Keith Park, as Dowding's Principal Staff Officer in 1938, and S/Ldr H. R. "Dizzy" Allen later agreed that the RAF should have chosen the Colt .50-caliber machine gun before the war instead of the Colt-Browning .303. The refusal to do so was based upon the .303 being common to the army's weapons and on what was erroneously believed to be the vast quantities of surplus World War I ammunition.[101]

The RAF believed before the war that if an enemy raid crossed the English coast at 16,000 feet, it would reach London ninety miles away before the British defenders could attack it, inasmuch as the Hurricane I, fitted with a three-bladed constant-speed propeller, needed 10 minutes to climb to 20,000 feet, plus scramble time of 1 to 3 minutes. For the ground observer, if a 180-mph

TABLE 8. Fighter Aircraft Throw Weights in Foot-Pounds per Minute*

AIRCRAFT	ARMAMENT	FOOT-POUNDS
Me-109E	(1 x 20 mm and 2 x 7.92 mm)	4,294,688
Hurricane and Spitfire	(8 x .303 in)	7,507,600
MS-406	(1.20 mm and 2 x 7.5 mm)	3,467,560
Hawk 75	(4 x 7.5 mm)	2,149,120

*The format used to compute the throw weight is $E = \frac{1}{2}$ mass x velocity^2 divided by 16 foot-pounds per minute. The calculations here are based upon the following, supplied by the RAF Museum: Hanfried Schliephake, *Flugzeugbewaffnung: Die Bordwaffen der Luftwaffe von den Anfängen bis zur Gegenwart* (Stuttgart: Motorbuch Verlag Stuttgart, 1977); John Tanner, ed., *British Aircraft Guns of World War Two: The Official Air Publications for the Lewis, Vickers and Browning Machine-Guns and the Hispano 20mm Cannon*, RAF Museum Series, vol. 9 (London: Arms and Armour Press, 1979); United Kingdom, AHB, Air Ministry, *Handbook of Foreign Aircraft Guns*, A.I.2 [G] (London, Nov. 1942) [typewritten material with tabulated information]; Clark Shore Robinson, *The Thermodynamics of Firearms* (New York: McGraw-Hill, 1943).

incoming enemy aircraft at 20,000 feet were sighted at thirty degrees 40,000 feet away (7.5 miles), doing three miles a minute, it would be overhead in 2.5 minutes. The great advantage of the British radar and the Observer Corps was that, combined with rapid reporting, plotting, and scrambling, the fighter—as it left the ground—had 14 minutes' advance warning with the enemy 42 miles away. With the Spitfire's 9.5-minute time-to-climb to 20,000 feet and the 10 minutes of the Hurricane, the defenders just had time to be vectored into position to meet a raid.

If an incoming raid was spotted at an elevation of 30 degrees, and if it was at 8,000 feet, it was 16,000 feet (3 miles) away, and if at 12,000 feet, it was 24,000 feet (4.5 miles) away. A Heinkel 111 cruising at 180 mph at 8,000 feet would be overhead in 1 minute, and if at 12,000 feet it would be overhead in 1.5 minutes, or 90 seconds. The He-111 P2 cruised at 230 mph at 16,000 feet, or 190 mph with maximum bomb load.[102] If Armée de l'Air fighters were on alert and scrambled at once, assuming that the pilots were already strapped in, it would take them 6 minutes to reach 8,000 feet and 9 minutes to reach 12,000 at their best climb speed of 278 mph. Inevitably they would be in a stern chase for many minutes and vulnerable both to the defending escort of Me-109s and to the bomber formation's protective rearward crossfire. Without early warning, the Armée de l'Air's Hawk 75 *chasseur*, with their climb rate of 6 minutes to 13,000 feet, were hopelessly outclassed.

Gun stoppages caused by the cold at high altitudes was a new phenomenon in May 1940. When the RAF encountered this frustration, an armorer suggested using the guns sans lubricant, because the cold and the very short bursts were quite different to conditions on the test-firing ranges where a continuous burst of three thousand rounds had to be proved not to damage the gun or cause it to stop. Elimination of lubricant worked. Faced with the same difficulty, the FAF sought an electrical heating solution, not found by 24 June. Given the above, then, what was the most likely Armée de l'Air tally in the Battle of France?

The Three Air Arms—Administration, Operation, and Personnel

The weakness of the FAF *chasse* was in part an administrative failure. Under Plan V, the manpower projection was to train 12,000 pilots, 3,200 observers, and 15,000 mechanics by April 1941. However, the necessary schools could not be established until late 1940. In June 1940 of the 5,500 cadets then in training, only 250 were fighter pilots, and these arrived at units already defeated, having already experienced great losses.[103] As the *chasseur* force was depleted and serviceability fell, so too did the number of sorties that could be launched rapidly decline while command and control became ever more chaotic and clogged, further reducing efficiency. A factor also to consider is the visual misconception of Me-109s shot down.

After a short peak of activity on 10 June, the Armée de l'Air withdrew to bases in southern France, which were soon packed with aircraft—targets the Germans largely neglected. Those *escadrilles* that had available aircraft with sufficient range were ordered off to North Africa on the eve of 17 June, and later that night Marshal Pétain asked for an armistice, which came into effect on 24 June. At that time it was believed that the Armée de l'Air had left in Metropolitan France 5,250 of all types and in North Africa 900 aircraft.[104]

The Germans and Italians allowed the French to retain 42,000 men and 769 aircraft in the Armée de l'Air de Vichy,[105] a force that had lost 16 percent of its total resources and had unfinished machines still at the factories; these, after 24 June, were reduced to scrap under the terms of the Franco-German armistice, with most aircraft factories placed geographically in German hands.

The disruption of the supply lines caused by a blitzkrieg against 1918-style thinking stopped the Armée de l'Air as much as the Armée de Terre in the forty-six critical days of 10 May–24 June 1940.

We have this problem for the Battle of France: while the records used by the SHAA's Patrice Buffotot and J. Ogier give the dates of killed or wounded, the authors only graphed this information. They indicate clearly that activity was heavy 10–20 May and 1–10 June, and show that the *chausseurs'* loss of 393 was 24.76 percent of the 1,587 aircrew officers plus another 16.25 percent wounded.[106] Of the 105 missing, it must be assumed that many either were made POWs, if they were not killed outright, or died of wounds in enemy hands. In this case, of other ranks eighty-eight pilots were killed or wounded and ninety-one missing. On that figure, a reasonable guess based upon the percentages above is that 314 officer pilots were killed or wounded, and an additional 320 were missing. Thus by 24 June, 634 fighter pilots were out of action, one way or another, bullets not being rank-conscious. With a service-ability rate of 30 percent and an accident rate of 25 percent, the Armée de l'Air was theoretically impotent, but apparently was not.[107] The French accident rate was more than double that of the RAF and the Luftwaffe and is a clear indication of the fatigue that the French aeromedical doctors had noticed in the 1936 maneuvers.[108] (See Table 7 herein.)

In early 1938, once La Chambre and Vuillemin were in charge at Boulevard Victor, they led the Armée de l'Air back into the ground war. They revived the conformities of the past, especially the 1934 structure in which operational commands were separated from service commands in peace and war. Reforms were delayed by the events at Munich and were only being completed as war began. When that came, General Vuillemin moved out to St. Jean-les-Deux-Jumeaux as Commandement of the Armée de l'Air, subordinate to the Commandement armée. Not satisfied with the command arrangements, he reorganized the field commands in April 1940, but in mid-May as his air units became overwhelmed, he again rearranged them. One result was that units were unsure of their overall commanders, their lines of communication, and their tasks, and always short of personnel and spares. Even before the Battle of France, in the rigid hierarchical system there was that lack of personal contact so essential to trust and swift responses. The evidence remains that the Armée de l'Air entered the battle in May 1940 without a clear doctrine or organization and with vastly inadequate numbers, overall inferior matériel, and inadequate training, not to mention lack of radar and control of the DCA.[109]

Until recently the importance of airfields as the bases of air strategy has been largely ignored. In prewar France there were five established main bases. All the rest of the two hundred stations in the northwest were really only landing grounds without permanent facilities. Even the elementary leveling, drainage, and sowing of seed had been neglected. This caused the loss of tailwheels and unnecessary accidents as machines were damaged when on the ground. Not only the French and British suffered, especially in the unusually severe winter of the Drôle de Guerre, but in May Me-109s and even Ju-52s were wrecked on unprepared fields. These two hundred airfields were linked by telephone, but that net from 10 May quickly became saturated and overrun. In addition the staff responsible had been just recently mobilized and were untrained, were billeted in nearby villages, and the aircraft were not in protected dispersals.

In order to see how the Armée de l'Air compared with its opponent, the Luftwaffe, and its ally, the RAF, this study looks also at the latter two. What will become apparent is that each of the three was preparing for a different war, though the French and the British, when at last they began an active alliance in 1939, both foresaw a long war. Given the precedent of the German Schlieffen Plan used in 1914 to deal with a war on two fronts—France on the west and Russia to the east—the Allies should have anticipated the blitzkrieg strategy, but instead they interpreted Intelligence evidence of such to conform to their own ethnocentric biases.

The stories of these air forces, covered in detail in *Two Roads to War: The French and British Air Arms from Versailles to Dunkirk* and in *Why Air Forces Fail: The Anatomy of Defeat*, provide the essential background to what happened in May–June and July–September 1940.[110] Ironically, all three emerged from World War I with different perceived lessons. The French, influenced by their dead and their exhaustion in a pyrrhic victory, saw a holding defensive action as the solution. The Germans, realizing they could not fight another devastating long war, were conscious of the need not to squander manpower and had the legacy of the offensive Schlieffen Plan and a Luftgeneralstab (air general staff) tradition of manning and running a war. Moreover, not allowed by the Treaty of Versailles to have an air force, they were given time to think, plan, and experiment and to engage in their ventures within the USSR. And the British, alarmed by the 1917 bombing of London, saw an independent RAF's primary role as Home Defence to be undertaken by a grand-strategic deterrent air offensive and defensive fighters. The RAF benefited from being led in the years 1919–1930 by offensive-minded and determined Marshal of the RAF Sir Hugh (as of 1936 Viscount) Trenchard.

General Lucien Robineau, late chef of the SHAA, had said that the French shot down 733 Luftwaffe aircraft and that the GAF lost another 450 in accidents, for a total of 1,183, or 69 percent of the GAF's 10 May strength (1,710) in fighters.[111] Robineau has further qualified this in a personal communication to the author of 24 November 2008.

We shall never know. I said that in a conference held in Freiburg in August 1988 under the official Luftwaffe historian Horst Boog's direction, which nobody then contested. It came from FAF archives and was consistent with the Buffotot-Ogier findings. Patrick Facon continued research in the German archives, which was not easy: German losses can be found but cannot be associated with particular days nor defined places. Moreover he had to deal with the claims of the British (821), French (853), Dutch (525), and Belgian (over 100), which all totaled were much more than the Germans had lost (1,390 to 1,470). Facon came to the conclusion that the actual number of aircraft shot down by the French in air combat (which should also consider tail gunners of reconnaissance and bomber aircraft, plus antiaircraft) should be in the range of about 600. A close review of the units' archives by a reliable author (Paul Martin, cited by P. Facon 1997) counted 594 aircraft shot down, not "victories" claimed.

We shall not consider some authors like Jean Gisclon and others, who are not historians and repeatedly assume one thousand "victories," imitating each other. Icare offered a very pleasant review, which brings interesting testimonies, which should be taken for what they are, not reliable sources, unless they confirm each other and cross-check with other sources.

In air warfare if claims are realistically adjusted and divided by three to five, they approximate the recorded enemy losses.[112] I had arrived at the figure of dividing claims by three from noting that the enemy losses admitted were about one-third of the other side's claims. Yet, in looking at the battles of 1940, it seems more realistic to use one-fifth. Using General Robineau's figures above totaling 1,183, and taking one-fifth of these, gives a possible Luftwaffe loss of 237, or 20 percent.[113] How, then, does this compare with the Luftwaffe quartermaster general's (LQMG) figure and how do we account for the discrepancy? For a variety of reasons there are disparities in the LQMG's figures, including perhaps clerical error when they do not add up. And in all of this it is useful to note that the Luftwaffe's bombers could outrun two-thirds of the Allied fighter force.[114]

The number of *chasse* pilots quoted for 10 May 1940 varies. Were there 632 out of 736 pilots in Metropolitan France? Or were there 438 or 378? d'Abzac-Epézy states there were 3,334 officers and *sous-officier* pilots in Metropolitan France and *outré-mer* (overseas) in October 1939.[115] Buffotot and Ogier's 1975 graphed figures of officers and reservists killed and wounded between 10 May and 24 June 1940, add up to 524 killed and wounded, of whom 200 (38 percent) were only wounded[116] (Table 7; Figure 3 from Buffotot and Ogier 1975).

Some 14 percent of the FAF was in fighter aircrew, of whom 700 were pilots. Of these, 40 percent (280) of the officers and 20 percent of the NCOs and other ranks were killed, missing, or wounded in the thirty days to 10 June, leaving on that date a few exhausted veterans and 250 unfledged/inexperienced new ones. Thus the effectiveness of the *chasse* was reduced to no more than 30 percent of its 10 May power and its aircraft as well.

Faris Kirkland asserts that the FAF and its allies outnumbered the Germans and had parity in quality, as well.[117] But the Germans were better trained. The eventual French defeat came in part from the failure of the French leadership to continue to train and organize new units; instead, they concentrated on preserving the professional cadre. The Haut Commandement had planned upon a long war, and so needed to preserve a nucleus cadre to man the future Armée de l'Air. In addition, in July 1940 they boasted they had more modern aircraft on 24 June than on 3 September 1939—yet many were not available because they were incomplete.

On 10 May the French had 637 fighters, the British Air Forces France (BAFF) 160, and the Dutch and the Belgians 43. The FAF had 2,517 modern fighters on charge as compared with the German 1,701 by the time Italy entered the war on 10 June, and when the best FAF units were being evacuated to North Africa. On the whole, however, the French committed only 1,095 modern aircraft of various types to the battle and the British about 500. The RAF committed 32 percent of its available fighters, while the FAF only put up 24 percent. The problem was command and control.[118]

The French long-war strategy required that there be large reserves. Yet on 10 May there were none, despite the fact that the Armée de l'Air leadership knew that air superiority was important. At the time, 46 percent of FAF units were in the process of conversion to modern types. In addition the FAF could not man all its aircraft. The theoretical FAF allocation was 796 pilots to *chasseur* units, which actually totaled more than the Armée de l'Air had. Because the Luftwaffe was training 12,000 or more pilots annually, replacements were not a problem for it; rather, serviceable aircraft were the limiting factor.

In September 1940, in the Battle of Britain, repaired single-engine fighters were roughly 16.5 percent of the serviceable machines. (See Table 34 herein.)

The Aces and the Claims

Patrick Facon, research chief of the SHAA, noted that in July 1940, following the May–June battle, General Vuillemin and General Mendigal at once sought recognition of the aces, the *chasseur* who had each shot down five enemy aircraft. The creation and recognition of aces was a necessary part of the Vuillemin plan to elevate *élan* and *la gloire* in order to personify the part the Armée de l'Air had played during the forty-six days in 1940 in contrast to that of its bête noire, the armée. During 1914–1918 the French system of recognizing aces actually had worked reasonably well owing to the fixed nature of the war front, which had provided many observers if not also the victims' wreckage for confirmation. And this was true still up to 10 May 1940.

For those designated as aces in 1940 there was no requirement to have their claims confirmed by fellow pilots and a viewing of the wreckage on the ground. In addition, postcombat talk and boasting by fighter pilots undoubtedly accentuated French—if not fighter pilots'—claims, for in many cases, as noted, there was evident a national predisposition to believe that if something simply had been talked about it had, in effect, been done—a view also noted early on, in 1928, by Oxford don Señor Salvador de la Madariaga in his study of Englishmen, Frenchmen, and Spaniards and by the historian of France Stanley Hoffman.[119]

After the Battle of France began, the situation was too fluid and unstable to allow a vigorous system of claims, as noted by Daniel Porret and Frank Thevenet in *Les As de la guerre 1939–1945*, the official SHAA publication on the aces.[120] The two volumes provide brief biographies of the aces and their victories, though unfortunately their tours are not given. The frequent assignment of "one victory for every flight member who had participated in the shooting down of one enemy aircraft" also was noted by Robineau in his December 2008 comments to the author. Obviously it was a system of accounting that inevitably led to the overmultiplication of total numbers and, as Robineau observed in commenting on this manuscript in July 2008, a "'gross exaggeration' of the total claims."[121] (See Tables 9–17.)

TABLE 9. Daily Victories Claimed by the FAF Aces, 10 May–20 June 1940[a]

DATE	VICTORIES	DATE	VICTORIES
10 May	34	1 June	18
11 May	37	2 June	4
12 May	41	3 June	18
13 May	24	4 June	2
14 May	28	5 June	34
15 May	38	6 June	29
16 May	24	7 June	24
17 May	25	8 June	20
18 May	42	9 June	15
19 May	29	10 June	26
20 May	20	11 June	5
21 May	11	12 June	3
22 May	3	13 June	5
23 May	3	14 June	7
24 May	10	15 June	22
25 May	16	16 June	12
26 May	29	17 June	—
27 May	—	18 June	—
28 May	7	19 June	—
29 May	—	20 June	5
30 May	—		
31 May	—		
Total: May	**421**	**Total: June**	**249[b]**

Source: Daniel Porret and Frank Thevenet, *Les As de guerre 1939–1945*, 2 vols. (Vincennes: SHAA, 1991). This does not agree with Patrice Buffotot and J. Ogier, "L'Armée de l'Air le française dans la campagne de France, 10 mai–25 juin 1940. Essai de bilan numerique d'une bataille," *Revue Historique des Armées* 3 (1975): 88–117 (see Figure 2 therein).

[a] From September 1939 to 5 September 1940, 80 victories.
[b] Total victories, 10 May–20 June 1940, 670.

TABLE 10. Early Allied Victory Claims and Actual Luftwaffe Losses in the Battle of France

DATE	ARMÉE DE L'AIR VICTORIES	RAF VICTORIES (ACBEF* ONLY)	GERMAN LOSSES	DATE	ARMÉE DE L'AIR VICTORIES	RAF VICTORIES (ACBEF* ONLY)	GERMAN LOSSES
10 May 1940	36	36	323	1 June 1940	9		20
11	24	21	58	2	2		22
12	34	20	38	3	17		13
13	25	8	45	4	1		5
14	46	12	52	5	55		35
15	25	35	30	6	28		19
16	18	18	39	7	20		18
17	17	20	16	8	24		22
18	24	8	50	9	24		18
19	17	16	63	10	12		18
20	17	7	25	11	6		10
21	16		20	12	2		22
22	11		46	13	10		18
23	1		15	14	5		16
24	8		25	15	14		7
25	11		20	16	5		11
26	22		22	17	1		4
27	1		38	18	0		10
28	1		15	19	1		7
29	1		13	20	2		7
30	0		9	21	0		3
31	0		14	22	0		2
				23	0		5
				24	1		2
				Total	**594**	**201**	**1,290**

* ACBEF: Air Component British Expeditionary Force.

TABLE 11. Correlation of French and German Claims

DATE	FAF CLAIMS	GAF LOSSES ADMITTED
10 May	50	299
11 May	46	60
12 May	48	53
13 May	42	38
14 May		55
15 May	57	34
16 May	30	37
17 May	22	45
18 May	23	49
19 May	39	53
20 May	23	28
21 May	22	27
22 May	22	23
23 May	2	11
24 May	20	24
25 May	20	25
26 May		37
27 May		37
28 May		21
29 May		20
30 May		10
31 May		15
Total	**466**	**1,001**

Source: From Patrice Buffotot and J. Ogier, L'Armée de l'Air française pendant la bataille de France, 10 mai a l'Armistice: Essai de Bilan numerique d'une bataille aerienne," Revue Historique des Armées 3 (1975): 88–117; reprinted in Recueil d'Articles et Études (1974–1975) (Vincennes: SHAA, 1977), 216; and United Kingdom, Air Ministry, CAB 106/282, 127.

TABLE 12. Luftwaffe Aircraft Shot Down Daily, by Types, over France and the Low Countries, 10–31 May 1940

DATE	ME-109	ME-110	HE-111	JU-88	JU-87	DO-17	JU-52	HE-126	DO-215	FI-156	HE-115	HE-59	HS-123	FW-189	TOTAL
10 May	9	2	54	16	8	23	162	1	2	22					**299**
11	5	6	26	1	10	3	4				5				**60**
12	9	4	17	3	4	7	2	5				2			**53**
13	8	10	2	5	1	12									**38**
14	15	6	9	4	11	3	6				1				**55**
15	4	10	3	2	7	8									**34**
16	5	7	7	1	4	8	4	1							**37**
17	9	3	5	4	7	8	3	6							**45**
18	11	1	13	1	4	15		2				2			**49**
19	6	7	24	7		8		1							**53**
20	5	1	9	4	1	4	3		1						**28**
21	5	2	5	3		5	1	6							**27**
22	5	2	3	1	3	3	3	2		1					**23**
23	2		2		3	2		2							**11**
24	7	3	4	2		3		5							**24**
25	11	3		3		6	1	1							**25**
26	7	5	7	4	7	6	1								**37**
27	3	5	6	5	1	9		2			1	5			**37**
28	5				1	9	2	4							**21**
29	4	2	4	4	2			4							**20**
30	1		1	2		2	2	1							**9**
31	6	3	2	3		1									**15**
Total	**142**	**82**	**203**	**75**	**74**	**145**	**194**	**43**	**3**	**23**	**7**	**9**	**—**	**—**	**1,000**

Source: United Kingdom, Air Ministry, CAB 106/282, 127.

TABLE 13. Luftwaffe Aircraft Damaged Daily, by Types, over France and the Low Countries, 10–31 May 1940

DATE	ME-109	ME-110	HE-111	JU-88	JU-87	DO-17	JU-52	HE-126	DO-215	FI-156	HE-115	HE-59	HS-123	FW-189	TOTAL
10 May	9	1	17	2	1	14	4								48
11	5	11	2	1	6	7					1				28
12	4		2		2	1	3	1				2	2		18
13	8		1		2	4									15
14	3	1	3		6	1									17
15	2	5	3			2									11
16	7	2	3	2		2		1							16
17	3	1		1		1									7
18	2		2	1		1									6
19	2	2	2			1	2								8
20	7	1		1	1					1					11
21	6	1				2	4			1					14
22	3		2			2	1								6
23				1	2	1			1						5
24	6		2	1		2		1							12
25	3		2		1	2	3								9
26	1			3	2	2	1		1						7
27			5			8			1						17
28	4		1					1							6
29	2		1					1							4
30								1							1
31	2						18								20
Total	**77**	**25**	**48**	**13**	**23**	**48**	**36**	**6**	**3**	**2**	**1**	**2**	**2**	**—**	**286**

Source: United Kingdom, Air Ministry, CAB 106/282, 127.

TABLE 14. Luftwaffe Aircraft Shot Down Daily, by Types, over France and the Low Countries, 1–18 June 1940*

DATE	ME-109	ME-110	HE-111	JU-88	JU-87	DO-17	JU-52	HE-126	DO-215	FI-156	HE-115	HE-59	HS-123	FW-189	TOTAL
1 June	7	3	10	3	3	3									29
2	2	3	5	1	6	1	1								19
3	9	1		2		2									14
4	1	2											2		5
5	9	3	10	7	2	2		2					3		38
6	12	6				2		3							23
7	10		2		1	2	3	1	1						20
8	5	4	2		7	1				1					20
9	8	1	2		1	2				1					15
10	2	2			2	2	2	4							14
11	1		1		2	1		2							7
12	1		5		1	3		1							11
13		2	1	1	1	1									6
14	2		2	1	2	2									9
15			4	2	1	5		3							15
16	1		1	2	2	1	1	2							10
17	2														2
18	4		2	3	2			1			1				13
Total	**76**	**27**	**47**	**22**	**33**	**30**	**7**	**19**	**1**	**2**	**1**		**5**	**—**	**270**

Source: United Kingdom, Air Ministry, CAB 106/282.

* These figures include all entries marked unknown. They do *not* include planes destroyed or damaged over Norway and the United Kingdom. A total of the planes on both tables would give the number destroyed and damaged during the whole campaign.

TABLE 15. Luftwaffe Aircraft Damaged Daily, by Types, over France and the Low Countries, 1–18 June 1940*

DATE	ME-109	ME-110	HE-111	JU-88	JU-87	DO-17	JU-52	HE-126	DO-215	FI-156	HE-115	HE-59	HS-123	FW-189	TOTAL
1 June	6		1	1	2	2		1							13
2	3	2		1	2										8
3	2			2		1									5
4			1			1									2
5	2		2				1	1					1		7
6	1					1		1					3		6
7	1		2	1	1										5
8	2		1												3
9		3				2		1							6
10	2			1		1									4
11	2		1	2		4									9
12			1										2		3
13		1	1				1								3
14	3		3	1		1		2		1					10
15	1						1			1					2
16	1		2												3
17	1														1
18	3						1								4
Total	**29**	**6**	**15**	**9**	**5**	**13**	**4**	**6**	**—**	**1**	**—**	**—**	**6**	**—**	**94**

Source: United Kingdom, Air Ministry, CAB 106/282 (Luftwaffe *Abteilung VI* [1945]).

*These figures include all entries marked unknown. They do *not* include planes destroyed or damaged over Norway and the United Kingdom. A total of the planes on both tables would give the number destroyed and damaged during the whole campaign.

TABLE 16. RAF Fighter Command Losses Allocated to Air Staff Categories 2 and 3, 10 August–28 September 1940[a,b]

DATE	HURRICANE	SPITFIRE	TOTALS
10 August			
Category 2	4	4	8
Category 3	16	12	28
17 August			
Category 2	21	11	32
Category 3	82	40	122
23 August			
Category 2	9	4	13
Category 3	53	21	74
31 August			
Category 2	4	7	11
Category 3	70	50	120
7 September			
Category 2	8	8	16
Category 3	84	53	137
14 September			
Category 2	6	10	16
Category 3	47	26	73
21 September			
Category 2	8	11	19
Category 3	34	21	55
28 September			
Category 2	11	5	16
Category 3	40	35	75

10–31 August, Total of Category 2: 63
10–31 August, Total of Category 3: 344
10–31 August, Total of Categories 2 & 3: 407

7–28 September, Total of Category 2: 67
7–28 September, Total of Category 3: 340
7–28 September, Total of Categories 2 and 3: 407

Source: Francis K. Mason, *Battle over Britain* (New York: Doubleday, 1969), 598; United Kingdom, Air Ministry, CAB 106/282, 127.

[a]Category 2: Wrecked beyond unit capacity to repair. Category 3: Lost or wrecked beyond repair; from United Kingdom, National Archives, AIR 2/5205 (31.7.40). See also Table 20, Luftwaffe Damage Assessment Categories.

[b] The second of the two six-week segments in the Battle of Britain, 10 August–21 September, is comparable in endurance to the forty-six-day Battle of France. The 114 machines in Category 2 during this time were repairable on the station or unit, while the 609 in Category 3, 10 August–21 September, were repairable either elsewhere in the Civilian Repair Organization or by the mobile Ministry of Aircraft Production teams in the latter part of the battle. These figures should be compared with the Luftwaffe's blitzkrieg German mentality.

TABLE 17. RAF 1942 Estimates of German Air Force Casualties, 1939–1942

DATE	SHOT DOWN	PROBABLE	DAMAGED	TOTAL
September–December 1939	15			15
January 1940	3			3
February 1940	10			10
March 1940	3			3
April 1940	6.5			6.5
May 1940	357			357
June 1940	143			143
July 1940	212	222	95	529
August 1940	960	389	437	1,786
September 1940	971	371	467	1,809
October 1940	211	103	157	471
November 1940	188.5	62	78	328.5
December 1940	40.5	16	24	80.5
Totals	**3,120.5**	**1,163**	**1,258**	**5,541.5**

Source: United Kingdom, National Archives, AIR 20/6208 (1942), Air Intelligence Joint Committee.

For years then, until it could be possible to put together all available archives from those who had participated in the 1939–1940 air battles, the so-called victory claims had been quite different from the reality. Today, in any air force, we are able to put a more correct assessment of the truth in the place of potential mythology. On FAF claims the reader also is referred to the chapter by Sebastian Cox about the RAF's Air Historical Branch, in Horst Boog, ed., *The Conduct of the Air War in the Second World War:* "In the RAF offensive of 1941–1942 over France it was difficult to corroborate claims as the usual sources were no good—wrecks were on the wrong side of the Channel."[122] In France in 1940, the wrecks were increasingly behind German lines.

In comparison with the French process of compilation of claims, the RAF had strict rules of verification by independent observers on the ground, yet though these had applied acceptably during World War I over a static front, in 1940 those verification procedures had overwhelmed the newly appointed, untrained squadron Intelligence officers due to the numbers involved. For a confirmed kill by an RAF pilot or gunner up to mid-1940 it had to be seen (1) by a crew member, a vessel, police, or the Observer Corps as on the ground; (2) while descending in flames (not smoking); or (3) while breaking up in the air.

However, from midnight of 13 August 1940 the categorization for confirmed kills was changed to "Destroyed, Probably Destroyed, Damaged," because pilots following victims down to observe the crash were vulnerable to enemy action.[123]

Another way to view the Armée de l'Air's claims of Luftwaffe machines shot down and damaged in the Battle of France is to look at the RAF's conclusions regarding their pilots' claims in the Battle of Britain from 10 July to 2 October 1940. The initial British claims were 2,071 destroyed, 1,464 probably destroyed, and 824 damaged for a total of 4,359. This figure for aircraft damaged was revised to 843, though the Germans only admitted to 692. The modified claim of 843 was only 19.3 percent of the original claims, while the German admission was only 15.85 percent. (Again, though initially I had used one-third of the claims as being close to reality, both the RAF and the Armée de l'Air numbers appear to have been five times reality.)[124] And the ultimate point, once again, is that combat claims in the days before universal camera-gun films often were likely to be highly exaggerated, especially when large numbers of pilots were involved.

The answer has to lie in the psychological effect of circumstance and events. The Armée de l'Air *chasse escadrille* were homogenous and trained and experienced in their own aircraft, units, and milieu. They were an élite, knitted together by unit pride and camaraderie, even among the pilots and the ground crew. With, I reckon, an average 750 flight hours each, the pilots had five times as many hours as new RAF pilots and roughly three times the average Me-109 or Me-110 German pilot. Professional pride and cohesion seem to be the answer to the paradox.

Delving further into the specifics of the *chasseur* pilots, the whole inflation of their reputation fits snugly into a typical Lost Cause myth. From both volumes of Porret and Thevenet's *Les As de la guerre 1939–1945* it can be noted that only 10 of the 101 aces in the Battle of France were credited with shooting down five enemy aircraft *unassisted*. Of the 142 pilots listed as aces in the Porret and Thevenet work, 1939–1945, some were not credited with five kills by French standards in 1940 because they only amassed that total during the whole war. Only 101 had qualified as aces in 1939 and in the forty-six days of the battle and these were assisted by 1,646 other pilots.

The 1,646 assists work out to be 16.3 pilots plus an ace (17.3) per enemy aircraft shot down. French pilots who claimed 50 percent of the kills comprised 4 percent of those pilots,[125] leaving 96 percent of them to share the other 50 percent. As for the 2,834 victories claimed, I totaled the 1,188 aircraft the aces claimed shot down and added the 1,646 assists (and alternatively, to get 100 percent of enemy losses to the aces—2,376). Multiplying that by the sortie rate per kill given by Paul Martin (15.5) yields 36,828 sorties flown, a figure way beyond the capacity of the Armée de l'Air in the Battle of France. If the serviceability rate was only 68 percent on 10 May, there would have been only 433 fighters available and these could only have flown at 0.9 sorties per machine per day, 390 sorties each day. At a kill ratio of 15.5, the FAF could only have shot down 25. And, as noted below, there were actually only twenty flyable days during the forty-six of the Battle of France, not to mention a shortage of *disponible* aircraft (down to 30 percent by 10 June) and of qualified pilots.

From 10 May to 5 June there were twenty-seven days, of which seven had no reports due to bad weather. The total sorties flown by the *chasse* on the twenty flyable days, using the numbers from Table 1, at 100 percent the average daily strength (*disponible* fighters) was 303 less losses, at 68 percent 206, and 30 percent 91. At 0.9 sorties per aircraft per diem, the latter two meant 185 and 82 sorties. And at the 15.5 kill ratio, only thirteen and six enemy aircraft shot down, respectively. It is interesting to note that Porret and Thevenet's *Les As de la guerre 1939–1945* was published in 1991; and forty years after the battle the myths were still being created.

If all 637 *chasseur* had been serviceable for the forty-six days, they could have put up 29,302 sorties, about 22 to 23 percent of the number needed. Using the average availabilities above, the total number of sorties flown on the twenty flyable days would be approximately 6,060 (303 x 20) at 100 percent, 4,120 at 68 percent, and 1,820 at 30 percent.

Complicating all this we must remember that these calculations are based upon the assumption that all the sorties of the Armée de l'Air were to engage enemy aircraft in flight, whereas in fact a large proportion were against Wehrmacht ground targets, resulting in many FAF losses due to flak. Paul Martin's work does not distinguish the nature of each sortie. With on average 50 percent serviceability, or six aircraft available daily for the twenty flyable days from 10 May to withdrawal from operations on 10 June, and at 0.9 sorties daily, the total generated by all thirty-one *chasse escadrilles* would have been 3,720 sorties .

Then if the assertion of both General Vuillemin and General Mendigal holds that only 30 percent were serviceable, the total sorties that could have been flown was only 3,822. And that total as divided originally by the RAF/GAF 36.5 sorties per kill points to only 105 enemy aircraft actually being destroyed, but if Martin's sorties per kill of 15.5 it is 251. And so doubling the figure of 2,376 losses to get the total FAF victories above means that the FAF fighters flew a total of 4,752 sorties during the Battle of France, or 0.86 (close to 0.9) sorties per diem per surviving aircraft.[126]

According to Porret and Thevenet's *Les As de la guerre 1939–1945,* on several occasions eighteen or more Armée de l'Air MS-406 aircraft were reported to have shot down a German Henschel Hs-126 two-seat observation plane, a fact indicative of ill-disciplined action, poor marksmanship, and lack of training—essentially unnecessary "overkill." Statistics indicate that it indeed had taken an average of sixteen *chasseur* to achieve the kill, and as many as twenty-one on occasion. If the Armée de l'Air only shot down between 369 and 400, rather than my original estimate of 218 and 232 German aircraft, why did the German Luftwaffe QMG issue so many replacement machines? The answer lies in the German definition of unserviceability. And that we will find in Chapter 2, "The Luftwaffe."

The Germans admitted the loss of only forty-nine Hs-126 in May and sixty in June.[127] The LQMG had issued only thirteen new Hs-126 machines in May and fifty-four in June.[128] Perhaps because the Hs-126 was highly maneuverable, a number may have escaped being shot down. Moreover the attacks on the Hs-126s show that the ill-armed *chasseur* were not fighting for air superiority, or even trying to frustrate the bombers, but rather were engaged in their third role, that of armée cooperation. Specifically the FAF aces claimed 173 Heinkel 111s shot down against the Luftwaffe admitted totals of 207, and 125 Hs-126s against the LQMG's issue of 144[129] (Table 4). In contrast to the FAF's claim of 710, examination of Peter D. Cornwell's very careful tabulations in *The Battle of France Then and Now* shows that 369 German air force losses occurred after contact with FAF fighters, though a good number of these Luftwaffe crashed upon their return flights or on their airfields and therefore were written off.[130]

Comparing the FAF action in the Battle of France with the RAF in the Battle of Britain, the RAF flew thirty-seven to fifty-six sorties per aircraft lost and the Luftwaffe thirty-six sorties.[131] Christienne and Lissarrague state that the Armée de l'Air lost all told 410 in the air, 200 on the ground, and 230 in accidents, for a total of 840 or 16.7 percent of the 5,026 strength on 10 May.[132] Earlier they noted that in the losses in the first phase to 16 May the erosion was 787, of which 473 were fighters.[133] What the FAF does not say is that the difference must have been that repairs were effected in those days before the front was broken and units were on the move.

Reconstruction of the Battle of France from several angles makes clear that the number of German Luftwaffe machines claimed downed has changed over time. Reconstruction also shows that the French air weapon was inferior not only in numbers but also technically, coupled with a shortage of trained aircrew and groundcrew. The last mystery of the Battle of France certainly must be how the gap between Luftwaffe losses and its LQMG's issues should be explained.[134]

And yet, in spite of its many deficiencies, from doctrine and command to matériel, the *chasseur* deserve accolades for their courage and conquests amid the general debacle of 10 May–24 June 1940.

The story of the Armée de l'Air in the Battle of France, in sum, is a classic tale of the numerical conundrums of air battle claims and losses, while at the same time showing a similarity of experiences of the Armée de l'Air, Royal Air Force, and Luftwaffe; each approached the coming war and battles according to national circumstances, grand strategies, experience, and beliefs. Regrettably the defeated Armée de l'Air followed the course taken by others in similar dismal situations, looking for scapegoats, blaming the politicians, claiming superior *élan* but insufficient strength, and attempting to create myths to support the Lost Cause.

Patrick Facon's 1997 Analysis

Patrick Facon, chief of research for the SHAA at Vincennes, went to the German Federal Military Archives in Freiburg im Bresgau and consulted the GAF statistical reports to the Wehrmacht Oberkommando. These daily reports signaled the losses in combats and in accidents, divided into those wasted and damaged on operations and those in the rear areas of the Fatherland (Heimat). The details included type, percentage of damage from 10 to 100, and the fate of the pilot or his aircraft. The great thing, noted Facon, was that these documents existed, but they were complex and full of errors. For instance the number for any given day might include those lost earlier and omit those of that day. Not until he reached the November 1940 records could a reliable answer be found. To overcome this problem, Facon counted one by one the Luftwaffe aircraft lost and so was able to create a definitive table. The result was not absolutely precise but did give an order of magnitude as close as possible to reality. Facon's conclusion was that the GAF lost between 1,290 and 1,300 machines in the Battle of France rather than the 1,389 to 1,471 that certain historians of the Luftwaffe have reported.

My own observation of the Luftwaffe mathematics is that if the records/accounts were in error in one column by 464, that would close the gap.[135] Why such a difference? It depends upon the sources.

The difference between my earlier calculated estimate of 232 Luftwaffe machines shot down by the Armée de l'Air and my analysis of Peter Cornwell's 2008 records is that in the latter case I included GAF aircraft that were written off after landing because of damage inflicted either in combat or in landing. That total was 369. Paul Martin's total was 400, so as noted earlier, I calculated the median as 384 and accepted Martin's 15.5 sorties per kill. At least after the Battle of France the Luftwaffe could salvage a lot of machines (more than 800) unserviceable for various reasons, and even those written off could become sources of parts. But in the Battle of Britain those GAF shot down or forced-landed in England or in the Channel were irretrievably lost.

Facon noted[136] that in 1975 two official historians published an article in the *Revue historique des armées*, based on the archives, which stated that the Armée de l'Air shot down 733 GAF aircraft and the antiaircraft defenses 120 for a total of 853.[137] These authors also reckoned that counting enemy aircraft that did not return to base or that crashed upon landing, the total was close to 1,300. Then Paul Martin published in 1990 a large day-by-day volume that put the total at 575 less 175 by the DCA, for a total of 400.[138] After it, in 1995–1996 Facon's additional inquiries at the RAF's own Air Historical Branch (AHB) added 201 by the Air Component, 131 for the fighters of the AASF and 489 for Fighter Command, 10 May–25 June 1940, for a total of 821 added to the French claim, equaled 1,674 destroyed said Facon, of which my 19 percent would be 328. So the total downed by fighters was: RAF, 821; FAF and DCA, 853; Netherlands, 525 (*chasse* and DCA); Belgium, 100 minimum; for a total of 2,299, as opposed to German known losses of 1,389–1,470. But if we include only the enemy accounted for by the RAF, the Belgians, and the Dutch (1,446), then the results change considerably.

Unhappily the British statistics are only daily for the Air Component, and then only to 21 May. The British Air Forces France (BAFF) were divided between the Air Component of the British Expeditionary Force (ACBEF) and the Advanced Air Striking Force of Bomber Command (AASF). The former contained four Hurricane fighter squadrons, which after 10 May were increased to sixteen. The AASF originally was composed mainly of light and medium bombers and two Hurricane squadrons.

The RAF flew an estimated 8,000 sorties in the Battle of France, according to the Air Historical Branch (AHB) history, even without radar vectoring, and only claimed 682 Luftwaffe aircraft, averaging one per every 11.8 sorties. During the Battle of Britain, 13–23 August 1940, Fighter Command flew 6,414 sorties and lost 114 aircraft (56.3 sorties per loss). During the Battle of Britain on 24 August–5 September, Fighter Command flew 10,673 sorties and lost 286, which equals 37.31 sorties per loss, or an average of 46.8 sorties per loss.[139]

Conversely all RAF units in France flew about 8,000 sorties; divided by 36.5, per GAF loss, it would be 219, rather than Facon's 821 noted above.

The Battle of France cost the RAF 396 Hurricanes and 67 Spitfires (463 total), and roughly 280 fighter pilots killed, missing, or prisoners of war.[140] The caveat here is that the RAF was much more efficient in the Battle of Britain than in the Battle of France due to radar, thus the number of sorties flown over France could have been higher, but not during the retreat and the evacuation to Britain of the squadrons.

If in fact the RAF flew only about 8,000 sorties in the Battle of France with, say, one-third of these flown by bombers (i.e., 2,667), then that leaves 5,333 roughly for fighters. If 5,333 is divided by 36.5 sorties per aircraft downed, the RAF might have shot down 146 German aircraft. And if the 682 total GAF aircraft claimed by the RAF is divided by three, the result is 227 German aircraft shot down by fighters, or if divided by five, 136.4 aircraft.

Lacking official records and figures in the Battle of France, I estimate that in those six weeks from 10 May to 19 June when the RAF was in France, as the Air Component British Expeditionary Force and the Advanced Air Striking Force, the loss rate of killed and presumed dead was 280. In the Battle of Britain in the nearly eight weeks from 10 July to 31 August the RAF flew 17,037 sorties and lost 400 aircraft for a rate of 45.6 sorties per machine lost. At the weekly rate of 2,434 sorties in the almost seven weeks of the Battle of France, the RAF generated a maximum of 12,170 sorties, but allowing for reduced activity, slightly below the July rate of 2,138 weekly, say 8,000 sorties total (i.e., what T. C. G. James stated).[141]

The BAFF lost 534 (L. F. Ellis [1954, p. 312] says 474) and Fighter Command 219 for a total of 753. The ratio of 280 killed and presumed dead to 8,000 sorties is 28.57 sorties per death and of the 753 to 8,000, is 10.6.[142] Thus I would argue that 8,000 sorties by the RAF for the Battle of France is about correct. Certainly the losses claimed inflicted by the Allies (682) exceeded reality by 528 (802 minus 384, the Martin–Cornwell average). Obviously the official figures were published as propaganda and were created in the heat of battle with uncertainties in confirmation procedures.[143] (Note, however, that Tables 10 and 11 herein show other figures.)

French Armée de l'Air records following the overrunning of their airfields, the retreat, and restrictions after 24 June when they moved to Unoccupied Vichy France are not available; no accurate count was possible then or later. (See Paul Martin's reconstruction.)[144] The difficulty with the presently accepted FAF figure is that it assumes that all GAF LQMG issues were to make good operational losses. But as I pointed out in my chapter on the Battle of Britain in B. F. Cooling's *Case Studies in the Achievement of Air Superiority*,[145] the production of new Hurricanes and Spitfires just equaled those aircraft shot down. So why, then, were those machines at repair and salvage units or aircraft storage units drawn down from 574 at the beginning of the battle on 15 August to 254 at the end a month later? The answer lies in the RAF's serviceability and repair categories. (See Table 32.) Category B was for aircraft to be repaired by the squadron's central hangar that would be ready at 1700 on that day. Aircraft in Category C, serviceable in twelve hours, or D, serviceable in seven days, were also repairable at the central hangar, as were Category E aircraft, which were repairable by the unit in more than seven days. Category F aircraft were repairable but beyond the unit's capacity, which meant a trip to a repair and salvage unit or a factory. Category G aircraft were a complete write-off, that is, struck off the unit's strength, to be picked over for spares. As the battle progressed, a field across the road from each station became cluttered with machines in Categories D and E while those in Category G went to the dump, to be picked over later. As far as the squadron's books were concerned, Categories F and G were taken off as no longer on charge. Thus it appeared that the losses were greater than was physically true.

If the Armée de l'Air only shot down between the 218 and 232 as I originally estimated or 384 German aircraft, the averaged Martin and Cornwell figures,[146] why did the German LQMG issue so many replacement machines? The answer lies in the German definition of unserviceability.

The statistics cited come from the historiography of the battle of 10 May–24 June. Of the 1,290 to 1,300 aircraft destroyed according to the German archives (actually 1,306, as noted by United Kingdom, Air Ministry),[147] the causes of GAF losses were 18 percent in aerial combat, 15 percent in accidents, 7 percent destroyed on the ground, and 7.3 percent by DCA; the wastage of the other 52.7 percent was due to "causes unknown."

According to Peter Cornwell with hindsight, for these efforts the Germans destroyed 1,067 RAF planes and the RAF 1,442 Luftwaffe machines. For defending fighters, this meant that it took 36.5 sorties to down a German.[148] The total of 1,442 repeats the total GAF loss of 1,814 less 232, which I conclude were downed by the Armée de l'Air and 120 by the DCA—or, if the Martin-Cornwell figure of 384 is used, with 15.5 sorties the total Armée de l'Air sorties in the Battle of France would be 5,952.

If the Armée de l'Air started with roughly 372 *chasse*, of which 75 percent were serviceable, the fighter force of 10 May would have been 279. Given the RAF ratio of sorties to destroyed, the FAF could not, at the most in undesirable conditions, have accounted for more than 232 Luftwaffe aircraft in six weeks. Or, if out of 637 *chasse* on 10 May only 68 percent were *disponible*, at .9 sorties daily, 390 sorties. At 36.5 sorties for each enemy aircraft shot down, the possible total of destroyed was only 449, but at 30 percent *bon de guerre*, 172 sorties and 4.7 Luftwaffe aircraft shot down (taking the base 637 *chasse*, at 68 percent serviceable, and at 0.9 sorties a day, divided by the 36.5 sorties to kill ratio for RAF and GAF).[149]

Regarding the question of how many GAF aircraft French fighters shot down in the Battle of France during May–June 1940, an attempt to answer was made, as noted above by Patrick Facon, by using the records of issues by the GAF quartermaster general.[150]

In France about one-tenth of all German aircraft were probably brought down by antiaircraft light machine guns (AALMG), as GAF bombers in summer 1940 were unarmored. At last, later, across the Channel in the Battle of Britain, British antiaircraft worked well, based upon the organization created in peacetime and the close liaison with Fighter Command.[151]

The relevance of the above to the Battle of France has several facets. First, the Armée de l'Air was unprepared in a number of ways for the increased wastage and consumption of war as opposed to that of the Phoney War (Drôle de Guerre) of September 1939–May 1940. Even so, the FAF failed to use the "lotus" months to prepare for the inevitable onslaught. Moreover, second, it was totally unprepared for the overrunning of its airfields in the northeast and east. RAF Fighter Command never faced that difficulty later in the summer. Third, the Armée de l'Air's lack of ferry pilots further degraded the FAF's recovery, whereas in the Battle of Britain the RAF could expect squadron Category G strike-offs and aircraft needing Category F repairs to be replaced within twenty-four hours. And because of planning from 1934 onward, the British had the ground crews, in general, and specialists, in particular, necessary to maintain the fighting force.

On 22 June the Franco-German armistice was signed and operations halted on 24 June. One last attempt was made to reach North Africa by the D-520s of Groupe de Chasse I/55, one of the Escadrille légerès de Defense, but when the planes reached Perpignan, in southern France, there was no fuel to take them further.

Conclusion

By the end of the final phase of the fighting the French Armée de l'Air had already lost 473 fighters, 120 bombers, and 194 reconnaissance machines (a total of 787) of which 410 were destroyed in combat, 202 on the ground, and 230 in accidents, for a total of 842 or 24.3 percent of the total first-line strength of 10 May of 3,454 modern machines, or in France 1,095 first line, or

TABLE 18. Comparison of German Losses, May and June 1940

AIRCRAFT	MAY 1940	JUNE 1940	TOTAL
Me-109	73	91	164
Me-110	56	7	63
Do-17	76˙	26	91˙
Do-215	7	3	10
He-111	83	31	114
Ju-88	4	9	13
Ju-87	24	18	42
Hs-126	51	40	91
Diverse	3	11	14
Total	**366**	**236**	**602˙˙**

Source: Paul Martin, *Invisibles Vainqueurs: Exploits et sacrifices de l'Armée de l'Air en 1939–1940* (Paris: Yves Michelet, 1990).

˙ Martin's totals do not add up correctly.

˙˙ Total includes losses to DCA.

77 percent.[152] The FAF could have replaced these, but 30 percent of those in the depots were unfit for service. Thus of the 852 aircraft accepted by the Centre de Réception des Avions de Series (Aircraft Reception Center [CRAS]) from 10 May to 5 June 1940, only 581 were sent to flying units, leaving a deficit of 271.[153] The general headquarters of the Armée de l'Air (GQGA) tried establishing a corps of expediting officers to close the gap, one at each of the five aircraft manufacturers, and depots were set up at Chateaudun to arm the new machines more rapidly, adding test and ferry pilots. But these measures were too late and insufficient.

Interestingly in Table 18 the comparison of German losses in the two almost equal periods of twenty-one days in May and twenty-four in June 1940 identifies, according to Paul Martin's tallies,[154] the German aircraft that fell to the Armée de l'Air.

CHAPTER 2

THE LUFTWAFFE

T he Luftwaffe and the Reichsluftministerium (German Air Ministry [RLM]) had come into being under Herman Goering from May of 1933 and included Generalstab (general staff) branches for operations, organization, training, flak, logistics, and signals comprised of officers transferred from the Wehrmacht (German army) and Reichsmarine (navy).[1] The Kaiser's Flying Corps had been abolished in 1920, after World War I, at the Allies' insistence. Yet General Hans von Seeckt had covertly impressed upon the Reichswehr, the armed forces of the Weimar Republic, that it had to remain air-minded. As Bart Whaley has noted, von Seeckt sought to "maintain a hidden reserve of trained pilots, aircrew, and ground staff . . . [and] a viable aviation industry"—all "until . . . safe and politic to reconstitute it."[2] Both von Seeckt and, later, Luftwaffe Chief of Staff General Walter Wever had imbedded Luftwaffe officers in ground units.

By September 1933, following Hitler's rise to power, German aviation and technician training programs had been consolidated and expanded, and by the summer of 1934 the inspectorate of flying schools controlled pilot, navigator, observer, and technician training including fighter, bomber, armament, and instrument instructional establishments. Concurrently the country was divided into six districts, each under the charge of a senior air commander responsible for everything in his district, including a full staff, procurement, and supply. By the time Air Minister Hermann Goering announced the Luftwaffe's existence on 1 March 1935, it had a fully developed organization. Joel Hayward, head of air power studies, Kings College London and at the Royal Air Force College, has described well that organization in a 2006 presentation at the biennial Air Power Conference at Hendon.[3] Hayward noted:

The Luftwaffe formed huge self-contained, multi-functional operational commands called *Luftflotten* (Air Fleets).

Each *Luftflotte* comprised all types of air combat units (reconnaissance, transport, fighter, ground-attack, dive-bomber, and bomber) as well as ground-based signals and flak units. . . . This mutually supporting integration of aircraft and anti-aircraft artillery was years ahead of its time.

. . . Each *Luftflotte* possessed one or more partnering *Luftgau* (Air District) . . . administrative organizations designed to manage the fleet's principal training, procurement, supply, repair and maintenance affairs, as well as its creation and upkeep.

. . . During wartime the *Luftgaue* served as the logistical life-line between the Reich and the various highly mobile in-theatre *Luftflotten* [and their] *Fliegerkorps*.[4]

———————————●———————————

The Luftgeneralstab (German air staff) in Berlin had to assist Goering in the Fuehrungstab—the operations staff—which dealt with all major operational and policy questions of GAF organization: air-raid precautions, flak, concerns in the field, weather, Intelligence, navigation, propaganda, security, the aircraft industry, and the manifold needs for planning Luftwaffe policy. A Generalstab was also established for administration and the maintenance of the Luftwaffe when policy had been laid down.

On 1 April 1935 flak forces trained by the Reichswehr came under Luftwaffe control, motorized and armed with 20-mm and 37-mm cannon and the valued dual-purpose 88-mm gun. At the same time, flak was incorporated into the Fatherland air defense with zones around vital industrial and military installations. While these zones were controlled by the Luftwaffe, the Wehrmacht determined the flak and fighter defenses in the field. General Wever of the Luftwaffe also oversaw the creation of that organization's paratroop force, inspired by Soviet developments in 1934 with their Tupolev TB-3 heavy bomber.[5] The Germans were particularly conscious of the relationships of technology to doctrine and many senior airmen saw the need for a long-range heavy bomber, which was a symbol of significant airpower.

On 1 April 1936 the nine regional Luftgau commands were created, and by 1937 the Luftwaffe had the infrastructure and organization to handle future expansion. Goering immediately had to build an officer corps for the expanding Luftwaffe, but he had to start with only 550 who had received pilot or observer training in the Reichswehr (Wehrmacht or Reichsmarine). Although these men from eleven different sources were very capable, they were far too few in number; and whether or not fliers, they soon were transferred to the nascent air arm. Some took pilot training in the German tradition of being able to lead from the front rather than command from the rear, and all those transferred to the Reichsluftministerium were commissioned, some for the second time.

A high proportion of the new Luftwaffe officers were gleaned from civil aviation; by 1945 they would constitute a quarter of the Luftwaffe's general officers. Others who had retired with distinction from the Wehrmacht—when it then had been the Reichswehr—were invited back and soon rose to be generals. At the other end of the scale, Wehrmacht and Reichsmarine cadets were encouraged to transfer to the new service. As a result, by 1938 the Luftwaffe had a solid corps of several thousand fully qualified officers, according to historians Horst Boog, E. R. Hooten, and James Corum.[6] Far from the antiquated clashes between the Prussians and the others, it was a homogeneous élite with the advantage of experience in modern aviation.

Technical Matters

Along with building the personnel side of the Luftwaffe, the air arm recruited Erhard Milch, former general manager of the Deutsche Lufthansa airline, to recreate the aircraft industry during 1933–1935. The goal was to produce 1,000 machines using the existing eight aircraft firms, as well as to license production to additional companies. By the end of 1933 the 3,200 employees at the beginning of the year had become 11,000. On 1 March 1935, the Luftwaffe already possessed over 800 operational airplanes. In 1936, when the really modern machines began to enter service, the industry's interim models were exported or relegated to training. The newer aircraft were the fruit of the January 1934 Rhineland program that had called for 4,021 of all types by the end of 1935, the majority of 1,760 being trainers. Milch had successfully moved the aircraft industry to where it was employing 124,878 by 1936.

The selection of aircraft types in these early days was based upon the technical office (TO) in the Reichsluftministerium drafting the performance specifications that it thought the Luftgeneralstab wanted. The TO engineers then made these into very detailed guidelines, which were sent to two to four manufacturers to develop into prototypes. The resulting two to four designs subsequently submitted were then tested at Rechlin and the winner selected for a production order. The German aircraft and engine firms were nationalized, with dictatorial decision-making.[7] Aircraft testing allowed engines to be run in for 2.5 hours at the factory, until 1944 when fuel shortages caused a reduction to thirty minutes. Guns also had been test-fired, until 1944 when a shortage of ammunition led to no firing trials before aircraft were delivered, complete with a warning that the guns had never been fired.[8] This contrasted strongly with the Armée de l'Air's convoluted and inefficient system. Each new aircraft had the engines run for two to five hours and the guns harmonized and fired before the machine was delivered to the Luftwaffe.

The whole was prioritized: first came heavy, long-range bombers; then a heavy dive-bomber; then mediums; and finally heavy fighters. These soon were followed by the Me-109, an all-metal, low-wing monoplane fighter that in Spain in 1938 was fitted with a metal three-bladed propeller.

In 1934 the TO had responded to a RLM call and had developed the innovative approach to what would become the Me-110, a twin-engine, long-range fighter for reconnaissance and for use as a fighter-bomber and an escort fighter. Interestingly this development was occurring at the same time that the French Armée de l'Air was creating the biplane BCR (bomber-combat-reconnaissance). The Me-110 first flew on 12 May 1936 as a two-cannon, five-machine gun, 285-mph fighter. It was the German attempt to obtain a long-range twin-engine fighter with single-seater characteristics. By March 1938 four prototypes had been produced, though these soon were replaced by aircraft with 1,100-hp engines versus the older 670 hp. Deliveries of the Me-110 began in February 1939, and the aircraft was engaged over Poland in the fall. But on 18 December 1939 it was 109s that scored heavily against RAF Wellingtons over the Heligoland Bight, the bay off the North Sea at the mouth of Germany's Elbe River.

The development of a German heavy bomber had been delayed by the lack of high-horsepower aero-engines. The initial 1936 prototype four-engine heavies (the Do-19 and the Ju-89) were under-powered, and thus the TO issued a new specification to succeed the terminated first-generation heavies. In the meantime the Luftwaffe concentrated on the excellent medium bombers such as the He-111 and upon long-range navigation, including guidance beams and automatic bomb-release over a target up to 400 km distant. By the time General Wever was killed on 3 June 1936 in an accident flying the Heinkel He-70 Blitz—a passenger, training, liason, and bomber craft—the Luftwaffe was on its way to being a well-rounded force. By mid-1937 it contained 178,000 men, including 46,000 flak personnel and 23,000 in the Luftzeichenkorps (air signal corps) And by then the Luftwaffe was being tested in Spain, where it learned, especially, the need for careful planning of air-ground operations.

On the control and management of production for the GAF see *The Supply Organization of the German Air Force, 1935–1945.*[9] The RLM was solely responsible for production for the Luftwaffe up to February 1944 when the

"Fighter Staff" was formed and Albert Speer took over all war production in the Third Reich.[10]

The Evolving Luftwaffe

The lessons of the Spanish Civil War, noted James Corum, were crucial to the development of the GAF. Over 39,000 GAF personnel served there during 1936–1939 in a complete war experience—strategic bombing, close air support, and air superiority. The campaign moved from a 1918-style static front to close support of mobile ground and armored actions and made it clear that airpower would play a decisive role in modern war. The Luftwaffe emerged victorious with more veterans of modern war than any other air force and with very few casualties from all causes—combat, accidents, or sickness. In addition, senior officers had experienced command and its problems, which prepared them for the Polish and Western campaigns of 1939–1940.[11]

Postwar study of the bombing of Madrid and Barcelona had convinced the Luftwaffe that proper civil defense (the British ARP, or air raid precautions) could protect civilian morale. Strategic-bombing initiatives in Spain also contributed to German understanding of the accuracy of high-level bombing and of the vulnerability of bombers to fighter attack. Hence the need to provide escorts was evident, and that required an increased production of fighters. And although the GAF leaders saw that a major strategic-bombing campaign was not feasible in Spain, they did not abandon the idea.

In Spain the loss of 160 aircraft in operational accidents including night flying and becoming lost, versus only 72 in combat, caused an emphasis on better training. In 1937 when General Hugo Sperrle (the future commander of the Third Air Fleet in the West in 1940) returned from Spain, he ordered intensive bad-weather and night-flying training. Neither the French nor the British had such proficiencies, though Lufthansa did.[12] The experience in Spain enabled the Luftwaffe to provide the close air support that was an essential of blitzkrieg victory.

With the 1936 death of General Wever, however, the Luftwaffe had lost not only its sole strategic-bombing visionary but the one man who had the respect of the air arm and the overall conception of airpower that made the GAF a world leader.[13] A power struggle ensued that had a deleterious effect upon the GAF until 1945. Wever was succeeded in 1936 by the able Albert Kesselring, who was amiable but tough and did not get along with either Goering or Milch. Goering became an active patron who began to interfere in Luftwaffe affairs. Milch meanwhile aimed to strengthen his position as state secretary of aviation as well as that of chief of staff of the Luftwaffe. Kesselring had been the Luftwaffe chief of staff (COS) from 1936 to 1937; Ernest Udet, the World War I ace, was appointed to the Technisches Amt (technical director-ate [T-Amt]). This had caused immediate fallout due to conflicting ideas and activities. General Wilhelm Wimmer, the brilliant head of the TO from October 1936 through May 1937, departed as did Colonel Wolfram von Richthofen. Kesserling[14] was soon fed up with Milch's actions and asked to be reassigned in June 1937. His successor, Werner Stumpff, soon pointed out to Goering that the Luftwaffe now had two conflicting chains of command. He advocated a clear division, separating operations from procurement. Milch had proposed three co-equal officers, but General Wever realized that supply from factory to units, including that of spares, was a Luftgeneralstab (air staff) responsibility, linked as it was closely to planning and operations.

In February 1939 the Luftwaffe was assigned a new chief of staff, Colonel General Hans Jeschonnek, a fighter pilot who worshipped Hitler. He also believed that the short-war blitzkrieg was the be-all and end-all of war and, therefore, that the GAF needed no reserves of pilots or matériel. He decreed that in war all the training staff should go on operations, and he vitiated the excellent reconnaissance and transport forces that General Wimmer ear-lier had created through the T-Amt. Jeschonnek had a limited vision of war, according to James Corum; he lacked the breadth of Kesselring and others who had served in the ground forces.

By 1939 the GAF's regional organization had become outdated by the need for uniformity and efficiency in war. The air districts then became only logistical and administrative commands responsible for total air and civil defense and the creation of the infrastructure of airfields, depots, and training schools. For war operations, Luftflotte (air fleets) were established and sup-ported by experienced Luftgeneralstab officers, their doctrine developed from 1935 by war games and exercises. These maneuvers were critiqued and the conclusions disseminated throughout the GAF. From 1936 on there had been major joint Wehrmacht/Luftwaffe exercises in which fighting for air superior-ity was an important part.

At that same time, Chief of Staff Kesselring had developed night fight-ers and in 1937 published Major General Helmuth Wilberg's 1935 Luftwaffe manual, *Luftwaffen Dienstvorschrift (L.Dv.) 16* (Luftwaffe *Regulation 16, The Conduct of Aerial War*). Maj. William F. Andrews, USAF, in a 1995 *Air Power Journal* article wrote:

Luftwaffe Regulation 16, *Luftkriegsführung* (Conduct of Aerial War), directed that "the enemy air force is to be fought from the beginning of the war. . . . An offensive execution of the battle in the enemy's territory is indispensable. The aerial battle will gain the initiative over the enemy." Offensive action by bomber units was intended to destroy enemy air units on the ground, simultaneously disrupting sortie generation and command and control. Fighter units would then hunt down units that were able to get airborne. Defense was not emphasized. In order to avoid diluting the air offensive, defense was left to flak units. This offensive counterair (OCA) effort was concentrated in time to neutralize the opponent's air force as quickly as possible.[15]

COS Kesselring and Stumpff, his successor, convinced Milch to approve a new heavy-bomber program, and Kesselring also demanded the development of two fighters, the Me-109, already in process, and the heavy Me-110. Concurrently the Luftwaffe recognized that the enemy's will could be broken by the destruction of his industry, and that was the role of the bomber. It was understood that Germany was vulnerable to air attack by her surrounding enemies, and that the Luftwaffe was her best means of defense. Major Hans-Detlef Herhudt von Rohden of the Luftgeneralstab noted this in articles published in 1937 and in his 1938 book, *Vom Luftkrieg (On Air War)*, all works accessible to the French and British Air Staffs, if they had cared to read them[16]—though the French did not. The Luftgeneralstab, however, had purchased 200 copies of von Rohden's book.[17]

It is interesting to note that in 1934, then-Colonel Charles de Gaulle in France had published his *L'armée de métier* (*The Army of the Future*) on a mobile armored force. Yet in Germany, following the 1935 Regulation 16, Major von Rohden had concluded that a campaign should open by an attack on enemy airfields, followed by the seizure of air superiority, and then the destruction of the enemy's aircraft industry. Though not genuinely Douhetian in approach, this broad bombing guide did aim to destroy the opponent's transport system, but lacked detailed strategic planning.

Expansion and Innovation

By 1938 the Luftwaffe had perfected the X-Gerät and Y-Gerät navigation systems of radio-beam guidance to a target at night in bad weather and had created Kampfgeschwader (KG) 100 as the élite Pathfinder force. During 1937–1939 fighter production was increased as a result of the lessons from Spain indicating the need for air support for troops as well as the value of the fighter-bomber role. By September 1939, 1,500 fighters had been produced compared with 2,000 bombers. During 1938 the plan had been for 335 fighters monthly. Thus during a campaign, replacements ready for action could be flown to operational units. During 1939–1940 the German aircraft industry had sufficient inspectors of their own in each factory to handle the necessary work, but the Flieger Inspektion (air ministry inspection office) also had representatives at each main factory where airframes and engines were produced and their stamp of approval was held in highest respect.[18]

Most remarkable of the German aircraft production program for 1939 to 1941–1942 was the restriction of its scope. It was only slightly increased from 133 to 150 fighters and 217 to 251 bombers per month during 1939 to 1940. The reason was the "overweening confidence and almost incredible optimism that percolated downwards from the Führer himself."[19] He considered the war in the west to be finished in October 1940 in spite of not achieving his objectives in the Battle of Britain. And Germany failed to use the interval to 22 June 1941 to increase aircraft production. When the war in Russia shifted from blitzkrieg to attrition, the already overextended Luftwaffe saw the master plan gone awry.

At the same time, the Reichsluftministerium was instituting no fewer than sixteen major revisions of the aircraft production program between 1 September 1939 and 15 November 1941. There was a failure to plan and think ahead in the Luftwaffe staff structure, due to overconfidence in the excellence of its materièl. The development of new types stagnated. On top of that, the technical department of the ministry meddled in design problems, for which it lacked competence. Moreover the manufacturers, operating on a cost-plus profit basis, were not efficient until fixed-price agreements were instituted in 1943. A third factor was the demand for modifications suggested by frontline commanders and pressed by Goering.

Luftwaffe losses came from enemy action, operational and nonoperational causes including flying into terrain in bad weather, stunting, mechanical failure, accidents on the ground, running out of fuel, and unserviceability that ground crews could not fix at once (an aircraft with more than 10 percent damage was a write-off), and the general effects of a very high-speed intense campaign, which may have brought on metal fatigue and at that time not a well-known or understood phenomena in a high-spirited, victorious force. Due to the fact that the Luftwaffe made no record of its salvage and repair operations during and after the Battle of France, we cannot tell why the Luftquartiermeister General (LQMG) had to replace certain machines.

The Germans had practiced the fighter-bomber role from 1936 on as part of cooperation with the ground forces. Low-level and bad-weather flying were employed to achieve surprise. With their new canon-equipped air-craft, tank- and truck-busting was a fresh role.[20] Air support of the Panzer and motorized divisions was believed by both the Wehrmacht and airmen to be essential to success, and for that it was to be concentrated on the decisive point in the battle as operations in Spain had made clear. In the Wehrmacht coopera-tion role there would be a commander of air and flak assets (*Koluft,* Luftwaffe air liaison officer) at the appropriate Wehrmacht Kommando headquarters. He also was responsible for the air logistical support, and he was backed by Fliegerverbindungsoffiziere (German air force liaison officers [Flivos]) who provided an accurate and quick picture of the GAF combat availability without placing Luftwaffe assets under Wehrmacht command. The system was estab-lished for the 1939 maneuvers under General Hugo Sperrle's Luftflotte 3. In contrast to the ponderous French chain of command the Luftwaffe in Poland had developed the system of embedding German air force officers in front-line units with direct wireless links to Luftwaffe Oberkommando (air head-quarters). This enabled strikes to be launched by *Fliegerdivisions* in minutes. The Fliegerverbindungsoffizier also advised field commanders of the air assets available. This was recognized by both General Jean Armengaud and by the Deuxième Bureau, but ignored by the French Haut Commandement.[21]

The Luftwaffe also supported the ground forces by air interdiction of enemy strong points, transport, and reserves, to break through and to isolate the battle-field. To accomplish this the Luftwaffe had to be as mobile as the Wehrmacht.[22]

The Luftwaffe was especially well prepared for war. Hitler's grand strategy was short wars, keeping the opponents off balance and avoiding the stalemate casualties of World War I. The Luftwaffe from its Generalstab at the top to its mechanics at the bottom was a highly trained force with men and machines partially blooded in the recent Spanish Civil War. It was a tactical close-sup-port body whose task was to buttress the Wehrmacht on land. For the tasks of August 1940 the GAF had 3,157 serviceable planes, pilots, and a full set of ground crew, plus very modern communications for command and control. The GAF's weakness was in sustainability.[23]

For the assault on the west, the Luftwaffe fielded 850 Me-109s, 350 Me-110s, 1,100 medium bombers, 400 Stukas, and 1,500 transports. He-111 and Ju-87 units had a strength each of thirty-eight to thirty-nine machines.[24] For the later attack on England in mid-July, Luftflotten 2 and 3 had 700 sin-gle-engine fighters, 220 twin-engine fighters, 1,200 medium bombers, 280 dive-bombers, 50 long-range reconnaissance aircraft, and 90 short-range machines.[25] Obviously the Battle of France had been costly. (See also Table 19. The numbers vary due to how many aircraft were serviceable.)

GAF bomber formations of up to one hundred aircraft escorted by a similar number of fighters were in sharp contrast to the raids sent over by the Allies. Compared with the flexibility, initiative, concentration, and numbers of the Luftwaffe fighters, the German bombers were hampered by their rigid formations, yet they achieved success by mass. They also enjoyed a settled prewar doctrine and stability of higher commanders.[26]

TABLE 19. Tally of GAF Strength in the West, 10 May 1940

AIRCRAFT	NUMBER
Long-range bombers	1,120
Dive-bombers	358
Long-range fighters	248
Single-engine fighters	1,016
Long-range reconnaissance	300
Short-range reconnaissance	340
Transports	475
Gliders	45
Total	**3,902***

Source: Table 21 herein, and United Kingdom, Air Ministry, CAB 106/282, 30–32.
*Out of almost 5,000 aircraft.

Strategy, Organization, and Operations

Luftwaffe planning was determined by the grand strategy of the Third Reich, and the Luftwaffe shaped its doctrine to specific threats. Clearly the enemies were France and its eastern allies, all of whom were within range of German medium bombers. It was not until early in 1938 that Hitler realized the admired British Empire might be an enemy, and thus the Luftflotte 2 (Second Air Fleet) under General Helmuth Felmy was ordered to plan for a possible enemy across the North Sea. But the Second Air Fleet had neither the airfields nor the logistics for such a campaign, as the GAF focus had been upon France and her allies. It had only nine airfields facing Britain versus the GAF's forty facing France and forty-three against Czechoslovakia and Poland. Until new air bases were built during 1941–1942 no serious campaign against the British was thought possible, and even then the bombers needed training for attacking naval vessels and shipping. In the spring of 1939 General Felmy reported his forces still far from effective for victory; he would not have the heavy Heinkel He-177 long-range bomber until 1942. In early 1940 he repeated his warning.

Luftwaffe analysis of the Armée de l'Air correctly saw the French weaknesses, foreseeing that if Germany attacked Poland, the French response against German industry could be parried and a grand-strategic bombing campaign against French industry initiated. In case of war, the GAF strategy was to destroy the weak Armée de l'Air infrastructure, including its aircraft unprotected by revetments, and to cut off France's importation of oil.[27]

The 1936 appointment of General Ernst Udet to the Luftwaffe TO had led to a total focus on dive-bombers to the detriment of future designs. The twin-engine Junkers Ju-88 had started life as a high-speed bomber design, but proved very versatile. Work started early in 1936 with construction of the first prototype in May and the first flight in December. Modified after tests at Rechlin, it had new 1,200-hp engines and soon carried 4,410 pounds of bombs over 621 miles at an average speed of 321 mph. Later that range was extended to more than 1,200 miles. Production of the ideal Junkers Ju-88 fast, long-range bomber was delayed from September 1937 to late 1939 while it was redesigned as a dive-bomber, though some 60 had been produced by the end of 1939. During 1940, as well as during the rest of the war, 300 per month were turned out. The Ju-88 needed 11,900 hours to complete in contrast to the 16,000 hours of the first MS-406 French fighter.[28] At a maximum weight of about 26,000 pounds, the Ju-88 could reach a 26,000-foot ceiling. In August 1939 the Luftwaffe had 4,201 operational aircraft (421 bombers; 361 dive-bombers; 788 fighters; 43 heavy fighters; 488 transports) and 373,000 personnel. It was not fully ready for war, yet far better off than the Armée de l'Air and the Royal Air Force, with the Soviet air force then in decline.[29] The Luftwaffe was the most formidable and best trained force of the day.

In the Luftwaffe each operational station (military airfield) was known as a *Fliegerhorst* and housed a *Gruppe* of twenty-seven aircraft in three six-plane *Staffeln* plus nine, these reserves   being units complete with crews who were available at all times to ensure that the *Staffeln* were at full strength in spite of unservice-abilities and routine maintenance. Units were joined together to form a *Geschwader* (wing) of four *Gruppen* in the bomber and two in the fighter wings. *Fliegerhorst* personnel ran the station with the operational *Gruppen* separate, highly mobile and able to move early and quickly. Each command contained one or more *Luftpark* (aircraft parks) and a *Zeugamt* (stores depot) as well as three to four recruit depots and attached *ab initio* flying schools[30] (Figure 3).

FIGURE 3. German Air Force Operational Station Establishment

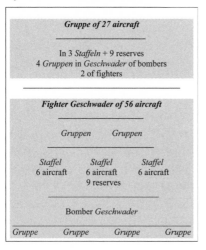

Planning for War—Britain and Poland

In February 1938 General Hellmuth Felmy was General Officer Commanding of Luftwaffengruppenkommando 2, which included the German North Sea. Matthew Cooper's *The German Air Force, 1933–1945*, aptly describes the situation.[31] Felmy was instructed to propose actions if Britain intervened in the war, and after the Munich Agreement of September 1938 was solidified he produced two memos noting (1) an air war against Britain could have only nuisance value, and (2) the range of Luftwaffe bombers from the Frisian coast was too limited, requiring bases in Holland and Belgium. The Luftgeneralstab also studied the problem and came to the same conclusions, inasmuch as the essential task of the GAF was to secure freedom of action for the ground forces.

In May of 1939 the Luftgeneralstab concluded again that the GAF could not hope for a quick, decisive victory over Britain. On 23 May, Adolf Hitler had told his chiefs that Great Britain would not be beaten by air alone and that war against her would be long and costly. On 24 May, he told the GAF that as soon as bases were available they should begin the effort to defeat the United Kingdom.[32] On 23 May 1939 Hitler also had announced to his service chiefs that he would invade Poland, and if Britain entered the war the Reichsmarine and the Luftwaffe were to deprive the United Kingdom of food supplies. With this economic blockade of the nation to become policy, the GAF was essentially forced into a war in which it did not believe and for which it was not prepared.

On 9 July 1939 Luftflotten 2 (LF2) was told to prepare to attack vital British targets, including the aircraft industry, ports, and oil storage. General Joseph "Beppo" Schmid advised Goering at that time that the RAF would equal the Luftwaffe in 1940 and thus the GAF would need to defeat not only the RAF but also the British aircraft industry, and then close the ports. Yet, Goering added, the GAF attack drive might not be enough when it came up against the British known ability to improvise and their mental toughness, and thus invasion and occupation would probably be necessary. However, as Matthew Cooper notes, War Directive No. 1 of 31 April 1939—and reconfirmed in Directive Nos. 2, 3, and 4 of September—contained instructions that there were to be no attacks on mainland Britain or on passenger ships. On 9 October 1939 Hitler issued Directive No. 6 to conquer Belgium and Holland in order to be able to strike the air industrial heart of the United Kingdom and its southwestern ports. Occupation of Belgium and Holland was believed necessary to protect German vital areas from the RAF and to shorten the distance to England, to save GAF fuel, and to enable more bombs to be carried. On 29 November 1939 these premises congealed into War Directive No. 9—war on the economy of the enemy—amended to make the British aircraft industry the primary target.

During that fall of 1939, after the start of World War II, the Luftwaffe was gradually authorized to attack the Royal Navy and its convoys but, Cooper notes, was ill-prepared for the task. Time was required to train GAF airmen and to develop their weapons. The 228 aircraft assigned to Kriegsmarinekommando (naval command) were obsolete, though modern aircraft were on the way. Early in the war, mine-laying operations were undertaken, and while losses were high, nevertheless success was considerable. During February 1940 the Reichsluftministerium (RLM) set up Flieger-Division IX and gradually pulled the GAF out of Kriegsmarinekommando. By then the division had two units, one with sixty-five HE-111 medium bombers and the other with eighteen Ju-88 heavies, but attacks on the Royal Navy were not as effective as those on the Merchant Marine. The result was the creation of Fliegerkorps X in February 1940, which undertook the Norwegian Campaign later that year and subsequently was involved with mine-laying and antishipping tasks. In the spring of 1940 the Focke-Wulf Fw-200 Condor transport was added, which had a radius of action of 1,000 to 1,400 miles and an airborne time of fourteen to sixteen hours.[33]

But while Germany had been preparing for an assault on Britain it also had its sights on Poland, which in September 1939, of immediate relevance on the Continent, should have warned France that dispersed aircraft deprived of their basic airfield facilities and DCA could not survive because repair facilities, fuel, and spares, as well as reserve aircraft and communications, needed to be at hand. The Luftwaffe destroyed Polish rail networks and pulverized fortresses, while the Wehrmacht overran airfields not already bombed into uselessness. Expeditiously, upon availability, mobile Luftwaffe logistics units converted the Polish airfields into advanced GAF bases, enabling sortie rates of three-plus per day per aircraft and quick reaction to requests for air help. Support and mobility were provided by fleets of Junkers Ju-52 transports. And as soon as the three-week Polish Campaign was over, the Luftwaffe staff critiqued the operations. Yet the French, meanwhile, still saw nothing instructive or of interest in the campaign.

As Williamson Murray has noted, military organizations tend to extract from experience only those materials that agree with their preconceived ideas.[34] The result is a lack of interaction of battlefield experience and doctrine—a critical difference between success and failure. The Wehrmacht Oberkommando (high command) and the Luftwaffe analyzed the Polish Campaign of September 1939, had commands of all units make a harsh critique of their units' deficiencies, and then instituted rigorous training and maneuvers up to May 1940 that sought to have adequate forces for their new combats. Officers and NCOs were detailed to special schools and new reservists were force-fed to get them to the same level as the regulars, while the unfit were weeded out.

Victory for the Luftwaffe in the west in 1940 owed much to the training and doctrine developed during the time of the Phoney War—after the invasion of Poland and before the May 1940 Battle of France. The GAF absorbed the lessons from its Polish action and rather than be congratulated on its successes,[35] analysis was followed by training to bring all the reserve units up to regular standards. In Poland the Germans defeated forty divisions with one million men. Yet the Oberkommando des Heeres (high command of the army [OKH]) judged the success as insufficient and inadequate, Williamson Murray notes.[36] The higher the headquarters, the more demanding and dissatisfied were commanders with operational performance (unlike the USAF in the 1960s, Murray adds), and yet this seems to have generated greater trust and harmony at all levels leading to the ability to critically evaluate troop performance, training, discipline, and doctrine. The Wehrmacht thus learned a great deal. The OKH paid tribute to the Luftwaffe, but noted that with air superiority the troops had become careless of their camouflage, which could be disastrous in fighting in the west before air superiority would be won.

The Polish Campaign confirmed Generalstab ideas of war despite some of those who opposed blitzkrieg. The Oberkommando did not want the World War I mistake again of the power of their fighting units being overestimated. It had opposed an attack on the west because at the time many units in the Wehrmacht were untrained or undereducated. But on 13 October 1939 the OKH issued a memo on "The Training of the Field Army," and by May 1940 these units had been brought up to standard. The Wehrmacht by May 1940 was far superior to its opponents.[37]

Clearly the German air arm had an excellent idea of the weaknesses of Poland and France—given that it had had two decades, from 1918 to 1939, to prepare. In comparison, it took the Allies nearly four years of warfare to know how to hurt Germany. The Luftwaffe had the benefit of being en cadre under the Weimar Republic (1919–1933), so that a great deal of its time had been spent in cooperation with the German Reichswehr and in thinking about and planning for its role in the next war. Hitler was in one sense almost the perfect political leader for Germany and its armed forces: he wanted to revise the 1919 Versailles Diktat; he knew the Fatherland could not stand another 1914–1918 high-casualty trench war; he accepted the Wehrmacht's concept of a blitzkrieg; and he was a promoter of aviation and of tank/mobile formations as in the 1935 military maneuvers.

The German grand strategy was for a quick decisive war, as compared with that of the French who were looking to a long holding struggle before victory, as in 1914–1918. The Germans were willing to take offensive risks and drew correct lessons from World War I. The French were more static and dilatory in responding to the pace of a protracted defensive infantry and artillery war. The French took their time; the Germans took France. And the British reverted to insularity.

Production, Logistics, and Resupply Issues

The German aircraft industry benefited from the Führer being the ultimate decision-maker, with most being quick. But it had the later disadvantage that the Führer regarded himself as infallible and so ignored professional advice.[38] Nevertheless on 10 May 1940 the Luftwaffe had a two-to-one advantage in personnel and machines against France. Moreover the GAF flew four sorties daily, in itself a force multiplier, against the 0.9 sorties of the Armée de l'Air.[39] (See Graph, German Aircraft Production 1934–1941.)

The Wehrmacht philosophy supported a short campaign with emphasis upon momentum. (The Wehrmacht was in general supplied by the railways and horse-drawn wagons.)[40] Thus an aircraft with more than 10 percent damage was simply to be pushed aside and a new one flown in from the depots (Table 20). The RAF had essentially the same rules; if a machine could not be repaired on the squadron within three days, it was to be replaced. The Luftwaffe had enough pilots to operate a resupply service and the RAF in Britain had service pilots to collect aircraft from the factories as well as the civilian air transport auxiliary (ATA) to deliver them; but the Armée de l'Air lacked such an effective system.[41] French prewar thought had ignored the resources needed for sustained operations; the RAF had not.[42]

Although wastage and consumption was made good in the Luftwaffe by flying the spares to airfields occupied by GAF advanced units, these units frequently were short of fuel, and GAF air transports were pressed to keep up with that demand. In addition, evidence of a combination of unprepared airfields and pilot fatigue is to be found in the high shrinkage rate of the serviceable Ju-52 transports, which had also suffered heavily in the invasion of the Netherlands. The Ju-52 transport fleet dropped from a high of 475 on 11 May 1940 to a low of 342 on 6 June, and serviceability fell from 99 percent to 59.9 percent or 201 machines.[43]

Logistics was not highly ranked in German military circles in spite of the lessons of World War I. However, during World War II, military specialist Generalfeldmarschall (Field Marshal) Erich von Manstein assumed responsibility for all his command, including personnel, Intelligence, and logistics.

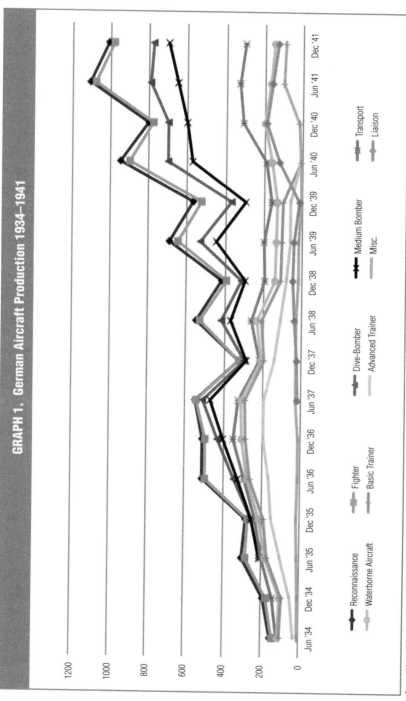

GRAPH 1. German Aircraft Production 1934–1941

Reconnaissance
Waterborne Aircraft
Fighter
Basic Trainer
Dive-Bomber
Advanced Trainer
Medium Bomber
Misc.
Transport
Liaison

Source: William Green, *The Warplanes of the Third Reich* (New York: Doubleday, 1970).

TABLE 20. Luftwaffe Damage Assessment Categories

CATEGORY	DESCRIPTION
100 percent	Total write-off
60–100 percent	"Write-off with varying degrees of cannibalization"
45–60 percent	Severely damaged and needing major replacements
40–45 percent	Major damage and engine replacement
25–39 percent	Major damage requiring major inspection at the unit
10–24 percent	Local damage from gunfire or shrapnel and possible replacements
< 10 percent	Minor damage unit could make good

Source: Francis K. Mason, Battle over Britain (New York: Doubleday, 1969), 129.

Note: Both sides mis-assessed, and that goes a long way to explain the discrepancy between pilot's claims and so-called official figures. The LQMG records are clearly inaccurate—often by a wide margin. Some losses were not reported until a week or more later, and it's doubtful that some returns were submitted at all. This challenges British statistics on losses.

Because of the German blitzkrieg philosophy, all aircraft drawn from the Luftwaffe quartermaster general (LQMG) were not simply to replace machines shot down but to replace all temporary wastage and consumption. Similarly, at the first Battle of the Marne in 1914 house stocks were soon depleted by the underestimation of the expenditure of ammunition. By the time many German battalions reached the Marne, they were only at half-strength due to wastage from rapid daily marches of twenty to twenty-five miles in hot weather. Essentially the same difficulties occurred in Russia in 1941, due again to over-optimism and neglect of logistics planning.[44]

According to Dr. Lutz Budrass (of the University at Bochum, and some-time Luftwaffe historian), in 1935 the Luftwaffe Generalstab (air general staff) estimated that the GAF would suffer 50 percent aircraft casualties. This was reduced in 1938 to 30 percent per month, of which only some 10 percent could be repaired. Then in 1937 Lieutenant Colonel Fritz Loeb of the Luftwaffe Generalstab suggested that any aircraft with over 10 percent damage be scrapped, which resulted in the GAF not setting up a repair organization. However, the 1940 Battles of France and Britain surprised the Luftwaffe with the large number of machines that returned to base with heavy damage. Yet the GAF's losses were less than 20 percent in combat (shot down), and the new damage assessments only led to scrapping if there was more than 80 percent damage. Thus a considerable number awaited rebuilding. A vast repair organization was set up, but only began to show results late in 1940. Light damage was repaired at improvised Front reparatur facilities. In 1940 the GAF received 7,700 new aircraft as well as 2,600 from both the Front reparatur and from the

Heimat (Fatherland) rear areas *reparatur* facilities such as Erle/Antwerpen in Belgium. The success was more marked in 1941 and onward (Tables 21–24).[45]

Prewar thought had ignored the question of the strength needed to sustain an air campaign, not just in the first line but also in the numbers of aircraft required to make up for wastage, salvage, repair, and maintenance. To overcome this stress on the availability of machines, the Ju-52 transport fleet, flown by instructors, was ruthlessly employed.[46] Royal Air Force Intelligence in 1941 had accepted that Luftwaffe serviceability was 50 percent, though according to Luftwaffe historian Horst Boog it was as low as 30 percent, as in France in 1940 where it equaled that of the FAF.[47] Initially flying units were highly mobile and not hampered by much technical apparatus, including machine shops, but frequent moves soon reduced efficiency by 30 percent per change of station. Moreover because Oberkommando did not see logistics as part of operations, supply was excluded from the Luftwaffengeneralstab (air staff) purview. The Luftwaffe was constantly short of spare parts, with the result that an aircraft could be grounded for lack of a single item. And shortage of parts meant that the LQMG had to issue large quantities of new and rebuilt aircraft to keep the frontline units up to strength. The void between the Luftwaffengeneralstab and the logisticians had resulted in a shortage of fuel on operations. The failure to take into account the increased fuel consumption of the newer, higher-horsepower engines effectively grounded the Me-109 fighters at Dunkirk during May–June 1940 (Table 24).

All air forces, however, endured a shortage of spares during the introduction of new types, and even more so in the early days of the Technological Revolution during the 1930s. In part it was due to general staffs failing to realize the importance of logistics and the critical need for spares in a new technological, mechanical service. Yet these shortages were also the result of manufacturers not being paid until an aircraft was complete, the peacetime practice of not assessing the spares requirements until after eighteen months of service, and the finance officers' fear of overspending.[48]

According to Horst Boog, regarding the tables in Ulf Balke,[49] "Ab 60%" refers to GAF planes damaged, between 60 and 100 percent, and which were no longer considered to be repairable. In fact we do not have an official summary of the German losses in the French Campaign. In May 1940 the total of all GAF types issued was 923 but the Luftwaffe quartermaster general had said 834, and in June 944. We do agree on the July figure of 673.[50]

On 4 May 1940 the Luftwaffe had 5,398 aircraft of which 3,928 (73 percent) were serviceable. On 18 May the Luftwaffe had 5,016 aircraft, with 3,035 (61 percent) serviceable. In those fourteen days, the strength had dropped 382

TABLE 21. Luftwaffe Strengths, 4 May–6 July 1940, Totals and Serviceable Aircraft*

DATE	CLOSE RECCE	LONG-RANGE RECCE	SINGLE-ENGINE FIGHTERS	TWIN-ENGINE FIGHTERS	BOMBERS	DIVE-BOMBERS	GROUND-ATTACK	COASTAL	TOTAL (EXCLUDING TRANSPORT)	TRANSPORT	TOTAL
4 May											
Strength	345	321	1,369	367	1,758	417	49	241	**4,867**	531	**5,398**
Serviceable	281	232	970	250	1,180	341	38	161	**3,453**	475	**3,928**
11 May											
Strength	335	322	1,356	354	1,711	414	50	240	**4,782**	471	**5,253**
Serviceable	280	216	1,076	246	1,084	345	45	152	**3,444**	330	**3,774**
18 May											
Strength	336	309	1,313	338	1,641	378	50	242	**4,607**	409	**5,016**
Serviceable	202	186	788	203	985	227	30	145	**2,766**	269	**3,035**
25 May											
Strength	333	299	1,366	345	1,631	381	50	249	**4,654**	410	**5,064**
Serviceable	200	180	820	177	897	229	30	149	**2,682**	246	**2,928**
1 June											
Strength	335	284	1,477	383	1,636	376	50	244	**4,785**	348	**5,133**
Serviceable	201	171	886	192	900	226	30	146	**2,752**	209	**2,961**
8 June											
Strength	334	272	1,436	376	1,621	344	44	236	**4,663**	342	**5,005**
Serviceable	200	163	862	188	892	206	26	142	**2,679**	205	**2,884**
15 June											
Strength	344	258	1,061	330	1,371	400	41	239	**4,044**	406	**4,450**
Serviceable	256	174	815	249	856	271	33	160	**2,814**	219	**3,033**

29 June											
Strength	312	257	1,107	357	1,380	428	55	233	4,129	408	4,537
Serviceable	264	187	856	261	841	297	40	151	2,897	301	3,198
6 July											
Strength	268	263	1,071	374	1,437	443	55	203	4,114	428	4,542
Serviceable	214	176	880	283	993	312	40	149	3,047	302	3,349

Source: United Kingdom, Air Ministry, Abteilung [Department] VI [Intelligence], CAB [Cabinet] CAB, 106/282, 30-32.

*Strengths on these dates computed by Abteilung VI from strength return on 11 May, casualty reports, and returns of new aircraft delivered to units. Serviceability is calculated as being 50-60 percent of strength.

TABLE 22. Luftwaffe Monthly Deliveries to Formations by LQMG, 1940

AIRCRAFT TYPE	JAN.	FEB.	MAR.	APR.	MAY	JUNE	JULY	AUG.	SEPT.	OCT.	NOV.	DEC.	TOTAL
Close Recce	27	21	42	25	60	84	5		23	18	40	32	**377**
Army Cooperation	3	6	6	22	18	20	11	4	5	3	9	19	**126**
Long-Range Recce	5	10	27	18	23	29	27	43	106	55	32	23	**398**
Single-Engine Fighters	81	46	115	150	310	354	162	222	338	238	91	64	**2,171**
Twin-Engine Fighters	44	46	62	89	95	126	112	93	203	137	95	65	**1,167**
Bombers	86	89	137	259	302	239	269	290	335	314	279	262	**2,861**
Dive-Bombers	19	52	43	35	65	8	17	84	68	30	43	42	**506**
Transport	35	60	39	55	50	74	70	130	109	65	65	56	**808**
Total	**300**	**330**	**471**	**653**	**923**	**934**	**673**	**866**	**1,187**	**860**	**654**	**563**	**8,414**

Source: United Kingdom, Air Ministry, Abteilung [Department] VI [Intelligence], CAB [Cabinet] CAB 106/282, 157.

TABLE 23. Luftwaffe Losses in France, May–June 1940

AIRCRAFT	NO. DESTROYED	NO. DAMAGED	TOTAL
Me-110	170	105	275
Me-109	149	30	179
Ju-88	100	22	122
Do-17	163	67	230
He-111	348	68	416
Ju-87	111	22	133
Hs-126	61	11	72
Total	**1,102**	**325**	**1,427**

Source: United Kingdom, Air Ministry. *Abteilung* [Department] VI [Intelligence], CAB [Cabinet] CAB, 106/282.

TABLE 24. Total Cumulative and Daily GAF Losses, 10 May–24 June 1940

DATE	CUMULATIVE DESTROYED AND DAMAGED	ACTUAL DESTROYED AND DAMAGED FOR DAY	DATE	CUMULATIVE DESTROYED AND DAMAGED	ACTUAL DESTROYED AND DAMAGED FOR DAY
10 May	347	347	2	48	18
11	454	107	3	64	16
12	525	71	4	70	6
13	578	53	5	108	38
14	650	72	6	132	24
15	695	45	7	153	21
16	748	53	8	176	23
17	800	52	9	193	17
18	855	55	10	207	14
19	916	61	11	216	9
20	955	39	12	228	12
21	996	41	13	235	7
22	1,025	29	14	244	9
23	1,041	16	15	259	15
24	1,077	36	16	269	10
25	1,111	34	17	273	4
26	1,155	44	18	287	14
27	1,209	54	19		
28	1,236	27	20		
29	1,260	24	21		
30	1,271	11	22		
31	1,288	17	23		
1 June	30	30	24		

Source: United Kingdom, Air Ministry. *Abteilung* [Department] VI [Intelligence], CAB 102/262, 15.

from all causes, including domestic nonoperational write-offs, but the critical serviceability had dropped 893. Between 4 and 18 May, LQMG figures indicate the Me-109 fighter force had dropped from 1,369 to 1,313, a loss of 56, with serviceability falling from 70 percent to 60 percent. On the basis of serviceability, with four sorties each aircraft per day, on 4 May the GAF had 668 serviceable Me-109s and generated 2,672 sorties; divided by 36.5—the average GAF and RAF sorties per enemy kill—these aircraft sorties could have destroyed 73 enemy aircraft. Fourteen days later, on 18 May, with 473 aircraft putting up 1,892 sorties, the enemy lost close to 52. Once the fighting stopped by 29 June, the Me-109 serviceability rate was up again to 77.3 percent. Of 1,711 bombers, however, on 11 May 1,084 were serviceable (63.4 percent); this dropped to 55 percent by 6 June, but rose to 69.4 percent when fighting ended.[51]

The LQMG issued 541 bombers in May and June and 269 in July. The average for the whole of 1940 was 434 per month, but the LQMG clerk gave the year's total as only 2,701 rather than 5,208, an error of 2,507, or 48 percent.[52] Horst Boog notes, "As to that [LQMG] error I have no information."[53] Francis K. Mason's 1969 *Battle over Britain* gives daily tallies and damage categories and notes the inaccuracy of German loss returns, especially when they used other (informal) channels rather than the required documentation listed to obtain replacement aircraft (Tables 25–27).[54]

According to Williamson Murray, the LQMG during the Battle of France lost 1,129 machines to the enemy of its initial establishment (IE) of 5,349, and a further 216 not due to the enemy, for a total of 1,345 and 81 destroyed not on operations, or 1,426 equaling 26.6 percent of the IE. Of the Me-109s, 169 were shot down and 66 lost from other causes, or 235 out of an IE of 1,369,

TABLE 25. Luftwaffe Strength and Serviceability, 5 October 1940

TYPE	TOTAL	SERVICEABLE	PERCENTAGE
Close Recce	361	290	80.3
Long-Range Recce	334	224	67.1
Single-Engine Fighters	859	667	77.6
Night Fighters	144	89	61.8
Twin-Engine Fighters	166	99	59.6
Bombers	1,427	836	58.5
Dive-Bombers	458	379	82.7
Transports	379	319	84.2

Source: United Kingdom, Air Ministry, CAB 106/282.

TABLE 26. Luftwaffe Strength, 11 May 1940, as Calculated by *Abteilung* VI[a]

AIRCRAFT	NO. SERVICEABLE[b]
1,356 Single-Engine Fighters	1,076
354 Twin-Engine Fighters	246, estimated at 50–60%

Source: United Kingdom, Air Ministry, CAB 106/282.

[a]*Abteilung* VI (Luftwaffe intelligence department) summarized the LQMG data at the end of the war for the British Air Ministry.
[b]For the GAF: If 55% serviceability = 746 at 4 sorties daily = 2,984 sorties ÷ 36.5 = 82 enemy aircraft shot down. For the FAF: If 55% serviceability = 348 x .9 = 313 sorties ÷ 36.5 = 8-9 shot down (or: Paul Martin notes, 15.5 sorties per aircraft shot down = 20 GAF shot down rather than 8-9).

TABLE 27. RAF and Luftwaffe Casualties, Aircrew and Aircraft—Losses, Actual and Claimed, August–October 1940

MONTH	RAF: AIRCREW LOST, ACTUAL/ VERIFIED	RAF: AIRCREW LOST, CLAIMED	RAF: ENEMY AIRCRAFT SHOT DOWN, ACTUAL/ VERIFIED	RAF: ENEMY AIRCRAFT SHOT DOWN, CLAIMED	GAF: RAF AIRCRAFT SHOT DOWN, ACTUAL/ VERIFIED	GAF: RAF AIRCRAFT SHOT DOWN, CLAIMED
August	176	154	389	298	1,101	694
September	173	150	358	150	629	1,097
October	120	53	185	118	118	379
Total	**469**	**357**	**932**	**566**	**1,848**	**2,170**
% Error	**131**		**164**		**117**	

Source: United Kingdom, Air Ministry, CAB 106/282.

or 17.2 percent.[55] The total number of Me-109s issued in May and June was 674, with 182 in July, for a total of 856.[56] In May the Luftwaffe lost 229 fighters (147 Me-109s, 82 Me-110s) and 169 Me-109 pilots, or 15 percent of the pilot total, with the POWs being returned after the armistice; 643 bombers were lost. Given the total number of single-engine fighters issued by the LQMG as 2,271, that figure should be 2,191, a discrepancy of 80.[57]

The German Aircraft Types

The story of the development of the German aircraft types is instructive, as it shows what the French Armée de l'Air's principal contemporary opponent was doing and what was possible.

The Bf-109/Me-109

The Messerschmitt Bf-109, for example, was a very successful fighter produced by a brilliant design team willing to move forward regardless of the skeptical attitude of the Luftwaffe TO in Berlin, questioning of the team's lack of experience in high-speed aircraft design. The result was a state-of-the-art machine that was still constantly evolving well after the 1940 Battle of France.[58] The Me-109, as the aircraft was commonly known during the war rather than as the Bf-109, was the most numerous and long-lived of Luftwaffe fighters. As William Green noted in 1970, it established the standard for international fighter design when it appeared in 1935, and it remained in first-line service until almost the end of World War II.[59] The Me-109E was notorious for breaking from an attack by rolling on its back and diving away trailing a plume of black smoke, fooling many into believing it had been shot down.[60]

The Me-109 designers, Willy Messerschmitt and Walter Rethel, made use of the most advanced ideas of the day to get the ultimate performance with the smallest possible airframe and the most powerful engine available, combining them with the new radical all-metal stressed-skin construction. The wings had slotted trailing-edge flaps and Handley-Page leading-edge slats; the fuselage had a retractable undercarriage and a fully enclosed cockpit, side-hinged for easy access, but less easy to exit in the air. Well-constructed and finished, the Me-109's handling characteristics were good throughout its speed range (from stalling at sixty mph to more than three hundred mph), and below ten thousand feet it could climb steeply at low speeds and dive better than the nearest competitor, the British Spitfire I.

The Me-109 had been conceived at the Bayerische Flugzeugwerke (BFW, Bavarian Aircraft Works) at Augsburg in early 1934 to Luftwaffe specifications, despite the Luftwaffe's technical office doubts that the company could compete with the established Arado and Heinkel Flugzeugwerken. Arado had developed the Ar-65 and 68 fighters and the Ar-66 trainer, among others, and Heinkel was the home of the renowned He-111 bomber. World War I fighter ace Erhard Milch, then state secretary of aviation, had made it plain that he would not award a contract to the Bavarian Aircraft upstarts, a consequence of earlier ill-will toward the firm. In 1929, as the managing director of the national airline, Deutsche Luft Hansa (Lufthansa after 1933), Milch had cancelled a contract for ten Messerschmitt M-20b transports then nearing completion. It was a move predicated upon crashes in 1928 of the early prototype M-20, and perhaps the resultant death of one of Milch's friends, and a crushing blow that had bankrupted the manufacturer. Nevertheless Messerschmitt reestablished his company in 1933 though, due to the adversarial Minister Milch, had to focus on foreign orders and exports.

Events began to turn in Messerschmitt's favor, however, after Milch had criticized the firm for foreign rather than German orders, leading to Messerschmitt's explanation that he sold abroad of necessity, which subsequently embarrassed the TO. Messerschmitt's revived Bayerische Flugzeugwerke (BFI) was then given a development contract to produce six aircraft for the 1934 Challenge de Tourisme Internationale. Messerschmitt later took his proto-type M-37 single-engine sports monoplane and converted it into a thoroughly modern tourer, the two-seat Bf-108. At about the same time, early in 1934, he received a development contract for a fighter. By that fall Messerschmitt had a new friend in charge of the TO, which saved the fledgling Bf-108 after it had experienced an unfortunate crash before the Challenge. But by then the design team at Augsburg was fully focused on the new Bf-109. The official specifica-tion had required two 7.92-mm machine guns, high rates of roll and turn, the ability to power dive, and perfect spinning. The Bf-109 team was so concerned that they would not get a production contract for the aircraft that they decided to extend themselves to produce a superior machine.

The Bf-109 was designed to take either of the new twelve-cylinder Daimler-Benz or Junkers Jumo engines, which were inverted Vs to give the pilot the best view possible. In August 1935, as the Bf-109a was being readied for taxiing trials, Ernst Udet, still a civilian and not yet part of the TO, visited Augsburg and subsequently expressed his disapproval of this modern machine. However, within a year he had a drastic change of mind as a result of its per-formance. The first flight in September 1935 had been with an available Rolls-Royce Kestrel engine, as the Jumo 210 was not yet ready. The Bf-109 prototype was soon ferried to Rechlin, the Luftwaffe's primary aircraft testing area, where Willy Messerschmitt had to explain its radical design features to skeptical test pilots. In spite of its 290 mph and 640 hp, the technical office staff preferred the more traditional Heinkel 112, as Messerschmitt was an upstart and they questioned whether or not his firm could handle a contract.

The second Bf-109 prototype flew in January 1936 with a Jumo 210A engine of 610 hp, and the third flew in June. By then attitudes had changed, as the Bf-109 had proved itself in tests, and an order for ten preproduction aircraft was received. In part this also was due to Intelligence discovering that the British Supermarine Aircraft Company had an order for 310 Spitfires. The TO acceptance commission had found the Bf-109 to be superior to the Heinkel He-112. (There was an He-113, but it was a cover name for the rebuilt He-112.) The 109 gave an impressive handling demonstration, including a dive from 24,600 feet. And Ernst Udet, then-Fliegerhorst Inspekteur (inspector of airfields), approved. The 109's undercarriage was the same track as that of the He-51; it allowed for minimal damage when landing with only one oleo leg of the undercarriage extended. In addition the wing attachment to the fuselage allowed it to be changed without having to disassemble the undercarriage. The Bf-109's two 500-rpg 7.92-mm machine guns were shortly supplemented by an engine-mounted 7.92 gun flown on the preproduction model in November 1936, but the engine-mounted gun seized after a few bursts due to cooling problems and was removed.

German volunteer pilots were sent to Spain in 1936, and in November of that year the Condor Legion air unit was formally assembled. However, its He-112 fighters were outclassed by the Soviet Polikarpov I-15 that had arrived in October, and therefore a Bf-109B was shipped out at Christmas, with two more test machines to follow. The Bf-109s proved themselves under service conditions and were returned to the factory at Augsburg for continued development work.

BFW's Augsburg works had been expanded to handle production of 90 Arado Ar-66 biplane trainers, 115 Gotha Go-145 gunnery biplane trainers, 70 Heinkel He-45 reconnaissance/light bomber biplanes, 35 He-50 reconnaissance/dive-bomber biplanes, and 32 Bf-109B fighters. However, because larger facilities were needed, a new Messerschmitt GmbH (limited liability) company was formed at Regensburg for building aircraft. By February 1937 production models were coming off the line and going to the renowned "Richtofen" *Jagdegeschwader* (fighter wing) JG-132 at Döberitz to be worked up to operational standards.

But first, JG-88 in Spain had to be equipped to overcome the Soviet biplane Polikarpov I-15 and monoplane I-16 fighters. This essentially enabled the Germans to "wring out" the new Bf-109 fighter under combat conditions and to develop suitable tactics from April 1937. Pilots converting from biplanes to the new monoplane fighter aircraft had to learn to use rudder to prevent port-wing stalling on takeoff and landing and to use the leading-edge slats in low- and high-speed turns. They soon thought they had the best fighter in the world with its two-speed supercharger on a 680-hp Jumo 210 engine for takeoff with fifty-five gallons of fuel. In mid-1937 the Bf-109-C3.2 appeared, with a variable pitch two-bladed U.S. Hamilton metal airscrew. It, too, was shipped to Spain and used for air superiority, escorts, ground strafing, and offensive sweeps.

Although the involvement of the Bf-109 in Spain was played down, the new fighter was widely displayed and admired at the 4th International Aviation meet at Zurich-Dübendorf in July 1937, where it took numerous honors; the

Reichspropagandaministerium (propaganda ministry) claimed this marvel of aviation design was already well into service. The new Bf-109C had a pair of wing-mounted 7.9-mm machine guns that became standard after successful tests. The B-109s sent to Spain in July 1938 also had radios. At the same time, a 20-mm cannon in each wing was tried, but took time to develop. Messerschmitt's success led him to become chairman and managing director of the BFW organization, and its name was changed to Messerschmitt AG with all Messerschmitt GmbH patents transferred to it. On 11 November 1937 a Messerschmitt Bf-109 with a special engine capable of short bursts of 1,650 hp captured the world speed record with 379.38 mph.

By March 1938 the Luftwaffe had twelve Me-109 *Jagd Gruppen* (fighter groups) and one more in Spain, and by 1 August 1938 this had increased to 643 first-line fighters, of which less than half were Me-109s. Production, however, was exceeding the ability of the Luftwaffe to absorb the new fighters. By 19 September factories had produced 583 Me-109s, of which 510 were serviceable. The Me-109D, with a three-bladed propeller, was an interim aircraft until the Daimler-Benz DB-601 engine could be installed in what would be the 109E series. However, the 601 had not yet attained sufficient reliability for single-engine installation, though it did have fuel injection with fuel capacity increased to 85 Imperial gallons. Armament was two 7.9-mm guns, with 500 rpg, and a 20-mm cannon on the engine, with 60 rounds. The Luftwaffe-Lehrdivision (international division) had been formed on 1 November 1938 specifically to develop operational tactics and techniques with Me-109s on strength.[61]

The Me-109E became operational in time for the September 1939 Polish Campaign; it had been delayed by the prolonged process of making the DB-601 engine reliable. On 1 September 1939, the Luftwaffe had 1,060 Me-109s in units versus only 171 a year earlier. But less than 200 Me-109s were included in the order of battle against Poland as the rest were faced to the west to deter any Anglo-French move. Few reserves of 109s were used on any lengthy campaign. When the attack on Poland began, the Luftwaffe had 1,056 Me-109s in the inventory, of which 946 were serviceable. During the period of 1–28 September 1939 the Luftwaffe lost 67 to combat, mostly in ground attacks, and another 67 with more than 10 percent damage. Of the 67 lost during 1–28 September, half were to antiaircraft guns.[62] By the end of 1939 the 109Es were being fitted with a 1,175-hp DB-601 engine and a crankcase-mounted 20-mm cannon firing through the propeller hub.

New manufacturing works run by Fieseler, Arado, Erison, and WNB made all but 147 of the 1,540 Me-109s produced in 1939. By January 1940 Me-109 production had peaked at 122 per month, but declined to 79 per month one year later. In the latter part of the Battle of France and again in the Battle of Britain, the numbers of the Luftwaffe single-engine fighter forces declined to dangerously low levels. At Dunkirk during 26 May–4 June 1940, for example, the Luftwaffe's Me-109 *Jagdflugzeuge* (fighter planes) were down to 30 percent serviceability, but they later entered the Battle of Britain during the summer and fall with 1,034, of which 805 (78 percent) were serviceable. But by October 1940 the Luftwaffe had only 957 Me-109s, of which 667 were serviceable, and replacements were hard to come by.[63]

During the Phoney War—3 September 1939 through 10 May 1940—the Me-109Bs were transferred to the *Jagdlfliegerschuler* (fighter operational training units [OTU]) and the 109Ds to night-fighter units. In early May of 1940 two of the Luftwaffe's latest Me-109s landed by mistake in France. They were sent at once to the RAF's Aircraft and Armament Experimental Establishment at Boscombe Down, and then on 14 May to the Royal Aircraft Establishment (RAE) Farnborough, which confirmed that the British Hurricane fighter was inferior, except in turning, and that the Me-109 was superior to the British Spitfire below 20,000 feet, from which it could escape by diving. On 10 May 1940, ten Me-109 *Gruppen* had easily seized air superiority; however, in early July only one Me-109 *Gruppe* faced Britain. All the others were resting and reequipping. A strengthened cockpit canopy and armor were being added, and the engine-mounted cannon was replaced by one in each wing, along with an auxiliary 66-Imperial gallon fuel tank that could be jettisoned—but it was never used.

The Me-110 in 1940

According to Chris McNab, the Luftwaffe had 247 Me-110s allocated to Luftflottes 2, 3, and 5 on 10 May 1940.

Counting shot-down and crashed 100 percent write-offs, it suffered 115 in Norway and the west from 10 May to 24 June 1940. From 3 July to 6 September, in the Battle of Britain, it suffered 269 losses, and from 7 September to 31 December a further 157 written off, plus another 75 with less than 100 percent damage. In other words, the total Me-110 cost for the April to December 1940 campaign was 541 machines, plus another 75 possibly repairables, for a grand total of 616, or a wastage rate of 60 aircraft per month for nine months (Map 1, Air Aspects of the April 1940 Invasion of Norway; Map 2, The Dunkirk Operation, May–June 1940).

A remarkable number of the twin-engine heavy fighters of that era could feather a dead engine's propeller, and if piloted by those sufficiently skilled to attempt to get back across the Channel on one engine, might either crash in

MAP 1. Air Aspects of the April 1940 Invasion of Norway

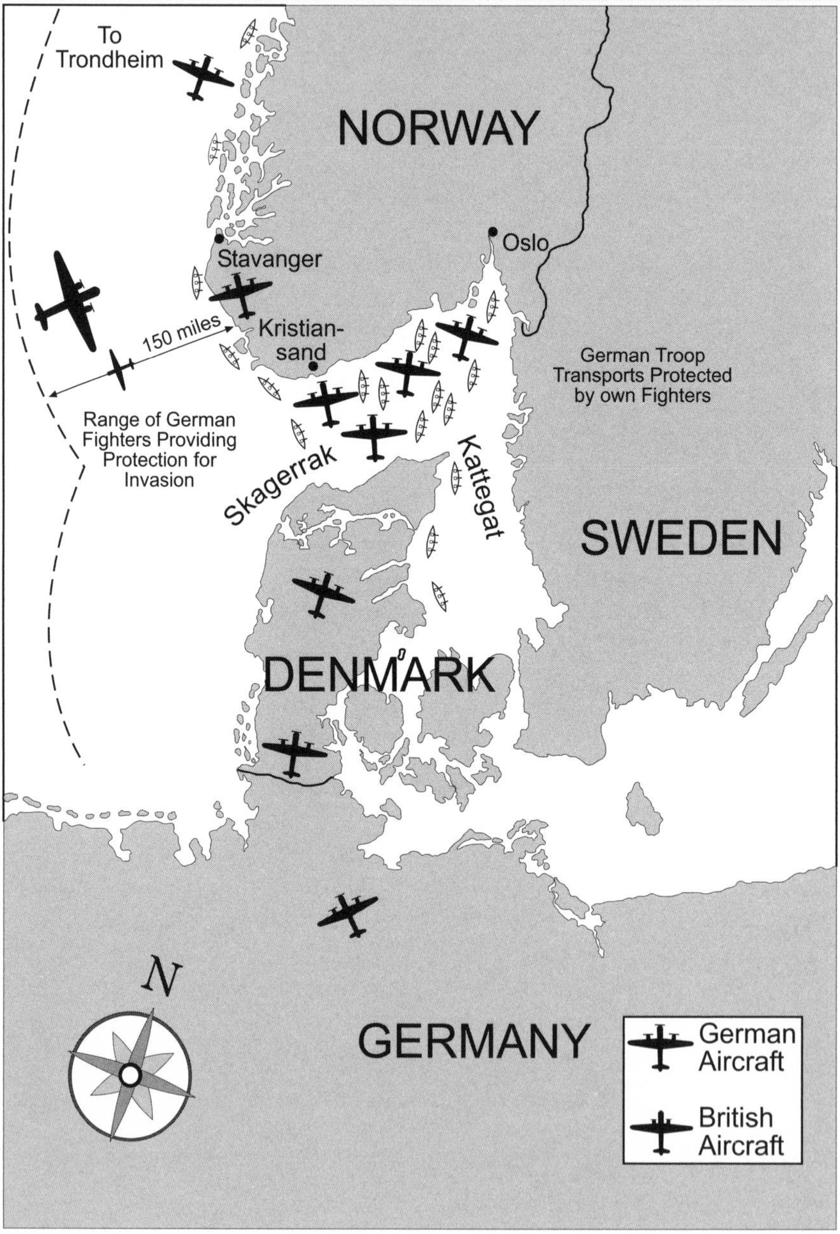

To Trondheim

NORWAY

Stavanger

Oslo

150 miles

Kristian-
sand

German Troop
Transports Protected
by own Fighters

Range of German
Fighters Providing
Protection for
Invasion

Skagerrak

Kattegat

SWEDEN

DENMARK

N

GERMANY

German
Aircraft

British
Aircraft

From Alexander P. de Seversky, *Victory Through Air Power* (New York: Simon & Schuster, 1942).

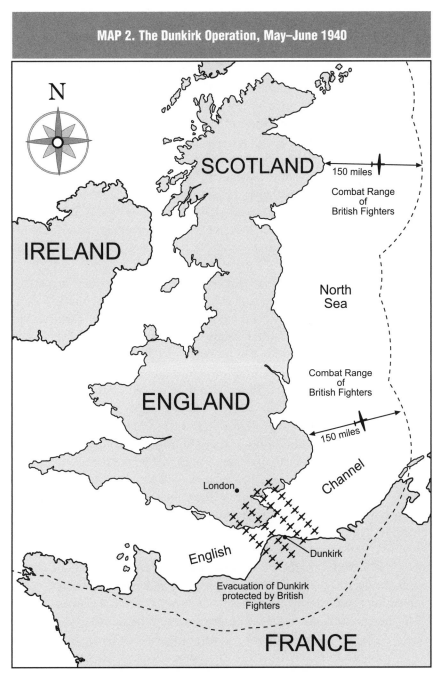

MAP 2. The Dunkirk Operation, May–June 1940

N

IRELAND

SCOTLAND

150 miles

Combat Range
of
British Fighters

North
Sea

Combat Range
of
British Fighters

ENGLAND

150 miles

London

Channel

English

Dunkirk

Evacuation of Dunkirk
protected by British
Fighters

FRANCE

From Alexander P. de Seversky, *Victory Through Air Power* (New York: Simon & Schuster, 1942).

France or be written off as unrepairable (though it is noticeable that after 1 July 1940 more sophisticated damage assessments were being made).

While in July 1940 only seven aircraft were in the 90 percent or less range—"written-off with varying degrees of cannibalization" (Table 20)—and where injuries were not recorded, this rose to fifty-seven aircraft in August to 6 September, with twenty-three more not recorded, and in the final four months of 1940 fifty-five, plus twenty unrecorded. By these last few months the repair and salvage system was beginning to function. For the Me-110, we have the careful tallies of Vajda and Dancey, as well as Cornwell, for the months of combat from 10 May to the end of December 1940.[64]

The Me-110 was intended as a long-range escort fighter and was blessed with a top speed of 340 mph, according to William Green's *The Warplanes of the Third Reich,* faster than the MS-406, and with a heavy armament of 2x20-mm cannon and four machine guns, as well as sometimes also a single 30-mm cannon.

In the opening phase of the campaign in the west, including Norway and the intrusions into Swiss airspace, the Me-110 force lost 35 shot down, 34 damaged in combat, 7 lost in fatal collisions in the air, and 6 otherwise damaged on landing, 7 to antiaircraft, and 18 missing. Of these 107, 80 were ruled 100 percent write-offs, one 90 percent, and for remaining no damage assessment was recorded by the clerk. The 100 percent figure certainly illustrates the Luftwaffe philosophy of not bothering with repairs during the campaign.

According to LQMG tallies, the Me-110 units received 241 new machines in the first four months of 1940, 96 in May, 126 in June, 112 in July, 93 in August, 203 in September, 137 in October, and 160 in November and December, for a total of 1,168 in 1940. On a twelve-month basis, that averaged 97.3 each month; but for the five months from May to September inclusive, a total of 630, or 126 monthly, the yearly average monthly wastage doubled.[65]

July was a moderate operational month, whereas the other four were intensive. By the scales laid down in *SD 98* (1936), the Luftwaffe should have lost 63 Me-110s from all causes.[66] *Geschwader* of Me-110s contained 34 to 37 aircraft, so according to the 1934 tables of RAF Air Staff Memorandum No. 50, against heaviest opposition the Me-110 units could expect to lose 100 percent of their initial establishment per month, or 68 to 74 aircraft. However, in all of 1940, the Luftwaffe averaged 97.25 monthly, and from May to September the rate was 126, or double the British Air Staff's calculation (Table 17).

Over the west the German Me-110s did not face serious opposition in the air. However, Dunkirk presaged the need for the escort fighters themselves to have to be escorted. Of the 248 serviceable Me-110s available on 10 May, 275 were lost or damaged, or 111 percent, were casualties.

On the other hand, there is an adverse trend of engine failures, which would indicate mechanics getting tired, being less skilled, or being less well supervised, in addition to wear and tear on machines.

Considering that these air fleets started with 247 Me-110s, the loss of 616 from all causes required the LQMG to supply 60 new machines on average for each of the latter nine months of 1940, according to the LQMG records supplied by *Abteilung* VI to the British Air Ministry in 1945 (CAB 106/282), which would have included the needs of the training establishments.

While the Me-110 proved vulnerable to the eight-gun fighters, it proved off Norway to be very effective against RAF Handley Page Hampdens. The latter had only one pilot, with two rear gunners, but their field of fire was limited to the 30-degree cone that the British air staff calculated would be the limit for fighters attacking from astern. Thus they could not shoot at an enemy abeam. The Me-110s, therefore, drew up alongside and shot the Hampden's pilot while they themselves remained immune.

Other GAF Aircraft

As for other Luftwaffe types, few Junkers Ju-87 Stukas were issued,[67] which seems surprising, except that the Ju-87 dive-bomber was a very rugged, fixed-undercarriage aircraft only vulnerable in the air to attacks from the rear or to antiaircraft fire. The aircraft had originated in Sweden in 1928, but was not developed in Germany until 1933. A two-seat all-metal monoplane first flew in the spring of 1935, and initial production machines left the works in early 1937. Some 952 had been produced and proved in Spain, and they were in Luftwaffe units by 1940. As small as a fighter, and with a pilot-gunner team free to take evasive action, it was hard to shoot down. Ironically the Stuka was to be phased out of production in late 1939, but its success in Poland received Goering's approval for 611 to be delivered in 1940.[68]

The Henschel Hs-123, designed in 1933 to meet a dive-bomber requirement, had first appeared in May 1935, but three of the four prototypes had shed their wings in dives. Loaded, the aircraft weighed 4,884 pounds. Its maximum speed was 212 mph, its ceiling 29,000 feet, and its range 534 miles. The Hs-123 had entered service in late 1936 as a close-support aircraft with the Ju-87 following in the spring of 1937, so that by the end of 1938 the Hs-123 was largely out of service, except for one *Gruppe* used in the invasion of Poland and then against France (and later also in the Balkans in 1941). But all tools and jigs for the Hs-123 were scrapped in 1940.

The Hs-126 was then a rapid redesign of the Hs-123 to incorporate a more powerful engine so that the fourth model, a production Hs-123, emerged as the Hs-126 powered in 1937 by a new 830-hp radial engine. This 200-mph observation machine had a capacious fuselage, a sliding cockpit canopy, and docile handling characteristics with a great short-field performance. It was a highly maneuverable two-seat reconnaissance biplane of all-metal stressed skin. The moncoque construction made the aircraft strong. Design had begun in 1936 and the aircraft flew before the end of the year, with production and deliveries beginning in 1938. The machine was well received by the Luftwaffe, both in Germany and in Spain. It had both short-field and high-altitude performance. The pilot and observer-gunner were seated close together, and in the gunnery mode deflector plates relieved the gunner of slipstream pressures. The pilot had a single, fixed, forward-firing 7.92 machine gun with 500 rounds; the gunner had a flexible 7.92 with thirteen drums totaling 975 rounds. A few Hs-126s were lost photographing the Maginot Line in 1939, but in 1940 casualties began to rise. Some 257 Hs-126 were in GAF service on 3 September 1939, and by 11 May 1940 the Luftwaffe had 277, with 234 serviceable. However, the type was being phased out of production.

The most numerous German bomber of the period was the Heinkel He-111, designed in 1934 as both a transport and a bomber. With a stressed all-metal skin, it was ordered into production in early 1936 and soon was built at the model factory estate at Marierche in Berlin. It was operational in 1937 in Spain, where it was faster than Republican fighters. At 30,000 pounds, the He-111 could do more than 200 mph over 1,121 miles. The Luftwaffe had 349 He-111P on the outbreak of war in 1939, of which 295 (84.5 percent) were serviceable; 400 He-111H, of which 358 (89.5 percent) were serviceable; 38 He-111E, of which 32 (84 percent) were serviceable; and 21 He-111J, of which 20 (95 percent) were serviceable[69] (Table 28). At that time, almost half of the 808 He-111s on strength were the He-111H model whose defensive armament of three 7.9-mm machine guns was woefully inadequate. After the invasion of Poland, where some 789 He-111s had been sent, three more machine guns were added as well as a tail gun.[70] Most of the 78 twin-engine bombers lost to fighters and flak over Poland were He-111s—a higher number than anticipated. Of the 1,120 twin-engine bombers serving in Luftflotte 2 and 3, about half were He-111s.

The German Air Force also had the Dornier Do-17 light bomber, often called the "Flying Pencil." Prototypes had flown in 1934, and though it had

TABLE 28. Heinkel 111 on 3 September 1939

TYPE	NUMBER	SERVICEABLE	PERCENTAGE
He-111P	349	295	84.5
He-111H	400	358	89.5
He-111E	38	32	84.2
He-111J	21	20	95.2

Source: William Green, *The Warplanes of the Third Reich* (New York: Doubleday, 1970), 295.

been known since 1935, it was actually only revealed when it won the Circuit of the Alps at Zurich in 1937, outpacing all extant fighters. This prototype was 56 mph faster than the bomber version then being delivered to Luftwaffe units. The original design was for a fast six-passenger commercial aircraft, however Lufthansa refused it. By chance it was referred to the RLM as a bomber, and it became the Do-17. Fitted with two water-cooled Hispano-Suiza 12Ybrs (improved) engines of 775 hp each, it attained 245 mph. Serial production began in 1936 with a bomber and a long-range photo-reconnaissance model. This was the first German warplane produced in subassemblies, the final going to the Luftwaffe in early 1937. The Do-17M could carry 2,200 pounds of bombs over 311 miles at 245 mph. On 3 September 1939 the GAF had 370/319 serviceable Do-17 bombers.[71]

Shortly thereafter one *Staffeln* of the Do-17 reconnaissance version was dispatched to Spain to gain combat experience where it quickly proved immune to enemy fighters, until the modern Soviet fighter craft appeared. One of the lessons gleaned from service in Spain was the need for better protection, and so the forward fuselage was redesigned to allow for a rearward-firing gun. Better crew accommodations were needed as well, all of which appeared in the Do-17Z of 1939. Yet by early 1940, Do-17 production was closed down as the He-111 and the Ju-88 were faster and carried a greater bomb loads. Some 520 Do-17s had been built. In the Polish Campaign of 1939 the Do-17 bomber units hit airfield and targets of opportunity; in the May–June 1940 Battle of France, they attacked Dunkirk; and in the 1940 summer and fall battle over Britain, they hit fighter command airfields. The Do-17's defensive armament, noted William Green, was "lamentably weak, but it could do 320 mph in a shallow dive."[72]

Also in the Luftwaffe inventory was the Junkers Ju-52, a 1929 civil transport design that the Germans also used as a medium bomber—a rugged corrugated-metal aircraft with three American radial engines. (The Swiss Air Force

Museum at Dübendorff still flies some of these aircraft.) Ju-52s of the GAF operated throughout World War II and on into peacetime, with a maximum loaded
weight of 22,000 pounds.[73] In the May 1940 attack on the Netherlands nearly 40
percent of the 452 Ju-52s were lost; 160 had crashed, of which 53 were repairable
and 47 were cannibalized for spares. By the end of June, 242 transports, almost
all Ju-52s, had been destroyed, but were replaced by 401 new machines.

The widely adaptable Junkers Ju-88 medium bomber was newly designed
during the mid-1930s and saw Luftwaffe service as a dive-bomber, night
fighter, torpedo bomber, and reconnaissance craft. The Luftwaffe had 110 on
charge at the end of 1939 and 2,124 a year later. The Ju-88 was used extensively
over France and Britain during 1940.

The Luftwaffe in Retrospect

Compared with the Armée de l'Air, the Luftwaffe by 1940 was a twice battle-
tested organization, having been blooded in Spain and Poland. Moreover it had
taken to heart the lessons learned and observed. Machines and their equipment
had been refined and strategy and tactics honed. In the Polish campaign of
1–28 September 1939 the Luftwaffe had lost 67 single-engine fighters, 12 twin-
engine fighters, 78 bombers, 31 dive-bombers, 63 reconnaissance machines, 12
transports, and 22 miscellaneous aircraft for a total of 285, plus 279 not quickly
repairable, for a grand total of 564, or 20 per day. Intensive operations in rough
conditions exhausted units.[74]

Horst Boog has stated that he knows of no German tallies of the total
number of sorties. But in *Das Deutsche reich und die Zweite Weltkrieg 2* he
gave the figures for bomber sorties against Britain in August, September, and
October 1940.[75] Research in Francis K. Mason, *Battle over Britain*[76] sometimes
gives the number of escorts, and by taking three of those days the average was
2.2 times the number of bombers sortied. (See also Tables 29–31.) Hence the
figures show Luftwaffe sorties (the October figures should be less due to the
switch to the night blitz):

Date	Bomber	Escorts	Total Sorties
August 1940	4,779	10,514	15,293
September 1940	7,260	15,972	23,232
October 1940	9,911	21,804	31,715
	21,950	48,290	70,240

By May 1940 the Luftwaffe was an instrument of policy, an accepted means to an end, guided by a grand strategy under a dictator who knew where Germany had to go in order to return to Great Power status. The French did not realize they had lost that Great Power status, but the British retained their supreme insular confidence.

TABLE 29. Battle of Britain, RAF and GAF Sorties and Losses, 1940

DATE	RAF SORTIES	RAF AIRCRAFT LOSSES	GAF SORTIES*	GAF AIRCRAFT LOSSES
10 July–12 August	18,016	150	15,293	286
13–23 August	6,414	114	23,232	290
23 August–6 September	10,673	286	31,715	380
Total	**35,103**	**550**	**70,240**	**956**

Source: T. C. G. James, *The Battle of Britain,* edited with introduction by Sebastian Cox, vol. 2 in the *Air Defence of Great Britain* series, Royal Air Force Official Histories (London: Frank Cass, 2000), 35,103; Basil Collier, *The Defence of the United Kingdom* (London: HMSO, 1957), 450–451, 456–460.

*The total is from Collier, but the three figures for the months were computed from Horst Boog, who provided bomber sorties; from Anthony T. Wood and Bill Gunston, *Hitler's Luftwaffe: A Pictorial and Technical Encyclopedia of Hitler's Air Power in World War II* (London: Salamander, 1977), 22 and 25; and from David Baker, *Adolph Galland* (London: Windrow and Greene, 1996), 109 and 112. It seems that the escort fighters were 2.2 times the number of bombers by months.

TABLE 30. Luftwaffe Write-Offs for All Causes in the Comparable Forty-Six Days of the Battle of France and of Britain, 12 August–25 September 1940

TYPE	AUGUST 1940	SEPTEMBER 1940	TOTAL
Me-110	124	75	199
Me-109	190	202	392
Ju-88	114	116	230
Do-17	192	68	260
He-111	102	156	258
Ju-87	59	9	68
Total write-offs	**781**	**626**	**1,407**
Repairables	**82**	**23**	**105 (7.5%)**

Source: After the Battle, *The Battle of Britain, II,* 259 (London: Battle of Britain Printing International, 1982), 556 ff; and United Kingdom, Air Ministry, CAB 106/282, 151, 157 (Table 29).

Note: LQMG replacements of Me-109s during May–July 1940 were 826; during August–October, 798.

TABLE 31. *Luftwaffe* Daily Losses, May/June 1940

DATE	NO. LOST	DATE	NO. LOST
10 May	4	1 June	
11May	14	2 June	
12May	8	3 June	26
13May	3	4 June	12
14 May	6	5 June	4
15 May	106	6 June	12
16 May	61	7 June	13
17 May	3	8 June	3?
18 May	25	9 June	10
19 May	6	10 June	5
20 May	10	11 June	12
21 May	14	12 June	5
22 May	1	13 June	9
23 May	2	14 June	10
24 May	8	15 June	4
25 May	54	16 June	3
26 May	4	17 June	8 (+2)
27 May	47	18 June	45
28 May	20	19 June	2 (+2)
29 May	12	20 June	2
30 May	28	21 June	"6"
31 May	2		
	457ˑ		**All totaled, 656 + 4**ˑ
			660 – 196
			464

Source: Ulf Balke, *Zusammergestelt nach Unterlogen aus RL Z III/707/Einsatz-bereitschaft der fliegenden Verbande,* an archival file provided by Horst Boog, Germany; *Der Luftkrieg in Europa: Die Operativen Einsatze des Kampfgeschwaders 2 im Zweiten Weltkrieg* (Koblenz, Ger.: Bernard & Graefe, 1989); and *Kampfgeschwader 100 Wiking: Eine Geschichte aus Kriegstagebuchern,Dokumenten und Berichten 1934-1945* (Stuttgart, Ger.: Motorbuch Verlag, 1981). See also, United Kingdom, National Archives, CAB 106/282.

ˑ Note the original errors in GAF recordkeeping and addition, as in column 1   (which should total 438 rather than 457), and an overestimation of losses.

CHAPTER 3

THE ROYAL AIR FORCE

The story of the Royal Air Force between the wars, 1918–1939, is quite different from that of the Armée de l'Air.[1] Before the end of World War I, the RAF had indoctrinated itself with the belief that the airplane was always an offensive weapon. The bombing of London from 1915, culminating in the daylight raids of mid-1917 by German Gotha biplanes, propelled the British government to create the Air Ministry as of 1 January 1918, followed by the amalgamation of the Naval and Military Air Services (the latter the Royal Flying Corps) into the Royal Air Force on 1 April. This new third service was guided from 1919 to 1930 by Air Chief Marshal (ACM) Sir Hugh Trenchard with Sir Samuel Hoare as Secretary of State for Air during much of that time.

In the interwar years British policy was limited liability and that governed strategy, a process rather than an event. The problem was that the Air Staff failed to adapt reflexively to changing policy and so lacked intellectual agility. The year 1940 provided relevant lessons, according to G/Capt. Alistair Byford, still applicable today regarding strategy making. Policy is executive direction in the national interest and which strategy is then designed to achieve.[2]

The Royal Air Force of Great Britain, still considered that of a Great Power, was in 1940 just hitting its stride in rearmament, with new modern fighters being grafted onto a refined, radar-equipped air-defense system. Moreover after the change of government of 10 May 1940, the country was led by a determined, decisive prime minister and Fighter Command by an equally confident air chief marshal. Neither the leaders in France nor Germany had this unhampered singleness of purpose to their advantage.

Air Chief Marshal Sir Hugh Dowding had in Fighter Command 960 single-engine well-tested modern fighters and 1,400 trained aircrew backed by a sustaining organization that included civilian ferry pilots—though the offensive-minded Air Staff still favored Bomber Command.

The Royal Air Force College was established at Cranwell in 1920 and the RAF Staff College at Andover in 1922, to develop a uniquely air-service concept of the RAF's role. This was to be distilled wisdom designed to shape the development and the intellectual envelope, to guide the officers in forming policy and means. By 1922 the disparate ideas and elements had evolved into the first Royal Air Force doctrinal manual, *CD 22, RAF Operations Manual.* For better or for worse, the RAF was separate from its ancestors in the defense community, the Royal Navy and the Army.[3]

Within the Air Ministry was the Air Staff (an ill-defined body), and gradually junior members were added to it from the Staff College at Andover. Many in the Air Ministry had been handpicked in 1919 by Trenchard and they tended to adhere to his beliefs, especially after 1923 accepting that the key weapon was the bomber offensive. The Air Staff also had an insular vision, which caused it to judge what other nations could do using RAF methods as a premise. Officers in the Air Staff served from time to time in the Empire, but were not posted to foreign countries. Nor did they work more than half a day until after 1934.[4]

The Air Staff was better organized and more independent than the General Staff Air Force of the Armée de l'Air in Paris, but not nearly of the organization nor quality of that of the Luftwaffe in Berlin. The RAF eschewed the thorough examination of World War I that the Germans undertook, arguing that the 1914–1918 experience was too short to provide useful lessons. This led to at first the failure to create a systematic approach to airpower. The Staff College provided a conformity of thought, but not of high quality. *CD 22* was issued to all officers of the rank of flight instructor and above and was patterned after the Army's *Field Service Regulations,* with Chapter VII on war at sea based upon the Royal Navy's limited-circulation confidential air orders. Only those of the original eleven chapters were new and focused upon air force operational concerns. These did sense the need to obtain air superiority, concluding that then concentrated raids could attack other targets, including cities and populations.

Home defense was not seen as a priority, despite the bombing suffered in 1917. The relationship of the RAF to the surface forces was discussed with those services, but of course not settled. *CD 22* saw the RAF as winning the counter-air battle against the enemy, acting in concert with the surface forces and then carrying out other actions such as army cooperation. The first course at Andover proceeded to rewrite the 1922 *Operations Manual,* but the replacement, *AP 1300,* was not published until 1928. However, as Neville Parton notes in "The Development of Early RAF Doctrine,"[5] the RAF did not concentrate solely on the grand-strategic bombing role, but rather on the Imperial function of air control in harmony with the army.

One legacy of the Great War was British refusal of another Continental Commitment. Linked to that was Disarmament, which finally collapsed at the Geneva Conference in 1934 in part over the issue of an intercontinental air force.[6] Prime Minister Neville Chamberlain's policy of appeasement tied into these two thoughts of peace and disarmament and saw the RAF's deterrent bomber strike force as the cheaper policy. Fortunately in 1936 the new Minister for the Coordination of Defence, Sir Thomas Inskip, switched the emphasis to Home Defence fighters. From 1936 to 1938 Air Staff plans undertook a reevaluation of the deterrent. This resulted, at the time of the Munich Conference of September 1938, in the conclusion that the RAF was impotent against Germany, a judgment reinforced by the Air Officer Commanding-in-Chief (AOC-in-C) of Bomber Command, Sir Edgar Ludlow-Hewitt, who said his forces could not reach German targets beyond the Ruhr nor find and strike Luftwaffe airfields. Moreover, until the end of Disarmament, British bombers had been limited to 6,800 pounds all-up weight. As soon as that restriction was lifted, the Vickers Wellington twin-engine, long-range medium bomber design shot up to 32,000 pounds, while the 1936 follow-on heavy bombers rolled down the runways in 1941 at 68,000 pounds with the range to reach Berlin.[7]

Developments in Britain were aided by the fact that Parliament had no specialist committees outside of those overseeing the accounts, so that the Air Ministry was able to make design and procurement decisions, which were approved by the Cabinet after being vetted by the Committee of Imperial Defence. Moreover the CID was supervised by the same Secretary (Sir Maurice Hankey) from 1912 to 1938 and from 1923 to 1940 there were only five different prime ministers, thus allowing consistency in policy and stable financing.

John Ferris' detailed study of RAF doctrinal development between the wars shows that during 1921–1934 while then–Chief of the Air Staff (CAS) Trenchard and his successors argued that the bomber would always get through, he was opposed by the former Air Officer Commanding (AOC) Home Defences T. C. R. Higgins and the AOC India, J. A. Chamier, who believed that developments in fighters and early-warning systems would force aerial combat, meaning that the fight for air superiority as during 1915–1918 would be renewed.[8] This view challenged the central theme of RAF thought. ACM Geoffrey Salmond as CAS in 1933 supported and Higgins advanced the idea of development of long-range escort fighters to gain air superiority. The RAF much earlier, in 1918, when fighters and ack-ack had stopped the unescorted raiding German bombers, who suffered 21 percent losses—the last of the battles showing that the defense could indeed master the offense. Some escorting by the RAF had been carried out over the Western Front during 1917–1918 but it was rare, as most penetration raids were made by either single machines, even over the German side, or by self-escorting DeHavilland DH-4 two-seat biplane bombers. One reason the RAF still kept to the disastrous Fighting Area attack formations (essentially close, tight formations) into 1940 was that since it was not interested in and never fully explored the idea of escort fighters, it had not worked out the problems that the presence of such enemy machines would pose. British fighter tactics in early 1940 were still those of 1917, as promulgated in the General Staff of the War Office's *Fighting in the Air, April 1918*.[9] The Air Staff remained hostile or blind to the need for escort fighters at least into 1940 when on 20 May the Air Staff expressed the opinion that escorts were useless if they did not down a single enemy, in spite of the fact that escorted bombers suffered no losses.[10] The Air Staff was still wedded to the unrealistic Trenchardian offensive-mindedness of 1917. Too often it seems the RAF assumed no enemy defensive air opposition, as in colonial operations or in the scheme to establish itself in the Low Countries to bomb Germany. One wonders why.[11] It was as a result of the fear of a French "air-menace," and Trenchard's determination, in 1923 that the RAF had been given the task of the Air Defence of Great Britain (ADGB). The new Home Defence Air Force (HDAF) was to be two-thirds an offensive deterrent bomber force and one-third defensive interceptors.

By 1934 the RAF's strategic Home air defense had the correct principles and was about to get the needed equipment—fighters and radar. Fighters were flown by regulars and according to Ferris, Fighting Area Headquarters in the Air Defence of Great Britain Command was the most professional in the world. The Hawker Fury I of 1931 could reach an altitude of 20,000 feet 7.5 miles from its airfield, and fighter squadrons were off the ground eighty seconds after the warning was given, though in 1935 exercises this more realistically was three to five minutes.[12]

Though the RAF budget was cut back year after year under the 1919 Cabinet rule—the Ten-Year Rule—that there would be no need to prepare for war for ten years, Chief of the Air Staff Trenchard steadily built a cadre Air Force. His memorandum of 25 November 1919, *Command Paper 467* (*Cmd 467*), laid down the structure of the RAF and the importance of training.[13] While the structure and training of the RAF were being upgraded, consideration of the British aircraft and aeroengine industries also became necessary. In 1918 they had reached a very strong industrial position but postwar economics and policies had cut them back severely. Trenchard's policy, however, was to keep sixteen airframe and four engine firms operating—the Ring—and to give them prototype and development contracts. At the same time, the Air Staff worked on specifications.[14]

Organization and Preparation

The Royal Air Force College for cadet officers at Cranwell, and a school for fitters and riggers at Halton, produced gentlemen pilots and educated mechanics, respectively. Cranwell was originally, from 1916, a Royal Navy station. By 1936, various reserve and short-service commission schemes culminated in the Royal Air Force Volunteer Reserve (RAFVR) to man the aircraft being bought under the Expansion Schemes launched in 1934. The Japanese threat in the Far East had caused the cancellation of the Ten-Year Rule, and the French threat and then that of the Germans, together with the failure of the League of Nations, led to a succession of "alphabetical" programs, such as the first, Expansion Scheme A, to increase the size of the RAF from 31,000 officers and men. The organization steadily grew into the 1940 average of 292,688 officers and men and a front-line establishment of 2,400 aircraft, with 2,000 pilots and 20,000 other aircrew being added annually. In addition, the number in reserve totaled 4,000 pilots and 9,250 aircrew, with the RAF authorized to accept up to 12,000 aircraft by 1940—a number the Air Ministry could not handle until facilities, including airfields, were built.[15]

In the meantime, the World War I educational system was in 1936 revived as the Empire Air Training Scheme, and at the same time Reserve Command came into being with seventy-five stations and 3,189 aircraft of fifty-nine types. In May 1940, Technical Training Command became a separate organization with 100 units to produce ground crew while the new Flying Training Command turned out aircrew. All of this expansion created a need for medical supervision and care of service members, but this was hampered by a variety of administrative difficulties. When war came, the pace of the RAF expansion by the end of September 1939 as compared with peacetime had increased to the point of human fatigue in the administrative HQ operations blocks and on the airfields.[16]

Unlike the Armée de la Air, the RAF had realized in May 1937 that it would also have to enlarge its ground crew training to meet the needs of Expansion. It thus was arranged to send ten to twenty airmen at a time to aircraft constructors' works. In addition, for the overall RAF service, an attempt was made to get 1,000 recruits each week after the Munich Conference of September 1938. Then in early 1939, in anticipation of World War II, the Military Training Act brought the RAF 25,000 to 26,000 men versus the army's 12,000, though it soon was realized that 900 recruits weekly would be needed until the end of the year. The 3 September 1939 declaration of war brought in an additional 17,000.[17]

In France the Armée de l'Air's selected opponent was the army, but across the Channel in Britain it was the Admiralty. Immediately post-1918 and for nearly a decade more the First Sea Lord in the person of Admiral of the Fleet Earl Beatty tried to reacquire the Royal Naval Air Service. The quarrel between the RAF and the Royal Navy on several occasions required the intervention of the prime minister. It resulted in the Salisbury Committee's 1923 recommendation of the Home Defence Air Force, a further reinforcement of the RAF's singular position, and the postponing of the creation of a truly naval air wing (the Fleet Air Arm) from 1924 to 1937.

Apart from taking over colonial policing in Iraq and along the Northwest Frontier, with strictly limited budgets, the RAF was molded into an élite force of air and ground crew, a cadre for future expansion and war. It made a name for itself at annual air shows, in exploration flights, and during 1927–1931 in winning the prized high-speed Schneider Trophy for Britain. Very slowly permanent RAF stations were built, but the real push only came after the start of the 1934 Expansion and a plentiful supply of funding. Instead of spending its energies on interservice quarrels, the Air Staff did some planning, but not so much as to relate ends to means until involved in the Technological Revolution.

With the Expansion Schemes came the need to restructure RAF administrative and operational tasks along functional lines. The umbrella Air Defence of Great Britain Command in mid-1936 was split into Bomber, Fighter, Coastal, and Training commands, but the RAF then lacked an overall commander in chief, as had existed under the ADGB, for the chief of the Air Staff was only the secretary of state for Air's adviser. At the same time the rapid ordering of new types such as the Hurricane and the Spitfire, and the need to disperse the aircraft industry in consideration of the threat of bombing, led to the "shadow factories," the many other manufacturing firms, especially the motorcar companies, that were involved in some form of aircraft production.

Yet the inexperience of RAF pilots and crew showed in Fighter Command's peacetime losses: 46 percent of the killed and 34.7 percent of the wounded occurred in accidents.[18] The RAF had noticed after 1937 that accidents in training had risen from the early 1930s rate of 500 machines (beyond unit repair capacity, including 200 write-offs) to 800 during the fall of 1939. In early 1939 with 1,780 operational and 1,400 reserve aircraft, the training organization had 3,180. By April 1940 the front-line strength had risen to 1,880 with 5,800 in various training establishments, of which 1,250 were modern operational types.[19] According to E. R. Hooten in *Phoenix Triumphant: The Rise and Rise of the Luftwaffe*, the British saw their accident rate grow steadily with 17,592 hours flown per crash in 1935 to only 7,552 in 1938. The equivalent French rate was 14,646 in 1935 and 5,591 in 1937, the last year available. Hooten also notes that while the British hours flown represents the Expansion of the RAF, up from 390,500 hours in 1934 to 1,057,400 in 1938, the Armée de l'Air only increased from 12,312 in 1934 to 17,672 in 1938, a clear indication of a lack of Expansion and training.[20]

All of this also led to the formation of RAF Maintenance Command in July 1938 with the Master Supply Scheme creating by May 1940 five universal supply depots, accompanied by a demand and transport plan. Distances were short in southern England between aircraft factories and aircraft storage units (ASUs) and the squadron, so pilots could be sent to collect new aircraft without the danger that, like French pilots, they would make a side trip to other temptations. (Paris, so near to French aircraft manufacturing, was a hazard of French resupply.) To move the British aircraft, on 12 September 1939 ferry pools were established with male and female pilots to deliver them to ASUs. A month's stock was held at an ASU in readiness to provide combat-ready replacements to squadrons. Early in World War II, aircraft were delivered to ASUs with "slave" engines, which then were returned to the manufacturers for another ferry flight. As new engines became available, the ASUs installed them. There were delays in the system, but on the whole it met war needs. Crashed machines were either transported to Civilian Repair Organizations (CRO) or to factories, or treated as "Christmas trees," stripped of all usable items which then went to ASUs via equipment depots and the remains as scrap to be smelted.

By September 1939, No. 41 Group planned to store 9,000 aircraft in twenty-four facilities; it had nine facilities available to receive 739 aircraft and issued 694. War wastage was estimated at 620 per month, but up to May 1940 the issues were for newly reequipped units and not for battle wastage. HQ Maintenance Command estimated in March 1940 that ASUs would have to issue monthly 800 aircraft for sustained operations, 1,120 for intensive actions, and lastly 1,480 during a maximum effort, which would deplete the reserves in two months.[21] But reality at that time was that in March the ASUs issued 408 machines of forty-eight different types. This rose in April to 777 out of 1,001 new aircraft received. At the same time, the perceived shortage of aircraft equipment led to authorization to order twelve months ahead. The pace of Expansion and war saw squadrons no longer self-supporting, much of their repair work being taken on by advanced teams and the write-offs being returned to the factories. A consistent theme in the first years of World War II was a shortage of tools and the unfamiliarity of reservists with the newer types of aircraft.

Lessons Applied—Resource Management

In the early 1930s the experiences of 1914–1918 were put together as *Air Staff Memorandum No. 50,* classified in 1928 as a secret document (*SD*), on wastage and consumption in war. It contained instructions and assumptions upon which staff could base the requirements for operations. In true service fashion, as new aircraft and equipment came to squadrons the publication was modified by pages being removed and new ones substituted. *SD 98* of 1936 enabled air officers commanding (AOC) and their staffs to calculate the number of aircraft and amounts of fuel and ammunition they would need, as well as the likely casualty rates, and thus the reserve and replacement requirements. It was an excellent planning document. Yet the one area in which *SD 98* underestimated was in "Maximum Effort." It assumed that this intense stage would only last fourteen days, whereas in the Battle of France it lasted forty-six and in the Battle of Britain fifty-six.

For the Battle of Britain Air Chief Marshal Dowding, AOC-in-C Fighter Command, utilized the figures in *SD 98* regarding wastage and consumption.[22] These told him that his fighter squadrons would fly 300 sorties in a twenty-eight-day month, or 10.7 sorties daily per squadron of twelve aircraft or less—less than one sortie per day per machine (0.9 sorties per aircraft), the same actual rate as that of the Armée de l'Air. *SD 98* figures showed that the wastage and consumption of 55 fighter squadrons would total 1,650 aircraft in six months, or 275 per month. In fact, in the three months from July to September 1940, 550 (183 monthly) were shot down, of which half (91.5) were repairable in two days—slightly above fighter production of ninety per month—or 549 repairable over a six-month period, and a six-month loss of some 1,100 machines. At the same time, the wastage of pilots over six months would be 1,074, or 179 per month.[23] The actual loss rate in battle and accidents was 482 killed and 429 wounded, 911 total.

According to Table 3 of *SD 98,* a twelve-aircraft IE (initial establishment) squadron needed seventeen aircraft in order to keep twelve on maximum operations continuously at 75 percent serviceability. The squadron required fifteen aircraft to maintain intensive operations and only nine for sustained operations. The necessary sortie rate seven days per week would have been 3.4 per day per aircraft at a maximum effort, 2.6 on intensive, and only 1.7 sorties daily per aircraft on sustained operations.

In the Battle of Britain the Luftwaffe faced an RAF Fighter Command trained and dedicated to air defense and not distracted by army cooperation. Unlike the Armée de l'Air in the Battle of France, the 75 percent serviceable 450 fighters of the RAF were warned by radar and guided by sector controllers. Fighter Command's aircraft were faster than the German bombers and the equal of the German Me-109E fighter.

If a twelve-plane sortie of RAF fighters all fired the whole of their ammunition, that would total 28,800 rounds. The squadron's ammunition supply of three million rounds thus would last 104 full squadron sorties or twenty days. In terms of mobility, a squadron needed 690 two-ton lorries to move the 150-pound boxes of unbelted rounds (at .5 pounds per round, 300 per box). Each two-ton lorry could carry twenty-nine to thirty boxes (twenty-four boxes at 150 pounds, not counting the weight of the box = 4,350 = 690 two-ton loads).[24]

During the winter of 1939 and the spring of 1940 British Air Forces France (BAFF) and the Air Ministry had argued as to the number of motor transports (MT) needed to move British squadrons and wings forward in accord with the French Dyle plan, whose purpose was to stop the advance of the German Wehrmacht in Belgium. Unfortunately, when retreat became vital, the units did not have what was needed. It was estimated that a single-engine fighter squadron, for example, needed 4 x 30 cwt (hundredweight) (1½ ton) trucks for petrol, a fire tender and another 11 x 30 cwt for equipment plus 14 x 3-tonners for stores, and 12 more of these and 2 motor coaches for personnel. In addition, the whole convoy of 44 vehicles needed another couple of 3-tonners of MT petrol, as well as three bulk-fuel carriers, 2 x 3-ton trucks for explosives, and as many as 20 additional 3-tonners.[25]

If the RAF's MT was inadequate in the Phoney War, from September 1939 to May 1940, it was completely so in the fluid situation that had developed even by 15 May 1940. Thus when No. 87 Squadron left Merville, France, it had to abandon everything but its serviceable aircraft and its personnel. The Air Ministry in this, as in other matters, was still slumbering in a 1918 fog. Although the British system worked pretty well to supply replacements to a much larger fighter force while keeping squadrons almost up to initial establishment throughout the following Battle of Britain, the force in France suffered heavily compared with that in Britain and came within two weeks of exhausting its reserves, perhaps due to an embryo salvage and repair system. Nevertheless the aircraft delivered to squadrons were ready to fly (Tables 32–34). In comparison, the German logistic stream similarly was sometimes chaotic and short-sighted. The Luftwaffe quartermaster general (LQMG) issued a total of 857 new airplanes in the period from 10 May to 24 June, but these covered not only those shot down, but also operational and nonoperational accidents and write-offs, as well as replacing unserviceable machines as both were unavailable due to the blitzkrieg.[26] (See Graphs 2 and 3.)

In the winter of 1939–1940 the RAF's Fairey Battle suffered breakage at Frames 23 and 41 (the latter the kingpost for the rudder) during hard landings on frozen ground, and Hurricanes lost tailwheels taxiing on such.[27] Losses in the air are unknown, but could have resulted from violent evasive maneuvers. Supermarine Spitfires lost their wings in the early days due to metal fatigue after a rapid rise in flying hours and combat strains.[28] And the early 1942 Hawker Typhoons shed their whole tail assemblies because of metal fatigue. Unfortunately the meticulous Germans did not keep the necessary records for us to know how their machines fared. The Fairey Battle was oversized and overweight with its 10,792-pound loads compared with the German Ju-87 Stuka, to the U.S. Navy's Douglas SBD dive-bomber and its contemporaries, or even to the British Boulton Paul Defiant interceptor fighter at 8,350 pounds.

The losses of Fighter Command in the Battle of Britain during July 1940 offer an example of sustained effort. Table 33 uses the numerical classification system that indicates the availability of British aircraft at ASUs on 13 July, 10 August, and 14 September 1940:

Category 1. Ready for immediate issue.

Category 2. Should be available within four days.

Category 3. Being prepared for issue.

Category 4. Aircraft on ground awaiting modifications or spares.

In the thirty-one days of July, the RAF endured seventy-three damaged (Category 3) machines, which either were repairable in a couple of days on the squadron, destroyed in combat or its aftermath, lost, or missing. The latter two events required fresh replacement aircraft for a total of almost 350 new Spitfires and Hurricanes.[29] As Table 34 shows, in August and September 1940 roughly 34 percent of Hurricane and Spitfire production was repairables. Table 33 shows that between 17 July and 14 September, the RAF maintenance unit categories would indicate 58 Hurricanes and 25 Spitfires in Category 2, and 297 Hurricanes and 76 Spitfires in Category 3. These classifications were different on squadrons, in those cases referring to what the squadron's fitters and riggers could do for serviceability (essentially patching bullet holes),[30] and in such instances were so reported to headquarters for the daily-state report (Table 32).

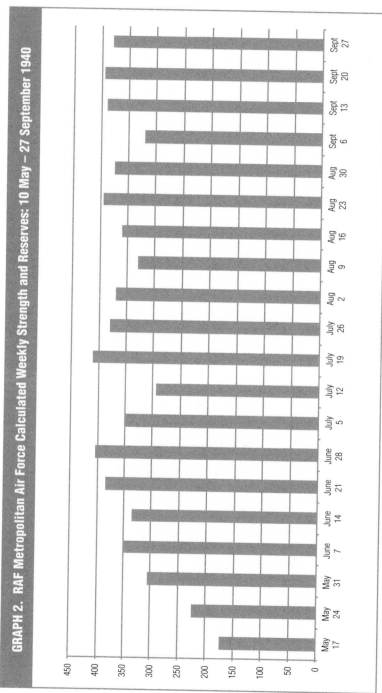

GRAPH 2. RAF Metropolitan Air Force Calculated Weekly Strength and Reserves: 10 May – 27 September 1940

Source: United Kingdom, National Archives, Air Historical Branch, AIR 2/5205.

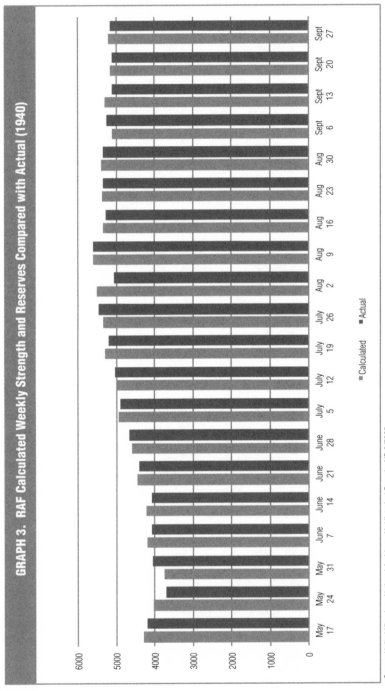

GRAPH 3. RAF Calculated Weekly Strength and Reserves Compared with Actual (1940)

■ Calculated   ■ Actual

Source: United Kingdom, National Archives, Air Historical Branch, AIR 2/5205.

TABLE 32. RAF Fighter Command Daily State Report Categories of Available Squadron Aircraft*

CATEGORY
A. Estimated IE (initial establishment) aircraft per squadron on 15 August 1940: Hurricane, twenty; Spitfire, sixteen.
B. Serviceable now
C. Serviceable in twelve hours
D. Serviceable in seven days
E. Repairable by unit, but in more than seven days
F. Repairable, but beyond unit's capacity
G. Struck-off

*As opposed to aircraft storage unit (ASU) stored, ready for issue, categories (Table 33).

TABLE 33. RAF Fighter Command Aircraft Storage Unit (ASU) Status on Selected Dates

AIRCRAFT TYPE — DATE	ASU CATEGORIES*	TOTAL
Hurricane — 13 July 1940	1. Ready for immediate issue	186
	2. Should be available within four days	18
	3. Being prepared for issue	79
Spitfire — 13 July 1940	1. Ready for immediate issue	122
	2. Should be available within four days	4
	3. Being prepared for issue	10
Hurricane — 10 August 1940	1. Ready for immediate issue	160
	2. Should be available within four days	23
	3. Being prepared for issue	150
Spitfire — 10 August 1940	1. Ready for immediate issue	132
	2. Should be available within four days	11
	3. Being prepared for issue	51
Hurricane — 14 September 1940	1. Ready for immediate issue	80
	2. Should be available within four days	17
	3. Being prepared for issue	68
Spitfire — 14 September 1940	1. Ready for immediate issue	47
	2. Should be available within four days	10
	3. Being prepared for issue	15

Source: Francis K. Mason, *Battle over Britain* (New York: Doubleday, 1969), 595.

*An additional classification, *Category 4, aircraft on ground awaiting modification or spares*, does not apply here.

TABLE 34. Aircraft Production of New Hurricanes and Spitfires and Aircraft Storage Unit (ASU) Category 2 Repaired Machines,[a] Summer 1940

DATE	HURRICANE			SPITFIRE		
1940	NEW	REPAIRED	TOTAL	NEW	REPAIRED	TOTAL
3 August	58	23	81	41	12	53
6 August	58	19	77	37	16	53
17 August	45	20	65	31	6	37
24 August	73	16	89	44	12	56
31 August	63	21	84	37	13	50
7 September	54	25	79	36	20	56
14 September	57	48	105	38	25	63
21 September	57	45	102	40	40	80
28 September	58	45	103	34	34	68
Totals[b]	**523**	**262**	**785**	**338**	**178**	**516**

Source: T. C. G. James, *The Battle of Britain*, edited with introduction by Sebastian Cox, vol. 2 in the *Air Defence of Great Britain* series, Royal Air Force Official Histories (London: Frank Cass, 2000).

[a]Category 1. Ready for immediate issue
Category 2. Should be available within four days
Category 3. Being prepared for issue
Category 4. Aircraft on ground awaiting modifications or spares

[b]Total of all Hurricanes and Spitfires, new and repaired, for dates noted: 1,301; Hurricane repairables: 33 percent of total Hurricanes; Spitfire repairables: 35 percent of total Spitfires. Total Hurricane and Spitfire repairables: 34 percent of total new and repaired.

SD 98's misassumption that half of the aircraft shot down would be repairable in two days was based upon World War I experience with canvas and wood aircraft of the pre–Technological Revolution era.[31] And thus one reason Fighter Command fell short of available machines and had to draw from reserves was that the planned rate of repair in *SD 98* was estimated at half that needed during intensive operations with all-metal machines. If the structure of maintenance and repair had been more attuned to the realities of the summer of 1940, Air Officer Commanding-in-Chief Dowding might have needed 598 fighters returned to service in four days, so that machines would not have to be consumed from reserves. However, the following conclusions can be drawn regarding RAF losses in July 1940:

(1) many aircraft (33 percent) shot down or damaged, if not over the sea, were repairable (RAF repairables in August and September totaled 524 and write-offs in the same period 672);

(2) few pilots were killed or even wounded; and

(3) a small percentage of losses were due to bad airmanship over water rather than being enemy related.

Parallel to the evolution of doctrine and the development of personnel was the steady improvement into the 1930s of the biplane fighters coupled to the Air Defence of Great Britain Command and then to the rapid evolution of the two principal monoplane RAF fighters, the Hurricane and the Spitfire. The new eight-gun designs were capable of well over 300 mph and replaced the two-gun single-seater that could not exceed 250 mph. The whole Hurricane development program cost no more than £50,000 at the time and production aircraft no more than £7,000 each.

The Hurricane's basic Hawker fuselage contained much empty space through which bullets could pass. Moreover bolted-together damaged parts were easily replaced by skilled tradesmen accustomed to working with the system since 1924; and the wood and canvas form of the fuselage was easy for craftsmen to repair with a standard toolkit. The all-metal monocoque fuselage of the Spitfire required repair and salvage unit (RSU) or factory professionals to make over. These blemishes help explain the serviceability and availability of the two types.

If a Hurricane was damaged, it could be repaired in a few hours at a satellite airfield, but a Spitfire had to be dismantled and taken back to base. In the Battle of Britain 1,700 Hurricanes flew and claimed 80 percent of the victories.[32]

The approach to both the Hurricane and the Spitfire marked a shift in Air Ministry practice from the past, which began with the invitation to submit designs; the competition then was judged, a short list of prototypes were built and evaluated, and finally perhaps only a small production contract made.[33] However, the revolution in technology and rearmament forced the Air Ministry to rely on the industry to make the vital leap. The vault to the monoplane was forced on the Air Ministry at Adastral House by the advent in 1930 of the Hawker Hart day bomber, a 1926 concept that could not be caught by contemporary fighters. Hawker's chief designer, Sydney Camm, then followed up with the private venture Fury I fighter, but its margin of speed over the Hart was only 20 mph. Yet this interim design had to remain in British front-line service until 1939.

In early 1930 Sir John Salmond succeeded "the father of the RAF" Lord Trenchard as chief of the Air Staff. Coming fresh from being air officer commanding, the Air Defence of Great Britain (ADGB), he was painfully aware of the need for fighters that could better the 155–174 mph of those then in service, which had no hope of intercepting the Hart. At the same time, the two-gun armament was incapable of destroying an enemy aircraft in the two seconds it might be in RAF sights. Moreover the then–Vickers Mark II 0.303 machine gun, with its one thousand rounds per minute rate of fire, was subject to jams and thus had to be cockpit mounted and its standard five hundred rounds per gun stored in the fuselage. As a result, Air Ministry Specification F 7/30 was issued, calling for radical changes for a machine that would be both a day and a night fighter, the latter needing to touch down at less than 65 mph.[34] But as no engine was available to power an F 7/30 prototype, the trials at Mantlesham Heath were put off from 1932 to 1934.

Unlike in France, engine development was taken very seriously in Britain, with cost-plus-ten-percent contracts and the ever present desire to win the Schneider Trophy. These stimulated both the Rolls-Royce and Bristol companies, but the latter had problems with the Mercury engine. Rolls-Royce first improved the 500 hp steam-cooled Kestrel engine and its super-charged derivative the Goshawk. But by 1934 this was displaced by the new in-line PV-12 design, later known as the Merlin. The Goshawk powered the interim 230 mph Supermarine Type 224 fighter, the link between the S-6B Schneider Trophy aircraft and the Spitfire. However, frequent modifications of Specification F 7/30 had confused the aircraft firms, and the secrecy surrounding the trials at Martlesham and Farnborough made for little progress. The Treasury and the contractors also safeguarded their concerns. Then from 1933 came German rearmament with the collapse of disarmament.

In 1933 Britain possessed thirteen ADGB squadrons with 280 first-line aircraft. At the same time, the director of technical development at the Air Ministry realized that Specification F 7/30 was indeed leading somewhere. Hawker now decided to create a new monoplane design based on its earlier Fury with an enclosed cockpit, and would have jumped the top speed to 275 mph. Sidney Camm of Hawker then designed the Hurricane around the basic primary fuselage structure developed from 1925 Hawker biplanes. In 1934 the Merlin engine appeared likely to have a 40 to 60 percent increase in power over the Kestrel V and flying test beds were put into commission. Besides adapting the monoplane design, Camm added a retractable undercarriage with a wide track and low-pressure tires for operation from rough grass airfields.

The estimated normal loaded weight in mid-1934 was 4,600 pounds with four machine guns. At about that same time, the Air Ministry issued a new Specification, F 5/34, for a six- or eight-gun forward-firing battery in order to have the assets and detriments explored.[35] Ralph Sorley (later Air Marshal Sir Ralph Sorley), while with the Air Ministry, was once thought to be credited with developing the Specification, though Colin Sinnott's *The Royal Air Force and Aircraft Design 1923–1939* indicates that the airman's memory does not accord with the documents.[36] The Hurricane design was strong enough to carry eight guns and ammunition. Wind-tunnel tests showed the aerodynamics suitable for up to 350 mph, so the Air Ministry issued F 36/34 to cover the Hawker design. A conservative specification for the Supermarine Spitfire followed, both using the same Rolls-Royce Merlin engine.

Hawker officially entered its F 36/34 design on 4 September 1934. In January 1935 the mock-up was approved, with the eight-gun installation dependent upon negotiations between the American Colt-Browning company and the English Birmingham Small Arms Co. (BSA) for licensed manufacture of the 1,200-rpm Colt 300 modified to use British .303-inch ammunition of which there were thought to be mounds (piles) available. On 21 February 1935 the Air Ministry ordered one prototype. In July 1935 BSA signed the licensing agreement with Colt-Browning USA and Hawker's was authorized to go ahead with the eight-gun installation. This led to a design study of metal stressed-skin rather than fabric-covered wings, which could balloon and rip off if damaged at high speeds. However, manufacturing concerns delayed the fitting of metal skins until 1939.

Critical at that time was the lack of factory floor space as workshops had to convert to production facilities. Nevertheless on 6 November 1935 the prototype Hurricane flew at Brooklands, the center of aviation training and manufacture in Weybridge, Surrey, which originally had been built as a motor course in 1907. After satisfactory test flights, the prototype was delivered to the RAF Aircraft and Armament Experimental Establishment at Martlesham Heath in Suffolk. At 5,672 pounds the new fighter's performance was quite satisfactory, and thus in March the company started preparations for producing one thousand. On 3 June 1936 a contract for six hundred was signed. Shortly thereafter the Hawker-Gloster combine took control of Armstrong-Whitworth and A. V. Roe airframe manufacturers and of the Siddeley engine company, forming the Hawker-Siddeley Group; that led at once to the erection of a new factory for Hurricane production at Langley, Berkshire.[37]

A change was made to the Merlin II in late 1936 that benefited production by 20 percent, but Hurricane cockpit hoods flew off and a remedy was not found until March 1938. Finally on 12 October 1937 the first production airplane flew at an all-up weight of 5,459 pounds. As the production aircraft came off the assembly lines they were test-flown and all the "wrinkles" removed so that when delivered to squadrons they were fully operational and armed. Four Hawker test pilots carried out 3,200 flights in 1938 to prepare the thirty aircraft per month of various types for delivery; they participated as well in experimental flying on two other types under development.

The first Hurricanes were delivered to No. 11 (Fighter) Squadron at Northolt. At that time Fighter Command's twenty-six squadrons either formed or forming were equipped with the intermediate phase of Expansion aircraft, mostly biplanes from Hawkers and Gloster's Gauntlets and Gladiators in January 1938. However, by the time of the Munich Conference in September there were only five squadrons of Hurricanes and some Spitfires in the now twenty-eight squadrons. When sent to France in September 1939 the Hurricane's rugged landing gear proved invaluable on the undrained grass French airfields. In January 1939 the first service aircraft was issued fitted with the new De Havilland-Hamilton two-speed, variable-pitch, three-bladed propeller. (The Luftwaffe's Me-109 had had a similar airscrew for well over a year.)

Hawker designer Sydney Camm's proposal of early 1939 for a 2x20-mm cannon armament to counter the German Me-109D was postponed by the Air Staff until early 1940 when firing trials validated the two-cannon installation. By 3 September 1939 the RAF had thirty-nine total fighter squadrons: sixteen Hurricane; ten Spitfire; seven Blenheim I; four biplane Gladiator; and one Hawker Hind and one Gauntlet, both obsolete biplanes.[38]

The Supermarine Spitfire was designed by R. J. Mitchell, the architect of the Schneider Trophy winners of 1927, 1929, and 1931.[39] Its immediate predecessor was the Rolls-Royce Goshawk-powered, open-cockpit F 7/30 monoplane, which met Air Ministry specifications but did not satisfy Mitchell. He proceeded to work on a private venture (PV) design. While this had an enclosed cockpit, it still used the Goshawk engine. Then the Air Ministry issued Specification F 5/34 for an eight-gun fighter and Rolls-Royce produced its new PV-12 engine. Built to F 37/34 requisites, the Spitfire first flew on 5 March 1936. It handled impressively and the Air Ministry at once placed an order for 310 to be completed by March 1939. The contract was finished in August 1939, when 4,000 more were ordered.

Production of the Spitfire began in 1937 with a new Merlin, a tailwheel instead of a skid, and a two-bladed wooden airscrew, then replaced with a three-bladed variable pitch and finally a constant-speed propeller. By the Battle of Britain, thirty Mark IBs with four machine guns and two 20-mm cannon were in service for trials. On the outbreak of war, 3 September 1939, Fighter Command had nine full squadrons of Spitfires. By July 1940 it had nineteen. During the Battle of Britain the average Fighter Command strength was 957 Spitfires to 1,326 Hurricanes. With a 1,050-hp Merlin and a loaded weight of

5,332 to 5,784 pounds the Spitfire could do 355 mph at 19,000 feet, climb to 15,000 feet in 6.2 minutes, and had a service ceiling of 34,000 feet, with a range of 500 miles on 85 Imperial gallons of petrol, or a full-throttle endurance of just over 1 hour. What made the Hurricane and the Spitfire successes was that their Merlin engines had been developed by the managers and the men of the dedicated Rolls-Royce motorcar firm, which had honed its engines to perfection in the Schneider Trophy races.[40] Peter Cornwell reports that turn-around times for fuel, ammunition, and oxygen were 9 minutes for the Hurricane and 26 minutes for the Spitfire, according to mechanic Eric Marsden at Tangmere.[41] This is perhaps explained by the fact that Sydney Camm of Hawkers had long designed RAF fighters and day bombers, whereas R. J. Mitchell had specialized in high-speed racing machines.

Other advances were in process as well. The RAF had been experimenting with radio at least since 1925. On and off from that time the weight of radios had been a trade-off in fighters with the time to climb to 20,000 feet. As a result, when airborne some fighters still communicated by hand signals. In the latter 1930s the Royal Aeronautical Establishment (RAeE) started work on ultrahigh frequency (UHF) radio sets, with a goal of 1942. But the trials went faster than expected. From January 1937 sets, though not fully meeting specifications, were accepted so that by the outbreak of war No. 11 and No. 12 groups had full ground installations and transmitters, and some 250 aircraft were also fitted. The new sets were the same size as the "tried and true" TR9 high-frequency radio, allowing squadrons to switch as needed. The new TR1133 was first fitted to Spitfires of No. 66 Squadron, giving them a 140-mile range at 20,000 feet and 100 miles air-to-air. In late fall of 1939 the chief of the Air Staff approved fitting the TR1133 to all Fighter Command aircraft. This made possible greatly improved sector control. But a shortage of sets resulted in the Dunkirk squadrons being ordered to refit the TR9, in part because Dowding did not want to lose one of the new sets over German-occupied territory.[42]

Initiatives in Air Intelligence

Air Intelligence was organized in peacetime on a geographical/country basis in which open and covert sources were supplied to a particular section, such as A13B concerned with Germany. It handled order of battle, aircraft, training, and production. It managed because reports were rarely required on more than one country at a time. With the 1940 German conquest of Europe, Air Intelligence underwent a long reorganization after the Battle of Britain, from November 1940 to August 1941. The change was driven also by the shift from open and clandestine sources to Sigint (signals intelligence) and PRU (photographic reconnaissance units).[43]

As Sigint and PRU became critical for Operational Intelligence, organizational changes were required to streamline the production of useful assessments. However, Air Intelligence remained a separate directorate within the chief of the Air Staff's department at the Air Ministry.[44] The reports produced, which sometimes criticized Air Staff strategy, were affected by prewar doctrine and what Cox called "mirroring." With the modernization of the Air Intelligence staff, intelligence in the RAF was highly regarded, partly because it was able to recruit from outside of the service. RAF interrogation of Luftwaffe POWs was conducted by Air Intelligence officers. Copies of those reports were widely distributed in the Air Ministry and disseminated to the operational commands as well as to Royal Navy and Military Intelligence, with extra copies sent to units having a special interest.

However, there is no evidence that Intelligence assessments affected RAF dispositions before the Battle of Britain began in July. This was because prewar Fighter Command doctrine and analyses had presumed there would be a German air attack on Britain and that after France had fallen to Germany an attack would be mounted from bases in Scandinavia and on the Continent as far west as Brest, France. But Air Intelligence did correctly evaluate the Luftwaffe's next moves; PRU showed new French runways, and low-grade Sigint enabled the location of German Luftwaffe units to be plotted. In addition, from the end of June 1940 the Enigma decryption machine began to reveal serviceability and readiness of the Luftwaffe. By then the prewar (1935) RAF listening services were delivering useful operational intelligence. Still, Air Intelligence tended to make "worst-case" assumptions, which weighted the scales against Britain until on 5 July 1940 Professor Frederick Alexander Lindemann, the prime minister's personal scientific adviser, questioned them. The expected German Luftwaffe bomb load then was reduced by 62.5 percent.

A weakness in Air Intelligence was the sending of Enigma signals to the section whose job it was to make long-term assessments of the Luftwaffe but which was not set up to handle the tactical signals received, and thus German Luftwaffe orders and results were not matched. On the other hand, the interception service had direct phone lines to RAF groups and could indicate which GAF units had taken off for a raid, and once Luftwaffe fighters moved to French airfields, their radio/telephone (R/T) chatter also could be dissected. But conversely, the French Deuxième Bureau—French military intelligence agency—had the best pre-1940 Armistice intelligence and assessments of the

Luftwaffe, and these were passed to London.[45] Of particular importance in all three air forces was Intelligence.

Equally important, however, the British government had not only decided in 1934 on the Expansion Schemes, but also decided to fund the Air Ministry so that the budget rose from £16 million in 1932 and to £106 million plus supplemental appropriations in 1939. Yet, interestingly, the result was that the RAF by July 1940 still was just barely prepared to defend Great Britain. And it was better off materially than mentally, for there was still a strong bomber mentality in the Air Ministry.

In 1969 the RAF identified 2,946 persons, both air and ground crew, eligible for the Battle of Britain Medal out of seventy-one units that participated between 10 July and 31 October 1940 of which the 537 dead equaled 18.2 percent. In the operation of six weeks to sixteen weeks, the RAF should have had twenty-seven times the force (637 x 2.7, or 1,720) personnel engaged, but instead it had an additional 1,226. So in spite of Dowding's cause for concerns regarding his shortage of pilots, he had a sufficient supply, especially as new ones were posted in to Fighter Command, as contrasted to a dwindling FAF corps.[46]

The new Dewoitine D-520 fighter, competitive with the Me-109E but tricky to handle both in the air and on landing. *SHAA, B80-2107*

From left to right, French General d'Astier de la Vigerie, German General Erhard Milch, and General Joseph Vuillemin inspecting the guard of honor during the psychological intimidation of the *Chef de l'Armée de l'Air*, August 1938. *SHAA, B82-1982*

Escadrille aircrew of a Potez 63, probably at a training unit *ca.* Spring 1940. The faces are older, the caps and kepis at various angles, and some coats are leather and others wool. *SHAA, B83-2591*

A Morane Saulnier 406 (MS-406), no. 428, during the Drôle de Guerre (Phony War), 1939–1940. The aircraft appears to belong to the first Escadrille of *Groupe Chasseur* I/2. The photo was taken at the Beauvais-Tillé in Fall 1939. Note the aerial masts above and below the fuselage—the FAF was just being equipped with radios. The MS-406 was inferior to the Me-109E. *SHAA, B83-4024*

Breguet Factory No. 4, 1 April 1939. *SHAA, B86-4997*

Breguet 693s under construction in June 1939, a three-seat fighter that reached units first in 1939 as a light bomber. *SHAA, B86-5096*

The Italian theorist Gen. Giulio Douhet, who advocated the invulnerable "battle plane" and the destruction of cities. *SHAA, B88-210*

French Army General Maurice Gamelin strapped into a backpack parachute walks out to an FAF aircraft for a flight to familiarize himself with the FAF's objectives. *SHAA, B90-507*

The Potez 63-11 was in the inventory on 10 May 1940, but 70 percent lacked spare parts and many were destroyed on the ground. *SHAA, B91-1750*

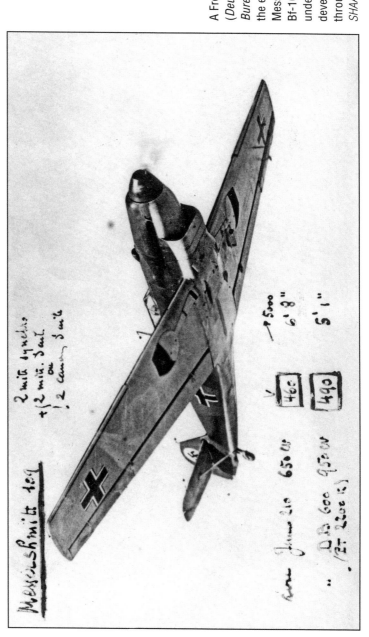

A French Intelligence (*Deuxieme Bureau*) card on the early German Messerschmitt Bf-109, still under continuous development through 1944. *SHAA, B92-3614*

Ministre de l'Air Guy La Chambre (in light coat) being shown an MS-406 at the Paris Salon de l'Aéronautique *ca.* 1938. The Morane-Saulnier M.S. 406 was the major Armée de l'Air fighter during the Battle of France. It normally carried one 20mm cannon and two 7.5mm machine guns. *SHAA, 92-4078*

A major redesign of the Bloch 200, the Bloch 210 dispensed with the earlier shoulder-mounted wing and huge fixed landing gear in favor of a more efficient low-wing and retractable main gear arrangement. Six groupes de bombardment flew 210s during the Battle of France. The more advanced LeO 451 was being introduced at the time of the Armistice and often, the units flew a mixed bag of the two types. *Peter B Mersky Collection*

This inflight view of the Amiot 143s of G.B. II/22 emphasizes the bombers' ungainly appearance. These bombers were also participating in 1937 exercises. During the 1940 campaign, Amiot 143s dropped leaflets, and flew reconnaissance and night bombing missions, especially against German railroad facilities in the Rhine valley, Belgium and France. *Peter B Mersky Collection*

The Bloch 152 was an honest fighter that never received the more powerful engine it needed. Five groupes de chasse flew it against the Luftwaffe in 1940. Its armament usually included two 7.5mm machine guns and two 20mm cannon. The wing on the far right of this photo displays the extended wing cannon inboard of the pitot tube. The 152's short range (barely 400 miles) precluded it being ferried to North Africa and it remained on the continent after the Armistice. *Peter B Mersky Collection*

A Curtiss Hawk 75A-3 of GC II/5, pre-Armistice. The export version of the P-36, the Hawk 75 was a popular fighter, strong and fairly maneuverable. The A-3 version also included two more machine guns bringing the total to six. After the Armistice in June 1940, the Hawk continued to serve in Vichy squadrons, colorfully marked in red-and-yellow stripes on their engine cowling and tail surfaces. Its most notable action came in November 1942 when Vichy squadrons in North Africa contested the Allied landings in Operation Torch. The Hawks gave good accounts of themselves and in fairness, many of their pilots fought with great reluctance against their long-time allies.

Peter B Mersky Collection

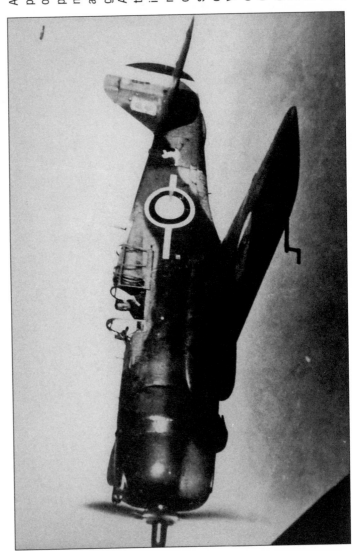

German ME 109
Courtesy Smithsonian Institution

German JU 87 Stukas entered service with the Luftwaffe in 1937, but were to be phased out in 1940. It was used as flying artillery in May–June 1940 and attacks upon British Channel convoys to lure fighter command up. *Courtesy Smithsonian Institution*

The Dornier DO-17 "Flying Pencil" was a fast, light bomber blooded in the Spanish Civil War. *Courtesy Smithsonian Institution*

The German Heinkel HE-111 was designed as a fast mail plane as well as a bomber. Many were in service in 1940 though being phased out of the Luftwaffe. It first flew in 1935. *Courtesy Smithsonian Institution*

Sir Philip Cunliffe Lister, newly appointed Secretary of State for Air, seated at his desk at the Air Ministry, 1935 *Charles Brown Collection, RAF Museum*

Pilots of 601 Squadron Royal Auxiliary Air Force standing in front of Hawker Demons, Hendon 1938 *Charles Brown Collection, RAF Museum*

Vickers Wellington I aircraft of 9 Squadron in flight, RAF Stradishall 1939. Though defeated in the Battle of Heligoland Bight 18 December 1939, they served throughout World War II as night bombers. *Charles Brown Collection, RAF Museum*

RAF Fairey Battle light bomber. Such ungainly aircraft, with a crew of three, were slaughtered in the Battle of France. *RAF Museum*

Hawker Hurricane Is of 111 Squadron with two-bladed wooden propellers as sent to France in 1939–1940. *Charles Brown Collection, RAF Museum*

Early Supermarine Spitfires in prewar markings, but fitted with the new all-steel three-bladed propellers.
RAF Museum

PART 2
THE BATTLES

THE BATTLE OF FRANCE

Introduction

The Battle of France was one of the most decisive in military history. It lasted forty-six days, from 10 May to 24 June 1940. It pitted the complacent Allied assumption that the new war would take up from where the victorious Allies had ended in November 1918 against the German determination to win a short economical war using the revolutionary blitzkrieg concept. Blitzkrieg meant breaking through the Allied Front and then rapidly disrupting the rear areas. The Allies were unprepared mentally or physically in May 1940 with a counter.

The roots of the defeat of the Armée de l'Air went deep. They included, among others, a lack of focus, lack of doctrine, and lack of communications. Northeastern France and adjacent Belgium, low-lying areas with a water table just over a foot below the surface, were long the scenes of battles and military campaigns before May 1940. Airfields during 1914–1918 and 1939–1940 were located on higher ground, but they were almost all grass and subject to weather, especially rain. There were days when even if it did not rain, drying airfields were unserviceable. Moreover the advancing Germans in their blitzkrieg mode, with aircraft designed to operate off of a natural surface, chose available open fields.

A consequence of this was a relatively high rate of accidents and damage. The Me-109 was the most vulnerable. About one-third of all of the type manufactured suffered take-off or landing accidents. Pilots had a Hobson's choice of taxiing and operating off of grass with the danger of bogging down, nosing over, upsetting, or losing control, or of using graveled taxi tracks and runways with consequent damage by stones to propellers, flaps, radiators, and fuselages.

Of the 600 Me-109s issued from 25 May to 30 June, 180 would probably have been sidelined for the above reasons.[1]

Vuillemin as chef d'état majeur de l'Armée de l'Air (French General Staff Air Force [CGSAF]) had predicted at Munich time that the FAF would not last two weeks in war. By 10 May 1940 the Armée de l'Air was much stronger, but the Luftwaffe was also more powerful and had proved itself in Spain and its strength and doctrine in Poland. In the event, the FAF experienced a logarithmic decline in effectiveness from 10 May until it ceased operations on 24 June.

Overview—10 May–24 June 1940

On 10 May the Germans struck the Netherlands, Belgium, and Luxemburg. Though alerted on 8 May, the Allies took no precautions. The attack converted Belgian neutrality into belligerency; but the Dutch succumbed in days. A Franco-British force, as planned by Gamelin, advanced into Belgium to the Dyle to protect industrial manufacturing in northeast France by fighting the battle away from French soil. A German airborne assault captured the key Belgian fortress of Eben Emael by landing inside and on top of it (Map 3).

On 12 May, Panzers and motorized infantry crossed the Meuse at Sedan, having penetrated the Ardennes, and attacked the joint of weak French reserve divisions. The next day Rotterdam surrendered and the following day the Dutch Queen took her government to exile in London as Dutch forces laid down their arms. On 17 to 21 May, the Germans raced down the Somme Valley to the English Channel, cutting off the Franco-British-Belgian forces in the northeast. The fall of Brussels and Namur forced the Allies to retreat to Dunkirk (Dunquerque) and Calais, from which they were evacuated 28 May till 4 June. All together, 200,000 British and 140,000 French troops were taken to Britain. Concurrently the Belgians were cut off and after eighteen days fighting, King Albert ordered them to lay down their arms (Map 4, The German Encirclement of the Allied Armies, Last Two Weeks of May).

In the meantime that consummate manager, General Maurice Gamelin, was replaced by his senior, General Maxime Weygand, recalled from Syria. But he was out of touch and unable to stop the Panzers, which renewed their attack along the Aisne and the Loire and quickly broke through. Solid French tanks were not wielded as an armored force, but like the air arm, allotted in packets to armies so they were not available for the counterstrike prior to 5 June that might have made a difference.

As the Germans poured through the gaps, on 10 June the Italians ineffectively entered the war. On 15 May Verdun of 1916 fame fell, and the next day

MAP 3. The German Attack, 9–10 May and the Allied Response

North
Sea

Amsterdam

The Hague

NETHERLANDS

Rotterdam

GERMANY

18th Army
Von Küchler

Antwerp

Ostend

6th Army
Von Reichenau

Dunkirk

7th Army
Giraud

Scheldt R.

Brussels

Cologne

BELGIUM

Aachen

Lille
B.E.F.
Lord Gort

Liége

4th Army
Von Kluge
12th Army
List
16th Army
Busch

Namur

1st Army
Blanchard

Mons

Sambre R.

Meuse R.

Arras

9th Army
Corap

Ardennes

Siegfried Line

Amiens

St. Quentin

FRANCE

Sedan

Luxem-
Bourg

2nd Army
Huntziger

Maginot Line

3rd Army
Condé

Marne R.

Paris

From Herbert R. Lottman, *The Fall of Paris: June 1940* (London: Sinclair-Stevenson, 1992), 16.

MAP 4. The German Encirclement of the Allied Armies,
Last Two Weeks of May

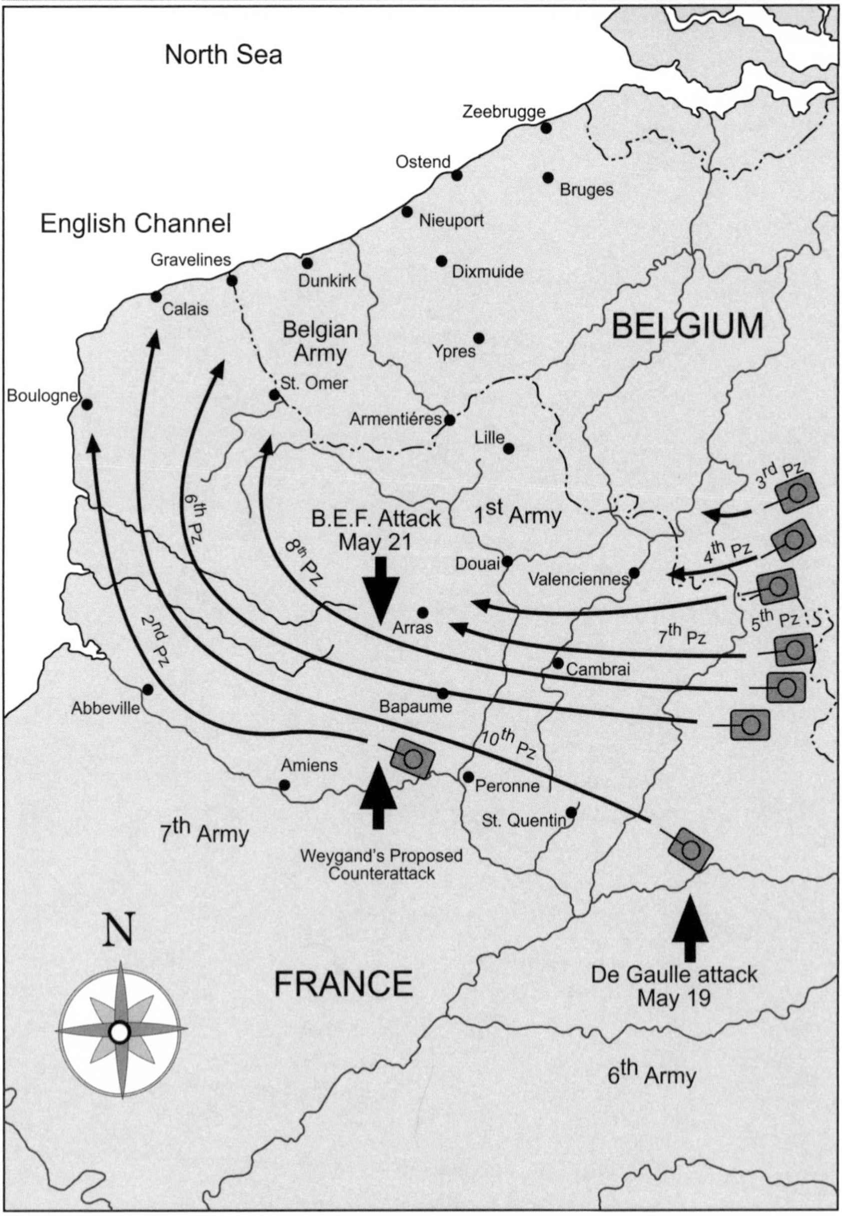

North Sea

Zeebrugge

Ostend

English Channel

Bruges

Nieuport

Gravelines

Dixmuide

Dunkirk

Calais

Belgian
Army

Ypres

BELGIUM

St. Omer

Boulogne

Armentiéres

Lille

3rd Pz

6th Pz

B.E.F. Attack
May 21

1st Army

4th Pz

8th Pz

Douai

Valenciennes

5th Pz

Arras

7th Pz

2nd Pz

Cambrai

Abbeville

Bapaume

10th Pz

Amiens

Peronne

7th Army

St. Quentin

Weygand's Proposed
Counterattack

N

FRANCE

De Gaulle attack
May 19

6th Army

From Herbert R. Lottman, *The Fall of Paris: June 1940* (London: Sinclair-Stevenson, 1992), 88.

Marshal Pétain became head of France in lieu of Paul Reynaud. On 17 May he asked for an armistice, which was signed at Compiègne on 22 May. Fighting stopped on 24 May, and Pétain moved the seat of government to Vichy in Unoccupied France.[2]

The British side of the Battle of France was directly affected by the pre-war policy up to spring 1939 of merely a token two-division Continental commitment with the emphasis upon naval and air action. The decision to send a British Expeditionary Force (BEF) with an Air Component and an Advanced Air Striking Force, resulted in neither the army nor the RAF being trained or equipped for the new war. Even with the Phoney War breather, neither was ready on 10 May.[3]

The assessment of Allied strength placed too much emphasis upon numbers and not nearly enough on command abilities and logistics arrangements. Too many decision-makers thought at 1918 speed. The British army lacked antitank guns and armor, and the RAF was wanting in aircraft, aircrew, and training for Army Cooperation work. The signals and intelligence systems were not geared to blitzkrieg.

Neither Gamelin nor Weygand had the quickness, grasp of the situation, nor the stamina for Supreme Commander, and on the air level Vuillemin was also over-matched. This was in stark contrast to the Wehrmacht and its associated Luftwaffe, well staffed and trained at all levels and with a common doctrine.

The Allies had not been able to weld a Supreme Command before the end of Belgian neutrality, but they had also failed to cement the BEF between the French First and Seventh armies in the Northeast. The cordial arrangements between General Georges as overall commander in the Northeast and Lord Gort, the GOC BEF, fell apart upon impact on 10 May. Gort was influenced by all three French commanders above him—Georges, Gamelin and Weygand.

The Supreme Command weakened the Allied Front by sandwiching the French 7e Armée (Seventh Army), between the BEF and the Channel, to adventure unsupported into Belgium to no purpose, and the whole advance to the Dyle to cover the weak French 9e Armée (Ninth Army), which allowed the German breakthrough at Sedan. And the French showed little ability to launch successful counterattacks. In October 1939 Gamelin had told the British chief of the Imperial General Staff (CIGS), Ironside, that the Germans would thrust through the Ardennes and along the Meuse. But Gamelin changed his mind and deemed the Ardennes an impenetrable route and so justified plans for the weak 9e Armée to block that line of approach.

After ordering the advance to the Dyle, Gamelin, sixty-seven, left the conduct of the battle to General Georges until on 20 May he was relieved by

Weygand, seventy-four; neither were notably fit. The latter made the third crippling mistake, to conclude that his forces were too weak and had no reserves and so could not hold the very long line from Switzerland to the Channel. "Perhaps," reckoned L. F. Ellis, the British official historian, "the time had already passed by May the 20th, when the situation could be retrieved. Perhaps in all the circumstances it never had been possible." Given French pessimism and the lack of a strong civilian government, defeat was inevitable.[4] Weygand's biggest failure was not to realize that time was against him. In contrast, British operations were carried out with foresight and speed. When action was ordered, movement followed. A second BEF, landed farther west under General Alan Brooke, was quickly reembarked when its commander telephoned the new prime minister, Churchill, and persuaded him that there could be no Breton Redoubt.

Air Marshal Barratt, the air officer commanding in chief, British Air Forces France, was not able to make his mark on the campaign as he was soon separated from the BEF and had not the power to support both the French and British armies, while the size of his forces was determined by the makers of grand strategy in London. His strength in the BAFF was also affected by the logistics of a long withdrawal amid refugees across a limited number of indifferently equipped airfields. His forces were defeated not by the Luftwaffe so much as by the Wehrmacht.[5]

The Germans had planned for a short war, and it showed. The Luftwaffe had air superiority in three days. Once across the Meuse, the Wehrmacht unleashed the bold blitzkrieg in which Stukas supported the lead units in lieu of artillery, and transports flew in fuel and matériel. The small RAF in France was supplemented both by Hawker Hurricane fighters and by Bristol Blenheim and Fairey Battle bombers from Home. But the British Air Forces France was not constituted for mobility and did not have the pilots to retrieve damaged but flyable machines. Moreover Luftwaffe air superiority caused the RAF to retreat to England, from which it shocked the GAF over Dunkirk.

On 10 May, the French Armée de l'Air had 2,787 aircrew officers and 2,897 NCOs, for a total of 5,684 aircrew; that day it lost 393 officers and 63 NCOs killed, 258 officers and 115 NCOs wounded, and 242 missing—a total of 1,071, or 19 percent. A shortage of mechanics in the Armée de l'Air explains its low serviceability (*disponible*) rates. This would have been especially true of the Bloch MB-151/152 fighter *escadrilles,* as the cylinder heads on their license-built American radial engines had to be replaced every ten hours or roughly every ten days. The lack of mechanics also meant that whenever an *escadrille* moved, its efficiency declined because of fatigue and of lack of manpower to pack and unpack. Moreover it also indicated that, as in the RAF squadrons in

France, any aircraft that could not be flown out (assuming a pilot was available) became part of wastage and consumption—abandoned.

The lack of doctrine, organization, and manpower were the Achilles heel of the Armée de l'Air. And whereas the RAF lacked mobility, the FAF's twenty-four *chasseur escadrilles* moved a total of 302 times from 23 August 1939 to 24 June 1940, 62 percent of those debilitating translations being after the end of May. The Allied Air Forces were not responsible for the collapse of France, but neither could they prevent that calamity.

The Air Campaign of 10 May–24 June 1940

The story of the air campaign of 10 May–24 June 1940 is quickly told. The Battle of France and the following Battle of Britain were unlike land campaigns or their accompanying battles, which are usually well defined and easily described in both broad and precise terms, or naval battles, which last but hours or days except for such struggles as the Battle of the Atlantic during World War II, really a six-year campaign. The May–June 1940 Battle of France and the following Battle of Britain consisted of a succession of actions between quite small forces. Hence their description becomes necessarily episodic (Map 5).

The nature of the French Campaign was essentially chaotic in unforecast fluidity that knocked 1918 assumptions into a cocked hat, in contrast to the subsequent Battle of Britain, which was fought along anticipated lines and was, as the Duke of Wellington said of Waterloo, "a damned nice thing—the nearest run thing you ever saw in your life."

By 15 May 1940 the Luftwaffe had air superiority. The Armée de l'Air exhibited a resurgence of activity during 18–22 May and again 5–10 June for the Battle of the Somme, but thereafter its *escadrilles* withdrew to southwest France. The units with the range were then dispatched to North Africa until stopped by lack of pilots, fuel, and the 24 June effective date of the Franco-German armistice.[6] Leading up to the Battle of France, on 21 March 1940 Air Minister La Chambre had been replaced by André (Victor) Laurent-Eynac, the 1928 air minister. On 19 May General Gamelin, commander of the French army, was replaced by his predecessor, General Maxime Weygand. On 13 June the French government left Paris and fled to Bordeaux after a brief sojourn at Tours, and on 16 June Marshal Pétain took over the government.

During the Battle of France wastage and consumption of RAF aircraft totaling 959 was heightened by lack of aircraft storage unit (ASU) Category 3 (being prepared for issue) repair facilities in France and by the dearth of building of airfields, as evidenced by the fact that only thirty-four Advanced Air

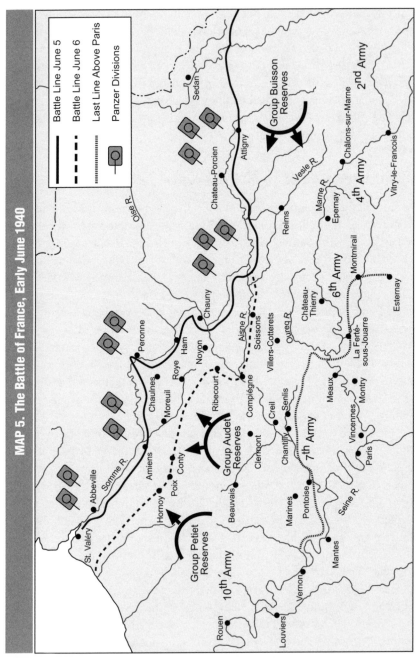

MAP 5. The Battle of France, Early June 1940

Battle Line June 5
Battle Line June 6
Last Line Above Paris
Panzer Divisions

From Herbert R. Lottman, *The Fall of Paris: June 1940* (London: Sinclair-Stevenson, 1992), 191.

Striking Force and seventy-five Army Cooperation (AC) Hurricanes were shot down—109 versus 386 casualties, or 28.2 percent.[7] In the lull from 25 May to 5 June, the Armée de l'Air concentrated upon rebuilding. Commanding General Joseph Vuillemin used the time to reorganize and consolidate his command. He then assumed control of all reserve forces in anticipation of a German advance toward Switzerland as of 31 May.

The French bombers during the Battle of France were divided into three divisions—one for the French Zone d'Opérations Nord (air zone of operations north [ZOAN]), one for the Zone d'Opérations Est (air zone of operations east [ZOAE]), and the third to hit objectives deep behind enemy lines. Thus, as of 2 June 1940 the ZOAN would have sixteen fighter and fourteen bomber *groupes*, while ZOAE would have seven *chasse* and twelve bomber *groupes*. In view of the likely Italian involvement, one fighter *groupe* was assigned to Air Operations Alps.

General Vuillemin's order for the three divisions deprived General Alphonse-Josef Georges, the ground commander in the northeast, of his air assets and he reacted strongly, noting that the difficulties of harmonizing air and ground operations was only increased due to the excessive centralization of the Armée de l'Air (and without the necessary communications). General Vuillemin and company were living in an unreal world where their ideas and resources had a canyon between them. Evidence of this can been seen: although 2,086 new planes had been supplied to the units in the first and second lines, only 599 were fit for combat; while the other 71 percent could not get off the ground, many machines were stacked on airfields or stored in depots. Over 60 percent of the fighters and bombers and over 86 percent of the reconnaissance planes were grounded because of mechanical, technical, equipment, or armament problems. The Armée de l'Air had already lost the spares and sustainability battles.

Armée de l'Air pilots and others had a cavalier attitude toward the German Me-109, the *chassers'* most dangerous opponent. They deluded themselves that they and their Morane-Saulnier MS-406 and Curtiss Hawk fighters could out-maneuver the Luftwaffe's single-seat fighter, for they had only encountered it in brief skirmishing during the Drôle de guerre (Phoney War). Additionally, the Gallic warriors were overconfident and did not train seriously, often believing a lively discussion was as good as rigorous training, while the detection of their own and their steeds' weaknesses and the correction of faults and omissions was set aside.

French assessments of the German Me-109E were singularly unrealistic. In spite of limited contacts with the Luftwaffe fighter in the winter of 1939–

1940, the Armée de l'Air should have been disabused of the idea that its MS-406 had superior maneuverability compared with the Me-109 and that the Curtiss Hawk, while inferior in firepower, was the 109's equal in other respects. This view probably came from the sincerely believed results of skirmishes, but was quickly discredited. Similarly, later during World War II, the Allies had dismissed the Japanese Zero, until it shot them down—a fatal ethnocentricity.

The Armée de l'Air had other problems as well. Besides the aged aircrew suffering fatigue, officers had other than flying duties, including the necessity at times to abandon and destroy their machines, and commanders had also to handle the organization, camouflage, and defense of the airfields. Moreover personnel were not only lacking, but ill trained, especially for flying in poor weather conditions. Table 35, courtesy of General Lucien Robineau, outlines in detail the French Armée de l'Air organization and order of battle on 10 May 1940, indicating the distribution and location of the Armée de l'Air day and night fighters, bombers, reconnaissance, and observation groups. Table 36 also shows the FAF order of battle and commanders, and Table 37 lists the allocation of aircraft on 10 May 1940.

Of the forty-six days of the Battle of France, only twenty to twenty-three were flyable. The *chasse* lost 574 aircraft in those forty-six/twenty days, which equates to 28.7 aircraft lost daily in twenty days. If the *chasse* total is 349 in forty-six days, the average replacement daily is 8.3; if the loss is in twenty days, daily replacement is 17.45. The French Armée de l'Air *chasse* needed 574 aircraft to make up wastage and consumption, but actually got 597 (Table 3). However, only 30 percent of those were *bon de guerre*, leaving a deficit of 418. Table 3 indicates that as the Battle of France progressed the *escadrilles* replacements started modestly, increased at various times mid-battle, then went back essentially to the numbers on 10 May. The cause is not specified, such as the human resources fatigued from the tempo of the battle.

Claude d'Abzac-Epézy in her 1997 work on the Vichy air force noted that on 10 May the Armée de l'Air had 5,025 total machines (Table 37): 2,402 *chasseur*, 1,159 bombers, and 1,464 reconnaissance aircraft. Of the Armée de l'Air's 2,402 total, 2,005 (83.5 percent) were modern—that is, of the new generation of all-metal machines. Overall, of the 5,025 total aircraft in the FAF, 68.7 percent were modern, though that included both first-line and second-line aircraft. First-line aircraft were ready to fly on four hours' notice, whereas the second-line were unserviceable (*indisponible*) due to routine checks and repairs from accidents or combat, or needing modifications.

Of the Armée de l'Air's total 5,025 aircraft, some on 10 May were categorized as "*aux armées,*" allocated to the air armies. Of these, in Metropolitan

TABLE 35. Armée de l'Air Order of Battle, 10 May 1940*

ZONE OF AIR OPERATIONS—NORTH (GROUP, AIRCRAFT, LOCATION)		
GROUPES DE CHASSE (GC) (DAY FIGHTER GROUPS)		
Groupement de Chasse 21		
GC I/1	Bloch MB-152	Chantilley les aigles
GC II/1	Bloch MB-152	Buc
GC III/3	Dewoitine D-520	Beauvais-Tillé
GC II/10	Bloch MB-151/152	Rouen-Boos
GC III/10	Bloch MB-151/152	Le Havre-Octeville
Groupement de Chasse 23		
GC II/2	Morane-Saulnier MS-406	Laon
GC III/2	Morane-Saulnier MS-406	Cambrai-Niergnies
GC I/4	Curtiss H-75	Wez-Thuisy
GC I/5	Curtiss H-75	Suippes
Groupement de Chasse 25		
GC III/1	Morane-Saulnier MS-406	Norrent-Fontes
GC II/8	Bloch MB-152	Calais-Marck
ESCADRILLE DE CHASSE DE NUIT (SQUADRONS OF NIGHT FIGHTERS) (ATTACHED TO GC 21)		
ECN I/13	Potez 631	Meaux-Esbly
ECN II/13	Potez 631	Melun-Villaroche
ECN III/13	Potez 631	Le Plessis-Belleville
ECB IV/13	Potez 631	Betz-Bouillancy
ESCADRILLE DE CHASSE MIXTE DE JOUR (SQUADRONS OF MIXED DAY FIGHTERS) (ATTACHED TO GC 21)		
ECMJ 1/16	Potez 631	Wez-Thuisy
1ÈRE DIVISION AÉRIENNE DE BOMBARDEMENT (1ST AVIATION BOMBER DIVISION)		
Groupement 6		
GB I/12	Lioré-et-Olivier LeO-451	Soissons-Saconin
GB II/12	Lioré-et-Olivier LeO-451	Persan-Beaumont
Groupement 9		
GB I/34	Amiot AM-143/AM-354	Montdidier
GB II/34	Amiot AM-143/AM-354	Roye-Amy
Groupement de Bombardement d'Assaut 18		
GB II/35	Breguet Br-691/Br-693	Châteauroux La Martinerie
GB I/54	Breguet Br-693	La Ferté-Gaucher
GB II/54	Breguet Br-693	Nangis

(continues)

TABLE 35. Armée de l'Air Order of Battle, 10 May 1940* (continued)

	Groupement de Bombardement d'Assaut 19	
GBA I/51	Breguet Br-693	Orléans-Bricy
GBA II/51	Breguet Br-693/Br-695	Bouard

GROUPES DE RECONNAISSANCE (RECONNAISSANCE GROUPS)		
GR I/14	Potez 63-11	Clastres-Saint-Simon
GR II/22	Potez 63-11/Potez 637	Couvron
GR I/24	Potez 63-11	Castres-Montescourt
GR I/33	Bloch MB-174/Potez 63-11/Potez 637	Athies sous Laon
GR I/35	Potez 63-11	
GR II/52	Bloch MB-174/Potez 63-11/Potez 637	Couvron

GROUPES AÉRIENS D'OBSERVATION (AIR OBSERVATION GROUPS)		
GAO 501	Mureaux 115/Potez 63-11	Dunkerque-Mardick
GAO 502	Mureaux 115/Potez 63-11	La Fère Courbe
GAO 503	Mureaux 115/Potez 63-11	Valenciennes
GAO 504	Potez 39/ Potez 63-11	Denain
GAO 505	Potez 39/Potez 63-11	Vestain le Quesnoy
GAO 507	Mureaux 115/Potez 63-11	Attigny
GAO 510	Potez 25/Potez 39/Potez 63-11	Attigny
GAO 511	Potez 39/Potez 63-11	Villers lès Guise
GAO 515	Mureaux 117/Potez 25/Potez 63-11	Avignon
GAO 516	Breguet Br-27/Potez 63-11	Aix en Provence
GAO 518	Breguet Br-27/Potez 25/Potez 63-11	Challerange
GAO 2/520	Mureaux 115/Potez 63-11	Challerange
GAO 545	Breguet Br-27/Potez 63-11	Denain
GAO 546	Breguet Br-27/Potez 63-11	Sézanne-St. Rémy
GAO 547	Breguet Br-27/Potez 25/Potez 63-11	La Malmaison
GAO 2/551	Mureaux 117/Potez 63-11	Tournes-Belval
GAO 4/551	Mureaux 117/Potez 63-11	Le Quesnoy-Vertain
GAO 552	Mureaux 117/Potez 63-11	St. Omer-Wizernes

ZONE OF AIR OPERATIONS—EAST (GROUP, AIRCRAFT, LOCATION)		

GROUPES DE CHASSE (GC) (DAY FIGHTER GROUPS)

	Groupement de Chasse 22	
GC I/2	Morane-Saulnier MS-406	Toul-Ochey
GC II/4	Curtiss H-75	Xaffevillers
GC II/5	Curtiss H-75	Toul-Croix de Metz
GC II/6	Morane-Saulnier MS-406/Bloch MB-152	Anglure-Vouarces

TABLE 35. Armée de l'Air Order of Battle, 10 May 1940* (continued)

GC III/7	Morane-Saulnier MS-406	Vitry le Francois
GC I/8	Bloch MB-152	Velaine en Haye

3ÈRE DVISION AÉRIENNE DE BOMBARDEMENT (3RD AVIATION BOMBER DIVISION)

	Groupement 10	
GB I/38	Amiot AM-143/Bloch MB-200	Troyes-Barberey
GB II/38	Amiot AM-143/Bloch MB-200	Chaumont-Semoutiers
	Groupement 15	
GB I/15	Farman F-222	Reims-Courcy
GB II/15	Farman F-222	Reims-Courcy

GROUPES DE RECONNAISSANCE (RECONNAISSANCE GROUPS)

GR I/22	Potez 63-11	Metz-Frescaty
GR I/36	Potez 63-11	Martigny les Gerbonvaux
GR II/36	Bloch MB-174/Potez 63-11	Neufchâteau-Azelot
GR I/52	Bloch MB-174/Potez 63-11/Potez 637	St. Dizier

GROUPES AÉRIENS D'OBSERVATION (AIR OBSERVATION GROUPS)

GAO I/506	Mureaux 113/Mureaux 117/Potez 63-11	Conflans-Doncourt
GAO 2/506	Mureaux 117/Potez 63-11	Chambley
GAO 2/508	Breguet Br-27/Potez 25/Potez 63-11	Mars la Tour
GAO 509	Breguet Br-27/Potez 63-11	Delme
GAO 512	Potez 39/63-11	La Perthe
GAO 517	Potez 39/63-11	Neufchâteau
GAO I/520	Mureaux 115/Potez 63-11	Gueblange les Dieuze
GAO 548	Mureaux 115/Potez 63-11	Epinal
GAO I/551	Mureaux 117/Potez 63-11	Etain
GAO 3/551	Mureaux 117/Potez 63-11	Senon-Spincourt
GAO 553	Mureaux 115/Potez 63-11	Nancy

ZONE OF AIR OPERATIONS—ALPS
(GROUP, AIRCRAFT, LOCATION)

GROUPES DE CHASSE (GC) (DAY FIGHTER GROUPS)

GC I/3	Dewoitine D-520	Cannes
GC II/3	Morane-Saulnier MS-406/Dewoitine D-520	Le Luc
GC II/6	Morane-Saulnier MS-406	Marseille-Marignane
GC II/9	Bloch MB-152	Marignane
GC III/9	Bloch MB-151/152	Lyon-Bron
GC I/145	Morane-Saulnier MS-406/Caudron C-714	Lyon-Bron

(continues)

TABLE 35. Armée de l'Air Order of Battle, 10 May 1940* (continued)

ESCADRILLE DE CHASSE DE NUIT (SQUADRONS OF NIGHT FIGHTERS)		
ECN 5/13	Potez 631	Loyettes

GROUPES DE RECONNAISSANCE (RECONNAISSANCE GROUPS)		
GR II/55	Bloch MB-174/Potez 63-11/Potez 637	Chambarand

GROUPES AÉRIENS D'OBSERVATION (AIR OBSERVATION GROUPS)		
GAO 1/514	Mureaux 117/Potez 63-11	Montbar-Trouillon
GAO 2/514	Mureaux 115/Potez 63-11	St. Etienne de St. Geoirs
GAO 581	Potez 25/ 63-11	Marignane
GAO 582	Potez 25 63-11	Valence
GAO 1/584	Potez 25/ 63-11	Valence
GAO 1/589	Potez 25/63-11	Le luc

GROUPES AÉRIEN MIXTE (MIXED GROUPS)		
GAM 550	Breguet Br-270/Potez 63-11	Calvi

ZONE OF AIR OPERATIONS—SOUTH (GROUP, AIRCRAFT, LOCATION)		

GROUPES DE CHASSE (GC) (DAY FIGHTER GROUPS)		
Groupement de Chasse 24		
GC III/6	Morane-Saulnier MS-406	Chissey sur Loue
GC II/7	Morane-Saulnier MS-406	Luxeuil-St. Sauveur

GROUPES DE RECONNAISSANCE (RECONNAISSANCE GROUPS)		
GR I/33	Bloch MB-174/Potez 63-11/Potez 637	Dôle-Tavaux
GR I/55	Potez 63-11	Malbouhans

GROUPES AÉRIENS D'OBSERVATION (AIR OBSERVATION GROUPS)		
GAO 1/508	Breguet Br-27/Potez 63-11	Romilly-sur-Seine
GAO 513	Potez 25/39/63-11	Belfort
GAO 543	Breguet Br-27/Potez 63-11	Montbéliard

SOUTHEAST AVIATION BOMBARDMENT INSTRUCTION GROUPS (GROUP, AIRCRAFT, LOCATION)		

Groupement 1		
GB I/62	Glenn Martin M-167F	Orange-Plan de Dieu
GB I/63	Glenn Martin M-167F	Orange-Plan de Dieu

Groupement 6		
GB I/31	Lioré-et-Olivier LeO-451	Lézignan
GB II/31	Lioré-et-Olivier LeO-451	Lézignan

TABLE 35. Armée de l'Air Order of Battle, 10 May 1940* (continued)

	Groupement 7	
GB I/23	Bloch MB-210/Lioré-et-Olivier LeO-451	Istres IV
GB II/23	Bloch MB-210/Lioré-et-Olivier LeO-451	Istres-Le Vallon
	Groupement 9	
GB I/21	Bloch MB-210/Amiot AM-354	Avignon-Châteaublanc
GB II/21	Bloch MB-210/Amiot AM-354	Avignon-Châteaublanc
	Groupement 11	
GB I/11	Bloch MB-210/Lioré-et-Olivier LeO-451	Arles-Mas de Rus
GB II/11	Bloch MB-210	Arles-Mas de Rus

*Table courtesy of General Lucien Robineau, former SHAA chief. See also Charles Christienne, Pierre Lissarrague et al., *A History of French Military Aviation* (Washington, D.C.: Smithsonian Institution Press, 1986), 361–363.

France, only 1,095 were modern first-line aircraft (609 *chasseur*, 128 bombers, 358 reconnaissance). Thus only 31.7 percent of the total modern French aircraft had to sustain the shock of the German onslaught. (Although the first-line fighters actually had totaled 637 on 10 May, 28 of these were obsolescent—*ancient*—leaving 609.) Of the FAF's 808 second-line aircraft, 15 were *ancient* and 303 out-of-date, a total of 318, or 39 percent.

On 10 May 1940 the Armée de l'Air had a total of 552 serviceable fighters out of 637: 278 MS-406, 36 D-520, 140 MB-151 and -152, and 98 Hawk 75. The RAF in France had a daily average of 40 Hawker Hurricane and 20 Gloster Gladiator fighters available. If only 30 percent of the FAF's *chasseur* were serviceable, then there were only 191 available and at 0.9 sorties daily per machine they could only put up 171.9 sorties, which at 36.5 sorties to a kill translates to just 4.71 enemy aircraft brought down, assuming they could reach the Germans, for the Luftwaffe's bombers could outrun two-thirds of the Allied fighter force.[8] However, if Paul Martin's 15.5 sorties per kill is accepted, then 10 to 11 Germans were destroyed.

On 10 May the Armée de l'Air had an inventory of 421 bombers *aux armées*, of which 233 (55.3 percent) were serviceable and 184 ready for combat (46 percent): 14 Lioré-et-Olivier LeO-451 heavy, 25 Breguet Br-693 light, 29 Amiot AM-143 heavy, and 6 Farman F-222 heavy, all together 74 bombers to face the Luftwaffe and the Wehrmacht. At dawn on 10 May, however, 5 AM-143s were destroyed on the ground.

The FAF on 10 May had eleven different aircraft types spread over two hundred airfields in northeast France.[9] But even the same types manufactured

TABLE 36. Order of Battle and Commanders of the Armée de l'Air, 10 May 1940

COMMANDER-IN-CHIEF, AVIATION FORCES: GENERAL JOSEPH VUILLEMIN		
AREA	AVIATION COOPERATION FORCES (WITH FRENCH ARMY UNIT): GENERAL MARCEL TÉTU	AVIATION RESERVE FORCES
Zone of Air Operations—North: General Henri d'Astier de la Vigerie	Forces Aériennes 107 (VII Armée): Colonel Chambe	Groupement de Chasse 21 (Fighter Group 21): General Pinsard
	Forces Aériennes 101 (l'Armée): General Cononne	Groupement de Chasse 23 (Fighter Group 23): General Romatet
	Forces Aériennes 102 (l'Armée): General Roques	
		Groupement de Chasse 25 (Fighter Group 25): Colonel de Moussac
		Commandant de Chasse de nuit de la region parisienne (Night Fighter, Paris Region): Lt-Colonel François Dordilly
		I Division Aérienne (Bombardement) (1st Aviation Bomber Division): General Philippe Escudier
Zone of Air Operations—South: General Robert Odic	Forces Aériennes 108 (VIII Armée): General Pierre Rousselot de Saint-Céran	Groupement de Chasse 24 (Fighter Group 24): Lt-Colonel Lamon
	Forces Aériennes 38 (45 Corps d'Armée): Commandant Toucanne	6 Division Aérienne (6th Aviation Divsion) : General Jean Hebrard
Zone of Air Operations—Alps: General Laurens	Forces Aériennes de l'Armée des Alpes: General Laurens	5 Groupes de Chasse Groupement mixte de Chasse de nuit No. 4 ?? (5 Groups of Mixed Night Fighters): Lt-Colonel Giraud
		11 Division Aérienne (11th Aviation Division): General Paul Gama

Source: Claude d'Abzac-Epézy, *L'Armée de l'Air de Vichy, 1940–1944* (Vincennes: SHAA, 1997), 136.

TABLE 37. Allocation of Armée de l'Air Aircraft, **10 May 1940**

AIRCRAFT TYPE	NORTH AFRICA AND COLONIES	INTERIOR FRANCE	FIRST-LINE AIRCRAFT	SECOND-LINE AIRCRAFT	TOTAL TO ARMIES	TOTAL: GENERAL
Fighters	237	1,176	637	352	989	2,402
*Modern**	*150*	*909*	*609*	*337*	*946*	*2,005*
Bombers	228	510	242	179	421	1,159
Modern	*111*	*233*	*128*	*103*	*231*	*575*
Reconnaissance	85	613	489	277	766	1,464
Modern	*57*	*228*	*358*	*231*	*589*	*874*
Total	**550**	**2,299**	**1,368**	**808**	**2,176**	**5,025**
Modern	***318***	***1,370***	***1,095***	***671***	***1,766***	***3,454***

Source: Claude d'Abzac-Epézy, *L'Armée de l'Air de Vichy, 1940–1944* (Vincennes: SHAA, 1997), 54.

* Modern aircraft were those of the new generation of all-metal machines.

in two different factories were not compatible, so that parts could not be inter-changed. (In this regard it is of interest to note that in America, even from 1878 onward, U.S. Army wagons had interchangeable parts, facilitating supply and maintenance.) In addition the French POL (petrol, oil, lubricants) system was inflexible with its pipelines supplemented with static depots, railway tank cars, petrol drums, and tins (the depots were set afire by the French as soon as they were forced to retreat).

In addition to unserviceable aircraft, the FAF also had a quantitative problem in air matériel. Because of an influx of orders, manufacturers' facili-ties became crowded, hampering production, and thus incomplete machines were moved to the Centres de Réception des Avions de Series (CRAS), which then had to test them and pass them onto the arsenals to be fully equipped to *bon de guerre* standards and to be declared finished, but not available for issue.

According to Buffotot and Ogier, on 10 May the Armée de l'Air had 637 *chasseur* and received 597 during the Battle of France. But of these, 349 (58.5 percent) were held at the arsenal (*Establishment de l'air armaments* 301) at Chateaudun,[10] and of the average thirty-two aircraft delivered daily by the con-tractors, ten stayed at the arsenals and twenty-two went to the units. By 1 June, 62 percent of the *chasseur* were unavailable (*indisponible*) and so the Armée de l'Air was thus ill supplied with modern aircraft.

On 10 May in Metropolitan France the Armée de l'Air had twenty-four groups of single-seat *chasseur* totaling 637 machines and four night-fighter *escadrilles* with Potez 631s. The latter were part of Groupement 21, which had five *groupes de chasse* to defend Paris and the lower Seine. Groupement 25 had two *groupes* to cover the French 7e Armée (Seventh Army) along the Belgian frontier, Groupement 23 with four *groupes* was to cover the 2e (Second) and 9e (Ninth) Armées along the Belgian-Luxemburg frontier south to Malmedy where Groupement 24 with seven *groupes* protected the Franco-German frontier all the way to Basle.[11]

Events in the May–June Battle

The episodes that follow in the Battle of France include only a selection of the sorties flown, and it is important for the reader to be reminded once again that in air actions a rule of thumb is that if claims are divided by three or perhaps five, the result equals about what the opponent admits he lost. (See Tables 38–40.)

The main Luftwaffe force employed in the west consisted of 380 bombers, 800 Me-109 and 640 Me-110 fighters, and 475 Ju-52 transports. Furthermore the Luftwaffe was clearly there to support and cover the Wehrmacht, and its units were controlled by two battle-experienced generals—Hugo Sperrle, a Luftwaffe officer, Luftflotte 3 Commander, and Albert Kesserling, a Wehrmacht veteran in charge of Luftflotte 2. The Wehrmacht attack in the west on 10 May surprised the Allies and quickly captured the key bridges across the Meuse at Sedan. The German Panzers and infantry poured across and soon broke through the French lines.

Although the Wehrmacht rumbled forward with 1,500 tanks in a one-hundred-mile-long column with infantry to follow, the Anglo-French air arms received no orders to attack. French fear of Luftwaffe reprisals limited orders to reconnaissance and fighter sorties. Only at 1100 hours were the Allied Air Forces released to attack German columns and airfields; but they were to avoid

TABLE 38. Allied Victory Claims by Country, Battle of France

COUNTRY	CLAIMS
Great Britain	821 (by fighters alone)
France	853 (fighter + DCA)
Netherlands	525 (fighter + DCA)
Belgium	No more than 100
Total	**2,299**

Source: Patrick Facon, "Les mille victoires de l'Armée de l'Air en 1939–1940: Autopsie d'un mythe," *Review Historique des Armées* 4 (Nov. 1997): Table D, 83–84.

built-up areas, including villages packed with Panzer units. The orders also put off-limits the industrial and communication centers, which Allied planning had designated as prime targets. When orders did arrive, the French day bombers were so visibly confused they stayed on the ground.

TABLE 39. Table of Victories, Battle of France, per *Chasse* Commander General Harcourt

GROUPES	CONFIRMED	PROBABLE	TOTAL
I/5	85	26	111
I/3	51	21	72
II/4	48	23	71
II/5	48	22	70
II/3	34	16	50
II/7	40	10	50
III/2	35	11	46
I/4	35	7	42
I/8	36	4	40
II/2	17	22	39
III/3	31	6	37
I/1	23	7	30
III/1	25	4	29
II/6	18	11	29
II/1	25	4	29
I/2	21	7	28
III/7	16	11	27
I/6	14	11	25
III/6	19	4	23
II/9	14	5	19
II/10	15	4	19
III/10	13	6	19
II/8	10	2	12
III/9	2		2
Total	**675**	**244**	**919**

Source: *Bulletin de renseignement de l'aviation de chasse, 20 juillet* 1940. SHAA 1D6. As cited in Patrick Facon, "Les milles victorires de l'Armée de l'Air en 1939–1940: Autopsie d'un mythe," *Revue Historiques des Armées* 4 (Nov. 1997): 87. According to General Lucien Robineau, Facon was quoting the World War II fighter pilot Jean Gisclon, *Les mille victoires de la chasse française mai-juin 1940*. Facon has come to believe the number of confirmed victories was about 600.

TABLE 40. After the Battle and Luftwaffe Tallies by Type of Losses for 12 August–23 September and May and June 1940

TYPE	GAF AFTER THE BATTLE MAY, JUNE	RAF AFTER THE BATTLE 12 AUG.-23 SEPT.	GAF TALLY, MAY: SHOT DOWN/ DAMAGED	GAF TALLY, JUNE: SHOT DOWN/ DAMAGED
Ju-52			209/18	7/4
Do-17	68	192	131/54	29/13
Ju-87	9	59	78/26	33/5
Ju-88	116	114	68/14	22/9
He-111	156	102	213/57	47/15
Me-110	75	124	71/14	27/6
Me-109	202	190	142/37	71/29
Total*	626	781	912/220**	236/81
Ratio, Loss:Damage			4.1:1	2.9:1
% Loss/ Damage			62.9/15.2	16.3/5.6

Source: After the Battle, *The Battle of Britain* (Mark II) (London: Battle of Britain Printing International, 1982), 536–705; United Kingdom, Air Ministry, CAB 106/282.

*Grand Total, GAF *After the Battle* Tally, May/June and 12 Aug.–23 Sept.: 1,407
 Grand Total, GAF Tally, Shot Down/Damaged, May/June: 1,449 [Original read 1,433]
**Original read 912/210.

In the Netherlands the Westhaven aerodrome at Amsterdam was taken in twenty minutes by German paratroopers and airborne units in Junkers Ju-52 transport/medium bombers, and shortly the Germans had air superiority over Holland. On 14 May Rotterdam was bombed when a recall signal failed to reach the German aircraft in time, and the Dutch surrendered that evening. The Royal Netherlands Air Force (RNAF) was finished, but the Germans had suffered the loss of 167 Ju-52s with another 98 damaged beyond repair. All told, the GAF lost about 500 machines.

Meanwhile German airborne forces had seized Belgian road junctions and landed inside Fort Eben Emael, forcing its surrender. By nightfall on 10 May the Belgian air force had lost almost one-third of its machines and by 14 May was virtually wiped out, though fifteen old Fairey Firefly biplanes flew until 16 May when the remnants moved to France. On 10 May the German forces hit before dawn at Metz, Dijon, Romilly-sur-Seine, and Lyon, in addition to Allied airfields.

The RAF in the Battle of France was under Air Marshal A. S. Barratt, the former AOC of Army Cooperation Command. By 10 May Barratt was AOC-in-C, British Air Forces France, which included the Air Component of the British Expeditionary Force (ACBEF) and the Advanced Air Striking Force (AASF) of Bomber Command in Great Britain. In the Battle of Britain all the fighters would be under ACM Sir Hugh Dowding of Fighter Command, as opposed to the Armée de l'Air's *escadrilles* being split between the air zones of operations north, east, and south—ZOAN, ZOAE, and ZOAS. And though in theory General Vuillemin was the commandant en chef des forces aériennes (air commander), in practice he and his forces were subordinate to the army's Grand Quartier Général ([GQG], Armée de Terre field headquarters), and the French GQG under General Georges.

On 10 May the ACBEF had four Hurricane and two Gladiator fighter squadrons (ninety-six aircraft). The Gloster Gladiator biplane fighters of No. 607 and No. 615 squadrons were due to be replaced with Hurricanes, but that was postponed when the campaign started. By 20 May the Gladiators had made an exaggerated claim of 72 enemy destroyed and 56 damaged (probably of the total 128 some 43–27), but their records were lost in the subsequent evacuation. By 15 May the ACBEF total was eighteen serviceable Gladiators and twelve Hurricanes, but that same day their airfield was heavily bombed and the fuel dump destroyed. The remaining unserviceable five to six Gladiators were destroyed by the RAF, and the ground crew was returned to England on 21 May.

The ACBEF had been reinforced on 10 May by three more Hurricane squadrons and a third was added to the two attached to the AASF. No. 501 Squadron landed on an AASF field, refueled, and took off at once against a raid, returning to find that additional pilots and the ground crew had arrived by air from Britain. In two days they claimed eighteen enemy for their own loss of two. The eight Hurricane squadrons faced great odds, which were lessened on 13 May when a further thirty-two Hurricanes were flown to France. Then Air Chief Marshal Dowding dug in his heels. The Hurricanes were to protect the BEF. Unfortunately the Fairey Battle and Blenheim bombers of both the AASF and of the ACBEF suffered greatly when sent out unescorted on 14 May. The RAF's bomber offensive in support of the Battle of France, in Robert Jackson's words, "wholehearted though it may have been, failed to influence the outcome of the Battle of France in the slightest."[12]

The RAF only began to develop salvage and repairs in 1940 in spite of the lessons of the Royal Flying Corps/Royal Air Force experience of the 1914–1918 period. Some 172 Hurricanes were left behind in France during May–June

1940 for want of pilots to fly them home. Only 74 had been shot down of the 261 sent to France all told. Still, once the repair organization in England functioned, by October some 200 Hurricanes per month were being returned to service there.[13]

The Luftwaffe in the Battle

It is difficult to find an account of the Luftwaffe in the campaigns in the west that details individual raids. In general, the German Luftwaffe operated bomber formations of roughly 100 Dornier Do-17 light and Heinkel He-111 medium bombers. For the crossing of the Meuse on 13 May, the GAF flew 310 bomber and 200 Ju-87 Stuka dive-bomber sorties, and after the crossing and breakthrough, attacks were concentrated along the path of the advance so as to eliminate roadblocks, strong points, supply depots, and airfields. The French railways were disrupted and the Allies prevented from mounting a counterattack with armor on particular targets.

On 23 May operations were halted short of Dunkirk to allow the Wehrmacht to consolidate gains, to rest, repair, and refuel, and enable the infantry to catch up. The GAF was still operating from bases in Germany, so while Goering boasted that the Luftwaffe could destroy the Allies around Dunkirk and Calais, his forces in fact could not do it. They flew many sorties, but at a very reduced rate after three weeks of intensive campaigning.

General Karl Rudolf Gerd von Rundstedt's 24 May halt before Dunkirk was caused by a fear of a counterattack to the south. He had about 1,500 tanks in running order and many others on the verge of repair. But Goering's Luftwaffe was incapable of filling the gap and reducing Dunkirk. Most of the bombers' impotence was due to being unserviceable and unable to operate at night, while fighters had to await establishment of forward airfields. As for the Battle of Britain, the Germans had no long-term strategy; they had not intended to invade and so lacked plans and wanted Intelligence on the island. The British thought German industry was near collapse while greatly overestimating the Luftwaffe's strength.

The Luftwaffe could only operate fully on 2.5 of the 9 days of Dunkirk, from 26 May to 4 June, and then faced the new Spitfire opposition. Attacks had also to be made on Calais, Lille, and Amiens, and the effort cost the Germans 200 aircraft. From 1 June the Luftwaffe also attacked the Armée de l'Air in the south of France, then carried out an especially large raid against the aircraft industry and aerodromes in the Paris region in Operation Paula on 3 June, which included high- and low-level bombing and strafing by Me-109s.

But on the night of 9–10 May the starlit sky was clear (Table 41). When Luftwaffe aircraft began to take off at 0500 hours, French and British ground crews were relaxing in the pleasant spring weather on forty-seven bases in eastern France. The dawn attacks destroyed four French MS-406 fighters and damaged thirteen. Other *chasseur* were soon in action before their fields were attacked, but the Luftwaffe claimed forty-nine destroyed and ten probables. The lack of a Spitfire photo-reconnaissance unit (PRU), as opposed to the single such aircraft sent out in June on sorties from the United Kingdom, allowed the BEF to be surprised on 10 May.

TABLE 41. Weather, 10 May–24 June 1940, and Operations for the RAF and the Armée de l'Air

DATE	CONDITIONS
10–12 May	Clear: CAVU (ceiling and visibility unlimited)
13 May	Not a good weather day
14 May	
15 May–21 May	Hazy, but flyable
22 May	Bad weather—rain and low clouds; all operations cancelled by AASF
23 May	Bad weather and heavy clouds
26 May	Driving rain
27 May	Good cloud cover
28 May	Weather poor: solid cloud cover, heavy-rain
29 May	Low cloud patches
30 May	Bad weather, but some operations
31 May	Weather terrible
1-6 June	Good flying weather
7 June	Very hot and dry
8 June–10 June	Early fog
11 June	Sea fog, haze and smoke
12 June	Low, heavy clouds and industrial haze—could shield/hide aircraft (low, heavy clouds "blinded" flak)
13 June	Poor visibility all night
14 June	Weather terrible; low cloud obscured targets; by mid-afternoon intense activity and to England

Source: Compiled from Norman L. R. Franks, *Valiant Wings: Battle and Blenheim Squadrons over France 1940* (London: Crécy Books, 1994).

The Luftwaffe had a 78 percent serviceability rate, with 3,530 first-line planes compared with 1,368 of the French—nearly a 3:1 advantage over that enemy.[14]

The British Air Campaign

The air campaign was both in France and from England in four phases:

- 10–15 May 1940. The Air Component of six, later sixteen, squadrons fought successfully to protect the BEF in its move to the Dyle. At the same time, the AASF suffered heavily trying to stem the German advance, aided by squadrons of Bomber Command from England. Air reconnaissance was important in these opening days.
- 16–22 May. The Air Component was further strengthened by six squadrons operating from British bases. When the northern airfields in France were overrun, the ACBEF was sent back to England. At the same time the AASF was forced to move further south; it continued to harass the enemy, but after heavy daylight losses only at night. Bomber Command aircraft were more suitable and they continued both day and night attacks and the bombing of strategic targets in Germany. AASF fighters primarily defended the force's airfields, also patrolling over the French on the Aisne, and executing reconnaissance sorties.
- 23 May–4 June. The Air Component fighters moved to England and No. 11 Group Fighter Command fought to defend the beaches at Dunkirk. In the south the AASF sought to prevent the Armée de l'Air from being dive-bombed, protect the airfields, and cover day bombers. AASF bombers continued their night attacks on enemy forces, while Bomber Command from Home attacked the enemy pressing the withdrawal from Dunkirk.
- 5–24 June. The RAF continued to help the Allied armies with Air Marshal Barratt having control of all of Bomber Command's medium bombers in No. 2 Group operating from Britain.[15]

The British and the French in Combat

During the morning of 10 May, AOC-in-C Barratt of the British Air Forces France decided on his own to order the Advanced Air Striking Force off to support General George's hard-pressed ZOAN troops. Four waves of Fairey Battles of eight aircraft each were escorted by five Hurricanes each of No. 1 and No. 73 squadrons, RAF, which patrolled at 13,000 feet while the Battles went into attack. Of the thirty-two attackers, thirteen were shot down by the enemy's very effective flak. Later in the afternoon, another thirty-two Battles, unescorted, went in, and the German Me-109s shot down a further ten and the rest were badly damaged. On 11 May a low-level attack by eight more Battles never reached the target bridges. Next came the turn of the Blenheims. No. 114 Squadron was to take off shortly after dawn on the 12 May for the same target, but a low-level Do-17K surprise attack destroyed the aircraft on the ground while still in peacetime fashion parked in line. The Belgians then sent their nine Battles also to strike the bridges over the Albert Canal in northeast Belgium, connecting Antwerp and Liège, and lost six to flak en route, while the one-hundred-pound bombs of the remaining three did no damage.

According to plan, immediately on 10 May, upon hearing of the German attack, General Vuillemin, as commanding general of the Armée de l'Air, turned over to General Marcel Tétu, commander of the northeast assault forces, all the strategic reconnaissance: the Breguet 693, the assault *groupes*, and all the *chasseur* on the northeast front. Tétu also was authorized to use from ZOAN the heavy LeO-451 bombers and the reconnaissance Br-693 light attack machines. However, these units were not effective on 10 May as they were busy changing station. Still the *chasseur* flew 360 sorties with only 200 pilots (averaging 1.8 sorties per pilot) and claimed forty-four enemy downed with a loss of twenty-two of their own. That night two *groupes* of French Farman heavy bombers struck three German airfields.

The Armée de l'Air had based its thinking and planning on the Armée de Terre assumption that in a long war it would parry the opening enemy offensive and then stay on the defensive for several years à la 1918. The French had learned nothing at all from the 1918 experience. The theory was that airfields would remain in fixed locations and that the FAF could rely upon a stable logistics system. Fierce fighting took place during 10–12 May and then exhaustion began to set in. By 15 May 1940 all of the above misassumptions had been swept away.

On 16 May General Vuillemin decided to withdraw and regroup, and this was done on 17 May, by which time the *groupes de chasse* were seriously depleted. *Chasseur escadrilles* were fatigued by constant uncertainties as to the channels of command, movement of bases (which was also an RAF problem), improvised quarters and lack of rest, and shortage of spares. Although fatigue had been noted during prewar maneuvers, nothing had been done to alleviate it. The night-bombing program had started in great frustration during the darkness of 10–11 May when an Amiot 143 bomber returned from reconnaissance over the Ardennes to report German convoys roaring through the mountains with their headlights on. But the commanding general of the 1e Division Aérienne (1st Air Division) had refused to order a strike as no such target was on the agreed Allied list worked out during the winter of the Phoney War. Instead he sent a small force to bomb the German airfield at Bonn-Hangelar, which the planes could not locate. On the night of the 11–12 May single aircraft were dispatched with discretionary orders to attack targets of opportunity outside built-up areas. But even operating at full throttle, enemy flak took its toll, and by 14 May only twenty-one of forty-five bombers were still available, a number that was further reduced by making daylight attacks on the various bridges.

Yet because morale remained high, night operations continued through 23 May, by which time bomber Groupement 10 had flown 107 sorties. Bomber units reequipping in the south were ordered up in the emergency with a mixture of equipment—Bloch 210s and Amiot 354s. In all fourteen Blochs and ten unarmed Amiots arrived at the front. By the end of May, eighteen Amiots had been lost. More surprising was the loss of only seven Bloch 210s, which were unsuitable for combat and could not get off the ground with a full load even after a 1,500-yard run. So on 26 May the commander of GB 1/11 of Groupement 11 ordered the units sent to training and the crews to LeO-451 conversion courses. Bloch bombers remained on operations in two other *escadrilles*, but their disastrous record urged they be withdrawn. Nevertheless until the end of May the Bloch and the Amiot 143 units still received replacement aircraft to keep them up to strength until mid-June. By then GB I/21 and II/21 of Groupement 9 had flown 677 sorties and logged 2,000 hours in the air, mostly in the Bloch 210.

While the focus here is on the *chasse*, the fighters, the Armée de l'Air did have other types, too, but not many of them. Of the heavy bomber, the LeO 451, there were very few, and their engines were so fragile they had to be changed every eighteen hours.[16] There were also 25 Farman F222 four-engine bombers that flew only at night, and then only two sorties, and lost 2 in accidents. Of the modern Potez 631 reconnaissance machines, there were 700, and of the 630–637 variants, 1,100, most of which had been withdrawn by 10 May. And the majority of these were unfit for daytime operations, easy victims of the German Me-109 and Me-110, a lesson the RAF had learned by the end of 1939.

But on the morning of 19 May the theoretical front-line strength of three LeO-451 French bomber *groupes*, said to total fifty-two, was reduced to ten by the Luftwaffe as the aircraft were parked in line at Persan-Beaumont. The LeO-451 force then lost four more on 20 May and was withdrawn to regroup having suffered sixteen losses in 140 sorties (11.5 percent); and twenty-five more were written off (a rate of 4.5 sorties per aircraft lost, as compared with 33 sorties per aircraft lost for the fighters).[17] The Amiot 143 bombers flew until 16 June. Notable was an attack by six aircraft singly on the Badische Anlin factory at Ludwigshafen, Germany, which was a success. But on 17 June, fearing retaliation, general headquarters of the air force (GQGA) banned further such attacks, even though the Luftwaffe had already hit Paris and other cities. Once the Germans crossed the Aisne River, the Amiots were sent to disrupt German lines of communication (LOC), but to little effect.

On 14 June the Amiots had begun to move south, but were severely handicapped by a general shortage of munitions, fuel, and spares, which prevented sustaining air drops to the French encircled in the Vosges Mountains near the German border in eastern France. In six weeks the Amiots lost forty-nine of the unarmored machines, yet GB I/34 and II/34 of Groupement 9 flew 197 sorties while losing only four machines in combat. The best loss rate was that of the Farman 222 and 223, which in the nine months lost only one, and that in an accident. The LeO-451s did some night bombing throughout the campaign, most notably of the BMW factory in Munich.

The War Cabinet in London by 14 May had decided that with little more than fighters being sent to France, the way to influence the struggle was to interdict German communications through railway junctions, marshaling yards, and the lines along the Rhine, especially in view of the Luftwaffe's raid on Rotterdam. On the night of 15 May a mixed force of Vickers Wellington, Armstrong-Whitworth Whitley, and Handley Page Hampden bombers attacked rail lines and other targets in the Ruhr. From 11 May to 15 June the RAF made twenty-seven major night attacks upon German targets from the Rhineland to the Somme. But as it was all done on an individual crew basis, these strikes lacked focus and coordination.

Both 11 and 12 May were very active and confused days of alerts and sorties in constant uncertainty, which quickly fatigued pilots. French Curtiss Hawks claimed sixteen Ju-87 Stukas in a few minutes over the Ardennes, twenty-two on 12 May, thirty-eight in the first three days of the Battle of France. Groupe I/14 had thirty-four Hawks on 10 May, but had been reduced to seven by the following morning. Yet, in spite of inferior armament, the seven Hawks held their own that morning. This was followed on 12 May by eighteen Breguet 693 bombers escorted by eighteen MS-406 fighters. It was a sortie delayed because a number of Br-693s lacked bomb-release gear, which had arrived by truck only before dawn on the same day—eight months after the war had begun. Eight Breguets were lost in this tree-top attack. However, later that day twelve LeO-451s bombed unscathed.

Ten of the Armée de l'Air's eleven MS-406 *groupes* (Table 35) had constant engine problems and their 7.5-mm machine guns froze up at altitude. The 20-mm cannon above the engine stayed warm enough to be reliable, but carried only sixty rounds. The MS-406 fighters had the disadvantage of being 60 mph slower than the Me-109s, which flew in a circle five thousand feet above the Moranes and then attacked in pairs as they had learned to do in Spain. The Moranes lost five out of nine aircraft. On 21 May, GC III/7 of Groupement de Chasse 22 ZOAE, put up all of its fifteen MS-406s, met fifty Luftwaffe Me-109s, and lost four and had three badly damaged. Losses in both pilots and machines weakened III/7 even as mechanics cannibalized older aircraft to try to maintain the serviceability of others. On 29 May five replacement aircraft were delivered to III/7 but, as the British would say, they were found to be "clapped-out" and unfit for operational flying. In the hands of a skilled pilot such as Le Niger, the MS-406 could survive and conquer, but many succumbed from inexperience and lack of R/T for warnings and commands.

Meanwhile GC III/3 of Groupement de Chasse 21, ZOAN, on 25 May had been withdrawn to Toulouse to reequip with the "dream machine," the Dewoitine D-520. On 10 May only GC I/3 of ZOAA (air zone of operations Alps) was operational on the Dewoitines, and a second had only begun to convert on 9 May. Though considered the dream machine, the D-520 had needed—as was normal with a brand-new type—some one hundred modifications since December 1939. The cause was hasty production from an excellent design, but a lack of a thorough testing and inspection program at the factory and at the Armée de l'Air reception centers—a serious flaw in the FAF's preparations for war. GC I/3 was moved on 11 May from Cannes to Wez-Thuizy near Perins with thirty D-520s and thirty pilots. It was soon in action and giving a good account of itself. It lost its first two pilots on 15 and 16 May, respectively, and on 17 May lost seven machines destroyed on the ground and was at once ordered to Estaly. That field was bombed twice, but fortunately the D-520s were on sorties. The attack would be repeated on 22 May, and one D-520 was shot down.

At noon on 12 May, French General Gamelin phoned General François d'Astier de la Vigerie, commander of the air arms in the zone of air operations north, and ordered him to do everything possible to stop the Germans, even to bombing the villages with Panzers in them. Thus on 12 May GB I/12 and GB II/12 of Groupement 6, 1ᵉ Division Aérienne de Bombardement (1st Aviation Bomber Division) were ordered to launch their ten LeO-451 modern bombers against the Meuse bridges. However, the bombers achieved little, losing one with the rest *hors de combat*—out of action—while the MS-406 escort claimed five enemy aircraft for a loss of four. A follow-up in late afternoon by twelve Home Defence–based Blenheim light bombers from Britain at three thousand feet cost four of the aircraft and all the rest damaged, for no result.

A similar disaster also occurred on 12 May when No. 139 Squadron dispatched seven Blenheims to the Meuse and lost five to Luftwaffe fighters. AOC-in-C Barratt, hard pressed, again had to send in the Battles during daylight. Five took off and were soon surprised by heavy flak—Intelligence did not know the Germans were already so far west. At the same time, the Battles' escort of eight Hurricanes tangled with one hundred enemy fighters and lost six. All five Battles also died, though the river crossing was put out of action for thirty minutes by bomb damage. Then ten of twenty-four Blenheims from England were lost to the Luftwaffe fighters and another six Battles, the latter losing 62 percent of establishment in three days.

The Armée de l'Air fighters were also badly mauled. *Groupes* had been pulled out of the reserves, and then on 13 May Vuilleman had been forced to disband the Basse-Seine defenses, sending its *chasseur* groups to ZOAN with other fighter and bomber groups also being placed at General Tétu's disposal. The overall air commander of ZOAN, General d'Astier de la Vigerie, had to meet the new German threat between Dinant and Sedan with a small attack by LeO-451 bombers, followed by ancient Amiot 143 bombers at night, in an attempt to allow General André-Georges Corap's weak 9ᵉ Armée to recapture the bridgeheads across the Meuse. All day on 13 May operations were paralyzed by lack of reliable target Intelligence. But still, the bombers had suffered heavily. Of the LeO-451s only five of the fourteen original machines in two *groupes* remained, though eight new ones had been flown up as replacements, while Groupe GBA 18 had only twelve of its initial establishment of twenty-five serviceable on 13 May.

So it was that early on 14 May sixty-seven Fairey Battles of the British Advanced Air Striking Force were sent again to the bridges over the Meuse, and thirty-two of them fell to German flak and fighters. In the afternoon thirteen Amiot 143 and six LeO-451 bombers followed, and they too suffered heavily. On the night of 15–16 May the AM-143s again went in. By 18 May the French bombers were impotent and incapable of affecting the struggle.[18] On 14 May, under urgent French appeal, two flights of Battles also attacked without loss the pontoon bridges across the Meuse at Sedan, but with little result. That afternoon all the French bombers attacked the three bridgeheads across the Meuse.

The AASF was now down to sixty-two Battles and eight Blenheims, all battered. All seventy were ordered to attack. The cauldron burned up thirty-five more Battles and five Blenheims. Two pontoon bridges were destroyed and two damaged. The RAF lost a total 102 aircrew killed, wounded, and POW. At dusk twenty-eight No. 2 Group Blenheims from Britain attacked and lost seven.

That evening, 16 May 1940, the AOC-in-C Fighter Command, ACM Dowding, stood his ground before the Cabinet in London and refused to send another 120 Hurricanes to France on the valid grounds that they could not stem the tide and to send them would seriously jeopardize the defense of Great Britain against the "German air menace." From Headquarters Fighter Command, Bentley Priory, Stanmore, Middlesex, on 16 May, Dowding wrote a classified "Secret" letter to Prime Minister Churchill:[19]

Sir,

I have the honour to refer to the very serious calls which have recently been made upon the Home Defence Fighter Units in an attempt to stem the German invasion of the Continent.

2. I hope and believe that our Armies may yet be victorious in France and Belgium, but we have to face the possibility that they may be defeated.

3. In this case I presume that there is no-one who will deny that England should fight on, even though the remainder of the Continent of Europe is dominated by the Germans.

4. For this purpose it is necessary to retain some minimum fighter strength in this country and I must request that the Air Council will inform me what they consider this minimum strength to be, in order that I may make my dispositions accordingly.

5. I would remind the Air Council that the last estimate which they made as to the force necessary to defend this country was 52 Squadrons, and my strength has now been reduced to the equivalent of 36 Squadrons.

6. Once a decision has been reached as to the limit on which the Air Council and the cabinet are prepared to stake the existence of the country, it should be made clear to the Allied Commanders on the Continent that not a single aeroplane from Fighter Command beyond the limit will be sent across the Channel, no matter how desperate the situation may become.

7. It will, of course, be remembered that the estimate of 52 Squadrons was based on the assumption that the attack would come from the eastwards except in so far as the defences might be outflanked in flight. We have now to face the possibility that attacks may come from Spain or even from the North coast of France. The result is that our line is very much extended at the same time as our resources are reduced.

8. I must point out that within the last few days the equivalent of 10 Squadrons have been sent to France, that the Hurricane Squadrons remaining in this country are seriously depleted, and that the more Squadrons which are sent to France the higher will be the wastage and the more insistent the demands for reinforcements.

9. I must therefore request that as a matter of paramount urgency the Air Ministry will consider and decide what level of strength is to be left to the Fighter Command for the defences of this country, and will assure me that when this level has been reached, not one fighter will be sent across the Channel however urgent and insistent the appeals for help may be.

10. I believe that, if an adequate fighter force is kept in this country, if the fleet remains in being, and if Home Forces are suitably organized to resist invasion, we should be able to carry on the war single handed for some time, if not indefinitely. But, if the Home Defence Force is drained away in desperate attempts to remedy the situation in France, defeat in France will involve the final, complete and irremediable defeat of this country.

> I have the honour to be,
> Sir,
> Your obedient Servant,
> [H. C. T. Dowding]
> Air Chief Marshal,
> Air Officer Commanding-in-Chief,
> Fighter Command, Royal Air Force.

At the time, Dowding had only thirty-nine fighter squadrons versus the approved fifty-two the Air Council said he needed. If he had not stood firm, the rate of loss of Hurricanes in France and Britain would have reduced that force to zero in fourteen days.

On 14 May the Amiot 143s had made noble efforts, but the mechanics servicing them were worn out and lacked spares. Out of the initial establishment of eleven, two *groupes* had only four *disponible*, one had seven out of twelve, and the other six out of eleven. Bomber Groupement 10 (GB 10) had five Bloch 200s, but was forbidden to fly over the front because of its initial losses. On the afternoon of 14 May, eighteen AM-143 bombers took off, escorted by twelve MS-406, twelve Bloch MB-151, and nine D-520 fighters. Six Amiots failed to rendezvous with their escorts and were ordered back to base. The remaining thirteen pressed on, only to dismay their escort by splitting into two groups, unaware due to radio difficulties that the target orders had been changed. Three Amiots were lost and the rest returned unfit for further action, thanks to flak and fighter damage. Of the eight unescorted LeO-451s, one was shot down and the rest were of no further use.

Late on 15 May the FAF launched a fifteen-plane bombing attack without loss. On that day, with the Germans across at Sedan, the French flew 150-strong patrols over the area allowing 12 and 16 sorties of Blenheims, each escorted by twenty-seven MS-406s fighters to attack. Four Blenheims were lost. By the end of 15 May, in only five days the RAF had lost 86 Battles, 39 Blenheims, 71 Hurricanes, and 9 liaison Lysanders (Army Cooperation machines) for a total of 205, plus 43 from No. 2 Group at Home—a total of 248, or 13.4 percent of the RAF's frontline force.[20] In the next few days the remaining LeO-451s were sent out singly or in pairs below 3,000 feet rather than at their best operating altitude of 15,000. As they lacked R/T, they could neither talk to each other nor to their escorts, whom they often failed to meet after their briefings. The bombers should have been based in the rear as they had ample range, but they were instead kept on undefended fields, close behind the front.

Two Fairey Battle squadrons were disbanded and the rest of the AASF sent back to Troyes to reorganize. Already on 16 May General Tétu's bases had been threatened by the German advance, and though he had launched an attack that afternoon, he lost four more bombers and the remainder were put out of action. On 17 May twelve Blenheims sent to attack German columns were jumped at six thousand feet and all but one downed. Also by 17 May the Army Cooperation Hurricanes claimed to have destroyed sixty-five enemy aircraft for a loss of twenty-two in the air and fifteen damaged on the ground, and fifteen pilots out of action. On that day, in addition, General Vuillemin and General Tétu agreed only to use the *chasse* to support troops in the front line and to tackle enemy bombers, hoping this would halt the increasingly heavy losses of fighters on escort duties. Thus during 16 and 17 May Armée de l'Air regrouped and reinforced, seven with an Aéronavale (French navy air arm) dive-bomber *groupe* bolstered by six *groupes* of fighters and aircraft and pilots from the training schools, so depleted were the *chasseurs*.

On 18 May twelve LeO-451 bombers that attacked the Avesnes-Landreines sector were smashed by flak; of the eight Breguet 693s that followed, four were shot down. On 19 May, all the LeO-451 bombers at Persan-Beaumont airfield were caught taking off and more or less damaged. Later in the day three of four-teen Breguet 693s were shot down trying to support the retreating Cinquième Armée (Fifth Army). All five night-fighter *escadrilles* were equipped with Potez 631s, and from 10 to 17 May had frequent alerts but sighted no Luftwaffe air-craft. Thus the GQGA decided to shift the planes to the daylight assault role.

Eighteen 631s were dispatched to attack enemy columns, but only two returned to one base and six to another, all those latter eight shot to pieces. On 18 May one night fighter scored a daylight kill. The next day the night fighters shot down another Luftwaffe He-111 bomber. But on the evening of 19 May two Potez were attacked by their own D-520s—the 631 did look like an Me-110 in the dusk. And amicide mistakes continued. Just before the end of the battle in June, ECB IV/13, Escadrille de Chasse de Nuit, received the new heavier armed Potez 631 fighter, which had been in process for two months. By 20 May there were no more left.

The Potez victims were the focus not only of French Armée de l'Air fighters, but also the concern of the French *défense contre avions* (DCA). In the second week of June the night-fighter bases were under constant Luftwaffe attack and lost several aircraft on the ground before being withdrawn on 10 June. Their last operation was on 23 June when only seven out of fifteen managed to take off from a rain-soaked airfield; six attacked enemy columns and returned to base.

Another of the Armée de l'Air workhorse machines, the Breguet 693— with 106 on charge on 10 May—had flown roughly 407 sorties and lost 59 aircraft with only 26 surviving into the Vichy regime from July onward—a rate of 6.9 sorties per aircraft lost. However, of the 254 Breguets manufactured up to the Franco-German armistice of 24 June, only the 106 had been delivered. For many days in early June these machines remained on airfields awaiting orders; then, after the Somme offensive began on 5 June, it was too late for the 693s to be effective.[21]

Yet before all this had transpired, on 19 May the BEF had begun to retreat to Dunkirk for evacuation. With the Air Component's bases threatened by the German advance, the Air Component AOC, Air Vice Marshal Blount, by 21 May regarded the situation as hopeless and ordered the Hawker Hurricane fighters evacuated to England. There two squadrons were sent north to rest and reequip while two fresh squadrons took their places on patrols over Dunkirk. Poorly armed, unescorted reconnaissance aircraft were easy victims of the German Messerschmitts. Some seventy-two were lost during 10–15 May. Even though the Potez 63-11 reconnaissance/observation craft was highly maneuverable, its three MAC (Manufacture d'Armes de Châtellerault) 1934 machine guns were unreliable and froze. On 19 May of eight Potez sent out, only two accomplished their mission; four were shot down, and two turned back damaged. And of the new high-speed Bloch 174 reconnaissance/bomber, only twenty-four had reached a front-line unit by 10 May. Groupe II/133 received its first Bloch on 29 March and was the only Bloch 174 unit completely up to establishment before the armistice.[22] The 174 was faster at 331 mph than the D-520 *chasseur,* so it could escape fighters. Its few losses came from flak.

General Lucien Robineau has noted the travels of GC II/154 between September 1939 and the end of June 1940. It changed fields eighteen times, came under three different administrative organizations, seven ground commanders, and twelve maintenance parks.[23] The twenty-four *chasse escadrilles* moved a total of 300 times from 25 August 1939 to 24 June 1940, with 187 (62 percent) of those translations being after the end of May.[24] The RAF squadrons had similar trials and tribulations. No. 85 Squadron was at Mons et Chaussée during 10–26 April; Lille/Seclin 26 April–19 May; Menille 19–20 May; Boulogne, 20–23 May; and then to the United Kingdom. No. 87 Squadron was at Amiens 15 April–3 May 1940; Senon 3–10 May; Lille-Seclin 10–20 May; Merville 20–22 May; and to the United Kingdom.[25]

The French airline pilots' excellent magazine *Icare* published a series of issues on the Battle of France, and from these and Paul Martin's work it is possible to report at *escadrille* level.[26] Armée de l'Air pilot Pierre Courteville attended the *chasse* school at Oran on the MS-406 fighter in early 1940 and returned to France with 250 hours, but was posted to a Bloch 152 unit. The 152s had two 20-mm cannon in the wings and two fuselage-mounted 7.62-mm machine guns. He thought the aircraft to be huge and robust, yet gross as compared with the nimble MS-406. (The Luftwaffe's Me-109 was 80 to 100 kph faster.) Not until 3 June did Courteville see real combat. When sent to Villacoublay to bring back replacements, the pilots found plenty of Bloch 152s, but none with propellers.[27] Another Bloch 152 unit, GC II/10, had lost "a terrible number of pilots" by late May. The replacements were twelve Poles. Henri Gille wrote in *Icare* regarding the Bloch 152, which he described as a very good aircraft, much better than the MS-406, but one hundred km slower that the German Me-109, which could only be fought by diving on it as dogfighting was fatal.[28] By early June the pilots of these machines were physically and nervously fatigued as well as overwhelmed.[29] Although the pilots of GC II/3 had 300 to 350 hours or more, some had not yet fired their guns in the Bloch 152 by 19 May 1940.[30]

Escadrille GC II I/5 was mounted on Curtiss H-75s, which had for them many new features but lacked manuals and nonmetric tools. The result was that training was difficult, as the machines were frequently unserviceable, all not helped by a shortage of young mechanics. The pilots thought that H-75 Hawks were a delight as their engines did not leak and thus there was no need for oil pans on the hangar floors. But the French bureaucracy insisted on peacetime habits of maintenance in the open because of the lack of hangars, even though the aircraft park was but twenty-five miles (forty km) away at Reims.

As a result, the very cold winter of 1939–1940 caused damage to the engines though the oil was diluted. After 10 May the *indisponible* rate rose rapidly in spite of the best efforts of an old French soldier familiar with metal aeronautical production who repaired wings and empennages but let the fuselages go.

The FAF began to adapt the American system of specialization, as the Hawk was an advanced machine with, for instance, electric constant-speed propellers. Soon cannibalization began to keep some machines flying by stripping parts from others.[31] Groupe I/5 was well below its fifty-four mechanics establishment and was especially short of armorers, equipment trades, and electricians. The *groupe* had an initial establishment of twenty-five aircraft and had reached twenty-six on 18 May, but of these only three were serviceable out of seventeen in GC I/34.[32]

Pilot Performance

During the Dunkirk operation, RAF medical officers observed that extreme individual effort over several days resulted in "gross fatigue" or mental exhaustion of pilots. That could only be overcome by twelve to forty-two hours of uninterrupted sleep. After severe periods, pilots were put on nonoperational duties.[33] Pilot fatigue was a common problem in all three air forces. With the Luftwaffe's pilots flying four sorties a day, their acuity would have declined, much as RAF medical officers observed in Fighter Command pilots. Four hours per day or more for five days was the equivalent of eighty hours per twenty-eight-day month. Such a pace could only be maintained with adequate rest, a situation not possible camping out during a blitzkrieg campaign. Medical officers did not keep statistics on fatigue at first as they regarded it as a natural phenomenon for which the obvious cure was sleep. And the same problem was even more true of French pilots who were at readiness for hours awaiting orders or on the move to new and strange surroundings and flying machines that were not only inferior, but in doubtful working order.[34]

During the later Battle of Britain, which began in July, conditions for RAF pilots were comparable to those in the six weeks in France. Sorties were not scheduled, but were sporadic, depending upon enemy actions. Pilots therefore were at readiness for much of the day, unless stood down by weather, nightfall, command decision, or unserviceability. Compared with patrolling over Dunkirk, sorties were around fifty-one minutes. A few pilots flew several sorties per day, but still only averaged one hour, thirty-six minutes of flying daily.[35] The Armée de l'Air in May and early June did not have the luxury of reserve pilots to allow the frontline airmen to be rested. Claude d'Abzac-Epézy, in *L'Armée de l'Air de Vichy, 1940–1944*, indicated some of the consequences in casualties.[36]

The 1915–1918 Royal Flying Corps commanding general, Hugh Trenchard, told his biographer in 1956 that during World War I it took seven days after a request was made to London to get new pilots and fourteen more days to train them in formation flying. Moreover the strength of twenty-one pilots on a squadron was really only twelve on any given day because two were on leave, four in training, two in a hospital, and one in a mental facility in Britain, with the lack of the other four being due to an unanticipated shortage of these airmen.[37] British historian R. J. Overy writes that the Luftwaffe suffered heavier losses in the Battle of France than it did in the first six weeks of the Battle of Britain and that by the end of September, the GAF was reduced to 735 available single-engined fighter pilots compared with the RAF's 1,492 in Fighter Command.[38]

The wear and tear of the campaign in France may be judged by the state of the Fighter Command squadrons that returned to Britain as of mid-July: all were resting. No. 73 Squadron had only seven pilots remaining, no serviceable Hurricanes, and only 45 percent of its ground crew establishment. No. 242 Squadron was grounded for lack of spares and equipment and could not even put up enough aircraft for combat training. No. 87 had twenty-three pilots but only half its ground crew and no armorers. No. 605 was still flying fabric-winged Hurricanes that should have been scrapped, but there were no replacements available. No. 245 (Hurricanes) and No. 611 (Spitfires) squadrons were so low on aircraft they had to be withdrawn to reequip.[39] Added to all this, one of the quiet disasters of 1940 was the sinking of the Cunard-White Star's 20,000-ton liner *Lancastrian* on 16 June while she was evacuating a large number of RAF ground crew among the some five thousand aboard.[40]

During the intense coverage of the Dunkirk evacuation, 27 May–1 June 1940, only about 16.5 to 17 squadrons were on patrol each day. The average was 1.8 patrols per day per squadron, and only 7 flew all six days; of the remainder, 4 flew on five days, 5 on four, and the rest for only three days. Fighter Command covered Dunkirk with 1,793 patrols averaging 165 sorties per day, and lost 106 aircraft, or one every 17 sorties.[41] Dunkirk involved a lot of over-water flying, and the missing probably went into the sea before RAF air/sea rescue was fully established. Losses were higher as operations over Dunkirk were beyond the range of radar and ground controllers, and thus of warnings of enemy aircraft, and over-water flying and operating at the limit of flying endurance added to anxiety and fatigue as did fuel exhaustion and the stress of maintaining efficiency. However, patrols were regularly scheduled, and so adequate sleep was possible. Over Dunkirk the RAF claimed 258 enemy, but German losses actually were less than half that. The same misrepresentations occurred during the Battle of Britain. Yet the Germans were also guilty during the campaign in the west, claiming on 10–15 May 1,418 victories. (See Table 17.) Both sides exaggerated.[42]

In the period from 10 May to 18 June, RAF Fighter Command lost 260 pilots killed, missing, or POW, and 60 wounded or injured. During the campaign in France and Belgium, medical records were poorly kept according to the RAF medical history, but casualties have been estimated by aircraft losses.[43] Enemy action in the air 10 May to 19 June, when the RAF was withdrawn from France, cost 140 RAF dead and 433 wounded. RAF dead and wounded from 3 September 1939 to 19 June 1940 were 362 killed and 560 wounded, 922 total. An additional 318 were presumed dead and 70 died and 104 were injured in accidents. This gives a grand total of RAF casualties in the campaign in France of 1,414 from all causes, or 9.3 percent of a total strength there of 15,172. In addition, of interest regarding casualties and medical concerns, four percent of those sent to France suffered from venereal disease, and the force was also weakened by 7,218 hospitalizations of an average 17.3 days each, largely for upper respiratory infections, which especially stopped aircrew from flying. Of these hospitalizations 740 were invalided home, 131 were medically discharged from the service, and—according to morbidity and mortality statistics—789 died.

The Exiles

Polish pilots who had escaped from their homeland were trained in France, starting in March 1940, where they converted to the MS-406 and to the stopgap Caudron-Renault lightweight CR-714 fighters, coming under what might graciously be called the Armée de l'Air's "rigorous training system." On 1 May the École de Chasse et d'Instruction at Lyon-Bron had two *escadrilles*, one with perhaps fifteen pilots and the other with thirty or more. Because the FAF's MB-152 fighters did not materialize, the Poles were ordered to train on the eight CR-714s available of the forty-six on the inventory. By 28 May at Villacoublay the Armée de l'Air had thirty-four 714s. At that time the Poles had yet to practice formation flying, firing exercises, or scrambles.

On 2 June the new fighter group GC 1/145 of ZOAA went to Dreux, in north-central France, with 31 out of 34 serviceable aircraft, 37 pilots, and 125 ground crew. But there was no fuel at Dreux until nearly nightfall. Still, the next day there were 28 serviceable machines. On the 4 June and on the following days GC 1/145 patrolled over the airfields. The experienced Poles managed several kills with their CR-714s. On 10 June it was decided to reequip GC I/145 with MB-152 fighters, but the armistice intervened. The decline of the FAF was such that by 10 June it could not put up more than a handful of sorties. The 637 *chasseur* of 10 May, of whom only 430 were serviceable at 68 percent, or 190 at 30 percent, had been consumed and wasted far faster than estimated, but not as fast (in fourteen days) as Vuillemin had forecast prewar. On 11 June GC I/145 moved to Ètampes, some twenty-five miles south of Paris, burning 11 unserviceable aircraft. In a short time in action in France the Poles had scored seven victories and two probables for 4 shot down and 20 destroyed on the ground.

No. 303 (Polish) Fighter Squadron, RAF, in late August and September 1940 appears to have had a record comparable to that of a French *escadrille*. Its pilots were mostly prewar graduates of the Polish flying schools and so probably averaged perhaps three hundred hours going into combat. Between 30 August and 7 October (thirty-eight days) they claimed 104.5 aircraft destroyed, 14 probably destroyed, and 9 damaged, for a total of 127.5.

Divided by five, the real total of destroyed aircraft would have been twenty-one in thirty-eight days, just a week shorter than the Battle of France.[44]

Machines and Men in Action

On 20 May, Armée de l'Air Fighter Group GC II/3 in ZOAA finally and hastily became operational but was delayed seeing action because the base to which it was assigned was totally unserviceable. It stayed three weeks on the next base, but due to the incomplete training, many landing accidents occurred. GC II/7 of ZOAS became operational on the Dewoitines at the end of May as it could spare only a small numbers of pilots to go to Toulouse and collect machines from the factory. Not until early June were GC II/7 and GC III/3 (ZOAN) able to send D-520s into action. Seven *groupes de chasse* were equipped with Bloch 152s, but one did not enter the Battle of France until 19 May and two others were converting from the MS-406 in May. Not only was the Bloch MB-152 inferior to the German Me-109, it was also slower than the Me-110. Losses were in the order of 75 percent per sortie, partly due to fuel exhaustion in forty-five minutes. In six days Groupement 21 had only 51 serviceable aircraft of the 102 it had had started with on 10 May. On 14 May alone, GC II/1 had lost all but 3 of its initial establishment of Bloch MB-152s. Replacements could not be brought forward fast enough for the MB *groupes* to keep up with wastage.

Meanwhile, on 21 May the French and British High Commands had agreed that since the ZOAN air support was now based in the Paris area and the distance to the Somme entailed too great a risk, the Anglo-French forces being encircled in Flanders would be protected by both RAF Bomber Command from Britain and the Air Components of the BEF, by then also in England. RAF Bomber Command had been committed to the Battle of France from 11 May when it had launched 20 aircraft to distant targets, such as the Ruhr, then 95 on 15 May, 80 on 17 May, and 97 on 17 May (Table 42). After the lull from 28–31 May, 65 sorties were launched on 1 June and a maximum effort of 146 on 3 June as the Battle of the Somme began. A much greater effort in France started on 10 May with 80, then down and up again, and then down on 15 May to 7. But thereafter, the number rose steadily to a peak on 22 May of 192 and remained above 100 daily, to peak again on 31 May at 184 and then dropping to zero on 4 June, and one last effort of eighty sorties on 5 June.

On 22 May the Germans pushed bridgeheads across the Somme in spite of the Armée de l'Air. The next day bad weather prevented reconnaissance,

TABLE 42. RAF Bomber Command Sorties, 10 May–5 June 1940

DATE	TO DISTANT OBJECTIVES	TO LAND BATTLE OBJECTIVES	DATE	TO DISTANT OBJECTIVES	TO LAND BATTLE OBJECTIVES
10 May	0	80	25 May	15	139
11 May	20	45	26 May	2	129
12 May	2	80	27 May	97	145
13 May	0	35	28 May	0	113
14 May	14	65	29 May	0	120
15 May	95	7	30 May	0	149
16 May	10	25	31 May	0	184
17 May	80	55	1 June	65	116
18 May	35	68	2 June	60	51
19 May	50	30	3 June	146	40
20 May	0	145	4 June	64	0
21 May	0	192	5 June	50	80
22 May	0	161	**Totals**	**805**	**2,519**
23 May	0	145	**Grand Total: 3,324 Sorties**		
24 May	0	120	**24.2% To Distant Objectives**		
			75.8% To Land Battle Objectives		

Source: From General Charles Christienne, "La R.A.F. dans la Bataille de France au travers des raports de Vuillemin de Juillet 1940," *Recuiel d'Articles et Études, 1981–1983* (Vincennes: SHAA, 1987), 333.

though the *chasseur* claimed ten enemy for a loss of two. The Armée de l'Air's logistics were disrupted by 1 June because the roads were clogged with unforeseen refugees, the *escadrilles* were always on the move, airfields had been overrun, and on 21 May the German blitzkrieg had reached the Channel at Abbeville, cutting off the zone of air operations in the north, whose armies were already defeated. The worst possible case was far more serious than the planners with their 1918 mindset had envisaged.[45]

In the meantime, losses had been great, and attempts to replenish units on their airfields abandoned. Observation groups had been merged and the impossibility of replacing the *chasse* MS-406s led to their *escadrilles* being sent to the rear to reequip with D-520s and Curtiss H-75s. Bomber *groupes* found themselves sent back to the battle with their old machines. On 23 May "Grouping" 6 with over 50 percent personnel and 75 percent aircraft losses was sent to the rear to rebuild. Given its tripartite responsibilities—support, air defense, and escort—the *chasse* never could concentrate effectively on any one role, though when allowed to focus on air defense, the FAF did prove equal to the task.

Concurrently, the bomber crews were being converted to new types in southern France, but by 19 June only two units, GB I/62 and I/63, had completed the transition and they had no impact on the battle. The Martin 167 light bombers had been in North Africa and for the nonstop 9 May flight to France they had had long-range fuel tanks installed in place of the nonexistent bomb racks. However, by 19 May the bomb racks still had not arrived, so it was not until 23 May that the aircraft were at last *bon de guerre*. Still they lacked harmonized guns and cockpit armor-plate. By the end of May there were six light bomber *groupes* in southern France. The other eleven bomber *groupes* had LeO-451 mediums and a few Amiot 351 mediums and Amiot 354 heavies. The Douglas DB-7 light bomber *groupes* flew over later on in June 1940.

Between 10 and 25 May the French lost 50 bombers in action, plus 36 to bombing on the ground and 26 in accidents, for a total of 112. By 28 May these losses had been made good with 18 Amiot 351/354 mediums and heavies, 10 Breguet 691 lights, 39 Br-693 lights, 23 Douglas DB-7 lights, 14 Martin 167 lights, and 74 LeO-451 mediums. On 28 May, the Belgians surrendered and the Allies had to speed up the retreat to the Channel coast, while the Germans were massing to cross the Somme and the Aisne.

On 31 May these new bombers went into action with eighteen 167s on the attack, all of which returned to base. Twelve DB-7s then sortied and lost three. Late in the afternoon six Breguet 693s made a successful assault on a tank concentration and managed to fight off Luftwaffe Me-109 fighters on the way home, losing only one. Early in the evening twenty-one LeO-451s took off unescorted to the Abbeville-Amiens area, where eight were lost. Over Dunkirk, the presence of RAF fighters distracted the Germans from protecting their bombers, which suffered considerably in consequence.

If standing patrols were to be flown in the fourteen daylight hours of May by 150 fighters of one-hour's endurance, the total number of sorties would have needed to be 150 x 14 or 2,100—plus 2 x 27, or 54 more than on escort duty. Allowing for, say, a 62 percent *disponible* rate, there would need to be 2 x 27 additional, or 54, aircraft to bring the standing patrol up to full 150-aircraft strength. Assuming 4 sorties daily per pilot with a serviceability of 68 percent, or 8 aircraft per 12-aircraft *escadrille*, means each such unit had to fly 32 sorties that day and that would have required 66 *escadrilles* to maintain the patrol (2,100 sorties per fourteen-hour day with each escadrille flying 32 sorties daily equals 65.625, or 66, *escadrilles*). It is assumed for these calculations the reality of mid-May, that each *escadrille* had only 12 aircraft. (Note, elsewhere, with depleted *disponibles* each needed 40!)

On 10 May the Armée de l'Air had only thirty-one *escadrilles* equipped with modern compatible fighters—MS-406s and Bloch 151s/152s, H-75s, and one *escadrille* of D-520s; only twenty-four of the total thirty-one *escadrilles* were in the Battle of France. Sorties of two-hours' duration would have cut the number of *escadrilles* to thirty-three, a number still not possible—beyond the FAF's capability. If serviceability, as Vuillemin maintained, was but 30 percent, that would have required more than seventy *escadrilles*—not at all possible.

On 27 May the British AASF Hurricanes had fought a pitched battle and claimed fifteen Luftwaffe Heinkel 111 bombers and one fighter. On 1 and 2 June almost all of France was covered in fog and drizzle allowing the *chasseur* an extra two days for their late May reorganization. By 3 June the available *chasseur* were redeployed to fields from which they could defend Paris, the airfields, and aircraft industry nearby. At dawn on 3 June half of the effective fighters of Groupements 21, 22, and 23, some sixty in all, were placed on alert, and pilots spent all morning sweating in their cockpits with threat of thunderstorms. Finally they were ordered to take off in early afternoon to greet five hundred enemy bombers and fighters of Operation Paula, already almost overhead. It was a fiasco. Orders were garbled by German radio jamming. The D-520 fighters had to battle for their lives against the Me-109s, while the MS-406s, having made a head-on pass at the bombers, could not catch up to them again and had instead to fend off more 109s. At Plessis-Belleville a three-pronged Luftwaffe high and low bombing attack and low-level fighter strafing left the MS-406 fighters helpless. The MB-152s suffered an almost similar fate, littering the Chantilly area with wrecks. The fifteen MB-152s from Bretigny were not much more successful, nor were the six from Claye-Souilly. To the south, MS-406s had little better luck and lost four pilots. And the well-trained H-75 Hawks of Groupement de Chasse 23's GC I/5 intercepted homeward-bound Luftwaffe bombers, only to be jumped by their escort. During the Battle of Paris the *chasse* flew 243 sorties and claimed twenty-six and lost seventeen aircraft shot down, with twelve pilots killed and eight wounded (the actual claim should have been six to seven).

The Luftwaffe had attacked thirteen French airfields around Paris, but had only destroyed sixteen aircraft on the ground and damaged another seven. All the fields attacked were serviceable again within forty-eight hours. Twenty-two railway stations were out of use for less than twenty-four hours, and only three of fifteen aircraft factories received more than minor damage. But 254 civilians were killed and 652 wounded.

On 5 June the now-reinforced 70 Fairey Battle bombers of the AASF and Bomber Command's 230 aircraft slowed the German Panzers along the Somme by attacking the enemy lines of communication. Meanwhile the French were making a maximum effort of 126 sorties including a dawn strike along the Somme by 19 Br-693 bombers escorted by 15 H-75s, the latter being involved in a fierce fight on the return with Me-109s and 110s of which they claimed seven for a loss of one. Two hours later, 12 more 693 bombers struck another bridgehead and then went in low against a convoy of trucks. However, they failed to guard their tails, were surprised, and lost 5 of the 693s to enemy fighters. In the afternoon, 18 Martin 167 bombers made a medium-altitude raid on a German armored column for a loss of 2. In the evening, the Breguet 693s made further bombing assaults in two waves of 7, followed by 12 DB-7s, which lost one. The final Armée de l'Air activity of 5 June 1940 was a dusk strike that returned without having been able to see the targets.

When the Germans attacked across the Somme River on 5 June, the *chasse* flew 438 sorties, claiming forty enemy (though more likely the real tally was twelve to twenty-eight) for a loss of fifteen French fighters. There followed twelve MS-406 cannon attacks upon enemy tanks. The FAF machines available could only operate in penny packets of less than a dozen at a time and suffered the consequences. Early on the same day, General Vuillemin had immediately handed over the reserve forces to General Tétu, but on 8 June had to provide air assets to the newly created air zone of operatioins center (ZOAC), yet the *chasse* remained with ZOAN. Four additional fighter *groupes* and twenty-four RAF Blenheim bombers from the AASF were added to ZOAN, but to no avail, as the front was broken by 7 June. On 8 June General Tétu asked for 50 percent of the assets of ZOAE. On 9 June Vuillemin sent all ZOAN's air assets to ZOAC for one day. By that evening the Germans were in sight of Rouen and the Grand Quartier Général Aerienn (general headquarters of the Armée de l'Air [GQGA]) left Saint-Jean-les-Deux Jumeax for a site close to Briare.

On 6 June LeO-451 bombers hit the bridgeheads along the Somme. But the 13 aircraft, as so often in the past, failed to meet their escort and lost 5. The belated escort claimed 2 Luftwaffe Me-109s. Thereafter, activity declined rapidly as operations were limited to nighttime or because friendly and enemy forces on the ground were not readily distinguishable. By 14 June the campaign was clearly over and the bombers were ordered withdrawn to southwest France in readiness to move to North Africa. The last sortie, by 11 LeO-451s in the Grenoble area, inflicted no damage, but the LeOs escaped the flak due to heavy cloud cover. Bomber Groupement 6 had flown roughly 450 sorties since 11 May and had lost 79 aircraft out of the total of 130 destroyed in the Battle of France, some burned on the ground to prevent their capture. Another 180 reached North Africa, mostly flown by crews who had seized them at the factory and acted on their own. Similarly the Martin 167s and DB-7s escaped under orders between 16 and 18 June with total losses of 40 167s and 20 DB-7s.

When Italy entered the fray on 10 June the air zone of operations Alps (ZOAA), created on 26 May, had only one fighter group, a part of which had D-520s, but no bomber forces. For a short period the RAF sent two squadrons of Wellington heavy bombers there, but the attempted operations were frustrated by politics—the local fears of retaliation. The fighters had been reinforced on 5 June with additional personnel and machines, but not until 12 June did the air forces clash, and the D-520s shot down three Regia Aeronautica Fiat BR-20 bombers. On 14 June about fifty Italian aircraft attacked French airfields, but lost heavily, particular to pilot Pierre Le Gloan who shot down five in thirty minutes, thus becoming an ace. Sporadic air activity followed, until the Franco-German armistice went into effect on 24 June and the FAF general headquarters disbanded the next day. From then on the whole campaign went downhill. The Armée de l'Air showed massive evidence of disorganization. It had no lookouts on airfields, while absence of "electromagnetic means of detection" made it impossible to concentrate because of lack of early warning.

On 15 June the last of the British Hawker Hurricanes were ordered to cover the western evacuation ports supported by the new squadrons temporarily in France. On 18 June refueled and serviceable remainders were ordered Home, those abandoned being burned. The Advanced Air Striking Force stayed in operation in France until 19 June when Franco-German armistice talks were in progress. The loss to the Air Component had been 279, to the AASF 299, with a total of aircraft lost of 1,029 and more than 1,500 personnel casualties.

On 15 June the French GQGA was forced to move from Bonny-sur-Loire to the Chateau Guyon. The ZOAE fell back toward the center of France, an area largely devoid of airfields. Yet General Vuillemin wanted all the fighters and also the bombers to be based south of the Loire, and around Dijon. Airfields became clogged with training and operational aircraft. Some fields soon had 250 to 300 planes. Fortunately the Germans did not attack these. On 16 June Vuillemin ordered that those planes with the range seek refuge in North Africa, but he wanted to keep nine fighter (40 percent) and eleven bomber (39 percent) groups in France.

On 19 June due to poor communications, the air operations areas were merged and the new commands created—air zone of operations west (ZOAW) and a new Alps, south of the mountains. Because of the fluid situation on the ground, roads clogged with refugees, and general uncertainties, operations dwindled to night attacks on specific targets.

As described, the air Battle of France was scattered, disorganized, repetitively responsive, and episodic. The French Haut Commandement lost control from the start and in, at most, four days the Germans had air superiority. The French response, with the aid of the RAF, was barely defensive, confined as it was by lack of clear doctrine, mission, and control and communications in an Armée de l'Air unprepared for combat.

Writing today, in 2011, it is no more possible to paint a clear picture than that uncertain one in the eyes of the 1940 commanders who were not at all sure at the time what was occurring. Even so, these comments must be presented.

CHAPTER 5

ANALYSIS AND THE PARADOX OF THE BATTLE OF FRANCE

By all tests, on 10 June 1940 the Armée de l'Air Chasse should have been impotent. Yet historians Peter Cornwell and Paul Martin show quite clearly that the Armée de l'Air and the Royal Air Force were still destroying Luftwaffe machines. Was this a paradox? The RAF—much better supplied and equipped, much better controlled, and with double the pilots—fared but half as well in the Battle of Britain only a few weeks later. Why?

The story of the Armée de l'Air in the Battle of France has been tinted and tainted by the disaster to the Armée de Terre, and by the shameful neglect by French historians of this part of their own history. In addition the tale has been skewed by the efforts of General Vuillemin and his cohorts to note how inadequate was the support given the FAF. On the one hand, contrary to myth, while their matériel was poor, yet on the other, the experienced pilots acquitted themselves very well.

So why was the Armée de l'Air comparatively more successful than the Royal Air Force or the Luftwaffe in 1940? The answer has to lie in the psychological effect of circumstances and events. The Armée de l'Air *chasse escadrilles* were homogenous, trained and experienced in their own aircraft, units, and milieu until mid-1940. They were an élite, knitted together by unit pride and camaraderie, even among the pilots and the ground crew. With an estimated average 750 flight hours each, the pilots had five times as many hours as new RAF pilots and three times the average Me-109 or Me-110 German pilot. Professional pride and cohesion seem to be the answer to the paradox. As d'Abzac-Epézy concluded, they fought for honor.[1] (In contrast, for the RAF, in the Battle of Britain both pilots and aircraft were still available on 15 September, though many were newly minted airmen and their casualty rates were high—a fact that *SD 98, Data for Calculating Consumption and Wastage in War* [1936], had not considered.) And with the Armée de l'Air, its training program, late in inception, only produced the first 250 pilots in May 1940, most of whom never reached the worn-out *escadrilles*.[2]

After the Battle of France, Dowding on 10 July had 134 percent of Hurricane pilots and 105 percent for Spitfires as compared with a serviceable fifty-four squadrons. The lowest Armée de l'Air figures then seem quite likely (Tables 43 and 44). As to aircraft, the *chasse* started with 637, but of those only 68 percent, or 433, were serviceable, or *bon de guerre*. Of these, 107 (25 percent) were lost in accidents by 10 June, so that the 433 were reduced to 326, of which only 97 (30 percent) by then were serviceable. (Hopefully, the unserviceable machines would return as *disponibles*.) If all twenty-four Armée de l'Air *chasse escadrilles* in the battle are considered, then at the serviceability rates of all twelve machines per *escadrille*, their victories per *escadrille* could have been no more than one per the full unit sorties here[3] (Table 45).

At 0.9 sorties daily at the 68 percent (433) *bon de guerre* aircraft, on 10 May the Armée de l'Air Chasse could put up 390 sorties and have shot down 25; on 10 June it could manage only 97 sorties with 6 GAF shot down. Given the fact that the *chasse* were often employed against enemy columns on the ground, and applying Paul Martin's 15.5 sorties per enemy aircraft destroyed, the FAF on 10 May could have shot down no more than 25 enemy aircraft without yet taking into account its operational deficiencies in speed and firepower. I estimate its likely number of kills on 10 June had been reduced to probably fewer than 6. Of 600-odd fighter pilots there were only 245 by 15 June, and to get them, General Vuillemin had pulled out instructors from the schools.

The FAF *Chasse* Units

In the Battle of France, some *chasse* units went almost unscathed at first, especially most Curtiss Hawks, but one Hawk unit had lost all but seven of its establishment of thirty-four machines by 15 May. Another, Groupe Chasseur I/12, started the campaign with thirteen aircraft and received no replacement aircrew. GC I/13 on 22 May had fifteen pilots for twelve aircraft, and on 10 June had ten pilots for eleven aircraft, of which no more than eight had radios. GC III/54 on 12 May had eight aircraft instead of twelve, and seven pilots instead of fourteen, seven gunners instead of nine, and sixteen mechanics instead of twenty-four; and by 9 June it had not a machine serviceable.

Escadrille GC 1/8 in 1936 had been equipped with sixteen older Dewoitine D-501 fighters and eight D-510s. In November 1938 it received its first Bloch

MB-152 fighters, but was not fully converted until December 1939. In May and June 1940 GC I/8 claimed thirty-two enemy aircraft for a loss of seven pilots, but it was slaughtered by German Messerschmitt Me-109s on 10 May, losing four aircraft. When attacking enemy bombers, GC I/8 was fended off by

TABLE 43. RAF Fighter Command, Daily Availability*

AIRCRAFT	INITIAL ESTABLISHMENT	SERVICEABLE	OPERATIONAL WITH PILOTS
10 July 1940			
Hurricanes	432	582	344
Spitfires	304	320	226
Others	128	131	86
Total	864	1,033	656
8 August 1940			
Hurricanes	568	645	370
Spitfires	328	335	257
Others	136	120	93
Total	1,032	1,100	720
31 October 1940			
Hurricanes	544	561	399
Spitfires	304	294	227
Others	136	100	58
Total	984	955	684
Total on 10 July, 8 August, and 31 October	**2,880**	**3,088**	**2,060**

*On average, Dowding had pilots to man only 66.5 percent of his serviceable fighters, or 71.5 percent of initial establishment aircraft (spare aircraft are ready also).

Source: United Kingdom Air Staff records.

TABLE 44. Hurricane and Spitfire Aircraft Lost and Pilots Killed, 10 July–30 September 1940*

DATE	AIRCRAFT	PILOTS
July	180	177
August	570	601
September	626	630
Totals	**1,376**	**1,408**

*From After the Battle, *The Battle of Britain (Mark II)*. 2nd ed. (London: Battle of Britain Printing International, 1982), 315–333.

TABLE 45. Relationship of Serviceability to Claims, Armée de l'Air, 1940*

PERCENTAGE SERVICEABLE (BON DE GUERRE)	INITIAL ESTABLISHMENT (IE)	AIRCRAFT AVAILABLE	WHOLE ESCADRILLE SORTIES NEEDED TO ACHIEVE A KILL	
			AT 15.5	AT 36.5
100	12	12	3	1.29
75	12	9	4	1.7
60	12	7	5	2.2
50	12	6	6	2.6
40	12	5	7	3.1
30	12	3-4	12+	3.9-5

*At 0.9 sorties daily, an *escadrille* needed two days at 100 percent *bon de guerre* to generate the 15.5 sorties needed for a kill. The point is that even at full strength of twelve serviceable machines and a kill-ratio of 15.5 flying only 0.9 sorties daily, they could only have shot down a very limited number of enemy aircraft.

Me-109 escorts. On 11 May the unit lost another pilot from a different *escadrille*. On 12 May it moved to Courbes. On 14 May it acted as escort to bombers against the Meuse bridges. Then on 16 May it had to leave Courbes in a hurry for Chantilly. On 17 May it lost two aircraft and on 18 May lost another (the pilot returned three days later). On 19 May GC I/8 lost another aircraft, ramming a German Dornier Do-17 bomber. Another pilot bailed out on 20 May and so the machine was lost.

Then GC I/8 moved to Claye-Souilly for four quiet days. On 25 May it was back in action and on 26 May was surprised by Me-109s. One pilot was shot down, one bailed out, and GC I/8 was then let out of the war. From 28 May to 2 June GC I/8 flew some thirty unfruitful sorties. On 3 June German Operation Paula against Paris took place. In the afternoon, Claye-Souilly was bombed and two MBs collided, with no grave consequences, and a pilot was killed testing a new aircraft. On 5 June GC I/8 lost two aircraft but no pilots. GC I/8's last big day was 7 June—twenty-four sorties, five confirmed kills, and one pilot lost. Bombed on the same day, the *escadrille* moved on 9 June to Bretigny-sur-Orge. On 10 June six MB-152 aircraft landed in the nearby river, probably mistaken for a wet runway. The following day the unit moved to Césarville near Pithivieu, and on 14 June to Chateauroux. A sergeant pilot was shot down by local peasants. On 20 June two pilots were killed in a mid-air collision in *pleine vol*—clear air. On 24 June GC I/8 was at Toulouse when the armistice came into force.[4]

GC II/8 had started in 1936 as a joint navy-air unit on Potez 63 fighters, but at the end of December 1939 was ordered to convert to Bloch 151/152, which took place in January 1940. During the Phoney War, and especially in February 1940, GC II/8 did little. By the end of March it had converted all four *escadrilles* to the Blochs. Largely unemployed due to bad weather, only on 10 May did it meet the Luftwaffe, when its airfield was bombed and it lost three MBs destroyed and nine damaged. In May–June 1940, GC II/8 had ten confirmed victories for zero losses. During the Phoney War and the Battle of France it moved ten times, including spending six days in Lympe, England, at the end of May.

At Calais-Marck three MB-152s were destroyed by bombs and nine were damaged. By 14 May the unserviceability rate was alarming, and from 15 May the unit received no more orders. The commander was shot down in flames by Me-110s on 16 May. Meanwhile, the unit was on the move. It flew a dozen sorties on 17 May toward Walcheren Island off Holland and Belgium. On 22 May it moved to Villacoublay, and on 27 May to Deauville St. Gatien where two were killed in landing accidents. The unit then operated from Lympne in Britain to cover the Dunkirk evacuations, but on 5 June it was back at Deauville. On 11 June it moved to a field south of Caen, and then on 14 June to Cherbourg. When it was out of POL and ammunition and scattered by weather, it seems to have been idle until it finally regrouped at Aix-les-Milles on 21 June[5] (Table 41) where the armistice found it.[6]

GC I/10, an MS-406 *chasseur escadrille,* was stationed in North Africa from 15 November 1939 to 25 August 1940. Its fourteen MS-406 aircraft were sent to GC III/5 in mid-May 1940. On 1 June 1940 the fighter school at Oran was reopened and the pilots gave instruction and patrolled off the port. On 10 June the *escadrille* was ordered to Djedida where four days later GC III/5 joined it.[7]

On 11 January 1940 GC III/5, still a training *escadrille,* with twelve Dewoitine D-501 became GC III/9, having been converted to Bloch 151s in November 1939, assigned to the air zone of operations Alps (ZOAA) to defend the Lyons area. They lived a very tranquil life, but on 20 April 1940 they were sent off against enemy bombers and shot down the first Ju-88 to fall to the FAF. On 10 May GC III/9 had only nine MB-151s *bon de guerre* and so had to patrol with its D-501s, hardly a match for the GAF. That night it moved to Satolas and on 16 June was attached to Groupement de Chasse 24. On 1 June the few *disponible* were sent up to defend Lyons. On 2 June GC III/9 was in action again, but on 17 June it went to Orange and on the following day to Vinon, and then on 19 June to Lac, where the armistice found it. In July, August, and September, minus its Polish pilots, the unit was amalgamated with other remnants to form a Vichy *escadrille.*[8]

The Organization of the Armée de l'Air

Overall, the Armée de l'Air had no doctrine of employment. There was instability in bases. The logistical system caused unserviceability and the loss of aircraft. The logisticians noted that at the time there were eleven types of fighters on 26 stations; twelve types of bombers at 18 bases; four types of reconnaissance machines on 12 airfields; and ten observation units on 47 fields, with eleven different types based on 200 airfields and landing grounds in the air zone of operations northeast (ZONE) alone. And the units were constantly moving; the whole was a nightmare. For fighter pilots, the constant shifting to a new airfield was disorienting and caused anxiety. The German seizure of airfields was a further complication. On 10 May alone, 47 airfields out of 113 were attacked and perhaps sixty aircraft lost.[9] By way of contrast Paul Martin says only fourteen aircraft were lost.[10]

In May and June 1940, according to Claude d'Abzac-Epézy, the Armée de l'Air *chasse* lost 276 shot down, 16 damaged in the air, 136 destroyed on the ground, and 137 destroyed plus 9 damaged in accidents, for a total of 574.[11] Assuming the losses were spread over the twenty flyable days, that meant 28.7 losses daily.

Given the fact that replacements were mostly not *bon de guerre*, the *chasse* serviceability declined (Table 1). On the basis of 378 enemy aircraft destroyed or probably destroyed, at 15.5 sorties per kill, the number of sorties flown 10 May–24 June by the FAF had to be 5,859. At 68 percent serviceability and 0.9 sorties daily per aircraft, that could have been no more than 387 sorties, and at 30 percent *bon de guerre*, at the most 171 in the first days and then declining (Table 5).

Claude d'Abzac-Epézy says that the French Armée de l'Air lost 1,179 aircraft destroyed and 387 damaged from 3 September 1939 to 25 June 1940, or a total of 1,566[12] (Table 5). In May and June alone, the totals destroyed and damaged were 1,033, of which 471 were shot down in the air, 77 damaged in the air, 254 destroyed in accidents, and 231 put out of action on the ground. Of the 1,042 new aircraft supplied 10 May–25 June, most were unavailable for lack of essentials such as propellers, radios, and guns, and so forth. The *chasseur* received the following 433 new aircraft: 10 MS-406s; 69 Bloch 151/152s; 237 Dewoitine 520s; 119 Curtiss Hawks.[13] Patrick Facon (1997) gives much smaller totals. Of the new *chasse* received by the units, only 104 were *bon de guerre*.[14] Of these new fighters, 321 were delivered in April, 657 in May, and 335 in June, for a total of 1,313. But with the serviceability supposedly 68 percent, or 893, but in reality of 30 percent, according to Vuillemin and Mendigal, only 394.[15]

By 10 June, there were 910 on charge—that is, on the units' records, of whom 338 were *disponible*, or 37 percent, by which time in the Somme offensive of 5–10 June, the FAF had lost 113 in a week, including 17 percent of its aircrew. At the same time, in a month the FAF lost 410 aircrew to flak. GAF losses claimed were 733 to fighters, and 120 to DCA for a total of 853, which included those brought down by the RAF. The FAF had lost 852 planes and its serviceability had been reduced to 30 percent, close to the GAF's as well. But the GAF had an unlimited supply of available machines ready for combat and healthy, well-trained young crews. Only 29 percent of French pilots were under 29 years of age, and only 40 were under 25. However, *Les As de la guerre* (1991) claims the French aces of 1940 averaged 24.5 years.[16] By June the FAF had lost 250 pilots or 71.8 percent of the 348 available on 10 May.[17]

By 10 June, if each pilot of the 120 French pilots had flown 1.8 sorties daily, double the RAF rate at Dunkirk, that would have amounted to 216 and (on the RAF sortie-to-kill ratio of 36.5) to the shooting down of 6 Germans. But perhaps one sortie daily per pilot was more realistic, leading to the loss of only 3.28 German aircraft daily, or, if Paul Martin's 15.5 sorties is used, to kill ratio of 1.29. Some of the fighter pilots counted above were *outré-mer* in the colonies, and thus a very small body of fatigued pilots was keeping the *chasseur* alive. But while on 10 June the FAF had 1,084 fighters on charge, on the next day it was described as disorganized and flew very few sorties thereafter because the movement to southwest France and North Africa was in process. (See also Table 1.)

The Armée de l'Air's accident rate of 25 percent not only indicates fatigue, but also a seriously depleted available fighter force. If the serviceability rate was only 30 percent and a quarter of these machines were unavailable and only 0.9 sorties were flown daily, then certainly by 5 June the Armée de l'Air could only launch about 180 daily sorties, a number far below the 899 needed to make good the claim of 58 enemy aircraft destroyed on 5 June, and a claim not supported by Luftquartiermeister General (LQMG) issues. However, if the ratio was Martin's 15.5 sorties per kill, then on 5 June the Armée de l'Air flew 899 sorties and could claim 58.

By 6 June, the FAF claimed it had destroyed 441 enemy aircraft. In spite of intensive operations, the FAF had grown from 2,176 on 10 May to 2,357 on 10 June, yet had losses of 852 (36 percent). One-quarter of those machines lost were in accidents, or 10.5 percent of those "*aux armées*," often as the result of combat or of using out of necessity aircraft listed as *indisponible*. In war, of course, pilots have to take risks and they become fatigued, which causes crashes and accidents. The Luftwaffe accident rate was worse than that for the

Armée de l'Air at 33 percent, or 450 out of the total of 1,365. Luftwaffe losses due to fatigue are demonstrated by the loss in France of overworked Ju-52s as these were noncombat accidents. The operational crews of the fighters and bombers must have suffered fatigue also from constant operations, which saw the units down to 30 percent serviceability before Dunkirk at the end of May after barely twenty days of the campaign.[18]

For all air forces, accident rates were very important as aircrew not only were killed or disabled, but also aircraft and spares were wasted and consumed, as well as mechanics' time. Accident rates varied depending upon the weather, the state of airfields, training, navigation, and fuel on board, among other causes. Accidents generally accounted for 33 percent of all German losses and 25 percent of the French. Their effect was dependent upon the availability of new or rebuilt aircraft as well as of ground crews and specialists to salvage and repair the machines involved, and the means to ferry them both to units and back to the factories.

The *chasseur* lacked both numbers and modern aircraft. The first *escadrille* of the really competitive Dewoitine 520 (GC I/3) became operational only on 7 May. Of the 852 new fighters the FAF accepted 10 May–5 June, only 571 went to units because 30 percent remained at the depots as they lacked radios and armament. By the end of the first phase of the Battle of France the *chasseur*, scattered to support the Armée de Terre, had lost 473 machines.

For nearly five weeks GAF repairables were 7.1 percent of the 1,422 (1,620) casualties. Applying the Luftwaffe's own criteria that more than 10 percent damage put an aircraft aside in favor of a replacement, there were 781 write-offs in August and 626 in September for a total of 1,407 machines written off[19] (Table 30). Mis-assessments by both sides led to figures in official reports that differed sharply from pilots' claims. This tally left out aircraft types that did not suffer losses during the Battle of France.[20] Again this shows the GAF operational philosophy, which assumed that the campaign would be short and that the Luftwaffe could be restructured later.

Luftwaffe casualties had to include all aircrew and aircraft shot down or otherwise wasted over Britain and the coastal waters, though the Seenotdienst, the air/sea rescue service, recovered many aircrew. All aircraft that did not return to the Continent were treated as wasted. Of interest, the RAF losses noted earlier and Luftwaffe wastage here can be used to assess those of the Armée de l'Air in the Battle of France.

From Peter Cornwell's *The Battle of France* and After the Battle's *The Battle of Britain* and their tabulation of GAF losses, I used the following:

(1) Operational sortie was any one listed as such plus some crashes *or* accidents that seemed likely to have been operational, usually takeoff accidents.

(2) Any aircraft lost on an operational sortie was noted as shot down even if it was simply listed as missing. This was because I was counting logistical implications and not credits for shooting down a machine. A certain number of the missing no doubt ditched due to engine failure or fuel starvation. Apparently Luftwaffe pilots had not yet been taught how to fly a twin-engine aircraft on only one engine. The problem was that the early war twins were under-powered, lacked full-feathering propellers, and required great leg strength if the trim tab was inoperative.

(3) Crew losses were counted as killed for any crew member listed as missing because all such persons were no longer on GAF strength, as was true of POWs.

(4) If appropriate, aircraft that returned to German-held territory or were domestic losses were listed as crashed or damaged. The GAF then decided if they were write-offs, as were all aircraft lost over England or ditched, and assigned a percentage of damage to them. If under 10 percent, the machine was considered repairable at the unit. Greater damage resulted in setting it aside or being written off and drawing a new machine.

(5) Non-operational losses were apparently either the result of air tests, which had to be conducted in those days after repairs or inspections, or due to the crew being lost in bad weather, or occasionally training in Germany. In this report [i.e., the After the Battle report] the LQMG records seem strangely silent on losses in the educational system.

The Luftwaffe used three categories to describe losses: (1) *Feindflug*—war flight; (2) *bei Ensatz*—support flights such as air/sea rescue (A/SR), which should be considered combat flying; (3) *Heimat-danstic*—local noncombat flight (Table 20).

Francis K. Mason, in *Battle over Britain,* gives RAF Fighter Command losses in July as 73 damaged and repairable, 66 destroyed, and 51 missing for a total loss of 190. In August the figures rise to 117 damaged but repairable, 242 destroyed, and 133 missing for a total loss of 492. In September he changed the figures to daily states on squadrons Categories C, D, and E, repairable in the squadron, and Categories F and G, sent away, the totals being for the four weeks 67 of Categories C, D, and E and 340 of Categories F and G, for a combined total of 407. These totals differ on the high side from those that follow, which are judged to be more accurate.[21] This tabulation for ninety days in summer 1940 shows that the RAF lost fewer Fighter Command aircrew, mostly pilots, than did the Luftwaffe, but that the latter lost considerably fewer fighter aircraft. However, most of those the Luftwaffe did lose were write-offs while 38 percent of RAF Fighter Commands (318) were repairable. In terms of total aircraft, the Luftwaffe lost 851 bombers with 1,696 aircrew so that the drain of the Battle of Britain was very real, assuming that there was considerable unrecorded salvage from the Battle of France (Tables 16, 20, and 46).

RAF killed, wounded, and missing totaled 616, while uninjured though shot down, and so forth, 817. Of the aircraft, write-offs were 744 and repairables 632. Of the total of 1,376 shot down or otherwise damaged, 44–46 percent were repairable. In the same period new production and repaired aircraft totaled 1,301.

The comparable six weeks (forty-six days) of the Battle of Britain to the earlier period in France would be those from 12 August to 23 September 1940.

TABLE 46. RAF and Luftwaffe—Losses, July–September 1940

RAF LOSSES		LUFTWAFFE LOSSES	
Number	Type	Number	Type
JULY			
68	Aircrew	348	Aircrew [52 Me-109]
91	Aircraft	185	Aircraft [56 Me-110]
AUGUST			
176	Aircrew	993	Aircrew [233 Me-109]
389	Aircraft	694	Aircraft [330 Me-110]
SEPTEMBER			
175	Aircrew	829	Aircrew [191 Me-109]
358	Aircraft	679	Aircraft [321 Me-109]
Totals: July, August, September			
			Aircrew [797 Me-109 pilots]
419	**Aircrew**	**2,170**	**[386 Me-110 airmen]**
838	**Aircraft**	**1,558**	**Aircraft**

Source: Francis K. Mason, *Battle over Britain* (New York: Doubleday, 1969), 598.

In that period RAF Fighter Command lost 563 Hurricanes and Spitfires written off and 1,039 repairable in squadron Categories C, D, and E. But in the same period, the RAF lost only 244 aircrew killed, wounded, or missing.

These losses were lower than for the Luftwaffe in the Battle of Britain because of the latter being based on the Continent and having to cross and recross the Channel. These actions were much more intensive on a sustained basis during 12 August–23 September than in the comparable period of the Battle of France when in four days the Luftwaffe gained air superiority (Table 40). Of the total of 1,439 written off, 63.3 percent were in May and 16 percent in June; and of the damaged, 14.6 percent were in May and 15.2 percent in June. (See also Table 30.)

During the French Campaign the Luftwaffe fighter-bomber idea had surfaced and by August, special Me-109s were diving at speeds up to 403 mph and with four 110-pound bombs or one of 550 pounds.

By 10 August the GAF in the west had 934 Me-109Es of which 805 were serviceable out of the whole German holding of 1,011 (or 86 percent). But these machines had only twenty minutes of combat time over Britain, and London was the limit of their range. With fewer than 700 serviceable, the Me-109s could not both fight the RAF and escort GAF bombers.

Disastrous RAF tactics led to 1,172 RAF fighters lost, almost all to Me-109s, as the latter used explosive 7.9-mm shells, though at a slower rate of fire than the British Brownings.

As Table 24 shows, monthly deliveries to units by the LQMG in 1940 amounted in May, June, and July to 826 single-engined fighters and in May and June alone 1,857 new aircraft all told. Against these are Armée de l'Air real kills I originally estimated at around 232 and later at 384, RAF British Air Forces France kills of 71, and DCA of perhaps 120 or maybe only 40, for a total of 384 to 423 (using Cornwell's data). With Luftwaffe issues of all types in May and June totaling 1,857, that leaves between 1,434 and 1,474 unaccounted.[22] July was included above because in at least the first twelve days, losses were still being made good from the Battle of France. Thereafter there were casualties from the new struggle with the RAF.

No known figures are available for German battlefield salvage before or after 24 June 1940, but some ideas as to wastage and consumption can be outlined. In the forty-six days during the Battle of Britain, from 12 August to 23 September, roughly contrasting in intensity with 10 May–24 June, the Luftwaffe lost 1,211 on operational sorties and 217 on domestic (i.e., nonoperational) totaling 1,428. Of these, 1,422 crashed on the Continent, 101 were repairable as defined above, and 1,344 were written off. (See also Table 20.) Of the aircraft replaced in the Battle of France in May and June, 1,066 were Me-109s, of which probably one-third were to replace fighters wrecked in undercarriage-related accidents. Another 222 were twin-engine Me-110s. Total GAF losses in May and June were 1,857 out of a 1,940 total of 8,414 horizontal line and 8,354 in the right-hand column in Table 24.[23] (See also Tables 12–15, 22, and 26.)

This compares to German admission of 1,688 lost or damaged in the campaign in the west, 10 May–18 June. Because so many damaged GAF aircraft in the later Battle of Britain did not make it back across the Channel, the repairables were only 7 percent of the casualties[24] (Table 31).

Using just a rough average aircraft weight of 10,000 pounds, with 3,129 Allied—including Dutch and Belgian—and 2,289 Luftwaffe machines lost, for a total of 5,418 machines, the potential salvage for the German aircraft industry was 54,180,000 pounds or 27,090 x 2,000-pound tons. In the Battle of Britain, German losses from combat (i.e., shot down or force-landed in Britain or in the Channel) were roughly 1,344, though the LQMG stated 2,053. The difference of 709 can be assumed to be wastage and consumption with 14 percent salvageable and repairable. Overall German aircraft production included in the monthly totals about 22 percent repaired machines. Write-offs were probably cannibalized for parts and these were shipped back to the factories to be reconditioned and reissued. Crashed and burned machines were in part salvageable as scrap to be melted down and remade.[25] (See Tables 10, 14, 30, and 39 for *chasse* claims.)

What does this say about FAF claims? Cumulative Luftwaffe losses destroyed or damaged over France or the Low Countries in May came to 1,286, of which 1,000 were lost by the end of 21 May. The daily loss (shot down and damaged) for the first eleven days averaged 91 whereas for the last eleven days (21–31 May) the average daily loss was only 30. The heaviest German loss was 166 Ju-52s on 10 May with 71 He-111s the same day. Some 28 He-111s were lost on 11 May and 26 on 19 May. Otherwise daily losses by all types was less than 10.[26]

By 6 June, the FAF claimed it had destroyed 441 enemy aircraft. In spite of intensive operations, the FAF had grown from 2,176 on 10 May to 2,357 on 10 June, yet had losses of 852 (36 percent). One-quarter of those machines lost were in accidents, or 10.5 percent of those *aux armées*, often as the result of combat or of using out of necessity aircraft listed as *indisponible*. In war, of course, pilots have to take risks and they become fatigued, which causes crashes and accidents. The GAF accident rate was worse than for the Armée de l'Air at 33 percent, or 450 out of the total of 1,365. Luftwaffe losses due to fatigue are demonstrated by the loss in France of overworked Ju-52s, as these

were non-combat accidents. The operational crews of the fighters and bombers must have suffered fatigue also from constant operations that saw the units
down to 30 percent serviceability before Dunkirk at the end of May after barely
twenty days of the campaign.[27]

The Armée de l'Air paid a high material price in the Battle of France. Of
502 MS-406s deployed in October 1939 and the 500 on order, roughly half
were wiped out 10 May–10 June. Of the new D-520s, 36 were available on 10
May with 194 on order. By 24 June, 85 had been shot down. These machines
lacked the loiter time to oppose the Luftwaffe in a war the Armée de l'Air had
not anticipated.[28]

Air Commodore Peter Dye's study of No. 9 Squadron, Royal Flying Corps,
in 1917 is relevant in that it shows that during intense fighting (albeit on a stationary front), while 53 percent of the aircrew casualties were caused by enemy
aircraft, 20 percent were to ground fire, and an equal number to accidents. A
postwar study showed that the monthly wastage of RFC squadron pilots was
32 percent. Moreover, inexperienced aircrew suffered from stress, cold, fear,
drink, and fatigue, and sometimes were weeded out.[29]

Looking at 5 June 1940 as a typical day, the FAF claimed 55 to 60 enemy aircraft while the Luftwaffe lost only 35. As to claims, there remain 800–850, which
the French and the British have to divide between them. But the partisans of
the FAF have proceeded as though the RAF never existed.[30] Yet the British con-
tribution to the Battle of France was important. During the six weeks, the RAF
lost 1,029 aircraft, mostly in France, of which 299 belonged to the Advanced Air
Striking Force, 279 to the Air Component, 219 to Fighter Command, and 166
to Bomber Command—or 55 percent of the British frontline aircraft strength
of 1,873, together with 1,526 killed, wounded, or disappeared.

Contrary to what General Vuillemin and his Vichy entourage claimed, the
RAF was heavily involved in the Battle of France. Moreover, there is a certain
confusion between the terms "victories" and "real losses." The French system
of confirmations was rigorous enough at first in that it required the wreckage
of an aircraft shot down to be located. However, a victory was credited to each
of the pilots involved. Thus it is not possible to say accurately how many enemy
machines the FAF shot down. And so General Harcourt's figures (Table 39) do
not tally with enemy's real losses. Examination of the German archives (tabulations from Peter Cornwell, *The Battle of France Then and Now*) revealed 1,300
Luftwaffe shot down and another 500 damaged, but repairable, together with
write-offs totaling 813, or a total of 2,613.

On 25 June, 575 modern fighters, 250 modern bombers, and 200 reconnaissance aircraft, were under the command of General Vuillemin, many

stored.[31] French aviation was thus not annihilated, as one reads in British and German works.

Patrick Facon's myth of the 1,000 victories is important in that it gave the British time to recover their defenses while the Battle of France badly mauled the Luftwaffe. The latter lost 30 percent of its Do-17, He-111, Ju-88, and Do-215 bombers (521), 30 percent of its Ju-87 Stukas (122), 40 percent of its Ju-52 and He-115 air/sea rescue (A/SR) transports (213), and 30 percent of its heavy Me-110 fighters (221). (See Tables 12–15. The tables, however, do not agree with these numbers in parentheses as either the original was in error or the 1945 Luftwaffe clerks were not accountants—or, as Francis Mason noted in 1969, the figures simply just don't add up.) However, only 19 percent (235) of the Me-109s were lost. But the bombers at the end of the campaign still had more than 850 in line, in spite of the loss of 500. That the Luftwaffe did not immediately attack Britain after the campaign in France had less to do with losses than with other factors: it needed to rebuild airfields and logistics. Furthermore Hitler thought England shortly would sue for peace, so he had no invasion plan.

It is now time to eradicate the myths in the history of the Armée de l'Air in an honest and objective manner. The FAF fighters had other tasks, too. And this corroborates the German fighter leader Adolf Galland's postwar comment that on the rare occasions when his pilots saw French fighters, they were down low attacking Wehrmacht columns.[32]

If the figure of 775 GAF losses is divided by the usual three, the result is 258, close to the number of Luftwaffe aircraft I thought the *chasse* really destroyed, as shown below. And, given that the French generals noted that serviceable aircraft were only 30 percent during operations of the 637 French *chasse*, out of the Allied total of 733 (of which 96 were RAF Hurricanes), the actual strength on operations of the FAF was 184. Not much of a scattered force with which to face the Luftwaffe.

Aerial combat is known for its swirling intensity and fleeting moments. Gun bursts were short (two seconds) and by no means always deadly accurate, while postcombat reports are generally lacking in accuracy.[33] To assess the whole question, it is finally necessary to dissect the operations of the Armée de l'Air.

The FAF lost in six weeks in the Battle of France 541 killed, 364 wounded, and 105 disappeared, 40 percent of the officers and 20 percent of aircrew.[34] Losses were especially high for the FAF in the intense days of 10–21 May and for the élite. Some 32 *chasse* pilots were lost on 10 May and 104 more by 24 June. As to the losses of aircraft, Vuillemin said of all types 413 were lost in combat, 234 bombed, and 245 in accidents for a total of 892. The archives of the general headquarters of the air force (GQGA) put the figures at 410, 232, and 230 for a total of 872, the latter being close to reality. (See Table 5.) The logic is that air forces know better their losses than their victories—in this case, for example, losses of 800 to 900. Thus the Armée de l'Air lost 45 percent of its frontline strength of 1,972 on 10 May, or 70 percent of its 1,286 serviceable machines on that date, according to d'Abzac-Epézy.[35]

Recently she has noted that in September 1940 the Italians and Germans counted more than 2,800 machines in the Unoccupied Zone with a total of 5,250 on the eve of the armistice, indicating that France still had a considerable air force at that time and inspired the chiefs of the FAF to want to preserve that capital; she notes, in addition, that by a curious paradox France had in July 1940 more modern aircraft than on 10 May. This helped support the thesis that the Armée de l'Air, unlike the armée, had not been defeated.[36] Moreover, that 30 percent serviceability also supported the thesis that the FAF had fought gallantly against great odds and that the 982 Luftwaffe machines destroyed was proof that the Armée de l'Air had done so in spite of the failure of the politicians to supply what it needed. The Armée de l'Air had neither the foresight, nor the production system, nor the volume to ensure its survival in 1940. This, however, does not downplay the courage of the Armée de l'Air pilots in the intense struggle in which they fought well, as their losses prove.

Across La Manche on the north side of the English Channel, several small groups of officers and scientists, supported by leading politicians, had kept an eye on the future and saw it as shaped both by the same forces unleashed by the 1914–1918 war and by science. One result of this was the Air Ministry's Air Staff Memorandum No. 50 (*SD 98*) in 1936 on wastage and consumption in war. The French had no such document and thus were unprepared for sustaining the demands of the campaign.[37]

SD 98's tabulations, which Air Chief Marshal Sir Hugh Dowding used to prepare for the Battle of Britain, predicted a loss of 275 aircraft per month in intensive operations with fifty-five squadrons each flying 300 sorties in a twenty-eight-day month, or 10.7 daily. In 1940, including the Battles of France and Britain, Fighter Command and the BAFF lost 3,000 Hurricanes and Spitfires, but production and repair supplied the squadrons with 3,500. As AVM Dye has pointed out, the Luftwaffe had not digested the needs of grinding attritional warfare, nor had the Air Staff in London prewar.[38] Fortunately, of the RAF losses over Britain, 44 percent were repairable. (See Graph 4.)

According to *SD 98*, Fighter Command would in theory lose 179 pilots per month, or 537 in three months' operational flying in the Battle of Britain.

GRAPH 4. RAF Calculated Weekly Strength and Reserves: 10 May–27 September 1940 (Wastage)

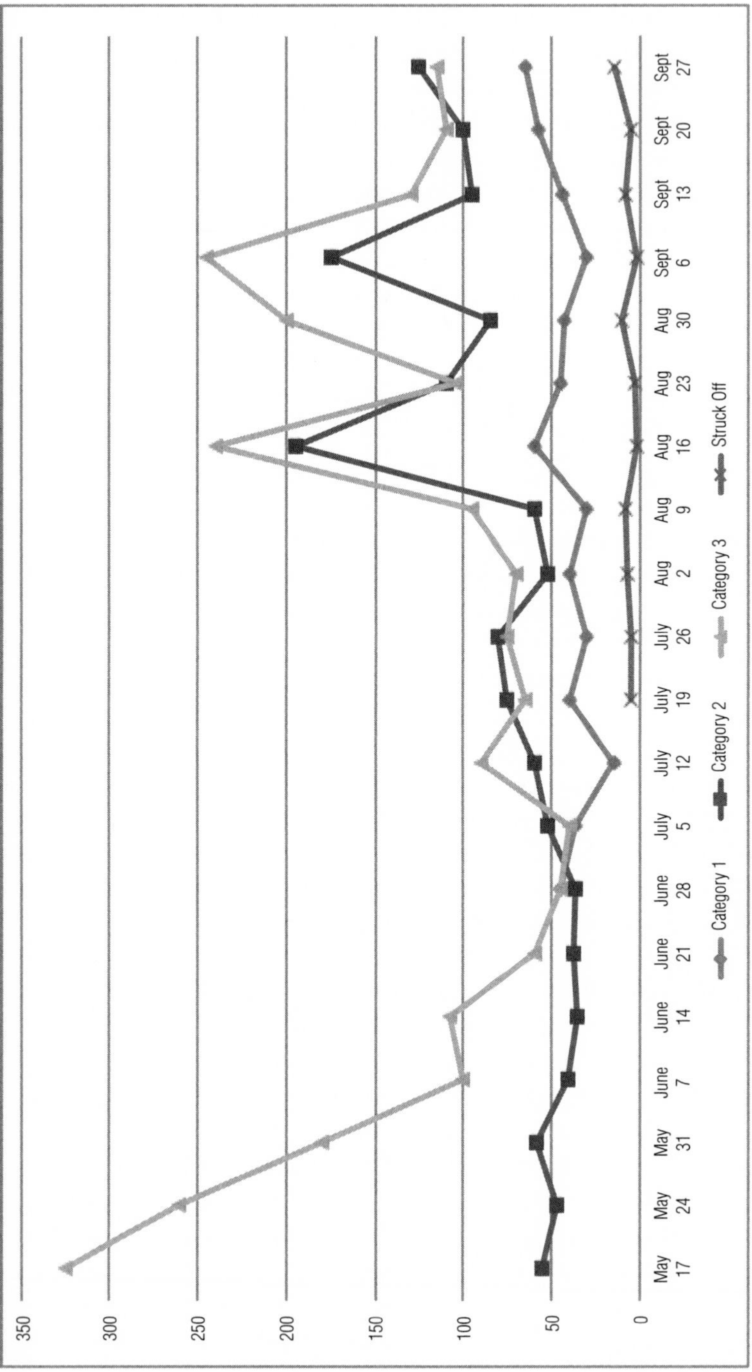

Source: United Kingdom, National Archives, Air Historical Branch, AIR 2/5205.

In the ninety days from 10 July to 30 September 1940, the RAF actually lost 332 pilots killed in action, and 248 wounded, to which can be added the 150 killed and 181 injured in accidents, for a total of 911, instead of the *SD 98* prediction of 1,073—or only 84.9 percent of expectation.[39] And 38 percent of the pilots shot down were fit to fight again.[40]

If the RAF destroyed all the Luftwaffe planes the LQMG issued, at 22 sorties per success, the British would have needed 38,126 sorties. The reality was by Basil Collier's figures,[41] 36.5 sorties per kill for a total of 35,105. And 18 percent of the British kills were by light antiaircraft,[42] which reduces the RAF sorties needed to 31,263. At the average of 37.6 RAF sorties per GAF loss, the Royal Air Force needed 46,090. The Germans lost 1,733 aircraft (later reduced to 1,460 or 23.9 percent) and the RAF 915, but also 1,007 pilots.

Fifteen percent of the Luftwaffe losses in the Battle of Britain were due to small-arms ground fire. In the Battle of France, Luftwaffe losses would not have been that high as there was very little French antiaircraft, and in 1939 French airfields were only protected by four light weapons each. So a guess would be that, say, seven percent or 190 German aircraft were downed due to small-arms damage.[43]

THE FAF, GAF, and RAF in the Battle of France

According to historian Ulf Balke's data,[44] in the weeks from 5 May to 29 June 1940 the Luftwaffe lost 410 officers and 68 NCOs at the front and 93 aircrew domestically, plus 175 in training, totaling 746; 2,499 officers and 449 NCOs were wounded in combat, plus 3 officers domestically and 5 in training, all together 3,702. Of this total, 742 were officers and 120 NCOs in combat, and 73 officers domestically and 167 in training, totaling 1,102 (30 percent of the total 3,702).

As to German aircraft losses in the same period, Balke gives the total of 1,513 in combat, 70 domestically, and 263 at schools plus 88 transferred from there to the front, of which 442 combat planes were repairable, as well as 199 training aircraft and 69 combat machines at the schools, or 38.5 percent of the 1,846 losses or 29 percent of the combat losses. Of the 1,513 then, 29 percent were repairable, and of the 351 school losses, 76 percent were repairable.[45]

Williamson Murray, *Strategy for Defeat: The Luftwaffe, 1933–1945*, noted that the German air arm lost 1,129 by enemy action and 216 due to other causes, for a total of 1,345, and with 83 not on operations for a total of 1,428, or 28 percent of the initial strength of 5,349 aircraft. Then there were 488 damaged for a total of 1,916, or 36 percent of the initial establishment[46] (Tables

23 and 24). Looking at Tables 23 and 24, which are based on figures from the *Abteilung* VI as supplied to the United Kingdom, Air Ministry, it seems that in quoting figures of German aircraft production, the number of repaired aircraft returned to service has been overlooked. In fact the rate for this category overall was roughly 22 percent, but higher for certain types. In the case of the Me-109 in the first six months of 1940, 811 new machines were produced to which were added 520 repaired, for a total of 1331, of which 39 percent were rebuilds. In the whole of 1940, of the 2,754 total production of single-engine Luftwaffe fighters, 48 percent were rebuilds. In the case of the Ju-52 transports, of the 831 total production, 360 or 43.3 percent were rebuilds.[47] The Luftwaffe rebuild rate exceeded the accident rate even during the Battle of France.

Monthly deliveries of all types to the Luftwaffe in the west in the first four months of 1940 amounted to 1,754, followed by 1,857 in May and June and a further 673 in July 1940 (Table 24). In August and September 2,053 were added, with a further 860 in October. May, June, and July totaled 2,530 (923, 934, and 673, respectively) in the Battle of France as compared with July, August, September, and October for the Battle of Britain of 3,586, or less the 860 in October of 2,726. From these figures it must be concluded that the Battle of France was slightly less intensive for the Luftwaffe than the subsequent Battle of Britain in spite of the water hazard of the English Channel in the latter case; over Gaul the Germans faced little opposition.[48]

Overall Luftwaffe serviceability in the west, as calculated in 1945 by the Luftwaffe's *Abteilung* VI from 13 April to 11 May 1940, averaged just over 70 percent, but dropped by 18 May to 60 percent (Table 21). On 13 April there were 1,338 single-engine fighters, of which 946 or 70.7 percent were serviceable. The latter could have flown 3,784 sorties at 4 daily per Me-109; using as a basis the Battle of Britain's 36.5 sorties per enemy aircraft destroyed, the 3,784 could have accounted for 104 Allied machines. On 18 May, with 788 single-engine fighters available, the tally for Germany could only have been 22 or at 15.5 per kill 51.

Luftwaffe casualties in the period 10 May through 18 June, the Battle of France, are also of interest, from 347 destroyed and damaged on 10 May to a maximum of 1,288 by 31 May, a low of 30 on 1 June, then 287 on 18 June (Table 23).

Regarding the number of salvageable and repairable Luftwaffe aircraft in the west, we have to include all those aircraft shot down because they could have yielded at least scrap metal, and at perhaps 60 percent recoverable, that would be 369–400 due to the Armée de l'Air, 120 due to DCA, 65 due to the RAF, and 300 due to the Belgian and Netherlands air arms and antiaircraft, for a total of 854–885. From Cornwell it is possible to glean the fact that the Luftwaffe in the Battle of France suffered 1,290 write-offs of machines, with more than 10 percent damage, and in the Battle of Britain 2,150.[49] But there were also 521 repairables during 10–31 May 1940 and 215 in June, for a total of 736 (122.6 weekly), while during July through September there were only 212 (15.1 weekly).

On 10 May, 347 of the Luftwaffe were lost to enemy action and 66, or 19 percent, to nonoperational causes and damaged on 10 May. After that first day, losses never exceeded 107 daily (Table 23). After 11 May, no GAF losses were higher than 72 (on 14 May). But the RLM documents indicate that nonoperational losses rose to 26.6 percent by 31 May and in the first eighteen days of June these losses rose to 43.2 percent. No doubt there were multiple causes including both pilot and ground-crew fatigue, the unprepared nature of forward landing grounds, fuel exhaustion, and so on.[50]

From the above we can perhaps conclude that the Germans had a salvage and repair organization that was the purview of the Luftwaffe Generalstab, but which functioned quite efficiently, at least in terms of recovery of accident victims. In reality, salvage was the province of the Wehrmacht engineers and therefore outside the ken of the Luftwaffe. It may also be presumed that salvaging from the French countryside proceeded during the summer of 1940, but that the repaired may not have been ready for reissue until 1941.

According to Buffotot and Ogier, German operational losses (destroyed or badly damaged) in France totaled 1,469 and would have included aircraft shot down and those that crashed either on or off the airfield, which were then categorized as repairable or write-offs.[51] As for German and British fighter production during this time, June through December 1940, the German was 1,219 versus the British 3,225, giving the RAF a 265 percent advantage.[52]

Within weeks of the fall of France, the Armée de l'Air was grounded by the terms of the armistice of 24 June, or because it had flown to North Africa where it was also impotent for want of spares, and was still part of the air force of Vichy France. The exceptions were the few patriots who had elected to join the Free French under General Charles de Gaulle in Britain. Only the latter played a role—albeit minor—in the Battle of Britain of 10 July–30 September 1940.

CHAPTER 6

AFTERMATH—
THE BATTLE OF BRITAIN

Air Chief Marshal Sir Hugh Dowding won the Battle of Britain because it was in many ways a 1918-style contest with the English Channel a trench line behind which he had fixed airfields unmenaced by Wehrmacht forces. He had command and control, comparable machines, reserves of planes and pilots, a functioning supply system, and an aircraft industry in high gear.

Dowding, the air officer commanding-in-chief (AOC-in-C) of RAF Fighter Command, started out with at least 570 Hurricanes and Spitfires and 924 officers and 300-plus NCO pilots. He ended the battle with 935 fighters and 1,400 pilots.[1] According to Basil Collier in *The Defence of the United Kingdom*, the Germans launched 22,080-plus night-attack sorties against Britain and the RAF responded with 34,553 sorties. From 10 July to 31 October the Germans lost 1,391 aircraft versus the RAF's 792. As a measure of the differences in the first forty-six days of the battles of France and Britain, the initial 637 FAF pilots averaged about 1.6 kills while the 1,325 RAF pilots averaged about 4.

After the intensive weeks of the August–September battle over Britain, the Luftwaffe had to lick its wounds as it was running low of Me-109s and other aircraft, especially since losses beyond the coast of France were total. In the Battle of Britain the RAF was enabled to be victorious in large part by the fact that it had observers, a radar chain, sector stations, and fighter controllers, and both telephonic and radio communication—the whole based upon a system developed in 1918 and refined in the interwar years.[2] Until 1936 there was a single command, the Air Defence of Great Britain (ADGB); after 1936, as part of the expansion of the RAF, Fighter Command controlled only the defenses. Moreover the defensive scheme had always included searchlights and antiaircraft guns, though these were not under the RAF. The General Officer Commanding (GOC) Antiaircraft Command and the AOC-in-C Fighter

Command worked closely together as timing was extremely important.[3] In addition, there were the Observer Corps posts and their system of reporting directly to Fighter Command so that from spotting to scramble required less than five minutes versus the public PTT-based (Postes, Télegraphes et Téléphones) net in France. Fighter Command aircraft needed ten minutes to climb to 20,000 feet while being directed onto the enemy by ex-fighter pilots in sector control.[4]

The Battle of Britain had three phases: Phase 1: 13–23 August, Phase 2: 24 August–6 September, and Phase 3: 7 September–31 October. In the period of 1–31 July 1940, Fighter Command had 54 squadrons (972 aircraft as of 10 July), 56 squadrons on 8 August (1,008 aircraft), and 61.5 (1,107 aircraft) on 31 October, so that it started the Battle of Britain with 23 more squadrons (414 aircraft) than the French Air Force's 31 *escadrilles* had serviceable on 10 May (372) at the start of the Battle of France. In addition Fighter Command ended the Battle of Britain with almost exactly twice as many squadrons as the FAF had at end of the Battle of France. On 10 July 1940, each Fighter Command squadron had an initial establishment of eighteen Hurricanes or Spitfires and a serviceability rate including spares of 134 percent for Hurricanes and 105 percent for Spitfires, but with only commissioned pilots for 80 percent of the Hurricanes and 74.3 percent of the Spitfires, with 71 squadrons all told certified as having served under Fighter Command in the Battle of Britain.[5]

On 8 August, 113.5 percent of Fighter Command's Hurricanes and 102 percent of its Spitfires were serviceable, because even the two spare machines were ready, but only 65 and 78.4 percent, respectively, had qualified pilots available. Although by 31 October there were 34 Hurricane squadrons as opposed to 28.5 on 8 August and 399 pilots versus 370, the number of Spitfire squadrons remained constant at 19 from 10 July when there were 226 pilots, peaking on 8 August at 257, but dropping back to 227 on 31 August. Pilots were always Dowding's shortage, but when NCO pilots were counted the total deficit was less than ten percent. It was experienced ones who were in short supply.[6] The reserves of Spitfires and Hurricanes were down to 161 by late August, but the shortage did not worsen because tactical lessons had been learned, production remained stable, and a solution to the repair of bombed airfields had been worked out. (See Table 47 and Table 32.)

The Battle of Britain[7]

The Battle of Britain, from 15 August to 25 September, is the classic first case of an air force being defeated by another air force alone. The differences with the Battle of France are not as great as they are significant.

As explained in *Two Roads to War: The French and British Air Arms from Versailles to Dunkirk,* unlike in France, the whole of the British temperament, system, governance, and leadership was very different to that south of La Manche. On 10 May, Winston Churchill, an experienced soldier with pilot's

TABLE 47. RAF Fighter Command Order of Battle 1 July 1940, Aircraft and Pilots per Squadron

GROUP	INITIAL AIRCRAFT ESTABLISHMENT SERVICEABLE	INITIAL AIRCRAFT ESTABLISHMENT UNSERVICEABLE	PILOTS
No. 11 Uxbridge			
Biggin Hill	51	19	88
North Weald	51	19	83
Kenley	44	19	75
Northolt	48	19	74
Hornchurch	33	15	54
Tangmere	43	17	64
Filton	34	16	60
Middle Wallop	21	6	36
Debden	14	4	129
Total	**339**	**134**	**663**
No. 12, Duxford	19	12	47
Colltishall	22	8	46
Kirton Lindsey	12	4	21
Digby	28	19	53
Wittering	32	13	61
Total	**113**	**56**	**228**
No. 13, Church Fenton	43	17	87
Catterick	21	10	40
Usworth	30	14	61
Turnhouse	57	26	94
Dyce	3	2	7
Wick	24	6	33
Total	**178**	**75**	**322**
Total, Fighter Command	**630**	**265**	**1,213**

Source: Francis K. Mason, *Battle over Britain* (New York: Doubleday, 1969), 130.

brevet and a national leader, had become prime minister, Britain's "man on horseback." In addition Dowding, as AOC-in-C of Fighter Command, had long been involved in planning to counter the "air menace," had the air defense system refined from 1918, had fighters comparable to the Me-109, and had radar.

German Panzers could not overrun RAF airfields nor overwhelm the antiaircraft defenses. The RAF had a working and refined air-defense system backed up by the Royal Observer Corps, the postal telecommunications links, radar, filter rooms, and fighter controllers with radios. The Air Ministry was providing a replenishment system bedded upon the aircraft industry, sufficient ground crew, and a system of reporting the daily state of serviceability of all aircraft based upon realities and not upon an elaborate system that hid real lack of readiness.

The Battle of Britain was what the Battle of France might have been. The English Channel was the completed Maginot Line that the Panzers could not disrupt to move to the airfields. This allowed a just-sufficient RAF Fighter Command to beat off the Luftwaffe, a tactical air weapon being used as a grand-strategic one. But the RAF had the additional advantage that at Home Fighter Command had authority, and an executive tactical commander, whose basic organizational structure had been honed since 1918. AOC-in-C of Fighter Command Dowding also was in close contact with General Sir Frederick Pile, the commander of the antiaircraft forces, which was the *defense contre avions* that the French did not have.

Dowding was lucky in that the chief of the Air Staff, unlike the First Lord of the Admiralty, did not have executive authority in 1940. The prewar proposal to create an AOC-in-C RAF died because Dowding was the logical candidate and various of his immediate juniors did not wish to see so knowledgeable an officer in such a powerful position. In contrast, General Astier de la Vigerie had to report to Vuillemin, who on the outbreak of war had shifted from *chef* GSAF (commander, General Staff Air Force) to *général commandant* Armée de l'Air (commanding general) in the field. But even then he had to get General Gamelin's permission to issue orders. British commanders were autonomous within their mandate and could threaten to resign if the Higher Direction overstepped its bounds, as Wavell made plain to Churchill in 1941.[8]

In the Battle of Britain the RAF was not shackled either by a doctrinal requirement to protect army units or by a divided command (with the exception of Park versus Leigh-Mallory) with layers of authority that stultified action. In contrast to the experiences in France, where the FAF was ill-prepared to meet the blitzkrieg in the air and on the ground, the RAF was limited by its dual role, defensive and offensive, by its lack of full authority, and by security concerns regarding radar and Spitfires.

The RAF on 4 June 1940 had only 30 fighters in reserve depots with about 1,000 available and new aircraft at 15 per day, plus 1,200 trained pilots with new ones at six per day.

After the Battle of France, Dowding on 10 July had 134 percent of Hurricane pilots and 105 percent for Spitfires as compared with a serviceable fifty-four squadrons. On 30 June 1940 RAF Fighter Command alone had an operational strength of 1,200 out of an establishment of 1,482 pilots, and on 15 June it had 405 operational Hurricanes and 357 Spitfires. By 15 August, at the start of the Battle of Britain, Fighter Command had 673 Hurricanes and 367 Spitfires for a total of 1,040 manned by 1,379 pilots, only 179 below establishment. Even at the end of the Battle on 15 September there were 608 Hurricanes and 333 Spitfires manned by 1,492 pilots. Earlier lower figures of pilots were influenced by the failure to include both NCOs and foreigners. The Luftwaffe started on 1 August with 869 fully operational single-engine fighter pilots and ended on 1 September with 735.[9]

Normal RAF squadrons in Fighter Command flew a total of about 1,500 sorties (one flight by one aircraft) weekly. Once the battle was joined, the sortie rate rose to more than 4,000 by the end of July, with a drop to 3,000 in the bad weather during early August and a rise to 5,000 just before the end of the month. Both sides took about 36.5 sorties to shoot down an enemy aircraft. On the 5,000-sortie day, the total possible Luftwaffe aircraft lost to the RAF would have been about 136 (Table 48).

RAF daily state lists clearly show that many RAF losses were repairable, the number being struck-off being quite small, and from early October the number of rebuilt returned-to-service machines rose dramatically with two hundred Hurricanes alone (Table 49). On the other hand, Luftwaffe losses over Britain were gone forever and more machines ran out of fuel and did not return to their airfields in France and Belgium. On top of this the traditional German disinterest in logistics led both in France and later in the summer of 1940 to lack of action to salvage machines.[10] Yet 22 percent of German aircraft production up to the summer of 1940 were rebuilds; in the Battle this dropped to 8 percent.

The German enemy air forces in France from 10 May to 24 June and over Britain from 7 August to 15 September were basically the same—bombers heavily escorted (about 2.2 fighters per bomber). Neither of the Allies had contemplated having to defend against heavily escorted bombers. Certainly British thinking, as Colin Sinnott has shown, was devoted to defending against unescorted enemy aircraft.[11] In addition, no air arm had devoted much thought to operational fatigue and its draining effects upon aircrew, mechanics, antiaircraft gunners, and radar operators.[12]

TABLE 48. Weather, 12 August–23 September 1940, during the Battle of Britain

DATE	CONDITIONS	DATE	CONDITIONS
12 August	Fine	3 September	Flyable
13 August	Bad weather until p.m.	4 September	Flyable
14 August	Flyable	5 September	Flyable
15 August	Cloudy, clearing p.m.	6 September	Flyable
16 August	Early coastal mists	7 September	Fine and warm
17 August	Fair	8 September	Flyable
18 August	Fair	9 September	Flyable
19August	Mainly cloudy	10 September	Dull weather
20 August	Weather deteriorating	11 September	Weather deteriorating
21 August	Poor weather in UK	12 September	Flyable
22 August	Cloudy	13 September	Flyable
23 August	Unsuitable, low cloud	14 September	Temperature deteriorating
24 August	Clear and fine	15 September	Fine weather
25 August	Fine	16 September	Rain clouds
26 August	OK	17 September	Flyable
27 August	Drizzle and low cloud, cleared later	18 September	Flyable
28 August	OK	19 September	Rain showers
29 August	Reasonable	20 September	Flyable
30 August	Fine	21 September	Flyable
31 August	Fine	22 September	Dull and foggy, clearing later
1 September	Flyable	23 September	Flyable
2 September	Flyable		

Source: Francis K. Mason, *Battle over Britain* (New York: Doubleday, 1969), daily.

During the opening phase from 7 July to 7 August, the Luftwaffe was recouping from the campaign in France, which had units down to 30 percent availability. Thus limited operations were undertaken against the coastal convoys in the Channel. The RAF's protective patrols consumed hours and fatigued pilots. RAF losses over water were real as pilots had at first no dinghies and there was no British AS/R service.

Neither side picked the better targets. The convoys were small-fry. The RAF was correct to go for the bombers, especially the vulnerable Stukas. The Germans should have concentrated on the radar chain, the RAF's forward

TABLE 49. RAF Daily States Categories

RAF DAILY STATES CATEGORIES	
A.	Estimated initial establishment (on 15 August 1940): Hurricanes at twenty aircraft per squadron, Spitfires at sixteen
B.	Serviceable now
C.	Serviceable in 12 hours
D.	Serviceable in 7 days
	Total
E.	Repairable by unit, but in more than 7 days
F.	Repairable, but beyond unit's capacity
G.	Struck-off

Source: United Kingdom, National Archives, AIR 22, Daily States.

Note: The "initial establishment" was the paper strength, whereas operational readiness counted only serviceable machines.

airfields, and the Hurricane and Spitfire factories in southern England. The RAF missed using No. 2 Group of Blenheim medium bombers against the fifty German airfields in northern France and Belgium, upon which there were an average of fifty unrevetted aircraft each. The problems were that No. 2 Group was in Bomber Command, not under Dowding, and RAF doctrine was focused on attacks upon enemy industry, which was mostly out of range, and the RAF's bombing accuracy such that little damage could be done by these raids.[13] Moreover, the insistence that Blenheims fly at 12,000 feet and not on the deck made them vulnerable.

The Germans from 12 August, when the offensive really started, assumed they could knock out the RAF in four days. The two GAF fleet commanders, Kesselring, a former ground-forces man, and Sperrle, a flier, argued about London being the proper target. Hitler ruled out London, and thus the Luftwaffe was dispatched to attack the RAF's airfields and factories to make the British rise and fight so that they could be shot down. By the end of July, Dowding had been able to refit the twelve squadrons ravaged in the Battle of France and to make good most of the 296 Hurricanes and 67 Spitfires lost in that campaign as well as most of the 340 pilot casualties. The fresh British pilots had fifteen hours at the new operational training units (OTUs), which replaced training on the squadron, but were lacking in gunnery practice and saddled still with the "vic" tactics instead of the German pair and finger-four formations learned in Spain. The RAF also needed cannon or .50-caliber machine guns rather than .303 machine guns.[14]

And if the Germans had disputes as to the proper targets, the RAF had the professional differences between fighter pilot AVM Keith Park of the key

No. 11 Group in southeast England and AVM Trafford Leigh-Mallory, a World War I reconnaissance pilot, who commanded No. 12 Group in the Midlands. When Park moved from being Dowding's senior air staff officer (SASO) to No. 11 Group, AVM D. C. S. Evill succeeded him and failed to stop Leigh-Mallory's determination to oust Dowding. The ostensible "burr under the saddle" was the Big Wing controversy, No. 12 Group's tactical solution of massing squadrons to meet the German attacks. No. 11 Group, with its airfield only fifteen minutes from the enemy, could not do that. In the end, this quarrel became a political intrigue in the Air Ministry.

Park launched his squadrons singly because of his limited warning time, while Leigh-Mallory tried to form three squadrons into Big Wings. But of the thirty-two occasions when these did coalesce, they found the enemy only seven times and only once intercepted a raid before other defenders. On that occasion the forty-eight fighters involved shot down not the claimed 57 enemy, but only 8. Park said that at the same time his fighters had destroyed 211 enemy, the "Balbos" from Duxford had shot down 1. Leigh-Mallory was deliberate and did not scramble his squadrons in time and wasted precious minutes forming up his Big Wings. Additional friction was caused by Leigh-Mallory's alleged dumping of his dud pilots into No. 11 Group when asked for replacements.[15]

Fighter Command was faced with totally unforeseen conditions. With the fall of Norway in April and May and then of the Low Countries and France, the Luftwaffe was able to station its forces in a semicircle to the north, east, and south of Britain, whereas prewar the air menace was expected, unescorted, from Germany alone. By August 1940 fifty German airfields were within striking distance of Great Britain, which was short of airfields. The RAF had had fifty-two in 1934, and though a vast expansion had begun, the new airfields took three and a half years each to build and Bomber Command demanded many of them. The result was that Fighter Command had eighteen when the battle opened, rising to twenty-three as the number of squadrons went from fifty-two on 10 July to fifty-seven on 7 September.[16]

The Germans had in the interval after the Battle of France reequipped the Luftwaffe. It was in reality not as strong as the Air Ministry in London claimed until the Singleton Report of spring 1941, when its estimated strength was reduced from 14,000 to 5,000 in all activities.[17] In terms of single-engine fighters, the ratio was 760 serviceable Me-109s to Fighter Command's 700 Hurricanes and Spitfires[18] (Table 50).

Park, at No. 11 Group, was a former fighter pilot who still flew. He was very conscious of his limited forces and his instructions to controllers emphasized this. On 19 August he ordered that fighters were to be scrambled only to

TABLE 50. GAF Fully Operational Single-Engine Fighters

DATE	NUMBER
1 June 1940	906
1 August 1940	869
1 September 1940	735
1 November 1940	673

Source: United Kingdom, CAB 106/282.

meet large enemy formations over land or within gliding distance of the coast. He could not afford to lose any pilots[19] (Table 51). By keeping his squadrons over Britain, Park not only ensured that pilots forced to bail out would be recovered but also that some 44 percent of the aircraft shot down could also be returned to service shortly because they had landed safely.

In France the RAF had lost twenty-five Hurricanes per day, but over England the newly armored Hurricanes were lost at the rate of only eight per day, and many were repairable and back in service in two days.[20] However, during the forty-three days in the Battle of Britain from 10 July to 21 August 1940, the RAF with fifty-five squadrons of eighteen aircraft IE put up 5,448 sorties (130 daily) with 990 aircraft total and at 75 percent serviceable, or 742 for 5.7 sorties daily per serviceable aircraft.[21]

The Luftwaffe began serious attacks on RAF airfields on 7 August, but due to bad weather the main assault did not come until 15 August. So compared with the situation in France, where observers' reports trickled along the PTT to command centers that then had to telephone to squadrons that did not have the initiative to launch sorties without orders from above in what was a far more anarchic situation, Fighter Command could respond at once (Table 51).

Unlike the Armée de l'Air's situation in May and June, Fighter Command had an excellent telephonic and teleprinter communications network, experienced former pilot controllers, and the ability to make quick decisions and to relay these by radio telephone to airborne squadrons. Sorties lasted no more than fifty-five minutes at full throttle, and combat only a few minutes with fifteen seconds of firepower.

TABLE 51. RAF Fighter Command Pilot Strength

DATE	ESTABLISHMENT	OPERATIONAL STRENGTH
30 June 1940	1,482	1,200
27 July 1940	1,456	1,377
17 August 1940	1,558	1,379
14 September 1940	1,662	1,492
19 October 1940	1,714	1,752
2 November 1940	1,727	1,796

Source: United Kingdom, National Archives, AIR 22, Daily States.

Both the Luftwaffe and the RAF normally had 25 percent of their aircraft on the ground unserviceable, making airfields a potentially lucrative target. The problem was that the Germans often hit airfields other than those of Fighter Command and that Dowding did not command the bomber forces, especially the Blenheims of No. 2 Group, Bomber Command, which might have struck at the crowded Luftwaffe airfields. Bomber Command's belief that the crews could not find and strike GAF airfields was based upon those aerodromes in Germany and not on those in France and the Low Countries whose locations were familiar from the recent campaign of May and June. Dowding and Park could not take the risk with Fighter Command, which was a defensive arm, but Bomber Command was an offensive weapon. Part of the weakness lay in the failure to appoint an AOC-in-C RAF. Vuillemin was the French GOC air force appointee, but his hands were tied to the armée. In the summer of 1940 an AOC-in-C RAF would not have been so handicapped.

Being so oriented to the Wehrmacht's needs, the Luftwaffe had not asked itself what were the strengths and weaknesses of its own Freya radar, nor in defense how it would control fighters. This was a double blindness—assuming that the enemy thought as you did and that he was less capable. The Germans, as also the Allies, were overly sanguine as to the damage they were inflicting because, unlike in 1914–1918, they had no troops on the ground to report the enemy's losses. Goering accepted the pilots' claims without dividing by three or five, and the pressure to produce results, to eliminate the RAF so that the invasion could take place, put a cloth over the picture. In addition, the Panzers were unable to seize aerodromes as they had in France.

After several days of bad weather, intense activity resumed on 24 August and lasted until 6 September. The regrouped GAF fighters, then stationed close to Cap Gris-Nez to increase their time over Britain, tried to overwhelm the defenders; but the latter had regrouped and were better at reporting the heights of raids.

The GAF fighter pilots under Adolf Galland were getting fatigued, as were those of the RAF. Goering's advisers believed they were winning the battle of attrition, claiming a score of 791 for a loss of 353. But Goering's four days to victory had stretched to four weeks, and victory was still not in sight. By then, the British chief of the Air Staff reckoned in spring 1941 that the RAF would get its second wind. Both planes and pilots were becoming available to replace reserves.

On Saturday, 7 September, Hugo Sperrle, the airman who commanded Luftflotte 3, lost the argument to attack airfields to Reichsmarschall Kesselring, who launched the attacks on London. On that Saturday, Fighter Command's airfields were saved. The day before, Dowding had divided his command into three letter groups—A, for those in No. 11 Group and those fit enough to reinforce it; B, for those in the other three groups, 10, 12, and 14, which could reinforce Park; and C, for those too weak to fight, but from whom experienced pilots could be posted into No. 11's exhausted squadrons.

In the meantime, production and wastage of Spitfires and Hurricanes were about equal, though losses by damage and forced landings had consumed the reserves. On 10 August the storage units had 160 Hurricanes and 129 Spitfires to replace a wastage in the previous week of 64. However, wastage in battle and accident rose to 240 per week for the next four weeks. On 7 September only 86 Hurricanes and 39 Spitfires were ready for issue. At that moment the Germans could have won. On 4 August the GAF had smashed one Sector Control apparatus. And in August Park had lost over 300 pilots, creating a deficit over training of 40. Of the original roughly 1,000 officer pilots Fighter Command had at the start of the war, only 250 remained in action.[22]

The GAF assault on London was not the devastating blow of the air menace so feared prewar. London was forty miles in diameter, and 60 percent of the Luftwaffe bombs fell in open spaces—streets, parks, and countryside.

From 8 September Park's squadrons scrambled in pairs, the Spitfires going for the escorts and the Hurricanes for the bombers. The apex was reached on 15 September. Park fought the Battle of Britain with Prime Minister Churchill and his wife, Clementine, in the control room. When at one point the knowledgeable "PM" asked about reserves, Park said there were none. He had gambled that his squadrons would all be rearmed and refueled before the Germans returned again that victorious day when the RAF claimed 183 shot down (later found to be 56) for 26 RAF aircraft lost. As a result, Goering's boast was pricked and the invasion of Britain (Operation Sea Lion) postponed indefinitely. Though the night Battle of Britain would continue into the spring of 1941, Britain was safe from the "air menace."

All told in the Battle of Britain, from 10 July to 31 October (though sometimes given as 12 August to 15 September), the RAF, Dominion, and Allied Air Forces lost 414 pilots and 35 other aircrew.[23] In the preliminary phase of operations, 10 July to 12 August, the RAF put up 18,026 sorties and lost 150 aircraft, or 0.8 percent, to the German 286.[24] In the next phase, from 13–23 August, the RAF launched 6,414 sorties and lost 114 aircraft, or 1.8 percent compared with the Luftwaffe's 290 losses.[25]

From 28 August to 6 September, Fighter Command put up 10,673 sorties and lost 286 aircraft to the GAF's 13,724 sorties, with a loss of 380 or 2.7 percent to 2.8.[26] On 7 September the GAF had 669 Me-109s in northern France and southern Holland, of which 533, or 80 percent, were serviceable.[27] From 7 September to 31 October, Fighter Command lost 242 aircraft to the Luftwaffe's 433.

These casualty figures, however, are only for aircraft shot down and do not include forced landings and accidents, from which many were salvageable.

During the Battle of Britain an immobile Luftwaffe was able to maintain a serviceability rate above 71 percent until the week of 31 August when it dropped for two weeks to 68.8, but by 14 September was back up to 72.6 percent. During the week that ended 13 July the GAF had 1,077 Me-109s in the west of which 899 (83.5 percent) serviceable. A month later there were 1,036 with 853 (82.3 percent) serviceable. But by 31 August there were only 921, with 692 (75 percent) serviceable. However, thereafter the number of serviceable Me-109s rose, then dipped down again by 28 September to 764. With 899 able to fly four sorties daily, the tally of enemy machines could have been 98.5 (3,596 divided by 36.5). With only 692 sortieing, the likely enemy destroyed was reduced to 76 daily.[28]

Although the RAF lost more fighters than the Luftwaffe, 44 percent were repairables versus the Luftwaffe's 7 percent of all 1,407 (Table 30). In total casualties the RAF came out more than 330 ahead and was able to sustain itself against the much larger enemy.[29]

The Fighter Command pilot story has been consistently skewed by referring only to the 924/925 commissioned pilots. However, these represented only 73.1 percent of Fighter Command's pilot strength in early July 1940, and only 66 percent by the end of the battle on 30 October.[30] Why the discrepancy? Prewar RAF NCO pilots had up to five years' flying experience but could not be flight leaders because they were not commissioned officers. They also reverted to their ground trades at the end of five years. The RAF during 1939–1940 was still an élite fighting club. The *Air Force List* gave the names of commissioned pilots in a squadron but only noted the number of NCOs. It seems apparent that the 924 were officer pilots and that the differences between the initial establishment of 1,430 less 197 and the 924 was 309 NCO pilots. Fighter Command had a consistent 924/925 commissioned pilots throughout the Battle of Britain supplemented by 340 to 505 NCO pilots. On that basis, the start was 1,265 pilots all told, and in that case NCO pilots were 26.9 percent of establishment, rising to 35.3 percent (925 + 505). In contrast, the FAF had possibly only 637 pilots (including *sous-officiers*) but should have had 3,218.[31]

Of the Hurricane and Spitfire pilots, 10 July to 30 September there were 1,433 of whom 817 (57 percent) were unhurt while 616 were killed, wounded, or missing (42.9 percent), and of their 1,375 machines, 632 or 45.9 percent were repairable and 744 or 54 percent were write-offs.

During the Battle of Britain in August 1940, RAF training produced 260 fighter pilots, but Fighter Command lost 304. By 6 September Fighter Command was losing on average 120 pilots weekly from strength of 1,400.[32] Thus Fighter Command's AOC-in-C Dowding introduced A, B, and C squadron categories, with A to be kept at sixteen operational pilots. He had to stop rotating squadrons and keep tired pilots in 11 Group.[33]

The Battle of Britain was essentially one of attrition. By the end of August, the Luftwaffe single-engine fighter force was only 69 percent of that on 10 May.[34] Meanwhile RAF Bomber Command was directed to attack the invasion barges and neglected the GAF airfields.[35] After the Battle's search of cemeteries revealed more dead than the official records showed, and thus the official total is 537, but the actual is 551, an error of 2.6 percent.

Another view of the matter is to use After the Battle's list of RAF pilots killed during the Battle of Britain and categorized by rank. Of the 537 casualties, 195 were NCOs, or 15.4 percent of the IE of 1,265 and 34 percent of the killed. Based on the alphabetical list[36] of those who died in the Battle of Britain, July–October 1940, 537 were killed in the battle, all but a mere fraction of whom were pilots. The age breakdown was 2 with no age given in their records; 4 of forty years or older; 32 between thirty and thirty-nine years of age; 172 between twenty-five and twenty-nine years; and 329 between eighteen and twenty-four years—a total of 537. In contrast, the Armée de l'Air had only forty pilots under the age of forty on 10 May. The RAF had so many pilots in the twenty-five-to-twenty-nine-year age bracket because in 1940 these were still Regulars leavened with the products of the Royal Auxiliary Air Force and RAF Volunteer Reserve (RAFVR) programs. (The RAFVR had to be eighteen to twenty-five years of age to volunteer.)

Fighter Command had the advantage in July–October 1940 of having twenty-four to twenty-six pilots on each squadron, allowing some to get a bit of a rest, whereas the FAF escadrille had a minimum of about twelve pilots to start with, and that added to their exhaustion even at only 0.9 sorties a day, as well as constant moves. During the Battle of Britain, the use of parachutes and all-metal aircraft fitted with safety harnesses meant that fighter pilots who were shot down or in damaged aircraft had a fair chance of survival, in contrast to the experience of the chuteless Royal Flying Corps pilot casualties during World War I. The Sutton safety harness was developed in late World War I because lap belts gave way during aerobatics and in crashes pilots hit their heads. The two shoulder and two thigh webs were held together over the stomach by a quick-release pin.[37] Postwar the harnesses were fitted to aircraft notable for nosing over on landing. Not until about 1928 were they fitted to all RAF aircraft, when parachutes were also supplied. By then engines could handle the extra weight.

The Battle of Britain was the contemporary sequel to the Battle of France, but it was fought under significantly different circumstances by, however, two of the same players with the same equipment, plus radar, sector control, and antiaircraft. So the RAF fought against the "air menace" for which it had been preparing since 1918, aided immensely by the Technological Revolution—in aircraft, aircraft production, armaments, and electronics—as well as without the distraction of a ground blitzkrieg battle. Moreover, Fighter Command was only one-third of the RAF. On the other hand, the Luftwaffe was confidently thrown into a struggle with poor Intelligence, including a misapprehension of the British character and leadership and an infrastructure insufficient to support the campaign.

Dowding, AOC-in-C Fighter Command since 1936, could focus on defeating the Luftwaffe, in contrast to the Armée de l'Air's General Joseph Vuillemin's schizophrenic tasks and woefully inadequate command, control, and communications, based upon unsettled doctrine. on confused infrastructure, and lack of wireless sets. In the Battle of Britain, Fighter Command was able actually to expand its aircraft strength while in May and June of 1940, the French *chasse* squadrons declined in effectiveness—though not in aircraft on FAF charge—to the point where the remnant left the battle on 10 June 1940. As Prime Minister Churchill observed in that same month, "The growth of the machinery of organization must precede the growth of the organization itself." That truism does much to explain why the Armée de l'Air was so far behind in 1940.

What follows dwells on the Battle of Britain, because coming only a few short weeks after the Battle of France, it can be regarded both as a continuation of that campaign, as a comparison and contrast with operations in Gaul, and as an example of the differing cultural characteristics and approaches on opposite sides of the English Channel. The foresight in RAF training can be seen in the growth from September 1939 to September 1940 of the pilot strength from 9,721 to 11,750 and total trained aircrew from 12,257 to 19,648 in spite of losses, plus 15,296 more under training.[38] By and during the Battle of Britain, the RAF's operational training of pilots broke down as the squadrons were too busy to continue the Victorian regimental system of that being done on the unit. So operational training units (OTUs) were in the process of being established. These took six weeks in 1940 to give fresh pilots the feel of their new operational machines—generally, in the Fighter Command case, of Hurricanes and Spitfires—with all told some fifteen hours on type. Newly mined pilots joined squadrons with roughly 150 hours, in contrast to the Armée de l'Air's average pilot experience of 750 hours and the Luftwaffe's 250. The length of the RAF process was governed by the OTUs 59 percent serviceability rate and that was due to a shortage of spares and of fitters, riggers, and mechanics as well as armorers, and requirements for routine station duties.[39]

The very hard winter months of 1939–1940 reduced the output of pilots to 1,100 by April. Efforts were made to push pupils through to OTUs, though to produce in six weeks 1,200 pilots for Bomber Command, with forty hours of flight time, needed 2,000 OTU aircraft. Speed and pressure caused accidents, especially in units with new, modern machines. Poor weather and lack of navigation, wireless transmission (W/T) and meteorological (Met') training led to pupils flying into cloud-covered high ground. Newer aircraft were heavier and had higher wing loadings that inadequately prepared pilots could not handle, leading to an accident rate in squadrons with modern aircraft four times that of units with older machines. The rate was especially high in single-seat aircraft because of lack of dual instruction, and because the cockpits were ten times more complex than in the older biplanes. In addition, experienced operational aircrew were drained off to training and replaced in their units by less skilled personnel.

Even the "miracle" radar was only a technical development together with sector control, which was integrated into the Air Defence of Great Britain (ADGB) created in 1918 by Major General E. B. Ashmore and perfected by him to 1929. From 1936 ACM Dowding, who had been the air member for technical developments, integrated the ADGB, electronics, and sector controllers, and proved the combination worked in the 1937–1939 air exercises, themselves based upon the 1927 and following tests. Radar largely saved hours on machines and men having to be sent up on standing patrols,[40] as the AOC-in-C had always to meet any raids. Short of resources, he resisted creating a second group pool OTU until 25 September 1939. Due to shortages of camera guns and of fully equipped aircraft, as well as only a 59 percent OTU serviceability rate, production of trained fighter pilots was only 500 annually rather than the planned 1,100.

Fighter OTUs, of which there were four by the summer of 1940, were to have an initial establishment of 75 percent operational aircraft and 25 percent trainers, or 75 aircraft, with 25 operational machines in reserve. When 215 squadrons were operational, such establishments would require 2,000 fighters and 700 reserves manned by 2,750 officers and 40,000 airmen. Yet the training organization did keep up with the casualties in the Battle of Britain and ended with a surplus.

Dowding asked for and the Air Staff reluctantly accepted on 17 August 1940 that twenty experienced Fairey Battle pilots, and thirty-three Army

Cooperation pilots, were to take a six-day course at a fighter OTU; in addition, between seventy and eighty pilots just completing OTU would join in a week. The Air Ministry then had enough foreign and other pilots to fill the next OTU courses. The order that the four-week OTU course be shortened to two weeks was rescinded, and pupils passed out with only ten to twenty hours solo in the aircraft they would fly on squadrons.

Paradoxically the need to form Polish and Czech squadrons for linguistic reasons came when there was a shortage of aircraft, barely enough for existing units. To reach a compromise, it was agreed that one new Czech and three new Polish squadrons would be established, but with only half the usual IE of pilots and machines and that they, not the OTUs, would train themselves. Thus none were in full action until October of 1940. Otherwise there was no big new intake to Fighter Command until the early September OTU courses graduated.[41]

Spitfires and Hurricanes attacking in the 30-degree cone of fire made the aircraft vulnerable to enemy bombers' gunners, especially those of the twin-tailed Do-17. Many RAF fighters were hit in the glycol tank or in the gravity feed tank. These were unarmored and located above and in front of the engine, and behind on the firewall, respectively. Hurricanes suffered more losses from bombers returning fire than did Spitfires because the former's job in the Battle of Britain was to try to smash the bomber formations before they could reach their targets, while the Spitfire's role was to tackle the escorts. When on routine patrols, on occasion both were surprised. As the battle progressed, it seems the German gunners and pilots became better shots—fewer RAF aircraft were repairable.

FAF fighters during the Battle of France were vulnerable to the return fire from Luftwaffe bombers because the latter's rear gunners seem to have been effective, judging by RAF damage reports, and because the French relative rate of closure was less than a negative 100 mph. Their casualties can be assessed by applying the RAF's loss ratios in July, August, September, and October on operations—destroyed, missing, and lost to the Germans for that period (Table 29). According to T. C. G. James's *Battle of Britain*, the early Air Historical Branch study, from 10 July to 30 September 1940 RAF Fighter Command flew a total of 48,336 sorties by day in eighty-two days, or 589.5 daily, and 2,301 at night for about twenty-eight nightly—all told, 50,637 sorties for an average of 617 every twenty-four hours.[42] On the basis of 36.5 RAF sorties per kill, then the total Luftwaffe destroyed should have been 1,387 in eighty-two days.

James, writing early, estimates the GAF sorties as 14,645 from 24 August through 30 September.[43] Horst Boog in Militargeschliches Forschungamt (ed.), *Das Deutsche reich und der Zweite Weltkrieg*, shows for August, September, and October a total of 21,950 sorties by bombers. He does not know fighter sorties, but as escorts appear to have averaged 2.2:1 bomber, the total by escorts would have been 48,290 and all told 70,240.[44]

During the Battle of Britain of the summer of 1940, the RAF between 10 July and 6 September flew 35,103 sorties and shot down 956 Luftwaffe aircraft. This meant an average of 36.5 sorties for each downed aircraft, not allowing for damaged machines and operational accidents. But this 36.5 sorties can be applied as a measure against the French claims and losses. RAF losses at 550 were 57.5 percent of the 956 German losses. The 550 RAF losses were approximately 1.6 percent of their 35,103 sorties, one for every 64 sorties, whereas the GAF's 956 over 13,724 sorties had a loss rate of one every 36 sorties in the last phase only of 13 August–6 September. It took 48 GAF sorties for one RAF loss (Tables 52–54).[45]

The 117 aircraft that Fighter Command lost on sustained operations was 27 above monthly production, but 419 Hurricanes and Spitfires were in storage units, ready for issue within four days on 13 July. On 11 July, 186 Hurricanes were Category 1, ready for immediate issue, and 18 more ready within four days. Of Spitfires in ASU Category 1, there were 122; in Category 2 (should be available within four days) and Category 4 (aircraft on ground awaiting modifications or spares), 126; and on four days' notice another 89 (Table 33).

Losses in August were 117 damaged but repairable within four days on the squadrons, and 375 burned in raids, destroyed, or lost/missing over the sea. In spite of a total loss of 492 in the month, on 24 August Fighter Command hit its peak serviceability of 740 aircraft, a figure that included Gladiators, Defiants, and Blenheims. These latter three types on 8 August comprised only

TABLE 52. Total RAF and GAF Aircraft Losses and Aircrew Casualties by Month, July–October 1940

DATE	RAF AIRCREW CASUALTIES	RAF AIRCRAFT LOSSES	GAF AIRCREW CASUALTIES	GAF AIRCRAFT LOSSES
July	68	91	348	185
August	176	389	993	694
September	123	358	829	629
October	120	185	492	379
Total	**487[a]**	**1,023**	**2,662[b]**	**1,887[c]**

Source: After the Battle, *The Battle of Britain (Mark II)* (London: Battle of Britain Printing International, 1982), 259.

[a] Total of both aircrew and groundcrew: 537.
[b] Total Me-109/110 aircrew killed: 551.
[c] Total Me-109/110 aircraft lost: 873.

TABLE 53. Weekly Daily State of Spitfires and Hurricanes as Shown in Air Ministry War Room, October 1939–December 1940*

DATE	INITIAL ESTABLISHMENT	SERVICEABLE	OPERATIONAL WITH PILOTS
16 October 1939	432	466	n/a
15 November 1939	502	534	
15 December 1939	432	436	
15 January 1940	490		
15 February 1940	n/a	n/a	
15 March 1940	n/a	597	
15 April 1940	n/a	706	
15 May 1940	n/a	594	
14 June 1940	n/a IE now 20 for most squadrons, except four Spitfire squadrons at 16	762	
15 July 1940		1,012	
15 August 1940		1,040	
15 September 1940		941	
15 October 1940		974	
15 November 1940		993	
15 December 1940		1,013	

Source: United Kingdom, National Archives, AIR 20/4174, Summary. 26 October 1945, daily AIR 16/940-946, October 1939-December 1940.

Note: Tables 53 and 54 illustrate another of the perennial problems in military as well as air history—what were actual strengths?

*At 1800 hours the day before.

8.5 squadrons with 136 machines of which 83 (69 percent) were Blenheim Ia twin-engine fighters (Table 21). The 120 Blenheims represented only 10.9 percent of the 1,100 serviceable aircraft on 8 August. As only 720 aircraft had crews, and of these only 627 were Hurricanes and Spitfires, the 93 obsolescent machines with crews were 12.9 percent of Fighter Command's strength.

On 14 September 165 Hurricanes and 72 Spitfires were ready for issue within four days. By 31 October, after the daylight battle was over, thirty-four Hurricane squadrons (each with nearly 17 aircraft) totaled 561 serviceable aircraft, and the same nineteen Spitfire squadrons as in July with 294 service-

TABLE 54. Air Ministry War Room Hurricanes and Spitfires, Daily States, July–October 1940

DATE	INITIAL ESTABLISHMENT	SERVICEABLE	OPERATIONAL WITH PILOTS
10 July			
Hurricanes	432	582	344
Spitfires	304	320	226
Total	**736**	**902**	**570**
8 August			
Hurricanes	568	645	370
Spitfires	328	335	257
Total	**896**	**980**	**627**
31 October			
Hurricanes	544	561	399
Spitfires	304	294	222
Total	**848**	**855**	**621**

Source: United Kingdom, National Archives, AIR 20/4174, Summary, 26 October 1945, daily AIR 16/940-946, October 1939–December 1940.

able aircraft or 15.5 each. But the operational-with-pilots rate was 71 percent for the Hurricane squadrons and 75.5 percent for the Spitfires (Table 54). On 26 October the aircraft storage units had ready for issue within four days 252 Hurricanes and 108 Spitfires for a total reserve of 360. Part of the reason for this was that machines were not taken on RAF charge unless they were substantially ready to be issued to a squadron—*bon de guerre*.[46]

A second contributing factor was that the Ministry of Aircraft Production field repair teams (created in May 1940) were cleaning out the Category 4 aircraft—"aircraft on ground awaiting modifications or spares"—which had been pushed across the road from airfields as beyond squadron resources and thus beyond the ability to return them to service. Another point to consider is that in order to maintain its effort, Fighter Command needed expert ground crews and a resupply of serviceable aircraft. In nine weeks in August and September, production and repair of Hurricanes and Spitfires produced 1,301 fresh, serviceable, deliverable machines to sustain the effort.[47]

The difference between the number supplied by the LQMG and those written off from 12 August–23 September 1940, according to After the Battle's *The Battle of Britain (Mark II),* has to be wastage and consumption at 101 percent of operational write-offs. Looking at these figures, the RAF lost more pilots in six weeks in France and the first nineteen days of the forty-two-day segment of the Battle of Britain than did the Luftwaffe due to faulty tactics. In the latter twenty-three days these losses were reversed as the RAF adapted flexible formations and the Luftwaffe fighters were bound to close escort. (See Table 2.)

In the comparable forty-three days (12 August–23 September 1940) of the Battle of Britain, the Luftwaffe suffered 2,007 write-offs and repairables (Table 55). In addition there were 82 repairables in August and 23 in September, for a total of 105, bringing the total aircraft casualties to 1,407, of which repairables were only 7 percent.

The Battle of France was generally fought below 15,000 feet. The Battle of Britain was fought at heights up to 32,000 with Dowding calling by the end of the struggle for fighters capable of climbing rapidly to 43,000 feet with heated cockpits sealed against -50° drafts. Both technology and aeromedicine were being pushed to the limits.[48]

In the Battle of Britain the RAF demonstrated that repeated practice made for efficiency of a system, but at the same time the demands of war called for the abandonment of the squadron as both a weapon and as a training establishment in the Victorian manner. New pilots were coming through the system to make up casualties, but they lacked experience in formation flying and gunnery. Replacement aircraft were flown in by the air transport auxiliary (ATA). The Armée de l'Air had a nucleus of experienced pilots, but lacked the reserves and the ferry pilots to keep the *escadrilles* up to strength until June, when they were too late. RAF Fighter Command could have had even more pilots if xenophobia and anticolonialism, as well as ignoring NCOs, had not held sway at the Air Ministry in London.[49]

TABLE 55. LQMG Deliveries and Write-Offs by Types, August and September 1940

AIRCRAFT	AUGUST DELIVERIES	AUGUST WRITE-OFFS	SEPTEMBER DELIVERIES	SEPTEMBER WRITE-OFFS	TOTAL DELIVERIES	TOTAL WRITE-OFFS
Me-110	314	124	277	75	591	199
Me-109		190		202		392
Ju-88	467	114	349	116	816	230
Do-17		792		68		860
He-111		102		156		258
Ju-87		59		9		68
Total	**781**	**1,381**	**626**	**626**	**1,407**	**2,007**

Source: United Kingdom, Air Ministry. *Abteilung* [Department] VI [Intelligence], CAB [Cabinet] CAB 106/282.

Because British success in the summer of 1940 was due to an integrated system, the superiority of their technology must not be overlooked. The Spitfire and the Hurricane have become the victorious symbols together with their Merlin engines, combining to give the RAF what the FAF did not have, which was aircraft equal in combat to the Me-109E. And that benefit was derived from concepts and decisions made in the early 1930s when the Armée de l'Air was focusing on the BCR. While it is true that by May 1940 the Dewoitine D-520, now partially tested, was becoming available, almost none of them were operational. They were just reaching the stage that the Hurricane and Spitfire were at the time of Munich, eighteen months earlier. The D-520 was too few, too late. Moreover even if masses of them had been available to equip the *chasseur escadrilles*, there were no longer the pilots to man them nor the mechanics to maintain them. By June 1940 the FAF fighter serviceability availability (*disponible*) rate was about 30 percent and losses in the air with novice pilots versus the Luftwaffe would quickly have made the D-520 force impotent.

As compared with the Armée de l'Air's experience in the Battle of France from 10 May to 24 June, it is obvious that one road led to absolute defeat in 1940 while the other to a close-run victory. The reasons, as shown in *Two Roads to War*, went back to at least 1918, to two very different theoretical approaches to war, combined with cultural and organizational characteristics that led to a failure to do sums and calculate the costs and necessities of new technology, as well as to the critical factors of time, money, and manpower.

The British losses in the Battle of Britain have to be looked at in both fighting and logistics terms, which were not as they appeared. First, what is surprising is the more than 44 percent of British aircraft that were damaged were repairable. Second, the few pilots or aircrew who were injured seriously enough to be hospitalized even though they were in damaged—even occasionally "write-off" machines—still left 38 percent who were immediately available again. Third, the very rapid rise in aircraft needing repairs far exceeded the prewar estimates as laid down in the 1936 *SD 98* calculations on consumption and wastage, because the assumption was that they would be beyond repair because they would be lost over enemy territory. Fourth, "repairable" aircraft accumulated until the fall, when a streamlined approach to salvage and repair began to return many machines to service—two hundred Hurricanes in October alone. Lastly, all aircraft shot down, destroyed, ditched, or missing were counted as write-offs, meaning that replacement machines were needed.

CONCLUSIONS FROM THE AIR BATTLES OF 1940

The Armée de l'Air and the RAF

This book initially was given an irony-laced title—*Undefeated?*—questioning the July 1940 statement of the Armée de l'Air's commandant en chef (commander in chief) that his force, unlike France herself, had not been beaten. However, as the work expanded into an analysis of the air campaigns of 1940, the point of view changed. The *chasse*, from 10 May to 24 June 1940, was the honorable tip of the iceberg that coalesced to represent what was wrong with La France by the summer of that year.

My previous study, *Two Roads to War: The French and British Air Arms from Versailles to Dunkirk*, had detailed how those two organizations, victorious in 1918, had come to very different fates in the summer of 1940—different fates that involved two very dissimilar nations.

Moreover the early air campaigns of the ensuing World War II would involve very small numbers of aircraft, aircrew (mainly pilots), and casualties. Success in World War II depended not on the weather or human frailty, but rather on the logistical infrastructure created in peacetime. Neither air staffs nor historians, however, have taken this basic fact into sufficient account. What was presented therein, then, tried to measure both victories and casualties as well as supply systems.

The comparisons show that each of the three air forces involved in the air battles of 1940 had its own problems. The Luftwaffe was well prepared for blitzkrieg, but its Achilles' heel was salvage and repair or rebuild, as well as its short-term view that it could afford to ignore the fundamentals of logistics because the war would be short. The Battle of France was a walkover because the Luftwaffe did not exceed its capabilities, though only because it could pause to regroup and had the strength to do so still. However, in the Battle of Britain, logistics had a long-term influence, especially regarding the later campaign in Russia, which like the Battle of Britain proved to be another long war rather than a short campaign.

The RAF was sent to the Continent as part of a commitment the British had refused until early 1939. It was not prepared for its Army Cooperation role any more than were the French—both had 1918 mentalities, and both had failed to sort out inter-Allied relationships and the role, equipment, and preparations needed for ground warfare. In particular, they had ignored the nature and purpose of the Wehrmacht-Luftwaffe relationship. Withdrawn to fight the Battle of Britain, RAF Fighter Command was in its element, while impotent RAF Bomber Command largely stood by. The RAF's weaknesses in the Battle of France were that it had failed to consider both the enemy's and its own use of escort fighters—and probably more important, the need to ferry damaged but flyable machines, notably Hurricanes, back to Britain so that they could be made serviceable again. Nor had the Air Staff thought through the needs of a modern mobile repair organization, and in so doing left behind 174 repairable Hurricanes—34 percent of those sent to France. Nor was there until 1941 an Air/Sea Rescue Command. And the British Air Forces France was badly short of motor transport.

As for the Armée de l'Air, its fate in May 1940 was sealed by inappropriate decisions made prewar. It lacked doctrine, command, control, and communications, aircrew able to withstand the attrition of war, as well as competitive, thoroughly tested machines with suitable, reliable engines and an accountable production and delivery system.

In comparing the Armée de l'Air in the Battle of France with the RAF in the Battle of Britain, the French had the advantage of experience, but as the campaign of summer 1940 advanced, the RAF lost its experienced aircrew and was feeding into the hard-pressed squadrons late teenagers who had some 150 hours' training and perhaps 25 hours of an operational training unit before they reached a squadron in action. Armée de l'Air fighter pilots probably had four times the experience and hours in May, but not the vigorous training.

While the German onslaught of 1918 was sluggish as compared with its blitzkrieg of 1940, the historical lessons should not have been ignored. The worst possible case envisioned in 1940 was mild compared with reality because the French mindset was that it could not happen there.[1] In addition, there was a lack of French defensive imagination.[2] No one had been trained or given the initiative to consider what unpleasantness might have to be faced nor to think and plan ahead to prevent and overcome any such circumstance.

It seems unlikely we will face a blitzkrieg again, but USAF forces could well face UAVs (unmanned air vehicles) and rocket attacks combined with terror guerrilla tactics, which could include disabling the electronics upon which we are overdependent. Remember that in 1918 British General Sir Edmund Allenby's forces used deception to achieve surprise against the Ottoman army. One morning the Turkish headquarters awoke to find itself surrounded by British armored cars and its communications destroyed. In 1935 Allenby's former chief of staff, General A. P. Wavell, in the midst of the annual maneuvers, walked into his headquarters and announced it had just been "bombed," and sent his protesting staff on leave—the others, he said, would have to figure it out! In both cases there was an immediate need to cope with the unexpected.

As the Anglo-French forces learned in May–June 1940, nothing is impossible. But the Allied air Battle of France was reactive and spasmodic. Periods of intense activities were followed by lulls caused by weather, exhaustion, unserviceability, unit movements to new airfields, and paucity of sustaining replacements, as well as by the want of early warning and quick response, the whole being hampered by the Armée de l'Air's lack of wireless transmission (W/T) and its consequent reliance on the inadequate French PTT telephone system and the low number of sorties flown. On top of all was the choking of initiative from the top down.

It has been said that the air Battle of France was more intense than the Battle of Britain, but not only is this assessment a matter of impressions, it is part of the French "Lost Cause" myth. The forty-six-day air campaign may have appeared to the participants to have been very chaotic and stressful. And it was. But that was because the command and logistics structure collapsed and *escadrilles* were constantly on the move, ill-housed and ill-fed, overworked, and under the constant strain of uncertainty. Life was chaotic.

The Battle of Britain, in contrast, was fought from well-established aerodromes with comfortable messes, with a solid logistics base, and with the whole protected by antiaircraft. In addition, the entire well-trained Fighter Command fought, in theory, as a unit under a single commander aided by the Observer Corps, radar, and defending fighters that were guided by sector-controllers via radio-telephone (R/T), with which all the aircraft were equipped. Gallic chaos replaced by English phlegm faced German orderliness.

The two battles of the summer of 1940 were determined by prewar planning and actions. The French had blindly hoped that war would not come again and comforted themselves that it would start from where it had left off in 1918. The British, far from muddling through, saw in 1934 future war as being in the air through their offensive Home Defence Air Force—and so built up the

HDAF—as well as, especially after 1936, in Fighter Command's fighters, radar and sector-control, and antiaircraft capability to meet the German air menace. All of which, nevertheless, was part of the policy of appeasement. On 10 May 1940, that policy of Neville Chamberlain's having proved bankrupt, Winston Churchill's war government took power and provided the bulldog leadership needed to frustrate Nazi ambitions and lead on to final victory in 1945, as in 1917, aided by the United States. And Britain was protected by the "anti-tank ditch," the English Channel.

It is most probable that the FAF started on the morning of 10 May at 68 percent serviceability, but that by the end of 12 May, or certainly by 15 May, it was shattered, and that thereafter because of wastage and consumption the *bon de guerre* rate was, as Vuillemin stated, but 30 percent. Even so, how did the *chasse* do so well?

Moreover, it must be recalled that an air force's serviceability rate is a composite. There were units not yet affected by action whose rate remained for a while at 68 percent or above, while others were so decimated as to have fallen to zero.

In forty-six days the Armée de l'Air loss rate was logarithmic, because as the experienced leaders fell and less well-trained pilots took their places, the latter's rate of survival dropped. So, in fact, the FAF had lost 500 pilots by 1 June and could mount few sorties. It was ordered out of battle on 10 June. Thus the loss rate was really 634 in twenty-eight flyable days, or roughly 23 per day. Table 7's figures, from Buffotot and Ogier (see Chapter 1), provide a visual of the loss of officers and reservists killed and wounded from 10 May to 24 June. The FAF's losses were higher than in other air forces. During 3–10 June, in the Battle of the Somme, FAF lost 115, or 18 percent in one week of the original 637 due to combat, accidents, and the like.

Before the 1–10 June Battle of the Somme, almost 68 percent of the FAF was unavailable (1,487 out of 2,086; see Tables 5 and 6). In contrast, during the Battle of Britain, Spitfire squadrons never had less than 90 percent of their establishment, and Hurricanes never had less than 84 percent, in spite of wastage in accidents as well as exports of between 175 and 195 Spitfires and Hurricanes for four weeks during the battle.[3]

Looking at the records for the late 1930s, it seems that French accounting was self-deceptive. For example, the aircraft on charge—on the FAF's records—were nowhere near ready to go to units, and so reserves were not what they were thought to be. The budgeted personnel were not those on active service (*aux armées*), though the former may have been reservists on the books, but still at home.[4]

The Luftwaffe in the Battles

Looking at the Luftwaffe's strengths for the Battles of France and Britain, and for the campaign in Russia, it is evident that its aircraft strength was in a steady decline. The prewar assumptions as to rapid victory had led to restricted production. This same assumption led to neglect during the campaign in France of the need to salvage and repair the damaged machines, without apparently the realization that 22 percent of new production had actually been rebuilds. Salvage was belatedly available for the Battles of Poland, France, Belgium, and the Netherlands, but the aircraft lost over Britain and the surrounding seas were gone forever. Instead of 22 percent repairables, the Luftwaffe could salvage only 7 percent. Meanwhile the RAF was being supplied with three times the new machines that the GAF was getting.

Since, as noted earlier, the air Battles of France and Britain were part of the same campaign, comparisons can be made between the two countries. An earlier concern was how the Armée de l'Air stacked up against the Luftwaffe and its effects upon the latter. For Britain, the roles were reversed in what the Duke of Wellington would have called a "close-run" battle as the RAF held off the "air menace." Over France, the ground was pulled out from under the RAF, but not so over Britain. Thus the question: How did the Luftwaffe fare as an operational organization during May–June 1940 and then in July–September, especially in two comparable forty-odd-day periods? In France both sides were involved in a mobile campaign, whereas the fight for Britain was much more a 1918-style of fixed lines.

On 28 July 1948, J. C. Nerney, Air Historical Branch chief, Air Ministry, stated in a letter to Major L. F. Ellis that RAF fighters inflicted 1,284 aircraft destroyed on the Luftwaffe in six weeks during the Battle of France versus only 1,733 during the sixteen weeks of the Battle of Britain, or 214 per week versus 108. It is not surprising then that the RAF thought the Battle of France to be the more rigorous.[5] This forces the reader to do much more analysis of the LQMG reports and the inferences from them and from publisher After the Battle's tallies.

If I am correct that, for the various reasons cited above, the Armée de l'Air only shot down the averaged Martin/Cornwell 384 Luftwaffe aircraft during the Battle of France, plus those by the Allies and the DCA, then what happened to all the 1,846–1,847 machines that the LQMG issued as replacements? (See Tables 24 and 25.) Succinctly, the answer is that the Wehrmacht's blitzkrieg war, supported wholeheartedly by the Luftwaffe Chief of Staff Colonel-General Jeschonnek's view that the Luftwaffe could rebuild after victory, led to a ruthless commitment to support of the ground forces that resulted in high wastage and consumption from enemy action and operational accidents. The whole effort was bent to operations in support of the grand strategy and the ground-support air forces were pushed forward to the limit of their endurance, physically and mechanically. Although the Luftwaffe was built to operate from grass fields, many fields in France were especially rough and hard on the Me-109s. And Luftwaffe instructions were to set aside as a write-off any airplane with more than 10 percent damage. In addition, if the loss of transports in the attack on Holland is omitted, the total losses in France were quite reasonable at about 1,300 (Table 22).

Unfortunately the Luftwaffe kept records only of issues and not of post-campaign salvage. In fact, judging by the RAF in the Battle of Britain, where over 44 percent of the fighters shot down were recovered and rebuilt, such a percentage does not seem unreasonable for the Luftwaffe in France, reducing actual wastage and consumption to the 384 shot down plus 708 (55 percent of the replacements), or 1,092 (Table 24). The issues relating to the French claim that all the new aircraft issued by the German LQMG (quartermaster general) were to replace those shot down by French fighters has to be measured in the following ways. Was there a sufficiency of aircraft to sustain both sides' operations? The answer can be obtained by looking at the Luftwaffe's production resources, logistic philosophy, and practice. It can be checked against the Royal Air Force in the Battles of France and Britain in 1940, and finally by consideration of the Armée de l'Air 's own supply of aircraft.

In the two weeks of 10–24 May, among other causes Luftwaffe units were down from an estimated 70 percent serviceability to 33 percent. In other words, a unit of twelve aircraft would only have had four available by 25 May, quite comparable to the FAF's situation. And thus, of the ten Me-109 *Gruppen* engaged in the Battle of France with a total of 1,016 aircraft on 10 May, by 25 May only 305 were operational (Table 19). Given the landing accidents of the type suffered, especially on rough fields, 335 of the wastage of 711 would have been from that cause, leaving 681, with only 305 serviceable.

I started out to see if the claims made that the number of planes that the FAF shot down in May and June 1940 in the Battle of France can be accurately estimated; my method was to count the issues from the LQMG,[6] as there are few French records due to the pace of the retreat and the ultimate defeat. It turns out that there really are two answers. The first is noted above, and the second an examination of the German logistics system and philosophy.[7]

German aircraft production was predicated on having to replace losses of less than 25 percent as the result of a campaign.[8] In 1939 German aircraft production was 8,295 machines (691 a month) of all types, of which 1,541 or 18 percent, were single-engine fighters (at 128 per month). Twin-engine fighters numbered 1,840; dive bombers 611, and twin-engine bombers 2,744.[9] According to Peter Cornwell's tabulations in *The Battle of France Then and Now* the Luftwaffe suffered shot down or written off 953 in May and 337 in June totally written off now with 568 and 209 repairables (785), the latter comprising 38 percent of losses of available aircraft. In the Battle of Britain, the Luftwaffe lost 304 shot down 10 July to the end of the month, 948 in August, and 898 in September, with repairables being 38, 130, and 44 (212 total). Or, of the total of 3,440 shot down or written off, the latter were but 6.2 percent versus 38 percent.

Air Commodore Peter Dye, in 2000, noted that rather than producing about 150 single-engine fighters per month to meet wastage, the Germans needed 350.[10] As rebuilds made up 22 percent of that figure, with losses at 2,067 in France with 38 percent repairable—or 785 of all types—by 1941 German aircraft production would have recovered. However, in the Battle of Britain, Luftwaffe losses of all types—those shot down, lost, written off, or repairable—totaled 2,362, of which only 212 were repairables, and aircraft production was very deficient. With only 7 percent of the total rather than 22 percent as rebuilds, the GAF in mid-1941 was still deficient.[11]

In spite of this, however, as the Battle of Britain subsequently demonstrated, the Luftwaffe went to war without a coherent naval air-war doctrine and without an effective Luftkriegsmarine (naval air arm), for it lacked long-range aircraft and a supply of magnetic mines and torpedoes. What the German air force lacked in the Battle of Britain was not grand-strategic heavy bombers, but long-range escorts to allow the medium bomber to cover all of Britain. Germany had developed the escort fighter from 1936 because it did not believe the bomber would always get through. In addition, a major cause of the Luftwaffe's failure in the Battle of Britain was poor intelligence on the country, on British industry, and on the RAF. And this was due to Hitler and the political Oberkommando not seeing Britain as an enemy until eighteen months before the war.[12]

On 10 May 1940, Matthew Cooper notes that the Luftwaffe had massed 2,589 frontline aircraft against the 1,453 of the Allies in France, with 50 of the 130 GAF bombing sorties being against French airfields. The French lost 757 aircraft in the Battle of France, of which 229 were destroyed on the ground, mostly within the first few days of the conflict.[13] At the end of three days the GAF had air superiority. The blitzkrieg reports from the German army air-liaison officers with the Panzers—the *Kolufts* (Luftwaffe air liaison officers) and the Flivos (Fliegerverbindungsoffiziere, German air force liaison officers)—were transmitted by radio to the Panzergruppe headquarters. The air and ground commanders conferred and orders were issued in minutes, gaining air support for the Panzers from forward airfields within forty-five to seventy-five minutes of the request. As in Spain, constant, all-day air attacks demoralized the defenders and took out their artillery support. In France, then, the Luftwaffe "became the key element in a war of maneuver."[14]

At the same time that it was fighting the Armée de l'Air, on the night of 5 June 1940, the GAF launched fifty He-111s against RAF airfields and other targets, but little damage was done because the British aircraft were dispersed. On 18 June a bomb accidentally hit London but did little damage. The number of GAF aircraft had never exceeded seventy on these sorties as few crews had been trained in night operations. The ineffectiveness of the GAF's inaccurate bombing of factories led to the British decision to keep them in operation and thus save the man hours lost when workers went to air-raid shelters. Yet, despite the raids being unsuccessful, the training for the GAF was valuable and the new dual radio-beam Knickbein system of blind bombing—no visual target detection—was used.

In mid-1940, however, Goering, Milch, Udet, and Jeschonnek could not decide upon a plan for the invasion of Britain because Hitler carefully kept them at each others' throats.[15] On 25 June, Hitler unexpectedly gave that task to the Oberkommando der Wehrmacht (high command of the armed forces [OKW]), and on 13 July he decided to proceed, based on the Wehrmacht plans. The Luftwaffe thus was to switch back from an economic blockade to being the handmaiden of the army. Luftwaffe success against the RAF, unlike in previous land campaigns, was to be the one condition for launching an invasion assault, and all that the Wehrmacht required was air superiority over the Channel and southeast England, not over the whole country—an essential element, whether Hitler decided upon invasion or a return to economic blockade. The radius of the attack on Britain was limited by the range of the German Me-109 fighter, which could only be airborne for ninety minutes. Yet only the bombers could provide the threat that would pull Britain's Fighter Command into the air. Goering, however, believed the RAF already was weakened and thus his tactical approach of drawing Fighter Command up into battle was based upon that assumption.[16] Interestingly Matthew Cooper notes that RAF No. 11 Group, defending London and southeast England, had 40 percent of the Fighter Command aircraft, and in the eventual Battle of Britain the Luftwaffe lost some 12 percent of its machines to British antiaircraft defenses.[17]

Cooper describes well the Luftwaffe plan, which aimed at destroying the RAF in the air and on the ground, as well as trashing Britain's seaborne trade both on the water and in ports. For the first objective, Fighter Command was to be defeated south of a line from Gloucester to London, and then the bases in the rest of the country were to be subject to daylight bombing attacks. At the same time, the aircraft industry was to be attacked day and night. The Luftwaffe Oberkommando believed that after four days from the start of Eagle Day (*Adlertag*), 10 August 1940, the RAF would be destroyed. Luftflotten 2 and 3 were given the tasks.

In July of 1940 a restored and relocated GAF focused attacks on Britain, but the aircrew, and others, had doubts as to the effectiveness. Euphoria was soon tempered with realism. The effort was light until 6–15 August 1940. Until *Adlertag*, single raiders from formations of twenty bombers with fighter escorts had been penetrating inland to attack ports, or at sea to hit convoys, in daylight. The German problem in July and August was to get British Fighter Command to rise to the bait so that it could be destroyed. But when the RAF did respond to defend the convoys or mainland targets, it was under orders to avoid the German fighters because the need was to stop the bombers. Yet, during the six weeks of the *Kanalkamp*—the Channel battle from 1 July—the Luftwaffe destroyed 142 RAF fighters and damaged 51, for a total loss of 279 and 71 damaged over the period. Of the 142, the Me-109s claimed 128, for a loss of their own of 85.[18]

As early as 10 July the Germans had started to search over the Channel where they were met by RAF fighters. This led to ever-larger combined bomber and fighter forces. The RAF soon learned that its "night-fighting area" tactics were passé and adapted the GAF's more flexible formations, while also avoiding pure fighter melées.[19] To inflict higher casualties, from 8 August the Luftwaffe penetrated inland, though the GAF escorting forces thus had to be tripled. From 13 August it was a battle of attrition. Of the 1,485 sorties the GAF flew that day the results were not impressive. On 15 August, 1,786 sorties were flown, 520 by bombers in a twenty-four-hour period. Raids of 100 to 150 GAF aircraft were launched throughout the day, but losses were daunting: 75 in the south and 91 in the north. After 16 GAF Ju-87 dive-bombers had been lost on 18 August, the type was withdrawn. Overall Luftwaffe losses during 8–23 August totaled 403 shot down and 127 damaged. The RAF lost 54 Spitfires and 124 Hurricanes, with 94 pilots killed and 60 wounded.

Germany's Fw-200 Condor transport had been hastily converted to an antishipping bomber and began operations in August of 1940; by February of 1941 it had sunk eighty-five Allied vessels totaling 363,000 tons. However, the Reichsmarine (from 1935, the Kriegsmarine) was not interested in an effective attack on Britain and did not understand the potential for naval aviation.[20]

Nevertheless by September 1940 sixty Fw-200s were at Bordeaux, in southwest France, as a unit, to be the eyes of the U-boats. But only fifteen Fw-200s were available at one time, as serviceability was only 25 percent.

From 24 August to 6 September the Luftwaffe sought to eliminate the RAF, but at the same time was shackled to the close support of the bombers. Nevertheless random raids and fighter sweeps aimed to destroy RAF Fighter Command, which was beginning to suffer the loss of experienced squadron and flight leaders; 295 RAF aircraft had been shot down and 171 damaged, and 103 pilots had been killed and 128 invalided. The Luftwaffe had lost 378 aircraft and 115 damaged. However, on the night of 25 August, after the RAF bombed Berlin, Hitler was determined to hit London—a fatal blunder relieving Fighter Command. On 7 September 372 GAF daylight bomber attacks hit and 255 at night fell on East London, and although the attacks also struck Central London, they were not effective and cost too much.

The Armée de l'Air was doomed from the start because it never was able to settle upon a high command structure, upon a viable doctrine to accommodate its three missions, and upon suitable equipment, logistics, communications, and bases with which to implement these policies in war. The FAF needed time to establish, from the formation of the Air Ministry in late 1928 through the creation by decree of the Armée de l'Air in early 1933 through the Law of July 1934. The consequent alignments and realignments both within the French air force and within the Ministère de la Défense Nationale (ministry of defense) primarily related to the demands of Army Cooperation.

The German, British, and French air forces dealt with logistics in both similar and dissimilar ways. In aircraft production, all three had reached roughly eight hundred machines per month of all types by May 1940. But while the Germans had leveled off, assuming a short, victorious war, the British were still accelerating, and especially in fighter production so that a surplus was accumulating in their ASUs. And meanwhile the French industry was delivering uncompleted airplanes to government depots where a leisurely system prevailed due to shortages, resulting in planes "on charge"—on the FAF's records—being stored unready for operations.

Shortage of pilots in all three countries, though lesser in Germany, led to varying degrees of replacement of combat wastage. The Luftwaffe's blitzkrieg doctrine and lack of concern with logistics resulted in units in the Battle of France being worn down to 30 percent serviceability; but within less than two weeks after the Franco-German armistice of 24 June, they were back to their full complement of aircraft and pilots. The German nadir had been reached because the Luftgeneralstab (air staff) had not been in on planning the campaign and so had not set up a resupply system that constantly sent forward aircraft, crews, fuel, and spares. Nor did the system provide for larger maintenance crews to alleviate the fatigue caused by long hours, constant moves, and the need to make do without adequate spares. Indeed the weakness of Luftwaffe planning was evidenced in the shortages of fuel on forward airfields being such that the Ju-52 fleet, with 167 lost in the Netherlands, was stretched to carry POL forward.

The RAF, in spite of frequent moves from 10 May to 12 June, was adequately supplied from its immobile air stores parks, but it lacked pilots to take flyable, as opposed to serviceable, Hurricanes back to England as it retreated. In Britain itself, the situation had been well thought-out, though spares were a problem. At Home, the supply of pilots was not only just adequate, especially when NCOs were counted, but also sustainable, and both service and civilian fliers could deliver the reserves from ASUs to squadrons in Fighter Command. The difficulty was pilot exhaustion at a time when operational training units were new and the transition was being made from readying pilots for operations from squadrons to the OTUs. Whereas the Luftwaffe was training ten thousand or more pilots annually by 1940, the RAF was just working up to that level.

In the Battle of France, the German losses were sharply reduced by their rapid achievement of air superiority and the fact that aircrew casualties fell within their own lines and so were to a large degree recoverable. Aircraft were left where they fell. In the following Battle of Britain, the situation was reversed. Aircrew and airplanes that became casualties over Britain and its immediate surrounding waters were lost to the Luftwaffe. Aircrew not killed were captured by the British, and machines were salvaged and melted down to aid the British war effort.

The Three Air Arms Revisited

Of the three forces, the Armée de l'Air had the worst of all possible worlds. Its aircraft acquisition system was inadequate, and it had not begun to train new pilots until the war began so that the first 250 of these only completed their education in early June and were never blooded. In addition, the pilot shortage led to a rickety resupply system compounded by the overrunning of the FAF's airfields, POL, and supply depots. On top of that, only 30 percent of the replacement aircraft delivered were *bon de guerre*—operationally fit. Above all the totally inadequate number of pilots available to the *chasse* (432 to 632) in theory could not possibly cope with both their rapid losses and increasing fatigue, nor with the inadequacies of the command, control, and communications, and the multiple roles their unformed doctrine required them to play.

In contrast, in the Battle of Britain the RAF's Fighter Command had the doctrine, the command, and the support system, including operational control of Antiaircraft Command, whose commanding general was compatible, so that its air officer commanding-in-chief could concentrate on the long-anticipated task at hand.

In all three countries—Germany, Britain, and France—the roles of the political higher direction was also formative. Hitler planned for blitzkrieg and a short war; Chamberlain in Britain adopted the RAF as the cheapest defense and in 1937 accepted switching from an offensive bomber to a defensive fighter emphasis. Both Germany and Britain were at the forefront of the Technological Revolution that in the summer of 1940 pitted the German Me-109E versus the British Hurricane and Spitfire. The advantage was to the British, as they had the control apparatus developed since 1918 coupled to the brand-new radar warning system, sector control, and R/T.

In contrast French politicians dallied, impotent, and power was in the Comités d'Aviation (aviation committees) of Parlement, so that the Armée de l'Air and the infrastructure were starved of money (credits) until 1938. Doctrine was still unsettled. The army's Général Commandant Maurice Gamelin had undue influence in France. The role, command, and equipment of the air arms was still in flux and ultimately subordinated to the army, whose 1918-style thought had been conditioned by the pace and casualties of World War I. In Germany, however, the Luftwaffe was a tactical air force designed and trained to support the Wehrmacht (army, navy, and air force, but not the Waffen SS) on the ground. And in Britain, the RAF was principally divided between Fighter and Bomber commands, which were not mutually supporting, nor was there an AOC-in-C RAF to coordinate their actions. The chief of the Air Staff was an adviser, not an executor. Fighter Command was a tactical defensive force, while Bomber Command was a grand-strategic offensive one, still four years in 1940 from effective maturity. And so it can be said that the Germans and the British had settled their air forces' roles and necessities, while the French were still discussing them. Thus, apparently, it was that in July 1940 the Haut Commandement of the Armée de l'Air sought to deflect criticism for its May–June defeat by creating its own myth of the Lost Cause.

What follows, then, seeks to explain the above. While the French prided themselves that their *escadrilles* were mobile, this was a disadvantage logistically. The Armée de l'Air units were soon running low on fuel and spares; their working hours were drastically shortened by having constantly to retreat to new and strange fields; and the supply of replacement aircraft was cut sharply by lack of ferry pilots and wastage due to pilots getting lost or landing at the wrong, threatened, or even enemy airfields. The effort was diminished by air and ground crew fatigue and disorientation, by accidents, and by shortages of fuel. When the last planes tried to fly to North Africa they were unable to do so for want of petrol (*essence*).

Before the war France had completed a POL system of pipelines, storage depots, railway wagons, tankers, and drums, but the reliability of the system was predicated on a stationary war. Critical to success in a war of movement was an intimate and precise knowledge of which *escadrilles* were on which of the two hundred airfields in northeast and east-central France. After 10 May such certitude did not exist; logistics became a nightmare and efficiency rapidly declined. The same, of course, was true of the spares replenishment system, and added to all this, the roads were jammed with some six million refugees.

The Armée de l'Air obtained replacement aircraft from the Paris environs workshops or the depots there by sending *escadrille* pilots to collect them. After 10 May the demands for *escadrille* pilots made this system impractical. Until June the loss of 250 pilots showed it was a major flaw to assume *escadrille* self-replenishment. But neither newly graduated pilots nor the well-qualified foreign pilots languishing in non-flying or in training posts were utilized for ferry work. In addition, contributing to the stinginess of the resupply system was the lack of radio communication, and therefore the reliance upon the overburdened, thin national telephone system.

FAF and RAF logistics were disrupted after 10 May 1940 by the Luftwaffe overrunning of their airfields by 25 May and the bombing of roads and railways, which disorganized repair and maintenance—for these reasons the number of serviceable aircraft also fell rapidly. The condition of landing grounds in farmers' fields was not improved by bad weather in late May–early June.

Both in the Battle of France and in that over Britain, the defending fighters faced large, combined forces of enemy bombers and escorts. Neither the RAF nor the Armée de l'Air had thought much of escort fighters. The British had a bifurcated mental process in the Air Ministry in which fighters were thought of solely as *attacking* enemy bombers, and even in the first decade or so if the bombers were French, no thought was given to the fact that they could be escorted. And when the "air menace" was determined to be German, it was *assumed* that the distance from bases in the Fatherland was too great for any German fighters to be able to accompany that attacking force. Conversely, on the bomber side of the Air Staff, no attention was paid to fighter developments, as the assumption was that bombers would have to fight their own way in daylight without the consequences being considered.

For the fighters, the Battle of France was a distinct surprise when they began to have to tackle Luftwaffe bombers supported by Me-109 and Me-110 escorts, though this only became really clear after 10 May and unavoidable after 24 June when the coasts of Europe from Norway to Spain were in German hands. Meanwhile, when providing escorts to Blenheims and Battles over France led to those aircraft not being attacked, the British Air Ministry claimed such sorties were a waste of resources as no enemy aircraft had been shot down![21] The fact that the bombers sustained no losses as compared with their disastrous unescorted sorties to the Meuse bridges apparently did not sink into the Whitehall mentality.[22] For the RAF bomber barons, the engagements over Heligoland Bight in the fall of 1939 exposed their conceptions of the defensibility of even modern, power-turreted Wellington formations as fallacious.[23] Yet, rather than develop escort fighters, Bomber Command switched to night operations.

The fascination of the air side of the summer of 1940 is in what different circumstances the three air forces found themselves, why, and the results each saw and subsequent actions each took. Ironically and historically important is the fact that each emerged from World War I with different interpretations (and hopes) regarding that conflict—the French took the ostrich, the British the insular, and the Germans the Teutonic. After their 1940 experiences, the French created the myth of the Lost Cause (though the Free French did produce a modern viable air arm), the British persisted in the Home Defence Air Force mode with a return to the concentration on the bomber to the neglect of tactical air forces until the Middle East and North African campaigns forced that option. The Germans, having got that right, were overconfident. Moreover, because of bad accounting and the Nazi Grossegeneralstab (general staff) limited appreciation of the sinews of war, on both the Eastern Front from 22 June 1941 and in the defense of the Fatherland they had to overcome basic logistical and ultimately manpower problems.

All three air forces were forced ultimately to realize that not strictly military constraints vitally affected their war efforts. In this sphere the heads of government's attitudes, beliefs, knowledge, experience, and management skills played a vital part in controlling the "Bamboo Basket," the complex skeins from Cabinet to war sortie, delineated in Figures 1 and 2. Whereas the campaign in the west enabled the Luftwaffe to recover and salvage many of its losses and write-offs, the campaign against Britain did not. The result was that although

German aircraft production leveled off by 1941, the real effect was the loss of much of the 22 percent or more of repairables, which had made up pre-1940 production numbers.

The Battle of Britain caused a decline, especially in Me-109s, and a dearth of potentially repairable machines. At the time of the invasion of the USSR in June 1941, the Luftwaffe was below the strength its leaders believed it had. In part this was due to the blitzkrieg mentality, which was first challenged over the English Channel and then later, during 1941, on the Russian steppes. Ironically the three air forces should have been differently positioned. The Germans should have been in France, the French in Britain, and the British in Germany. The Germans had a Great Power air force, the French might just have been able to defend No. 11 Group's air space in southeast England, and the RAF in Germany would have had a grand-strategic target in Britain.[24]

The last puzzling question is: Why did the *chasseur* fight for so long? Their plight was hopeless. Yet, Peter Cornwell in *The Battle of France Then and Now* offers a fitting tribute to the Armée de l'Air: "the battle lost, their exploits were exemplary, fighting to the bitter end, and bravely risking their lives for France."[25]

It is my guess the *chasseur* averaged about 750 hours of flight time each versus the RAF's 150 to 300 hours, that they were professional, and that they fought on in their mental and physical isolation, as Claude d'Abzac-Epézy wrote in 1997, *for honor*. The Armée de l'Air left a legacy.

Apart from the influence of the national political systems and personalities, and their effect upon grand strategy as laid out in *Two Roads to War* and in the opening chapters herein, of critical importance in the outcomes of the air battles of 1940 was *sustainability*.

That vital, but much neglected, subject—as in the Bamboo Basket illustration—had to start with the national conception of "the next war." That then determined the aircraft types needed, their production and spares, their crews and their training, as well as their supply system.

The latter was a complex, synchronized organization that foresaw realistically the worst possible cases and included the transfers of vitals from raw material resources through factories to storage depots to delivery and issuance of *bon de guerre* items, including personnel.

War demanded at least double the normal establishments, a continuous replenishment system including allowances for "pipeline purdah" of all in transit, as well as salvage and repair. For the whole to function efficiently required both accounting and communications systems.

All of the above was required for *sustainability*.

As shown, the Gallic structure was deficient at many levels, including lead times. The Germans matched the strategic and tactical needs, but the grand strategy neglected the coming consequences of their success.

The British started with the fundamentals and followed through with overall plans, of which the Trenchardian bomber offensive was misguided, but the air defense of Britain itself was not. The Air Ministry War Room tallies for the week of 6 September clearly indicate how narrow was the margin, not of victory, but of salvation. Those who were killed or who died numbered 537 aircrew; but 1,100 aircraft had survived to be repaired to fly again. Still, on 6 September it had been a very "close-run thing."

Sholto Douglas' "Rhubarbs" in later months cost the RAF planes and pilots lost over France and the Channel—a legacy with uncalculated consequences on the road to ultimate victory.

Paradox

In retrospect, the Battle of France is a fascinating paradox.

My own research and estimates concluded, as noted, that the Armée de l'Air could only have shot down about 232 enemy machines. But I must concede that the careful researches of Paul Martin in *Invisibles Vainqueurs* (1990) and Peter Cornwell in *The Battle of France: Then and Now* (2008) have produced convincing evidence from both documents and crash sites that the Armée de l'Air downed between 400 (Martin) and 378 (Cornwell). My count, from the latter's data, included aircraft the Germans wrote off, but which the French did not claim.

The prime question is: How could the FAF have accomplished this victory when all rational conclusions are opposed?

The Armée de l'Air had two peak days—14 May, when they shot down 46 GAF, and 4 June, when they had 55 confirmed kills. In the forty-two days of the Battle of France the FAF accounted for 162 Me-109s, 56 Me-110s, 90 Do-17s, 124 He-111s, 42 Stukas, 80 Hs-126s, and another 40 of miscellaneous types. Up to 26 May the Luftwaffe, in seventeen days, lost 352 confirmed shot down, or 20.7 daily. These figures should be compared with those in Table 24, the LQMG's necessary reissues of replacements. In the period after the losses of 27 May to 4 June, kills were only 32, or an average for the nine days of 3.6 daily. However, on 5–10 June in the intense fighting over the Somme, 163 confirmed kills were achieved, or a daily average of 27. Of these, 76 were Me-109s, which showed that the by then experienced *escadrilles* had caught their breath. Only

15 Do-17s, 21 He-111s, and 20 Hs-126s were shot down. The struggle lasted only six days and then the Armée de l'Air left the field.

The impact of the Battle of 18 May–24 June was much greater on the Luftwaffe, which by the lull in late May generally was down to 30 percent serviceability. But by 5 June it had been rested and replenished. Yet in talking about the Armée de l'Air it must be kept constantly in mind that proportionally the Luftwaffe was as weak as its opponent, and so the French cannot, at least for 27 May to 4 June, claim that they were at an overwhelming disadvantage.

That still leaves the question: How could the Armée de l'Air have been so successful, given that its aircraft were inferior in engine power and reliability, speed, and armament, and that the FAF lacked radios and radar?

While it is true that some of the Luftwaffe had had experience in Spain and more in Poland, this was leavening amongst the *Jagdstaffel* (fighter squadrons). Although the French units were on the whole more experienced (averaging 750 hours), they did not take the war seriously. They wasted the Phoney War, and did not respect the Me-109 as an opponent. But we have to admit that they were the invisible conquerors that Paul Martin hails.

As to the questions of why and how, the answer must be the old one that, when cornered, animals and men will fight with desperate courage, and in this case also for honor. Like the Royal Air Force's Auxiliary Air Force squadrons, they were a social group who felt a common bond. Given the probable fact that they did not read, were poorly supplied with intelligence, and thus probably largely unaware of the real situation, they fought for their honor and mentally isolated *escadrilles*. This, I have to assume, was the *chasseur mentalité*. The few bomber crews were stoic. Men could not dwell on their likely fate and still go into battle.

Did Vuillemin and Mendigal, and even the Commission G, paint a worse picture of the Armée de l'Air in late June 1940 than was justified? The picture at the top is often not what is reality at the operational level, which both the French bureaucracy and the communication systems created.

In spite of the chaos of the record keeping during the retreat, did more *bon de guerre* machines reach the *escadrilles* than leadership knew or cared to acknowledge?

If we accept the Armée de l'Air's 15.5 sorties per enemy aircraft shot down, then the total sorties flown would be in the range of 6,000, all told, by the *chasse*. And the confirmed kill rate was 2.25 times that of the RAF and GAF in the Battle of Britain.

On 14 May, when 55 Germans were confirmed shot down, the FAF had to have flown a minimum of 825 sorties, and during 5–10 June some 4,490.

NOTES

Preface

1. The FAF figures are from Paul Martin, *Invisibles Vainquers: Exploits et sacrifices de l'Armée de l'Air en 1939–1940* (Paris: Yves Michelet, 1990), 458–461; while the Anglo-German is from Basil Collier, *The Defence of the United Kingdom* (HMSO, 1957), 456–460, 491–492, and Peter D. Cornwell, *The Battle of France Then and Now* (Old Harlow, Essex, UK: After the Battle, 2008).

2. E-mail communication, General Lucien Robineau to Robin Higham, 20 December 2008.

3. See Winston G. Ramsey, ed., *The Battle of Britain: Then and Now* (London: Battle of Britain Prints International Ltd., rev. 1982 [1980]), 234, 705.

Introduction

1. See, for instance, Williamson Murray, "Strategic Bombing: The British, American, and German Experiences," in Williamson Murray and Allan R. Millett, eds., *Military Innovation in the Interwar Period* (Cambridge: Cambridge University Press, 1996), 96–143, and in the same volume, Richard R. Muller, "Close Air Support: The German, British, and American Experiences, 1918–1941," 144–190.

2. Robert M. Citino, *The German Way of War: From the Thirty Years' War to the Third Reich* (Lawrence: University Press of Kansas, 2005).

3. See Robert I. Nelson, "Review Article: The Germans and the German Way of War," *International History Review* 31, no. 1 (Mar. 2009): 85–91.

4. Richard Vinen, *The Politics of French Business 1936–1945* (New York: Cambridge University Press, 1991).

5. Geoff Watkins, "Review Article: Recent Work on France and the Second World War," *Journal of Contemporary History* (2002): 637–647. Apart from the official histories of the Service Historique de l'Armée de l'Air (SHAA) at Chateau Vincennes and the various issues of the French airline pilots' magazine *Icare*, very little serious work has been devoted to the air side of the Battle of France. Joel Blatt's edited *The French Defeat of 1940: Reassessments* (Providence, RI: Berghahn Books, 1998) does not have a chapter on the Armée de l'Air and Martin Alexander's military operations chapter barely mentions it, nor does he devote much space to it in his biography of General Maurice Gamelin, *The Republic in Danger: General Maurice Gamelin and the Politics of French Defence, 1933–1940* (London: Cambridge University Press, 1992). But see also Alexander's "The Fall of France, 1940," *Journal of Strategic Studies* 13, no. 1 (1990): 10–49.

More relevant on the Armée de l'Air is Patrick Facon, *L'Armée de l'Air dans la Tourmente* (Paris: SHAA, 1998), written to wipe away the myths created by both General Gamelin and General Georges who argued that the blame for the 1940 defeat lay on the refusal of the Armée de l'Air officers to integrate the Armée de l'Air once again into the armée. Pierre Cot, Air Minister during 1933–1935 and 1936–1938, wrote "En 1940, ou étaient nos avions? Le preparation, la doctrine, l'emploi de l'Armée de l'Air avant et pendant la Bataille de France," *Icare* 57 (1991): 36–57, a special issue; and he was supported by Joseph Roos [Ingenieur-general de l'Air] with "L'Effort de l'industrie aeronautique français de 1938–1940: La Bataille de la production aérienne," *Icare* 59 (1971): 44–53, and by Roland Maurice de Lorris, "La politique economique et industrielle du Ministre de l'Air," in *Quinze ans d'Aéronautique Français (1922–1937)* (Paris: Chambre Syndicale des Industries Aéronautique), 497–516. For a contemporary view of the Armée de l'Air see United Kingdom, National Archives, AIR 10/1648, *SD 132, Handbook of the French Air Forces* (London: Air Ministry, January 1939). A special issue of the *Revue d'Histoire de la Deuxieme Guerre Mondiale* in January 1969 was devoted to aviation from 1919 to 1940 with the authors examining three themes: (1) the supposed and qualitative inferiority of the l'Armée de l'Air during May–June 1940, (2) the High Command's deployment of its assets, and (3) the state of aerial rearmament before the war. See also Patrice Buffotot and J. Ogier, "L'armée de l'air français pendant la bataille de France du 10 Mai 1940 à l'armistice: Essai de bilan numerique d'une bataille aérienne," *Revue Historique des Armées* 3 (1975): 88–117, as reprinted in *Recueil d'Articles et Études (1974–1975)* (Vincennes: SHAA, 1977): 197–226; and Patrick Facon, "The High Command of the French Air Force and the Problem of Rearmament, 1938–1939—A Technical and Industrial Approach," in Horst Boog, ed., *The Conduct of the Air War in the Second World War: An International Comparison* (Oxford: Berg, 1988, 1992), 148–168. In the same volume see General Lucien Robineau, "French Air Policy in the Inter-war Period and the Conduct of the Air War against Germany from September 1939 to June 1940," 627–657.

See also LTC de Cossé-Brissac, "Combien d' avions Allemands contre combien d'avions français le 10 Mai 1940?" *Revue de Défense Nationale* 4 (1948): 741–759; Claude d'Abzac-Epézy in her 723-page *L'Armée de l'Air de Vichy, 1940–1944* (Vincennes: SHAA, 1977), provides an excellent introduction and a very comprehensive bibliography of the background to General Henri-Philippe Pétain's fiefdom of Unoccupied France and for its history then and now. She explains why there is so little literature on the Armée de l'Air, especially from 1938, but does strangely omit Angot and Lavergne's biography of Vuillemin. On the whole, writers about France have ignored the air arm, in part because it was small, in part because there are few relevant memoirs or biographies, and in part because even the buffs have avoided the subject. Most of the work that has been done emanates from the Service Historique de l'Armée de l'Air (SHAA).

The following articles by U.S. Army Artillery Colonel Faris R. Kirkland reveal various facets of the Armée de l'Air and its performance: "Anti-military Group-Fantasies and the Destruction of the French Air Force, 1928–1940," *Journal of Psychohistory* 14, no. 1 (Summer 1986): 25–42; "Planes, Pilots and Politics: French Military Aviation, 1919–1940," *1998 National Aerospace Conference . . . Proceedings.*

(Dayton, OH: Wright State University, 1999), 285–291; "The Aristocratic Tradition and Adaptation to Change in the French Cavalry, 1920–1940," *European Studies Journal* 4, no. 2 (Fall 1987): 1–17; and "Military Technology in Republican France: The Evolution of the French Armored Force 1917–1940" (PhD diss., Duke University, Durham, NC, 1968). Jeffrey A. Gunsberg's "*Armée de l'Air* vs. *The Luftwaffe*—1940," *Defence Update International* (1984): 44–53, is now dated. See also Patrick Facon, "Le Plan V (1938–1939)," in *Recueil d'Articles et Études (1979–1981)* (Vincinnes: SHAA, 1986): 31–80. *Icare* devoted issues 91–92, 113, 121, 123, 150, and 159 to the Battle of France. See also Stuart W. Peach, "A Neglected Turning Point in Air Power History: Air Power and the Fall of France," in Sebastian Cox and Peter Gray, eds., *Air Power History: Turning Points from Kitty Hawk to Kosovo* (London: Cass, 2002), 147–172.

6. Talbot C. Imlay and Monica Duffy Toft, eds., *The Fog of Peace and War Planning: Military and Strategic Planning Under Uncertainty* (London: Routledge, 2006).

7. See R. J. Overy, "Air Power, Armies, and the War in the West, 1940," *The Harmon Memorial Lectures in Military History* 32 (Colorado Springs, CO: USAF Academy, 1989).

8. As quoted by General Luicien Robineau in *Letter of the Air and Space Academy* (Paris: June 2004), 3.

9. See Anthony Christopher Cain, "*L'Armée de l'Air*, 1933–1940: Drifting Toward Defeat," in Robin Higham and Stephen B. Harris, eds., *Why Air Forces Fail: The Anatomy of Defeat* (Lexington: University Press of Kentucky, 2006), 41–70.

10. For examples of lack of foresight see Robin Higham, "The Worst Possible Cases," *Australian Defence Journal* 100 (May–June 1993): 63–65.

11. Patrick Facon, "The High Command of the French Air Force," in Boog, *The Conduct of the Air War in the Second World War*, 148 ff.

12. E. Angot and R. de Lavergne, *Un figure legendaire de l'aviation francaise de 1914 à 1940: le General Vuillemin: la combatant, le pioneer de Sahar, le chef* (Paris: Palatine, 1965), 261.

13. AVM Peter J. Dye, the current RAF expert and historian, Director-General, RAF Museum, has written "Logistics and the Battle of Britain: Fighting Wastage in the RAF and the Luftwaffe," *[U.S.] Air Force Journal of Logistics* 24, no. 4 (Winter 2000): 1, 31–40; "Sustaining Air Power: The Influence of Logistics on Royal Air Force Doctrine," typescript, 4 Jan. 2005, published in *Royal Air Force Air Power Review* 9, no. 2 (Autumn 2006): 40–51; and "The Royal Flying Corps Logistic Organization," *[U.S.] Air Force Journal of Logistics* (Winter 2000): 60–73, and *Royal Air Force Air Power Review* 1 (2000): 42–59.

14. John B. Heffernan, "The Blockade of the Southern Confederacy, 1861–1865," *Smithsonian Journal of History* 12, no. 4 (Winter 1967–1968): 23–44.

15. Mark Hinchcliffe, "Commanding Air Power: Some Contemporary Thoughts," Air Power Development Centre Working Paper No. 30 (Tuggeranong, ACT, Australia: Air Power Development Centre, 2010), 18–19.

16. d'Abzac-Epézy, *L'Armée de l'Air de Vichy, 1940–1944*, 88–109.

17. See for instance Gary W. Gallagher, ed., *Lee, the Soldier* (Lincoln: University of Nebraska Press, 1996); Patrick Facon, "Les milles victories de l'Armée de l'Air en 1939–1940: Autopsie d'un mythe," *Revue Historique des Armées* 4 (1997): 79–91.

18. Charles Christienne and Pierre Lissarrague et al., *Histoire de l'aviation militaire française* (Paris: Charles-Lavauzelle, 1980); English edition, *A History of French Military Aviation* (Washington, DC: Smithsonian Institution Press, 1986), 261.

19. The Oxford don Señor Salvador de la Madariaga in his study of Englishmen, Frenchmen, and Spaniards correctly noted that when the French talked about something, they thought they had done it. *Englishmen, Frenchmen, Spaniards* (New York: Hill and Wang, [1928] 1969).

20. Wolfgang Schivelbusch, *The Culture of Defeat: On National Trauma, Mourning, and Recovery* (New York: Metropolitan, [2001] 2003), 122–123.

21. Jared Diamond, *Collapse—How Societies Choose to Fail or Succeed* (New York: Viking, 2005), 417–440.

22. E-mail communication, 20 December 2008.

Chapter 1. The Armée de l'Air

1. Faris R. Kirkland, "Planes, Pilots and Politics: French Military Aviation, 1919–1940," *1998 National Aerospace Conference . . . Proceedings* (Dayton, OH: Wright State University, 1999), 285–291; Anthony C. Cain, *The Forgotten Air Force: French Air Doctrine in the 1930s* (Washington, DC: Smithsonian Institution Press, 2002).

2. Claude d'Abzac-Epézy, *L'Armée de l'Air de Vichy, 1940–1944* (Vincennes: SHAA, 1997), 59.

3. E. Angot and R. de Lavergne, *Un figure legendaire de l'aviation française de 1914 à 1940 le General Vuillemin: la combatant, le pioneer de Sahar, le Chef* (Paris: Palatine, 1965), 251.

4. Patrice Buffotot and J. Ogier, "L'armée de l'air français pendant la bataille de France du 10 mai 1940 à l'armistice: Essai de bilan numerique d'une bataille aérienne," *Revue Historique des Armées* 3 (1975): 88–117; reprinted in *Recueil d'Articles et Études (1974–1975)* (Vincennes: SHAA, 1977): 197–226.

5. Henri Michel, *Le Procès de Riom* (Paris: Albin Michel, 1979).

6. Lord [William Sholto] Douglas of Kirtleside, *Combat and Command* (New York: Simon and Schuster, 1966), 350.

7. Robert Pois and Philip Langer, *Command Failure in War: Psychology and Leadership* (Bloomington: Indiana University Press, 2004).

8. Wolfgang Schivelbusch, *The Culture of Defeat: On National Trauma, Mourning, and Recovery* (New York: Metropolitan/Henry Holt and Co., 2001); Jared Diamond, *Collapse—How Societies Choose to Fail or Succeed* (New York: Viking, 2005).

9. Patrick Facon, *L'Armée de l'Air dans la Tourmente: La Bataille de france, 1939–1940* (Paris: SHAA, 1998, and Paris: Economica, 1998); "Les mille victories de l'Armée de l'Air en 1939–1940: Autopsie d'un mythe," *Review Historique des Armées* 4 (1997): 79–97.

10. Colin Sinnott, *The Royal Air Force and Aircraft Design 1923–1939* (London: Cass, 2001); Sq/Ldr. H. R. "Dizzy" Allen, *Who Won the Battle of Britain?* (London: Arthur Barker, 1974); and G. F. Wallace, *The Guns of the Royal Air Force, 1939–1945* (London: Kimber, 1972).

11. AVM Peter Dye, "Sustaining Air Power: The Influence of Logistics on Royal Air Force Doctrine," *Royal Air Force Air Power Review* 9, no. 2 (Autumn 2006): 40–51.

12. Cain, *The Forgotten Air Force*, 95–104.

13. Allen, *Who Won the Battle of Britain?*, 63–79; Vincent Orange, *Sir Keith Park* (London: Methuen, 1984).

14. Thierry Vivier, "La commission G entre la défaite et l'Armée de l'Air future, 1941–1942," *Revue Historique de l'Armée* 176, no. 3 (1989): 113–121.

15. Paul Martin, *Invisibles Vainqueurs: Exploits et sacrifices de l'Armée de l'Air en 1939–1940* (Paris: Yves Michelet, 1990), 329–330 and 387–388 on accidents to the FAF; for GAF shot down by *chasse* 575, less 175 machines to DCA equals 400 (daily total 594) (also pp. 460–461). (See graph opposite p. 237 and caption 19 on p. 220.)

16. Peter D. Cornwell, *The Battle of France Then and Now* (Old Harlow, Essex, UK: After the Battle, 2008), 528–529.

17. Ibid.

18. Ibid.

19. General Lucien Robineau, e-mail, 19 January 2000. For the totals by types of aircraft received by the FAF from 3 September 1939 to 24 June 1940, see Charles Christienne and Pierre Lissarrague et al., *Histoire de l'Aviation militaire française* (Paris: Charles-Lavauzelle, 1980); English edition, *A History of French Military Aviation* (Washington, DC: Smithsonian Institution Press, 1986), 363. See p. 360 for losses of the Armée de l'Air.

20. See Buffotot and Ogier, "L'armée de l'air française pendant la bataille de France."

21. United Kingdom, National Archives, AIR 10/1594, 10/1595 (3rd ed., *SD 98*, Sept. 1936), *Air Staff Memorandum No. 50, Data for Calculating Consumption and Wastage in War*, tables 1, 8, 16, 17.

22. Dye, "Sustaining Air Power."

23. Colonel Ferruccio Botts, "Amedeo Mecozzi," *Actes de Colloque International* (Paris) (8 Oct. 1990): 131–150.

24. Pierre Cot, "En 1940 ou ont nos avions? Le preparation, la doctrine, l'emploi de l'Armée de l'Air avant et pendant la Bataille de France," *Icare* 57 (1991): 34–57; Ingeneur general de l'Air Joseph Roos followed with "L'Effort de l'industrie aeronautique français de 1938–1940: La Bataille de la production aérienne," *Icare* 59 (1971): 44–53; and Roland Maurice de Lorris, "La Politique economique et industrielle du Ministre de l'Air," in *Quinze ans de l'Aéronautique Français (1932–1947)* (Paris: Chambre Syndicale des Industries Aéronautique), 497–516.

25. Henri Michel, *Le Procès de Riom* (Paris: Albin Michel, 1979).

26. John Ellis, *Brute Force: Allied Strategy and Tactics in the Second World War* (New York: Viking, 1990), vii–6.

27. See F. H. Hinsley et al., *British Intelligence in the Second World War.* Vol. 1. *Its Influence on Strategy and Operations* (London: HMSO, 1979), 102, 177, 254n, 299, 301.

28. Christienne and Lissarrague, *A History of French Military Aviation,* 330; Dominique Breffort and André Joineau, *French Aircraft from 1939 to 1942—Fighters, Bombers, and Observation Types.* 2 vols. (Paris: Histoire et Collections, 2004), 8–19.

29. James S. Corum, "The Spanish Civil War: Lessons Learned and Not Learned by the Great Powers," *Journal of Military History* 62 (1998): 313–334.

30. Cot, in *Icare* (1971), see note 24 above.

31. Facon, "Les mille victories de l'Armée de l'Air en 1939–1940"; Patrick Facon, "The High Command of the French Air Force and the Problem of Rearmament, 1938–1939: A Technical and Industrial Approach," in Horst Boog, ed. *The Conduct of the Second World War: An International Comparison* (Oxford: Berg, 1988, 1992), 158–160. See also his mature work, *L'Armée de l'Air dans la Tourmente: La Bataille de France, 1939–1940,* on Vuillemin, 13–17; on assault aviation and doctrine, 57–60, 62–65; on DCA, 60–62.

32. E-mail communication, 22 February 2009.

33. Facon, "The High Command of the French Air Force," 148–168, esp. 150–151.

34. d'Abzac-Epézy, *L'Armée de l'Air de Vichy, 1940–1944,* 59.

35. Ibid., 60.

36. Breffort and Joineau, *French Aircraft from 1939 to 1942.*

37. United Kingdom, National Archives, AIR 41/22, app. 13–14. John Ellis, in *Brute Force: Allied Strategy and Tactics in the Second World War,* vii–6, claims the French had more available fighters than they did.

38. For one pilot's opinion of the MS-406 see Pierre Boillot, "Premièrs vols et premièrs batailles d'un jeune chasseur en 1939–1940," *Icare* 145, no. 16 (1993), "La Chasse, 3e partie," 28–34.

39. Owen Thetford, *Aircraft of the Royal Air Force Since 1918,* 8th ed. (London: Putnam, 1988), 88.

40. Christian-Jacques Ehrengardt, "Le chasseur à la française: la famille Dwoitine D.500–D.510," *Aero Journal* 40 (Dec. 2004–Jan. 2005): 8–37.

41. Ibid., 146.

42. Eric Brown, *Testing for Combat* (Shrewsbury, UK: Airlife, 1994), 57–59.

43. Ibid. See also, for a recent example, George Marrett, "Don't Kill Yourself: F-4 Testing Over the Mojave," *Flight Journal* (June 2008): 62–67, on a fatal flaw in the McDonnell F-4 Phantom II, reminiscent of the D-520.

44. Breffort and Joineau, *French Aircraft from 1939 to 1942.*

45. Peter M. Bowers, *Curtiss Aircraft 1907–1947* (London: Putnam 1979), 349, 362; Herschel Smith, *A History of Aircraft Piston Engines* (Manhattan, KS: Sunflower University Press, 1981), 130 ff; James McVicar Haight, *American Aid to France, 1939–1940* (New York: Athanaeum, 1970).

46. Haight, *American Aid to France*; Thetford, *Aircraft of the Royal Air Force*; Bowers, *Curtiss Aircraft 1907–1947*.

47. For the whole story see "Le Brewster Buffalo," *Aero Journal* (Paris), 7 (May 2004): 4–39.

48. Ibid. I am grateful to Col. Carl Finstrom, USAF (Ret.), for calling my attention to the Finnish use of the Brewster Buffalo.

49. d'Abzac-Epézy, *L'Armée de l'Air de Vichy*, 59, Table 1-5, notes some 97,000 *aux armées*.

50. Christienne and Lissarrague, *A History of French Military Aviation*, 359; see preceding note.

51. d'Abzac-Epézy, *L'Armée de l'Air de Vichy*.

52. Martin, *Invisibles Vainquers: Exploits et Sacrifices de l'Armée de l'Air en 1939–1940*, 328.

53. Christienne and Lissarrague, *A History of French Military Aviation*, 345.

54. Buffotot and Ogier, "L'armée de l'air française," 36.

55. Martin, *Invisibles Vainquers*, 381.

56. Christienne and Lissarrague, *A History of French Military Aviation*, 359.

57. d'Abzac-Epézy, *L'Armée de l'Air de Vichy*, 40, 57, and fn.

58. Boillot, "Premièrs vols et premièrs batailles d'un jeune chasseur en 1939–1940."

59. *Icare* 145 (1993/2): 40–45. On all of the above see also Robert Jackson, *The Air War over France, May–June 1940* (London: Ian Allan, 1974).

60. Thierry Vivier, *La Politique aéronautique militaire de France: Janvier 1933–Septembre 1939* (Paris: Editions Harmattan, 1997), 434–437.

61. Smith, *History of Aircraft Piston Engines*, 77–84.

62. Christienne and Lissarrague, *A History of French Military Aviation*, 353–354, 363.

63. See Emmanuel Chadeau, *L'industrie aéronautique en France, 1900–1950* (Paris: Fayard, 1987), which tells the story from a finance angle.

64. Christienne and Lissarrague, *A History of French Military Aviation*, 329; and Dye, "Sustaining Air Power."

65. Christienne and Lissarrague, *A History of French Military Aviation*, 326.

66. Arnaud Teyssier, "L'Appui aux forces de surface: L'Armée de l'Air et la Recherche d'une doctrine (1933–1939)," *Colloque Internationale Histoire de la Guerre* (Paris: SHAA, 10–11 Sept. 1987): 248–277.

67. Christienne and Lissarrague, *A History of French Military Aviation*, 325–328; Emmanuel Chadeau, "Government, Industry and Nation: The Growth of Aeronautical Technology in France (1900–1950)," *Aerospace Historian* (Mar. 1988): 26–44; Haight, *American Aid to France, 1938–1940*. See also Ian Lloyd, *Rolls-Royce: The Merlin at War* (London: Macmillan, 1978), 11–19.

68. Patrick Facon, "C'était hier—logistique—un impératif? Approvisionner l'Armée de l'Air," *Air ACTU* 534 (Aug.–Sept. 2000): 44–45.

69. Teyssier, "L'Appui aux forces de surface."

70. d'Abzac-Epézy, *L'Armée de l'Air*, described it as a "lamentable imbroglio," 135–137.

71. On the Duval Division see Patrick Facon "Aperçus sur la doctrine d'emploi de l'aeronautiques de militaire francais. 1914–1918," *Recueil d'Articles et Études* (1984–1985) (Vincennes: SHAA, 1991): 125–131.

72. Christienne and Lissarrague, *A History of French Military Aviation*, 340–341.

73. Cain, *The Forgotten Air Force*, 96, 99–200.

74. See Sir Edward Spears, *Assignment to Catastrophe*, 2 vols. (London: Heinemann, 1954); General Sir James Marshall-Cornwall, *War and Rumors of War* (London: Leo Cooper, 1984); and David Fraser, "Les transmissions de 1919 à 1959," *Revue Historique de l'Armée* 23, no. 1 (1967): 51–56.

75. Martin, *Invisibles Vainquers*, 236, 460–461.

76. Ibid.

77. Ibid.

78. Facon, "C'était hier—logistique—un impératif?"; Daniel Porret and Frank Thevenet, *Les As de la Guerre 1939–1945*, 2 vols. (Vincennes: SHAA, 1991).

79. After the Battle, *The Battle of Britain (Mark II)* (London: Battle of Britain Printing International, 1982); Christian-Jacques Ehrengardt, "Les unités: La couronne t'attend . . . Les écoles de l'Armée de l'Air, 1939–40," *Aero Journal* 37 (June–July 2004): 40–46; d'Abzac-Epézy, *L'Armée de l'Air de Vichy*, 59.

80. Christienne and Lissarrague, *A History of French Military Aviation*, 345; Buffotot and Ogier, "L'armée de l'air française pendant la bataille de France," 201, Table II, and 204.

81. See d'Abzac-Epézy, *L'Armée de l'Air de Vichy*, 52–53, n. 35. *Anciens* aircraft were those that were obsolescent; modern aircraft were of the new generation of all-metal machines.

82. Buffotot and Ogier, "L'armée de l'air française pendant la Bataille de France," Table III, 202–203.

83. Ibid., 204.

84. d'Abzac-Epézy, *L'Armée de l'Air de Vichy*, 36, 64.

85. 599 *chasseur*, 309 bombers, and 116 reconnaissance machines; Christienne and Lissarrague, *A History of French Military Aviation*, 363–365; Buffotot and Ogier, "L'armée de l'air française pendant la bataille de France," 36; and d'Abzac-Epézy, *L'Armée de l'Air de Vichy*, 58–68. See discussion of total losses earlier.

86. Buffotot and Ogier, "L'armée de l'air française pendant la bataille de France," 211–212; Facon, "C'était hier—logistique—un impératif? 44–45.

87. Buffotot and Ogier, "L'armée de l'air française pendant la bataille de France," 214.

88. d'Abzac-Epézy, *L'Armée de l'Air de Vichy*, 55.

89. United Kingdom, National Archives, AIR 29/802.

90. United Kingdom, National Archives, AIR 10/1594, 10/1595 (*SD 98*).

91. Marc Bloch, *Strange Defeat: A Statement of Evidence Written in 1940,* trans. Gerard Hopkins (New York: Octagon Books, 1968), 57 ff.

92. Buffotot and Ogier, "L'armée de l'air française pendant la bataille de France."

93. William Green, *The Warplanes of the Third Reich* (New York: Doubleday, 1970), 537; Richard Townshend Bickers et al., *The Battle of Britain: The Greatest Battle in the History of Air Warfare* (New York: Prentiss Hall Press, 1990), 87; Allen, *Who Won the Battle of Britain,* 67 ff; Orange, *Sir Keith Park,* 70; Anthony G. Williams, *Rapid Fire: The Development of Aeronautic Cannon, Heavy Machine Guns and Their Ammunition* (Shrewsbury, UK: Airlife, 2000), 224–254; G. R. Wallace, *The Guns of the Royal Air Force, 1939–1945,* 54–68; and W. H. B. Smith and Joseph E. Smith, *Small Arms of the World* (Harrisburg, PA: Stackpole, 1962), 716; Pamela Liflander, *Measurements and Conversions* (London: Running Press, 2002), 61.

94. An experienced pilot, thirty-six years old in 1940, has stated that the wing mounted 7.62s fired at only 300 rpm. Henri Gille, "A un contre cinq au GCII/10," *Icare* 145, no. 2 (1993): 75–79.

95. See Sinnott, *The Royal Air Force and Aircraft Design 1923–1939,* 16, 91–92, 98–102, 111–118.

96. Allen, *Who Won the Battle of Britain,* 63–69.

97. On the throw weight of FAF aircraft see Buffotot and Ogier, "L'armée de l'air française pendant la bataille de France," 206, Table IV.

98. Bickers et al., *The Battle of Britain,* 41.

99. H. F. King, *Armament of British Aircraft,* 1909–1939 (London: Putnam, 1971).

100. G. F. Wallace, *The Guns of the Royal Air Force, 1939–1945,* 15, 54, 58, 63.

101. Orange, *Sir Keith Park,* 70; Allen, *Who Won the Battle of Britain?,* 63–69; C. H. Keith, *I Hold My Aim: The Story of How the Royal Air Force Was Armed for War* (London: Allen & Unwin, 1946); United Kingdom, Air Ministry, CAB 102/355, *Cabinet History of .303 Ammunition,* 1 April 1939.

102. Green, *The Warplanes of the Third Reich* (1970).

103. General Lucien Robineau, "French Air Policy in the Interwar Period and the Conduct of the Air War Against Germany from September 1939 to June 1940," in Boog, *The Conduct of the Air War in the Second World War,* 627–657.

104. d'Abzac-Epézy, *L'Armée de l'Air de Vichy,* esp. 40, 57, and fn.

105. Ibid., 123 ff.

106. Buffotot and Ogier, "L'armée de l'air français pendant la bataille de France, 197–226.

107. However, see d'Abzac-Epézy, *L'Armée de l'Air de Vichy,* 67.

108. Cain, *The Forgotten Air Force,* 90; S/Ldr S. C. Rexford-Welch, ed., *Royal Air Force Medical Services,* vol. 2, *Commands;* vol. 3, *Campaigns.* History of the Second World War, United Kingdom Medical Series (London: HMSO, 1955, 1958).

109. For a more detailed account see Cain, *The Forgotten Air Force;* also see Major General R. B. Pakenham-Walsh, *History of the Corps of Royal Engineers,* vol. 8, *1938–1945—Campaigns in France and Belgium, 1939–40, Norway, Middle East, East*

Africa, Western Desert, North West Africa, and Activities in the U.K. (Chatham, UK: The Institution of Royal Engineers, 1958), on France and Belgium, 8–46.

110. Robin Higham, *Two Roads to War: The French and British Air Arms from Versailles to Dunkirk* (Annapolis, MD: Naval Institute Press, 2012); and Robin Higham and Stephen J. Harris, eds., *Why Air Forces Fail: The Anatomy of Defeat* (Lexington: University Press of Kentucky, 2006).

111. Robineau, "French Air Policy in the Interwar Period and the Conduct of the Air War against Germany from September 1939 to June 1940," 627–657.

112. United Kingdom, National Archives, CAB 106/282; Robin Higham, *100 Years of Air Power and Aviation* (College Station: Texas A&M University Press, 2004), loss ratios.

113. Lucien Robineau, "L' Armée de l'Air dans La Battaille de France," *Recueil d'Articles et Études, 1984–1985* (Vincennes: SHAA, 1991): 183–200; and T. C. G. James, *The Battle of Britain,* edited with an introduction by Sebastian Cox, vol. 2 of *Air Defence of Great Britain* Series, Royal Air Force Official Histories (London: Frank Cass, 2000), 392.

114. Francis K. Mason, *Battle over Britain* (New York: Doubleday, 1969), 110–111.

115. d'Abzac-Epézy, *L'Armée de l'Air de Vichy,* 59.

116. Buffotot and Ogier, "L'armée de l'air français pendant la bataille de France, 197–226.

117. LTC Faris R. Kirkland, "The French Air Force in 1940: Was It Defeated by the *Luftwaffe* or by Politics?" *Air University Review* (Sept.–Oct. 1985); reprinted at http://www.airpower.maxwell.af.mil/airchronicles/aureview/1985/sep-oct/kirkland .html.

118. d'Abzac-Epézy, *L'Armée de l'Air de Vichy,* 53.

119. Señor Salvador de la Madariaga, *Englishmen, Frenchmen, Spaniards* (New York: Hill and Wang, [1928] 1969); and Stanley Hoffman, *In Search of France . . .* (New York: Harper & Row, 1965), 1–117.

120. Porret and Thevenet, *Les As de la Guerre 1939–1945.* See also the study of aviation leaders of 1914–1918 by Daniel Porret, *Les As de français de la Grande Guerre,* 2 vols. (Vincennes: SHAA, 1983).

121. E-mail communication, General Lucien Robineau to Robin Higham, 20 December 2008.

122. Sebastian Cox, "The Sources and Organisation of RAF Intelligence and Its Influence on Operations," in Boog, *The Conduct of the Air War in the Second World War,* 553–579, esp. 567.

123. James, *The Battle of Britain,* 394–395.

124. Ibid., 392.

125. Christienne and Lissarrague, *A History of French Military Aviation,* 163–266.

126. Williamson Murray, "The German Response to Victory in Poland," *Armed Forces and Society* 7, no. 2 (Winter 1980): 285–298.

127. United Kingdom, National Archives, CAB 106/282, 123–128.

128. LQMG records from James S. Corum, 25 Apr. 2005.

129. United Kingdom, National Archives, CAB 106/282, 127–128; Porret and Thevetnet, *Les As de la Guerre 1939–1945*.

130. Cornwell, *The Battle of France Then and Now*.

131. Calculations from the figures in Basil Collier, *The Defence of the United Kingdom* (London: HMSO, 1957), appendices, 450 ff.

132. Christienne and Lissarrague, *A History of French Military Aviation*, 360.

133. Ibid., 359.

134. Stated in United Kingdom, National Archives, CAB 106/262, GAF QMG issues.

135. In tables kindly supplied to me by James Corum and copyrighted by Ulf Balke, the total LQMG issues for May are given by day and types as 238. However, for June the total is said to be 196, whereas the vertical right-hand column tallies to 660 rather than 196, a 336.7 percent error! See also Green, *The Warplanes of the Third Reich*; and Table 31 herein.

136. Facon, "Les mille victoires de l'Armée de l'Air en 1939–1940, 79–97.

137. Buffotot and Ogier, "L'armée de l'air française pendant la bataille de France."

138. Martin, *Invisibles Vainqueurs*.

139. Collier, *The Defence of the United Kingdom*, 453.

140. T. C. G. James, *The Growth of Fighter Command, 1936–1940*, edited with an introduction by Sebastian Cox, vol. 1 of *Air Defence of Great Britain* Series, Royal Air Force Official Histories (London: Whitehall History Publishing/Frank Cass, 2002), 98.

141. James, *The Battle of Britain*, 123–124, 364, and *The Growth of Fighter Command, 1936–1940*, 98. See also Cornwell, *The Battle of France Then and Now*; Cornwell gives RAF losses as 1,067 aircraft and 1,127 personnel.

142. United Kingdom, National Archives, AIR 41/21, *The Campaign in France 10 May–18 June 1940*, 425; Cornwell, *The Battle of France Then and Now*.

143. RAF debriefers were recently mustered civilians in the summer of 1940 and were not trained until the fall; RAF claims standards were changed on 14 August 1940.

144. Martin, *Invisibles Vainqueurs*, 328–330.

145. *Case Studies in the Achievement of Air Superiority*, B. F. Cooling, ed. (Washington, DC: Center for Air Force History, 1994), 115–174; Facon, "Les mille victoires de l'Armée de l'Air en 1939–1940, 27.

146. This is Peter Cornwell's tally in *The Battle of France Then and Now*, including write-offs.

147. CAB, 106/282, 151.

148. Collier, *The Defence of the United Kingdom*, 450–461. From 10 July to 6 September, fifty-nine days inclusive, the RAF put up 35,105 sorties for a daily average of 595. For the fifteen days 24 August to 6 September, the Luftwaffe launched 13,724 or 980 daily. The daily RAF rate should have netted then 16.3 enemy aircraft shot down daily or for the whole fifty-nine days the total was 962 destroyed on that basis. The 36.5 sorties per kill is derived from dividing total RAF sorties by total German aircraft destroyed.

149. Ibid.

150. Facon, "Les mille victories de l'Armée de l'Air en 1939–1940," 79–97; United Kingdom, National Archives (PRO London), CAB 106/282, GAF archives of German strengths and losses.

151. Collier, *The Defence of the United Kingdom*, 489–490.

152. d'Abzac-Epézy, *L'Armée de l'Air de Vichy*, 59.

153. See Buffotot and Ogier, "L'armée de l'air française pendant la bataille de France."

154. Martin, *Invisibles Vainqueurs*.

Chapter 2. The Luftwaffe

1. What follows is from James S. Corum, *The Luftwaffe: Creating the Operational Air War, 1918–1940* (Lawrence: University Press of Kansas, 1997), 155–161. Corum may be supplemented with E. R. Hooten, *Luftwaffe at War: The Gathering Storm, 1933–1939* (Horsham, Surrey, UK: Classic, 2007). On the creation of the Luftwaffe see E. R. Hooten, *Phoenix Triumphant: The Rise and Rise of the Luftwaffe* (London: Arms & Armour, 1994); James S. Corum, *Wolfram von Richthofen: Master of the German Air War* (Lawrence: University Press of Kansas, 2008); Alfred Price, *The Luftwaffe Data Book* (London: Greenhill Books, 1997); Gordon Williamson, *The Luftwaffe Handbook, 1935–1945* (Charleston, SC: The History Press, 2006); Col. Raymond Tolliver and Trevor J. Constable, *Fighter General: The Life of Adolph Galland* (Zephyr Cove, NV: AmPress, 1990); Galland's own autobiography, *The First and the Last* (New York: Henry Holt, 1954); and Robert M. Citino, *The Path to Blitzkrieg: Doctrine and Training in the German Army, 1920–1939* (Mechanicsburg, PA: Stackpole, 1999, 2008). See also Robert I. Nelson, "Review Article: Germany and the Germans at War," *International History Review* 31, no. 1 (Mar. 2009): 83–95. See also R. J. Overy, *Goering: The Iron Man* (London: Routledge and Kegan Paul Books, 1984, 1987).

2. Bart Whaley, "Conditions Making for Success and Failure of Denial and Deception: Authoritarian and Transition Regimes," in Roy Godson and James J. Wirtz, eds., *Strategic Denial and Deception: The Twenty-First Century Challenge* (Edison, NJ: Transaction Publishers, 2002), 50–51.

3. Joel Hayward, "The Luftwaffe's Agility: An Assessment of the Relevant Concepts and Practices," presented at the Air Power Conference, Hendon, London, 19–20 July 2006.

4. Ibid.; see also C. G. Sweeting, "How the Luftwaffe Kept 'Em Flying," *Aviation History* (Sept. 2011): 36–41.

5. Robin Higham, John T. Greenwood, and Von Hardesty, *Russian Aviation and Air Power in the Twentieth Century* (London: Cass, 1998), 37; Stanley G. Payne, *Franco and Hitler: Spain, Germany, and World War II* (New Haven, CT: Yale University Press, 2008), 32–43. See also Edward B. Westermann, *Flak: German Anti-Aircraft Defenses, 1914–1945* (Lawrence: University Press of Kansas, 2005).

6. Horst Boog, fax communication, 8 April 2007, and "Luftwaffe and Logistics in the Second World War," *Aerospace Historian* (Summer/June 1988): 103–110; E. R. Hooten, *Luftwaffe at War*; Corum, *The Luftwaffe*.

7. Corum, *The Luftwaffe*, 241; Ferenc A. Vajda and Peter G. Dancey, *German Aircraft Industry and Production, 1933–1945* (Shrewsbury, UK: Airlife, 1998).

8. William Green, *The Warplanes of the Third Reich* (New York: Doubleday, 1970), 13.

9. United Kingdom, Disarmament Branch, *The Supply Organization of the German Air Force, 1935–1945* (London, 1946); reprinted by the Naval and Military Press (Uckfield, East Sussex, UK: n.d.), 15–35. This is followed by delineation of the Luftwaffe organization with diagrams. On repair and salvage, see pp. 45 and 227 ff.

10. See also Vajda and Dancey, *German Aircraft Industry and Production 1933–1945*. Vajda and Dancey, and Cornwell, based their data taking in the returns made to the LQMG, which were not always accurate. Moreover the aircraft repairable in the unit were not reported.

11. Corum, *The Luftwaffe*, 219.

12. Ibid., 223.

13. Ibid., 224.

14. Ibid., 227.

15. Major William F. Andrews, "The Luftwaffe and the Battle for Air Superiority: Blueprint or Warning?," *Air Power Journal* (Fall 1995): www.airpower.au.af.mil/airchronicles/apj/apj95/fal95_files/andrews.pdf.

16. Corum, *The Luftwaffe*, 230; and Hans Detlef Herhudt von Rohden, *Vom Luftkrieg* (Berlin, 1938).

17. Personal communication to the author from *Oberst* Manfred Kehrig, November 2008.

18. German aircraft from production and testing to issue to units is a mystery not covered in any of the following: Corum, *The Luftwaffe*; United Kingdom (Great Britain) Air Ministry, *Rise and Fall of the German Air Force, 1933–1945* (New York: St. Martin's Press, 2000; Edward L. Homze, *Arming the Luftwaffe: The Reich Air Ministry and the German Aircraft Industry 1919–1939* (Lincoln: University of Nebraska Press, 1976); Vajda and Dancey, *German Aircraft Industry and Production, 1933–1945*. Nor did Horst Boog have the answer in his fax to the author of 8 April 2007. However, this information is vital for an assessment of the actual strength of a German Air Force and its ability to sustain operations. See Green, *The Warplanes of the Third Reich*.

19. Green, *The Warplanes of the Third Reich*, 10–12.

20. Corum, *The Luftwaffe*, 244.

21. Matthew Cooper, *The German Air Force, 1933–1945: The Anatomy of Failure* (New York: Jane's, 1981).

22. Ibid., 249.

23. Price, *The Luftwaffe Data Book*, 30.

24. From Chris McNab, *Order of Battle: German Luftwaffe in World War II* (London: Amber Books, 2009), 46ff.

25. Anthony Terry Wood and Bill Gunston, *Hitler's Luftwaffe: A Pictorial and Technical Encyclopedia of Hitler's Air Power in World War II* (London: Salamander, 1977), 20.

26. *Icare* no. 112 (January 1985) and no. 116 (January 1986), on the Battle of France, deal with the Luftwaffe I and II. On Luftwaffe training see Price, *The Luftwaffe Data Book*, 226–229; on the flak arm, 230–233; and on fighter tactics, 12–153. For the 17 August 1940 daily state, see 30–41. The decline in the Ju-52 force was due to these aircraft and pilots reverting to their training role.

27. Ibid., 259.

28. Vajda and Dancey, *German Aircraft Industry and Production 1933–1945*.

29. United Kingdom, National Archives, AIR 10/1644, *SD 128, Air Ministry Handbook on the German Air Force* (July 1939), 56; Field Marshal Kesselring, *Memoirs* (London: Greenhill, 2007); Higham, Greenwood, and Hardesty, *Russian Aviation and Air Power*; McNab, *Order of Battle*.

30. United Kingdom, National Archives, AIR 10/1644; David Irving, *The Rise and Fall of the Luftwaffe: The Life of Field Marshal Erich Milch* (Boston: Little, Brown, 1973); W/Cdr. Asher Lee, *The German Air Force* (London: Duckwall, 1946), an Air Ministry expert on the Luftwaffe of the RAF Intelligence Staff, 1940–1945; Corum, *Wolfram von Richthofen*; Williamson Murray, *Strategy for Defeat: The Luftwaffe, 1933–1945* (Maxwell AFB, AL: Air University Press, 1983); McNab, *Order of Battle*; Homze, *Arming the Luftwaffe*; Cooper, *The German Air Force, 1933–1945*; Overy, *Goering*; Wood and Gunston, *Hitler's Luftwaffe*.

31. Cooper, *The German Air Force, 1933–1945*, 121–126.

32. Ibid., 127–134.

33. Ibid., 125–127.

34. Williamson Murray, "The German Response to Victory in Poland," *Armed Forces and Society* 7, no. 2 (Winter 1980): 285–298.

35. Ibid., 286.

36. Ibid., 285–298.

37. Ibid., 290–291, 294.

38. Vajda and Dancey, *German Aircraft Industry and Production, 1933–1945*, 105.

39. Murray, "The German Response to Victory in Poland," 271.

40. See Alfred C. Mierzejewski, *The Most Valuable Asset of the Reich: A History of the German National Railway*, vol. 2, *1933–1945* (Chapel Hill: University of North Carolina Press, 2000), 82–83.

41. Boog, "Luftwaffe and Logistics in the Second World War," 103–110; United Kingdom, National Archives, AIR 10/1644.

42. United Kingdom, National Archives, AIR 10/1595, Air Staff Memorandum 50, *SD98, Data for Calculating Consumption and Wastage in War*, 3rd ed. (Sept. 1936).

43. United Kingdom, Air Ministry, CAB [Cabinet] 106/282, 128.

44. Martin Van Creveld, *Supplying War* (London: Cambridge University Press, 1979), 122 ff.

45. Dr. Lutz Budrass to author, e-mail of 24 March 2009 and letter of 28 April 2009.

46. James D. Crabtree, *On Air Defense* (Westport, CT: Praeger, 1994), 46–47; Richard Overy, *The Air War, 1939–45* (New York: Stein and Day, 1980), 45; John Batchelor

and Ian Hogg, *Artillery* (New York: Charles Scribner's Sons, 1972), 64–76 on heavy antiaircraft guns and German 2-cm [20-mm] *Flakvierling*; Major General E. B. Ashmore, *Air Defence* (London: Longmans, Green, 1929); General Sir Frederick Pile, *Ack-Ack* (London: Harrap, 1949).

47. United Kingdom, National Archives, AIR 10/1595, *SD 98*, 50, 1–8; Basil Collier, *The Defence of the United Kingdom* (London: HMSO, 1957), 450–460; Boog, fax; Overy, *The Air War*.

48. See United Kingdom, National Archives (PRO), Ministry of Aircraft Production, AVIA 46/288, "Ministry of Aircraft Production through AVIA," on the history of RAF spares as seen by the Ministry of Aircraft Production, 1940–1945; Peter J. Dye, "Logistics and the Battle of Britain," *[U.S.] Air Force Journal of Logistics* 24, no. 4 (Winter 2000): 1, 31–40.

49. Boog, fax. Ulf Balke, *Zusammengestellt nach unterlagen aus RL 2 III/707/einstazbereitschaft der fliegenden verbände*, archival file from Horst Boog, Freiburg, Germany. See also Ulf Balke, *Der Luftkrieg in Europa: Die Operativen Einsatze des Kampfgeschwaders 2 im Zweiten Weltkrieg* (Koblenz, Germany: Bernard & Graefe, 1989); and *Kampfgeschwader 100 Wiking: Eine Geschichte aus Kriegstagebuchern, Dokumenten und Berichten 1934–1945* (Stuttgart, Germany: Motorbuch Verlag, 1981).

50. United Kingdom, National Archives, CAB 106/282.

51. Ibid.

52. Ibid.

53. Fax to author, 10 June 2005.

54. Francis K. Mason, *Battle over Britain* (New York: Doubleday, 1969), 129, 137n, 167n, 181n, 378n, and 384; Winston G. Ramsey, ed., *The Battle of Britain: Then and Now* (London: Battle of Britain Prints International Ltd., rev. 1982 [1980]), 707.

55. Williamson Murray, *Strategy for Defeat*; Wood and Gunston, *Hitler's Luftwaffe*. For the Luftwaffe QMG figures, see United Kingdom, National Archives, CAB 106/282. See also Green, *The Warplanes of the Third Reich*, and Peter D. Cornwell, *The Battle of France Then and Now* (Old Harlow, Essex, UK: After the Battle, 2008), 528–529.

56. United Kingdom, National Archives, CAB 106/282.

57. Ibid.

58. Armand von Ishoven, *Messerschmitt Bf-109 at War* (London: Ian Allen, 1977).

59. Green, *The Warplanes of the Third Reich*.

60. For details on the Me-109, see Green, *The Warplanes of the Third Reich*, 524 ff.; and Jeffrey L. Ethell, *The Luftwaffe at War: Blitzkrieg in the West, 1939–1942* (Mechanicsburg, PA: Stackpole, 1997), 40 ff. Peter Cornwell, in *The Battle of France* (p. 629) notes the German loss for 10–31 May at 1,476 and for the whole of that month at 1,830.

61. Ibid., 340.

62. Luftwaffe strengths were calculated by the Luftwaffe, *Abteilung* [Department] VI [Intelligence] for the British Air Ministry and are in CAB 106/282 (1945).

63. Green, *The Warplanes of the Third Reich*, 547.

64. Vajda and Dancey, *German Aircraft Industry and Production, 1933–1945*; Cornwell, *The Battle of France Then and Now;* After the Battle, *The Battle of Britain (Mark II)* (London: Battle of Britain Printing International, 1982).

65. United Kingdom, National Archives, CAB 106/282, 157.

66. United Kingdom, National Archives, AIR 10/1593 (2nd ed., SD [Secret Document] 78, Nov. 1934) and 10/1594, 10/1595 (3rd ed., *SD 98,* Sept. 1936), *Air Staff Memorandum No. 50, Data for Calculating Consumption and Wastage in War,* table 16.

67. Mason, *Battle over Britain,* 137, noted that Stukas/*Geschwader* were slow submitting their losses. Luftwaffe strengths were calculated by *Abteilung* VI for CAB 106/282 (1945).

68. Green, *The Warplanes of the Third Reich*, 432; J. R. Smith and Antony Kay, *German Aircraft of the Second World War* (New York: Putnam, 1972), 317, 121; Peter C. Smith, *Impact! The Dive Bomber Pilots Speak* (London: Kimber, 1981).

69. Green, *The Warplanes of the Third Reich*, 116, 287–297, 432, 450.

70. Ibid., 306–307; Heinz Nowarra, *Heinkel He 111: A Documentary History* (London: Jane's, 1980), esp. 102–154.

71. Green, *The Warplanes of the Third Reich*, 172. Based upon the percentages of fixed write-offs as against the operational losses of 1,814 machines, of which there were 73 Do-17s of the total 370 write-offs, then they contained 19.7 percent or 138 personnel; the 97 He-111s with a crew of 5 accounted for 182, the 40 Hs-126s for 77, the 17 Ju-88s for 32, the 22 Stukas for 42, the 90 Me-19s for 170, and the 31 Me-110s for 59. All told, these 370 aircraft were crewed by 1,068 airmen, of whom we have to assume 368 could have escaped capture, were already dead, or died of their wounds. See Cornwell, *The Battle of France,* 528–529.

72. Green, *The Warplanes of the Third Reich*, 113 ff.

73. Ibid.

74. Cajus Bekker, *The Luftwaffe War Diaries* (New York: Doubleday, 1968), 364; and British Air Ministry, Air Historical Branch, translation of *Abteilung* VIII, *The Luftwaffe in Poland* (11 July 1944) in CAB 106/282.

75. Militargeschliches Forschungsamt, ed., *Das Deutsche reich und die Zweite Weltkrieg 2* (Stuttgart, 1979), 407.

76. Mason, *Battle over Britain.*

Chapter 3. The Royal Air Force

1. See Robin Higham, *Two Roads to War: The French and the British Air Arms from Versailles to Dunkirk* (Annapolis, MD: Naval Institute Press, 2012).

2. G/Cpt. Alistair Byford, "Fair Stood the Wind for France: The Royal Air Force Experience in the 1940s as a Case Study of the Relationship Between Policy, Strategy, and Doctrine," *The Royal Air Force Air Power Review* 14, no. 3 (Autumn/Winter 2011): 35–60.

3. Air Commodore Neville Parton, "The Development of Early RAF Doctrine," *Journal of Military History* 72 (Oct. 2008): 1155–1177.

4. United Kingdom, National Archives, AIR 5/299, AP 882, *CD 22, Operations Manual for the Royal Air Force* (July 1922).

5. Parton, "The Development of Early RAF Docrtrine."

6. Roger Beaumont, *Right Backed by Might: The International Air Force Concept* (Westport, CT: Praeger, 2001).

7. Colin Sinnott, *The Royal Air Force and Aircraft Design 1923–1939* (London: Cass, 2001), 157–177.

8. John Ferris, "Fighter Defense Before Fighter Command: The Rise of Strategic Air Defence in Great Britain, 1917–1934," *Journal of Military History* (Oct. 1999): 845–884.

9. Republished in 2009 by the Naval and Military Press, East Sussex, UK, in association with the Royal Armouries Museum, Leeds.

10. Norman Franks, *Valiant Wings* (London: Crécy Books, 1994, 1998), 182.

11. Sinnott, *The Royal Air Force and Aircraft Design 1923–1939*; Sir Charles Webster and Noble Frankland, *The Strategic Air Offensive Against Germany*, vol. 1 (London: HMSO, 1961), 1–132.

12. Ferris, "Fighter Defense Before Fighter Command"; Raymond H. Fredette, *The Sky on Fire: The First Battle of Britain, 1917–1918*. Smithsonian History of Aviation Series (Tuscaloosa: University of Alabama Press, reissue 2006); see also David Zimmerman, *Britain's Shield: Radar and the Defeat of the Luftwaffe* (Stroud, Gloucestershire, UK: Sutton Publishing, 2001).

13. CAS Hugh Trenchard, *Memorandum, Cmd 467,* "An Outline of the Scheme for the Permanent Organisation of the Royal Air Force," 25 Nov. 1919.

14. Philip Jarrett, ed., *Biplane to Monoplane—Aircraft Development, 1919–1939*. Putnam's History of Aircraft (London: Putnam, 1997), 127–240; Robert Schlaiffer and W. D. Heron, *The Development of Aircraft Engines and Fuels* (Boston: Harvard Graduate School of Business Administration, 1950); Herschel Smith, *A History of Aircraft Piston Engines* (Manhattan, KS: Sunflower University Press, 1981); Ian Lloyd, *Rolls-Royce*, 3 vols. (London: Macmillan, 1978); Peter Pugh, *The Magic of a Name: The Rolls Royce Story, The First 40 Years* (Cambridge: Icon Books, 2000); the Putnam series on British aircraft manufacturers; and Sinnott, *The Royal Air Force and Aircraft Design 1923–1939*.

15. See Robin Higham, *The Bases of Air Strategy: Building Airfields for the RAF, 1915–1945* (Shrewsbury: Airlife, 1998); and Robin Higham, *Armed Forces in Peacetime: Britain 1918–1940* (London: Foulis, 1962), 147–190, 201–206. See also Air Commodore Neville Parton, "Historic Book Review. *Air Power in War,* by [MRAF] Lord Tedder," *Royal Air Force Air Power Review* 12, no. 1 (Spring 2009): 124–132; AVM Peter J. Dye, "RFC Bombs and Bombing, 1912–1918," *Royal Air Force Historical Society Journal* 45 (2009): 8–14; and Stuart Hathaway, "The Development of RAF Bombs, 1919–1939," *Royal Air Force Historical Society Journal* 45 (2009): 15–24.

16. S/Ldr S. C. Rexford-Welch, ed., *The Royal Air Force Medical Services,* History of the Second World War, United Kingdom Medical Series, 3 vols. (London: HMSO, 1954–1958), vol. 2, *Commands* (1955), 165–228.

17. United Kingdom, National Archives, AIR 10/5552, *CD 1131, Maintenance* (London: Air Ministry AHB, 1951), 6–54.

18. Rexford-Welch, *The Royal Air Force Medical Services,* vol. 2. *Commands,* 158, 168–187; vol. 3. *Campaigns,* 45 ff.

19. United Kingdom, National Archives, AIR 41/59, *History of Flying Training in the RAF* (London, 1952), vol. 1, 1–74.

20. E. R. Hooten, *Phoenix Triumphant: The Rise and Rise of the Luftwaffe* (London: Arms & Armour, 1994), 160.

21. "Sustained operations" are defined as average operational effort and expenditures over twelve months; "intensive operations" are those with a high degree of operations lasting two to three weeks; and "maximum effort" is the highest degree of operational intensity not exceeding one week. Source: United Kingdom, National Archives, AIR 10/1593, *SD 78, Air Staff Memorandum No. 50, Data for Calculating Consumption and Wastage in War* (2nd ed., Nov. 1934), table 1.

22. Vincent Orange, *Dowding of Fighter Command: Victor of the Battle of Britain* (London: Grub Street, 2008).

23. Basil Collier, *The Defence of the United Kingdom* (London: HMSO, 1957), 450–460; United Kingdom, National Archives, AIR 10/1594, 10/1595, *SD 98, Air Staff Memorandum No. 50* (3rd ed., Sept. 1936), *Data for Calculating Consumption and Wastage in War,* tables 1, 8.

24. From W/Cdr Ian R. Gleed, *Arise to Conquer* (London: Victor Gollancz, 1942), 46.

25. See United Kingdom, National Archives, AIR 35/120.

26. CAB 106/282, the *Abteilung* VI summary of Luftwaffe states during 1939–1945; and Ulf Balke, *Zusammengestellt nach unterlagen aus RL 2 III/707/einstazbereitschaft der fliegenden verbände,* archival file from Horst Boog, Freiburg, Germany. See also Ulf Balke, *Der Luftkrieg in Europa: Die Operativen Einsatze des Kampfgeschwaders 2 im Zweiten Weltkrieg* (Koblenz, Germany: Bernard & Graefe, 1989); and *Kampfgeschwader 100 Wiking: Eine Geschichte aus Kriegstagebuchern, Dokumenten und Berichten 1934–1945* (Stuttgart, Germany: Motorbuch Verlag, 1981).

27. United Kingdom, National Archives, AIR 29/802; (ORB, No. 85 Squadron), AIR 27/703 ORB (No. 1 Salvage and Repair Unit).

28. Air Commodore Allan Wheeler, *That Nothing Failed Them* (London: Foulis, 1963), 52–56. Wheeler was the commandant of the Royal Aircraft Establishment at Farnborough during the war.

29. Peter Dye, "Logistics and the Battle of Britain: Fighting Wastage in the RAF and the Luftwaffe," *[U.S.] Air Force Journal of Logistics* 24, no. 4 (Winter 2000): 1, 31–40; see also the tables in T. C. G. James, *The Battle of Britain,* edited with introduction by Sebastian Cox, vol. 2 of *Air Defence of Great Britain,* Royal Air Force Official Histories (London: Frank Cass, 2000), 12–17.

30. After the Battle, *The Battle of Britain (Mark II)* (London: Battle of Britain Prints International, 1982), 14–30. For the squadron "daily-states" categories see Table 11 herein.

31. *SD 98* started life as an Air Staff file in the late 1920s before the Technological Revolution, and this assumption, like that of the lethality of the .303 bullet," was carried over without thought to the all-metal era.

32. Orange, *Dowding of Fighter Command*, 270.

33. Francis K. Mason, *The Hawker Hurricane* (London: Macdonald, 1962); Sinnott, *The Royal Air Force and Aircraft Design 1923–1939*, 76–133; John W. Fozard, ed., *Sydney Camm and the Hurricane* (Washington, DC: Smithsonian Institution Press, 1991).

34. Sinnott, *The Royal Air Force and Aircraft Design 1923–1939*, 98.

35. Ian Lloyd, *Rolls-Royce, the Merlin at War*, vol. 3 (London: Macmillan, 1978), 11–19; Derek N. James, *Schneider Trophy Aircraft 1913–1931* (London: Putnam, 1959, 1981), 249–271, 232–239.

36. Sinnott, *The Royal Air Force and Aircraft Design 1923–1939*, 98–102, 111–118.

37. For a recent remembrance of the Hurricane, see G/Cpt. Billy Drake, "From Fury Biplanes to Hurricanes," *Flight Journal* (Dec. 2007): 22–30.

38. Basil Collier, *The Defence of the United Kingdom* (London: HMSO, 1957), 74.

39. The Spitfire and its early troubles were featured in *BBC History Magazine* and included an article by Anthony J. Cuming and Christina Goulter, "Ready or Not?" Cuming argued that Fighter Command was thoroughly unprepared for the German attack, concentrating on the lack of training and shortages in radar, with the real culprit being the Air Ministry's insistence upon the .303 Browning machine gun, a weapon overrated even by Dowding. Christina Goulter, a former Air Historical Branch historian, countered. See *BBC History Magazine* 8, no. 11 (Nov. 2007): 22–23.

    Many books are available on the Spitfire including Jeffrey Quill, *Spitfire—A Test Pilot's Story* (London: Arrow Books, 1983; Manchester, UK: Crecy Publishing, 1998). For the technical story behind the fighter's development see Sinnott, *The Royal Air Force and Aircraft Design 1923–1939*, and Jonathan Glancey, *Spitfire: The Illustrated Biography* (London: Atlantic, 2006).

40. Owen Thetford, *Aircraft of the Royal Air Force Since 1918*, 8th ed. (London: Putnam, 1988).

41. Peter D. Cornwell, *The Battle of France Then and Now* (Old Harlow, Essex, UK: After the Battle, 2008), 310.

42. United Kingdom, National Archives, AIR 10/5570, *CD 1116, Signals*, vol. 5, *Fighter, Control and Interception* (London: Air Ministry, 1952), 43–50.

43. Sebastian Cox, "A Comparative Analysis of RAF and *Luftwaffe* Intelligence in the Battle of Britain, 1940," in Michael I. Handel, ed., *Intelligence and Military Operations* (London: Cass, 1990), 427–435. See also Wesley K. Wark, "The Air Defence Gap: British Air Doctrine and Intelligence Warnings in the 1930s," in Horst Boog, ed., *The Conduct of the Air War in the Second World War: An International Comparison* (Oxford: Berg, 1988, 1992), 511–526.

44. F. H. Hinsley et al., *British Intelligence in the Second World War*. Vol. 1. *Its Influence on Strategy and Operations* (London: HMSO, 1979), 146–176, esp. 171.

45. Robin Higham, *A Handbook on Air Ministry Organization* (London: AHB, and Manhattan, KS: Sunflower University Press, 1998).

46. After the Battle, *The Battle of Britain*, 205, 252–301.

Chapter 4. The Battle of France

1. CAB 106/282 on Luftwaffe QMG issues, April–June 1940; and Air Commodore Peter J. Dye, "Logistics and the Battle of Britain," *[U.S.] Air Force Journal of Logistics* 24, no. 4 (Winter 2000): 1, 31–40; and Corky Meyer, "The Best World War II Fighter," *Flight Journal* (Aug. 2003): 30.

2. For a concise map of the Battle of France, see William L. Langer, ed., *An Encyclopedia of World History*, 5th rev. ed. (Boston: Houghton Mifflin, 1972), 1138; the maps used here are from Herbert R. Lottman, *The Fall of Paris: June 1940* (London: Sinclair-Stevenson, 1992), 16, 88, 191; Martin S. Alexander, "The Fall of France, 1940," *Journal of Strategic Studies* 13, no. 1 (1990): 10–44; Julian Jackson, *The Fall of France: The Nazi Invasion of 1940* (New York: Oxford, 2003); Ladislas Mysyrowicz, *Autopsie d'une Défaite: Origines de l'effondrement militaire français de 1940* (Lausanne: Editions l'Age d'Homme, 1973); Jean-Pierre Azéma, *From Munich to the Liberation, 1938–1944*. The Cambridge History of Modern France 6 (1984); Jeffrey A. Gunsberg, *Divided and Conquered: The French High Command and the Defeat of the West, 1940* (Westport, CT: Greenwood Press, 1979); Alexander Werth, *The Twilight of France 1933–1940* (New York: Harper 1942, 1966); William L. Shirer, *The Collapse of the Third Republic: An Inquiry into the Fall of France, 1940* (New York: Simon and Schuster, 1969); Jared Diamond, *Collapse—How Societies Choose to Fail or Succeed* (New York: Viking 2005); David Reynolds, "1940: Fulcrum of the Twentieth Century?" *International Affairs* 66, no. 2 (April 1990): 325–350; Capitaine de Frégale Lecreox, "Leçons Méconnues [Lessons Unknown], 1918–1940," *Revue Historique de l'Armée* 2 (1961): 65–74.

3. L. F. Ellis, *The War in France and Flanders, 1939–1940* (London: HMSO, 1954).

4. Ibid., 320.

5. United Kingdom, National Archives, AIR 16/1023 (July 1940).

6. Charles Christienne and Pierre Lissarrague et al., *Histoire de l'aviation militaire française* (Paris: Charles-Lavauzelle, 1980); English edition, *A History of French Military Aviation* (Washington, DC: Smithsonian Institution Press, 1986); *Icare* 57, 80, 94, 131, 143, 156 (1971–1996); and Robert Jackson, *The Air War over France, May–June 1940* (London: Ian Allan, 1974).

7. United Kingdom, National Archives, AIR 41/21, 277 and 282.

8. Francis K. Mason, *Battle over Britain* (New York: Doubleday, 1969), 110–111.

9. See Dominique Breffort and André Joineau, *French Aircraft from 1939 to 1942—Fighters, Bombers, and Observation Types*, 2 vols. (Paris: Histoire et Collections, 2004): Morane-Saulnier MS-406, Dewoitine D-520, Curtiss Hawk H-75, Caudron-Renault C-714, Bloch MB-151/152, Loiré-et-Olivier LeO-451, Breguet Br-693, Amiot AM-143, Farman F-222, ANF Les Mureaux, and Potez P-63.11.

10. Claude d'Abzac-Epézy, *L'Armée de l'Air de Vichy, 1940–1944* (Vincennes: SHAA, 1997), 52–58.

11. Patrice Buffotot and J. Ogier, "L'armée de l'air français pendant la bataille de France du 10 mai 1940 à l'armistice: Essai de bilan numerique d'une bataille aérienne," *Revue Historique des Armées* 3 (1975): 88–117; reprinted in *Recueil d'Articles et Études (1974–1975)* (Vincennes: SHAA, 1977): 197–226.

12. Jackson, *Air War over France, May–June 1940*, 109.

13. G/Capt. Peter Dye, "Royal Flying Corps Logistical Organization," *Royal Air Force Air Power Review*, 1 (2000): 42–59, esp. 50.

14. Christienne and Lissarrague, *A History of French Military Aviation*, 345.

15. See Michael J. F. Bowyer, *No. 2 Group RAF: A Complete History, 1936–1945* (London: Faber & Faber, 1974), 79–109.

16. Breffort and Joineau, *French Aircraft from 1939 to 1942*, vol. 2, 39.

17. Ibid., 40. Actual number of these aircraft is unknown, as few of the four hundred ordered were delivered by 24 June 1940.

18. Ibid., 346.

19. Dowding Papers (London: RAF Museum).

20. Ellis, *The War in France and Flanders, 1939–1940*, esp. 312, 325.

21. Breffort and Joineau, *French Aircraft from 1939 to 1942*, vol. 1, 60.

22. Ibid., 46.

23. Lucien Robineau, "L'armée de l'air dans la Bataille de France," *Recueil d'Articles et Études, 1984–1985* (Vincennes, SHAA 1991): 193–194; Christienne and Lissarrague, *A History of French Military Aviation*, 340–343.

24. Paul Martin, *Invisibles Vainqueurs: Exploits et sacrifices de l'Armée de l'Air en 1939–1940* (Paris: Yves Michelet, 1990), 389–407.

25. W/Cdr. C. G. Jefford, *RAF Squadrons: A Comprehensive Record of the Movement and Equipment of All RAF Squadrons and Their Antecedents Since 1912* (Shrewsbury: Airlife, 1988); United Kingdom, National Archives, AIR 41/22, 12–28. For the French view see General Charles Christienne, "La RAF dans la bataille de France au travers des rapports de Vuillemin de Juillet 1940," *Recueil d'Articles et Études, 1981–1983* (Vincennes: SHAA, 1987): 315–333; also Hanna Diamond, *Fleeing Hitler: France 1940* (London: Oxford University Press, 2007), esp. 341–345.

26. *Icare*, Les forces Aériennes Françaises Libres. Tome 5, 1943–45, Les chasseurs français en Angleterre, 2.143 (1992); La Bataille de France. Vol. 17, La Chasse français en 1939–1940, 1.156 (1996); 1939–40, La Bataille de France. Vol. 15, Les Tchèques, 4.131 (1989); 1939–40, La Bataille de France. Vol. 12, L'Aviation d'Assaut, La 54e Escadre Troisième, 3.94 (1980); 1939–40, La Bataille de France. Vol. 3, Le Bombardement, La Reconnaissance, 57 (1971); 1939–40, La Battaile de France. Vol. 10, L'Aviation d'Assaut, 80 (1977).

27. *Icare* 1939–40, La Bataille de France. Vol. 16, La Chasse, Le Troisième Tome Consacré à la Chasse Française au Cours de la Bataille de France, 1.145 (1993): 83, 87–88.

28. Gille, "A uncontre cinq au GCII/10," *Icare* 145, no. 2 (1993): 25.

29. *Icare* 156 (1996): 111–115.

30. *Icare* 131 (1989): 57.

31. *Icare* 1.145 (1993): 62–78.

32. *Icare* 80 (1977): 90.

33. Basil Collier, *The Defence of the United Kingdom* (London: HMSO, 1957); and S/ Ldr S. C. Rexford-Welch, ed., *The Royal Air Force Medical Services,* History of the Second World War, United Kingdom Medical Series (London: HMSO, 1954–1958), vol. 2, *Commands* (1955), 163 ff.

34. On pilot fatigue during the Battle of France see the memoirs of participants, all not much over eighteen years old: W/Cdr Ian Gleed, *Arise to Conquer* (London: Victor Gollancz, 1942); Roland Beamont, *My Part of the Sky* (Wellingborough, UK: Patrick Stephens Ltd., 1989); Brian Cull and Roland Symons, *One-Armed Mac: The Story of Squadron Leader James MacLachlan, DSO, DFC and 2 Bars, Czech War Cross* (London: Grub Street, 2003), based upon his diaries and letters; and the memoirs of the Armstrong-Whitworth Whitley night bomber (AW-38), by Chris Goss, *It's Suicide But It's Fun: The Story of No. 102 (Ceylon) Squadron, RAF, 1917–56* (Bristol, UK: Crecy Books, 1995); J. Beedle, *43 Squadron, Royal Flying Corps—Royal Air Force: The History of the Fighting Cocks, 1916–66* (London: Beaumont Aviation Literature, 1966); Jan Tegler, "From Fury Biplanes to Hurricanes: Group Captain Billy Drake's Adventures in Hawkers," *[U.S.] Flight Journal* (Dec. 2007): 23–30; Sebastian Cox, "The Air/Land Relationship—An Historical Perspective, 1918–1991," *Royal Air Force Air Power Review* 11, no. 2 (Summer 2008): 1–11.

35. Rexford-Welch, *The Royal Air Force Medical Services,* vol. 2, *Commands,* 107–108. See also Brian Cull, Brice Lauder, and Heinrich Weiss, *Twelve Days in May* (London: Grub Street, 1995), which tells in detail the story of the RAF Hurricanes in France in May 1940.

36. d'Abzac-Epézy, *L'Armée de l'Air de Vichy, 1940–1944,* 52–68.

37. Andrew Boyle, *Trenchard: Man of Vision* (London: Cassell 1956), 309.

38. Richard Overy, *The Battle of Britain* (London: Penguin, 2001), 162; Paul Addison and Jeremy A. Craig, eds., *The Burning Blue: A New History of the Battle of Britain* (London: Pimlico, 2000), 271. Overy notes that the British feared still in spring 1941 a massive "air menace" blow on the *Singleton Report;* see F. H. Hinsley et al., *British Intelligence in the Second World War.* Vol. 1. *Its Influence on Strategy and Operations* (London: HMSO, 1979), 102, 177n, 254.

39. Mason, *Battle over Britain,* 131–132; Ellis, *The War in France and Flanders, 1939–1940,* 312, 325, says the RAF lost 956 aircraft in the Battle of France. From the 43 fighter squadrons engaged, 474 aircraft were lost. Colin Sinnott, *The Royal Air Force and Aircraft Design* (London: Cass, 2001), 134.

40. Jonathan Fenby, *The Sinking of the* Lancastrian (New York: Carroll & Graff, 2005).

41. Rexford-Welch, *The Royal Air Force Medical Services,* vol. 2, *Commands,* 168 ff. See also Sean Longden, *Dunkirk: The Men They Left Behind* (London: Constable, 2008).

42. Collier, *The Defence of the United Kingdom,* 116, gives the German loss at Dunkirk as slightly less than half the 262 claimed by all parties, or 137 including 4 transport aircraft.

43. What follows is based upon S/Ldr S. C. Rexford-Welch, ed., *The Royal Air Force Medical Services*, vol. 1, *Administration*, vol. 2, *Commands*, History of the Second World War, United Kingdom Medical Series (London: HMSO, 1954, 1955). See also Ellis, *The War in France and Flanders, 1939–1940*, 307–327, esp. 325.

44. Arkady Fiedler, *303 Squadron: The Legendary Battle of Britain Fighter Squadron* (Los Angeles, CA: Aquila Polonica (U.S.) Ltd., 2010; reprint of the 1942 edition), 291.

45. See Robin Higham, "The Worst Possible Cases," *Australian Defence Force Journal* 100 (May–June 1993): 63–65.

Chapter 5. Analysis and the Paradox of the Battle of France

1. Claude d'Abzac-Epézy, *L'Armée de l'Air de Vichy, 1940–1944* (Vincennes: SHAA, 1997), 67.

2. James S. Corum, *The Luftwaffe: Creating the Operational Air War, 1918–1940* (Lawrence: University Press of Kansas, 1997), 137–161; Gordon Williamson, *The Luftwaffe Handbook 1939–1945* (Charleston, SC: The History Press, 2006); W. A. B. Douglas, *The Official History of the Royal Canadian Air Force*, vol. 2, *The Creation of a National Air Force* (Toronto: University of Toronto Press, 1986), 193–342; Lucien Robineau, "French Air Policy in the Interwar Period and the Conduct of the Air War Against Germany from September 1939 to June 1940," in Horst Borg, ed., *The Conduct of the Air War in the Second World War: An International Comparison* (Oxford: Berg, 1988, 1992), 627–657; United Kingdom, National Archives, AIR 10/5551, *AP 3233, Flying Training*, vol. 1, *Policy and Planning* (London: Air Ministry, AHB, 1952), 48–107, 272–273.

3. General Charles Christienne, "L'industrie aéronautique française de Septembre 1939 à Juin 1940," *Recueil d'Articles et Études, 1974–1975* (Vincennes: SHAA, 1974, 1977): 142–163; Anthony C. Cain, *The Forgotten Air Force: French Air Doctrine in the 1930s* (Washington, DC: Smithsonian Institution Press, 2002); Arnaud Teyssier, "L'Appui aux Forces de Surface—l'Armée de l'Air et la Recherche d'une doctrine (1933–1939)," *Colloque Internationale Histoire de la Guerre Aérienne* (Paris: SHAA, 10–11 Sept. 1987): 248–277.

4. Christian-Jacques Ehrengardt, "La chasse Francais, 1939–1945, Le GC I/8," *Aero Journal* (Paris) 34 (Dec. 2003–Jan. 2004): 68–71.

5. Christian-Jacques Ehrengardt, "La Chasse Francais, Le GC II/8," *Aero Journal* (Paris) 35 (Feb.–Mar. 2004): 68–71.

6. Christian-Jacques Ehrengardt, "Les Avions français au combat—le Dewoitine D-520," *Aero Journal* (Paris) 35 (May 2003): 68–71; *Les avions français au combat: le Dewoitine D.520*, (Paris: Aéro-Editions, 2004), published in *Aero Journal* (Paris) 40 (Dec. 2004): complete issue; "Le chasseur à la francaise: la famille Dewoitine D.500–D.510," *Aero Journal* (Paris), 40 (Dec. 2004–Jan. 2005): 8–37, and "La Chasse français, 1939–1945, Le GC II/8," *Aero Journal* (Paris) 35 (Feb.–Mar. 2004): 68–71.

7. Christian-Jacques Ehrengardt, "La chasse française: Le GC 1/10," *Aero Journal* (Paris), 41 (Feb.–Mar. 2005): 70–71.

8. Ehrengardt, "Dewoitine D-500–D-510," 68–70.

9. Christienne, "L'industrie aéronautique francaise"; Cain, *The Forgotten Air Force*; Teyssier, "L'Appiu aux Forces de Surface."

10. Paul Martin, *Invisibles Vainqueurs: Exploits et sacrifices de l'Armée de l'Air en 1939–1940* (Paris: Yves Michelet, 1990), 318.

11. d'Abzac-Epézy, *L'Armée de l'Air de Vichy*, 53–77.

12. Ibid., 55.

13. Charles Christienne and Pierre Lissarrague et al., *Histoire de l'aviation militaire française* (Paris: Charles-Lavauzelle, 1980); English edition, *A History of French Military Aviation* (Washington, DC: Smithsonian Institution Press, 1986), 330–331, 363, Tables 3, 5, and 6.

14. Patrice Buffotot and J. Ogier, "L'armée de l'air le français pendant la bataille de France du 10 mai1940: Essai de bilan numerique d'une bataille aérienne," *Revue Historique des Armées* 3 (1975): 88–117; reprinted in *Recueil d'Articles et Études (1974–1975)* (Vincennes: SHAA, 1977): 197–226.

15. Christienne and Lissarrague, *A History of French Military Aviation*, 360.

16. d'Abzac-Epézy, *L'Armée de l'Air de Vichy*, 62; Daniel Porret, *Les As français de la Grande Guerre*. 2 vols. (Vincennes: SHAA, 1983); Daniel Porret and Frank Thevenet, *Les As de la guerre 1939–1945*, 2 vols. (Vincennes: SHAA, 1991). See Table 7 herein: Killed and Wounded, L'Armée de l'Air, 10 May–24 June 1940.

17. Christienne and Lissarrague, *A History of French Military Aviation*, 360; see also Table 7 herein.

18. United Kingdom, CAB [Cabinet] 106/2782, *Abteilung* [Department], VI [Intelligence], the *Abteilung* VI summary of Luftwaffe states during 1939–1945.

19. The Luftwaffe assessed damage as 100 percent, total loss; 60 percent and over, a write-off with possibilities of cannibalization; 45–60 percent, severely damaged and requiring replacement of major components; 40–45 percent, needing engine and system replacement; 25–39 percent, local damage requiring inspection on unit; 10–24 percent, machine has local damage and requires only minor replacements. Less than 10 percent was minor damage reparable on the unit. See Francis K. Mason, *The Battle over Britain* (NewYork: Doubleday, 1969), 129n.

20. After the Battle, *The Battle of Britain (Mark II)* (London: Battle of Britain Printing International, 1982), 526–704.

21. Mason, *The Battle over Britain*, 598.

22. United Kingdom, CAB 106/282, 157.

23. Compiled from After the Battle, *The Battle of Britain*, 536–705.

24. United Kingdom, CAB 106/282, 127 ff.

25. Ferenc A. Vajda and Peter Dancey, *German Aircraft Industry and Production, 1933–1945* (Shrewsbury, UK: Airlife, 1998).

26. Ibid., 6–7, 127.

27. United Kingdom, CAB 106/282.

28. Cain, *The Forgotten Air Force*, 60–66; Dominique Breffort and André Joineau, *French Aircraft from 1939 to 1942—Fighters, Bombers, and Observation Types*, 2 vols. (Paris: Histoire et Collections, 2004).

29. Peter Dye, "The Aviator as Super Hero: The Individual and the First War in the Air," *Royal Air Force Air Power Review* 7, no. 3 (Autumn 2004): 64–74.

30. See Martin, *Invisibles Vainqueurs*.

31. Breffort and Joineau, *French Aircraft from 1939 to 1942*; Christienne and Lissarrague, *A History of French Military Aviation*, 366.

32. United Kingdom, CAB 106/282, 140. While evidence from *Les As* is that they concentrated on Hs-126 observation machines.

33. After the Battle, *The Battle of Britain*, 310–313.

34. L. F. Ellis, *The War in France and Flanders, 1939–1940* (London: HMSO, 1954).

35. d'Abzac-Epézy, *L'Armée de l'Air de Vichy*, 54.

36. Ibid., 56.

37. United Kingdom, National Archives, AIR 10/1594 and 10/1595, *SD 98, Air Staff Memorandum No. 50* (3rd ed., Sept. 1936), *Data for Calculating Consumption and Wastage in War*, tables 1, 8, 16, 17.

38. Dye, "Logistics and the Battle of Britain," 31–40, esp. 38.

39. United Kingdom, National Archives, AIR 10/1594 and 10/1595, tables 16, 17.

40. Basil Collier, *The Defence of the United Kingdom* (London: HMSO, 1957), 200 ff.

41. Ibid., 450 ff.

42. Ibid.

43. General Sir Frederick Pile, *Ack–Ack: Britain's Defence Against Air Attack During the Second World War* (London: Harrap, 1949).

44. See Ulf Balke, *Zusammengestellt nach unterlagen aus RL 2 III/707/einstazbereitschaft der fliegenden verbände*, archival file from Horst Boog, Freiburg, Germany; *Der Luftkrieg in Europa: Die Operativen Einsatze des Kampfgeschwaders 2 im Zweiten Weltkrieg* (Koblenz, Germany: Bernard & Graefe, 1989); and *Kampfgeschwader 100 Wiking: Eine Geschichte aus Kriegstagebuchern,Dokumenten und Berichten 1934–1945* (Stuttgart, Germany: Motorbuch Verlag, 1981).

45. Balke, *Zusammengestellt nach unterlagen aus RL 2 III/707/einstazbereitschaft der fliegenden verbände*.

46. Williamson Murray, *Strategy for Defeat: The Luftwaffe, 1933–1945* (Maxwell AFB, AL: Air University Press, 1983; Baltimore: Nautical and Aviation Press, 1990).

47. United Kingdom, CAB 106/282, *Handbook of Foreign Aircraft Guns*, A.I.2 [G] (London, Nov. 1942) [typewritten material with tabulated information], 154, 157, 159.

48. Ibid.

49. My own tabulations from the data on aircraft losses in the Battle of France and in the Battle of Britain. See also Peter D. Cornwell, *The Battle of France Then and Now*

(Old Harlow, Essex, UK: After the Battle, 2008), 92–499; and After the Battle, *The Battle of Britain*, 315–705.

50. United Kingdom, CAB 106/282, 151.

51. Buffotot and Ogier, "L'armée de l'air française pendant la bataille de France," 215–216; 733 by *chasse* plus Forces Terrestres Anti-Aerienne (FTAA) and 120 by 5 June, and a total GAF loss of 853 by 21 June, plus RAF victories and those lost by accident, plus 300 during the Battle of the Somme. The GAF admitted 634. The FAF said that despite its inferiority, quantitatively and qualitatively, it was superior in combat to the Luftwaffe fighters. However, see below on that.

52. Vajda and Dancey, *German Aircraft Industry and Production, 1933–1945*.

Chapter 6. Aftermath—The Battle of Britain

1. Francis K. Mason, *Battle over Britain* (New York: Doubleday, 1969), 595, 598; Basil Collier, *The Defence of the United Kingdom* (London: HMSO, 1957); After the Battle, *The Battle of Britain (Mark II)* (London: Battle of Britain Printing International, 1982).

2. Collier, *The Defence of the United Kingdom*, 66, 78, 101, 200, 450–459; John Ferris, "Fighter Defence Before Fighter Command: The Rise of Strategic Air Defence in Great Britain, 1917–1934," *Journal of Military History* (Oct. 1999): 845–884.

3. General Sir Frederick Pile, *Ack–Ack: Britain's Defence Against Air Attack During the Second World War* (London: Harrap, 1949).

4. Derek Wood, *Attack Warning Red: The Royal Observer Corps and the Defence of Britain, 1925–1975* (London: Macdonald's and Jane's, 1976); Patrice Buffotot and J. Ogier, "L'armée de l'air française pendant la bataille de France du 10 mai 1940 à l'armistice: Essai de bilan numerique d'une bataille aérienne," *Revue Historique des Armées* 3 (1975): 88–117, reprinted in *Recueil d'Articles de Études (1974–1975)* (Vicennes: SHAA, 1977): 197–226.

5. Fighter Command had the great advantages of airfields not liable to ground attack and of a single focus.

6. United Kingdom, National Archives, AIR 20/4174; Collier, *The Defence of the United Kingdom*.

7. The background is covered in Collier, *The Defence of the United Kingdom*; T. C. G. James, *The Growth of Fighter Command* (London: Cass, 2002); and T. C. G. James, *The Battle of Britain* (London: Cass, 2000). Dowding has been the subject of several books: Basil Collier, *Leader of the Few* (London: Jarrolds, 1957), and recently S/ Ldr Peter Brown, *Honour Restored: The Battle of Britain, Dowding, and the Fight for Freedom* (Staplehurst, UK: Spellmount, 2005). His successor's autobiography is Marshal of the RAF Lord [William Sholto] Douglas of Kirtleside, *Combat and Command* (New York: Simon and Schuster, 1963, 1966). The definitive detailed overall history is Mason, *Battle over Britain*, to be supplemented by the After the Battle, *The Battle of Britain*. See also Robin Higham, "The RAF and the Battle of Britain," in B. F. Cooling, ed., *Case Studies in the Achievement of Air Superiority* (Washington. DC: Center for Air Force History, 1994), 115–178. (nb. This chapter

was written in 1985, but publication of the book was delayed until 1994.) More recent general accounts are Richard J. Overy, *The Battle of Britain: The Myth and the Reality* (New York: W. W. Norton, 2001); Vincent Orange, *Sir Keith Park* (London: Methuen, 1984); Adolph Galland, *The First and the Last* (New York: Holt, 1984); David Baker, *Adolf Galland—The Authorized Biography* (London: Windrow & Greene, 1996); Kenneth Macksey, *Kesselring: The Making of the Luftwaffe* (New York: McKay, 1978); David Irving, *Göring—A Biography* (New York: Morrow, 1989); John Ray, *The Battle of Britain: Dowding and the First Victory, 1940* (London: Cassell, 1994, 2000); Richard Townshend Bickers et al., *The Battle of Britain: The Greatest Battle in the History of Air Warfare* (New York: Prentice Hall, 1990; London: Salamander, 1999); Paul Addison and Jeremy A. Craig, eds., *The Burning Blue: A New History of the Battle of Britain* (London: Pimlico, 2000). The subsequent night Battle of Britain, the Blitz, is covered by John Foreman, *Battle of Britain: The Forgotten Months* (New Malden Surrey, UK: Air Research Publications, 1988), and in the After the Battle, *The Blitz: Then and Now*, 2 vols. (London: Battle of Britain Printing International, 1987–1988). For the Luftwaffe side of both Battles see Williamson Murray, *Strategy for Defeat: The Luftwaffe, 1933–1945* (Maxwell AFB, AL: Air University Press, 1983; Baltimore: Nautical and Aeronautical Publishing Co., 1986); James S. Corum, *The Luftwaffe: Creating the Operational Air War 1918–1940* (Lawrence: University Press of Kansas, 1997); Edward L. Homze, *Arming the Luftwaffe: The Reich Air Ministry and the German Aircraft Industry 1919–1939* (Lincoln: University of Nebraska Press, 1976); and William Green, *Warplanes of the Third Reich* (New York: Doubleday, 1970).

8. Robin Higham, *Diary of a Disaster: British Aid to Greece, 1940–1941* (Lexington: University Press of Kentucky, 1986).

9. Overy, *The Battle of Britain*, 162; United Kingdom, National Archives, AIR 16/943.

10. Horst Boog, "*Luftwaffe* and Logistics in the Second World War," *Aerospace Historian* (Summer/June 1988): 103–110.

11. Colin Sinnott, *The Royal Air Force and Aircraft Design, 1923–1939: Air Staff Operational Requirements* (London: Frank Cass, 2001), 199.

12. S/Ldr S. C. Rexford-Welch, ed., *Royal Air Force Medical Services*, vol. 2, Command History of the Second World War, United Kingdom Medical Series (London: HMSO, 1955), 168.

13. Michael J. F. Bowyer, *No. 2 Group RAF: A Complete History, 1936–1945* (London: Faber & Faber, 1974).

14. See the veteran S/Ldr H. R. "Dizzy" Allen, *Battle for Britain: Recollections of H. R. "Dizzy" Allen* (London: Arthur Barker, 1973); Derek Robinson, *Piece of Cake* (London: H. Hamilton; New York: Knopf, 1984), and the video with Spitfires for the no longer available Hurricanes; and Corum, *The Luftwaffe*.

15. Report by AOC, No. 11 Group, 7 November 1940, in United Kingdom, National Archives, AIR 2/5246; Orange, *Sir Keith Park*, 91–119.

16. Robin Higham, *The Bases of Air Strategy: Building Airfields for the RAF, 1915–1945* (Shrewsbury, UK: Airlife, 1998), 74.

17. See F. H. Hinsley et al., *British Intelligence in the Second World War.* Vol. 1. *Its Influence on Strategy and Operations. I* (London: HMSO, 1979), 200 ff.

18. Ray, *Dowding and the First Victory, 1940,* 42.

19. James, *The Battle of Britain,* 339.

20. United Kingdom, National Archives, AIR 41/14.

21. Brian R. Sullivan, "Downfall of the Regia Aeronautica, 1933–1943," in Robin Higham and Stephen J. Harris, eds., *Why Air Forces Fail: The Anatomy of Defeat* (Lexington: University Press of Kentucky (2006), 163; Collier, *The Defence of the United Kingdom,* 453–493.

22. On these figures see Mason, *Battle over Britain,* 595 and 598; and see graphs in Higham, "The RAF and the Battle of Britain," 136–137.

23. Collier, *The Defence of the United Kingdom,* 493.

24. Ibid., 456.

25. Ibid., 457.

26. Ibid., 460.

27. Ibid., 465.

28. United Kingdom, Air Ministry, CAB 106/282, the *Abteiling* [Department] VI [Intelligence] summary of Luftwaffe states during 1939–1945, Luftwaffe QMG figures.

29. After the Battle, *The Battle of Britain (Mark II),* (1982), 708–709.

30. Collier, *The Defence of the United Kingdom,* 453–493.

31. RAF casualties in the month 8 July–8 August were 94 killed and 60 wounded; total RAF pilots killed 1 July–1 November 1940 were 284 on operations and 159 in accidents (Overy, *The Battle of Britain* [London: Penguin, 2001], 155). Deficiency of pilots in Fighter Command (Collier, *The Defence of the United Kingdom,* 200) for 8 July, 197, and 8 August, 160; casualties, 8–18 August 1940: killed or missing, 94 + 50 injured. Hurricane and Spitfire write-offs, 175; Hurricane and Spitfire repairs other than at unit, 65; Hurricanes and Spitfires destroyed or damaged on the ground, 30. Of the 2,945 aircrew who served RAF Fighter Command in the 122-day Battle of Britain, 487 (16.5 percent) were killed and about 500 wounded, or all-told about 1,007 or 34 percent were "lost." From Bickers et al., *The Battle of Britain,* 187, total pilot losses, 487 (from p. 259: 68 in July, 176 in August, 123 in September, 120 in October; from all causes 537). Air Ministry Order 416 of 27 June 1940 promoted wireless operator and air gunners to sergeant with effect from 28 May. But 8 were still AC-2s when killed in the Battle.

32. James, *The Battle of Britain,* 124–125 and 225–226.

33. Overy, *The Battle of Britain,* 60.

34. Ibid.; Peter D. Cornwell, *The Battle of France Then and Now* (Old Harlow, Essex, UK: After the Battle, 2008), 528–529.

35. Overy, *The Battle of Britain,* 70–71.

36. After the Battle, *The Battle of Britain (Mark II),* 260–297.

37. Louise Geer and Anthony Harold, *Flying Clothing: The Story of Its Development* (Shrewsbury, UK: Airlife, 1979).

38. United Kingdom, National Archives, AIR 10/5551, AP 3233; *Flying Training I Policy and Planning* (London: Air Ministry, AHB 1952), 272–273, 48–107.

39. United Kingdom, National Archives, AIR 33, *Reports of the Inspector-General*; AIR 41/65, RAF monograph, *Manning: Plans and Policy,* n.d.; AIR 41/21, *The Campaign in France 10 May–18 June 1940,* 273–285.

40. Ferris, "Fighter Defence Before Fighter Command"; Robin Higham, "British Air Exercises of the 1930s" (Dayton, OH: Wright State University, 1998 National Aerospace Conference Proceedings, 1998, 1999): 303–312; see also, Robin Higham, *The Military Intellectuals in Britain, 1918–1940* (New Brunswick, NJ: Rutgers University Press, 1966), 119–234, and *Armed Forces in Peacetime: Britain 1918–1940* (London: Foulis, 1962), 146–190, 201–207, and 241–284; David Zimmerman, *Britain's Shield: Radar and the Defeat of the Luftwaffe* (Stroud, Gloucestershire: Sutton Publishing, 2001); Ronald W. Clark, *Rise of the Boffins* (London: Phoenix House, 1962) and *Tizard* (London: Methuen, 1965); C. P. Snow, *Science and Government,* rev. ed. (London: Oxford, 1961); United Kingdom, National Archives, AIR 10/5551, AP 3233, *Second World War 1939–1945: RAF Flying Training,* Vol. 1, *Policy and Planning,* 66–74; United Kingdom, National Archives, AIR 43/21, 278, MS 466, Fighter protection of bombers was not well managed in the first days because the Air Staff, based upon experience in the Great War, had "the idea that close fighter escort was an uneconomical method of protecting the bombers." So fighter patrols were flown irregularly to maintain air superiority. "There can be no doubt that the system was ineffective."

41. Alan Brown, *Airmen in Exile: The Allied Air Forces in the Second World War* (Stroud, Gloucestershire, UK: Sutton, 2000); and Michael A. Peszke, "The Polish Air Force in the United Kingdom, 1939–1946," *Royal Air Force Historical Society Review* 11, no. 3 (Winter 2008): 54–74.

42. James, *The Battle of Britain.*

43. Ibid., 364, 376–377.

44. Horst Boog, *Das Deutsche reich und der Zweite Weltkrieg,* Vol. 2, *Militärgeschlichtes Forschungsamt* (Stuttgart, 1979), 407; and Horst Boog, *Die deutsche Luftwaffenführung: 1939–1945* (Stuttgart: Deutsche Verlags-Anstalt, 1982).

45. Collier, *The Defence of the United Kingdom,* 456–466.

46. United Kingdom, National Archives, AIR 20/4174, Summary. 26 October 1945, daily AIR 16/940–946, October 1939–December 1940.

47. James, *The Battle of Britain,* 335–337, 340, 364, 376, 389, 394–395; AVM Peter Dye, "Logistics and the Battle of Britain: Fighting Wastage in the RAF and the Luftwaffe," *Air Force Journal of Logistics,* 24, no. 4 (Winter 2000): 37. Bickers et al., *The Battle of Britain,* 89, noted that no records now exist and gives a monthly total for June, July, and August of 903, but this overlooks rebuilds and repaired. Francis K. Mason in his earlier 1969 *Battle over Britain,* 595, totals 1,137 Hurricanes and Spitfires from 10 August to 30 October, and adding 200 Hurricanes, totals 1,337.

48. See Peter Garrison, "Hypoxia at Your Fingertips," *Flying Magazine* (July 2011): 88–91.

49. Allen, *Battle for Britain*; and Frank Robinson, comp., *The British Flight Battalion at Pensacola and Afterwards* (Manhattan, KS: Sunflower University Press, 1984).

Conclusions from the Air Battles of 1940

1. Robin Higham, "The Worst Possible Cases," *Australian Defence Forces Journal* 100 (May–June 1993): 63–65.

2. Robin Higham and Charles D. Bright, "Failure of Defensive Imagination," *Australian Defence Force Journal* 117 (Mar.–Apr. 1996): 49–55.

3. United Kingdom, National Archives, AIR 20/1835 (11.6.45).

4. Claude d'Abzac-Epézy, *L'Armée de l'Air de Vichy, 1940–1944* (Vincennes: SHAA, 1997), 59.

5. United Kingdom, Cabinet, CAB 106/282, *Abteilung* VI, 144.

6. General Lucien Robineau, "L'Armée de l'air dans la Bataille de France," *Receuil d' Articles et d'Études (1984–1985)* (Vincennes: SHAA 1991): 183–200.

7. Martin van Creveld, *Supplying War* (London: Cambridge University Press, 1979); James Corum, *The Luftwaffe: Creating the Operational Air War, 1918–1940* (Lawrence: University Press of Kansas, 1997); Horst Boog, "*Luftwaffe* and Logistics in the Second World War," *Aerospace Historian* (June 1988): 103–110; William Green, *The Warplanes of the Third Reich* (New York: Doubleday, 1970); Williamson Murray, *Strategy for Defeat: The Luftwaffe 1933–1945* (Maxwell AFB, AL: Air University Press, 1983).

8. Edward L. Homze, *Arming the Luftwaffe: The Reich Air Ministry and the German Aircraft Industry 1919–1939* (Lincoln: University of Nebraska Press, 1976).

9. Richard Overy, *Bomber Command, 1939–45* (London: Harper Collins, 1997), 215.

10. AVM Peter J. Dye, "Logistics and the Battle of Britain: Fighting Wastage in the RAF and the Luftwaffe," *[U.S.] Air Force Journal of Logistics* 24, no.4 (Winter 2000): 31–40, esp. 33.

11. Ibid.

12. Corum, *The Luftwaffe*, 283.

13. Matthew Cooper, *The German Air Force, 1933–1945: The Anatomy of Failure* (New York: Jane's, 1981).

14. Ibid., 102.

15. Vincent Orange, *Dowding of Fighter Command: Victor of the Battle of Britain* (London: Grub Street, 2008), 132.

16. Cooper, *The German Air Force, 1933–1945*, 130–131.

17. Ibid., 133–134.

18. Ibid., 129.

19. For a diagram of the fighting area formation see Alfred Price, *Blitz on Britain: The Bomber Attacks on the United Kingdom, 1939–1945* (London: Ian Allan, 1977), 182.

20. Corum, *The Luftwaffe*, 280–282.

21. Norman Franks, *Valiant Wings: Battle and Blenheim Squadrons over France 1940* (London: Crecy Books, 1994, 1998), 182.

22. Colin Sinnott, *The Royal Air Force and Aircraft Design 1923–1939* (London: Cass, 2001); Sq/Ldr. H. R. "Dizzy" Allen, *Who Won the Battle of Britain?* (London: Arthur Barker, 1974); and G. F. Wallace, *The Guns of the Royal Air Force, 1939–1945* (London: Kimber, 1972).

23. Franks, *Valiant Wings*, 267–268; Sir Charles Webster and Noble Frankland, *The Strategic Air Offensive Against Germany*, vol. 1 of The History of the Second World War Series (London: HMSO, 1961); and Eric W. Osborne, *The Battle of Heligoland Bight* (Bloomington: Indiana University Press, 2006).

24. O. F. G. Hogg, *The Royal Arsenal Woolwich: The Background Origin and Subsequent History*, 2 vols. (London: Oxford University Press, 1963), 723–1465; 995–1030; E. B. Haslam, "How Lord Dowding Came to Leave Fighter Command," *Journal of Strategic Studies* 4, no. 2 (1981): 175–186; A. L. Gropman, "The Battle of Britain and the Principles of War," *Aerospace Historian* (Sept. 1971): 138–144; After the Battle, *The Battle of Britain (Mark II)* (London: Battle of Britain Printing International, 1982), 259. RAF casualties day by day: July, 68; August, 176; September, 173; October, 120. Total, 537 killed. See also Air Commodore Russ La Forte, "The Strategic, Moral and Conceptual Significance of Victory in the Battle of Britain," *Royal Air Force Air Power Review* 13, no. 2 (Summer 2010): 55–66.

25. Peter D. Cornwell, *The Battle of France Then and Now* (Old Harlow, Essex, UK: After the Battle, 2008), 477.

GLOSSARY

Abteilung: department (Ger.)

Abteilung VI: Luftwaffe intelligence department (Ger.)

Adlertag: Eagle Day (Ger.) 10 August 1940, the official, decreed start of the Battle of Britain

Aéronavale: naval air arm (Fr.)

Anschluss: Hitler's annexation of Austria, 1934 (Ger.)

appareils périnés: obsolete, unrepairable machines (Fr.)

Arme Aéronautique: French air arm (Fr.)

armée: army (Fr.)

Armée de l'Air: air force (Fr.)

Armée de l'Air Chasse Escadrille: fighter force (Fr.)

Armée de Terre: army (Fr.)

attaque brusque: blitzkrieg, sudden attack (Fr.)

aux armées: allocated to the (Air) Armies (Fr.)

aviation d'assaut: army cooperation (Fr.)

bei Ensatz: support flights such as air/sea rescue (A/SR) (Ger.)

blitzkrieg: sudden attack (Ger.)

bon de guerre: war ready (Fr.)

bourgeois: mercantile middle class (Fr.)

bourgeoisie: French middle class

Centre de Réception d'Avions de Série: center of reception of airplanes of a series (Fr.)

chasse: fighter aircraft or force (Fr.)

chasse escadrille: fighter squadron (Fr.)

chasseur: fighter pilots (Fr.)

chasseur aérienne: French fighters

Chef d'état majeur: chief of staff (Fr.)

Cinquième Armée de l'Air: Fifth Air Army (Fr.)

Comité Permanente de la Défense Nationale: standing committee on national defense (Fr.)

Comités d'Aviation: aviation committees (Fr.)

Commandant en chef des forces aériennes: air commander (Fr.)

Commandement en chef: general in chief (Fr.)

Commandement d'Armée: army command (Fr.)

Commandement de Région Aéronautique: regional air command

Conseil Supérieur de l'Air: Supreme Air Council (Fr.)

cwt: hundredweight

Deuxième Bureau: French military intelligence agency (Fr.)

deuxième semester: (second half) (Fr.)

Diktat: reference to the Treaty of Versailles, 1919 (Ger.)

disponible: serviceable, available (Fr.)

Drôle de Guerre: strange or "Phoney War," September 1939–May 1940 (Fr.)

École de Chasse et d'Instruction: School for Fighters and Instruction (Fr.)

École de l'Air: air school (Fr.)

escadre: wing (Fr.)

escadrille: squadron (Fr.)

état majeur: air staff (Fr.)

état majeur de l'Armée de l'Air: general staff air force (Fr.)

Feindflu: war flight (Ger.)

first line: Up to WWII, those aircraft in Regular units ready to go (Br.)

Fliegerhorst: military airfield (operational station) (Ger.)

Fliegerhorst Inspekteur: inspector of airfields (Ger.)

Fliegerkorps: air command (Ger.)

Fliegerverbindungsoffiziere (Flivos): air liaison officers (Ger.)

Front reparatur: Forward repair unit (Fr.)

Fuehrungstab: operations staff (Ger.)

Général Commandant: commanding general (Fr.)

Generalfeldmarschall: field marshal (Ger.)

Generalstab: general staff (Ger.)

Geschwader: air wing (Ger.)

Grossegeneralstab: great general staff (Ger.)

Groupement d'Air Observation: air observation group (Fr.)

groupes chausseurs: fighter groups (Fr.)

groupes de chasse: fighter groups (Fr.)

Gruppe: group (Ger.)

Haut Commandement: high command (Fr.)

Heimat: Fatherland (Ger.)

Heimat-danstic: local noncombat flight (Ger.)

hors de combat: out of action (Fr.)

Inspector-génèral: inspector general (Fr.)

Jagd Gruppen: fighter groups (Ger.)

Jagdegeschwader: fighter wing (Ger.)

Jagdflugzeuge: fighter planes (Ger.)

Jagdlfliegerschuler: fighter operational training unit (Ger.)

Jagdstaffel: fighter squadron (Ger.)

Kanalkamp: the English Channel battle from 1 July (Ger.)

Koluft: Luftwaffe air liaison officer (Ger.)

Kriegsmarine: navy (from 1935) (Ger.)

La Royale: navy (Fr.)

l'état majeur: general staff (Fr.)

Little (Petite) Entente: French bloc—Poland, Czechoslovakia, Romania, and Yugoslavia (Fr.)

Luftflotte: air fleet (Ger.)

Luftgau: air district (Ger.)

Luftgeneralstab: air general staff (Ger.)

Luftkriegsmarine: naval air arm (Ger.)

Luftpark: aircraft park (Ger.)

Luftwaffe: air force (Ger.)

Luftwaffe Oberkommando: air headquarters (Ger.)

Luftwaffengeneralstab: air general staff (Ger.)

Luftzeichenkorps: air signal corps (Ger.)

Ministère de l'Armée de Terre: ministry of the army (Fr.)

Ministère de la Défense Nationale: ministry of national defense (Fr.)

Ministère de l'Air: air ministry (Fr.)

Ministère de l'Armement: ministry of armaments (Fr.)

Ministère de la Guerre: ministry of war (Fr.)

Ministre de l'Air: air minister (Fr.)

Ministre de la Guerre: war minister (Fr.)

Nazi: National Socialist German Workers Party

Oberkommando: high command (Ger.)

on charge: on a unit's records (aircraft)

outré-mer: overseas (Fr.)

Parlement: parliament (Fr.)

patronats: wealthy capitalist French class

petit bourgeoisie: the conventional French lower middle class

Phoney War: See Drôle de Guerre

pleine vol: clear air (Fr.)

Reichsmarine: navy (until 1935; thereafter Kriegsmarine) (Ger.)

Reichspropagandaministerium: propaganda ministry (Ger.)

Reichswehr: armed forces of Weimar Republic (to 1933) (Ger.)

rentiers: those on fixed incomes (Fr.)

procès: legal process (Fr.)

secrétaire d'État à l'Air: secretary of state for air (Fr.)

Seenotdienst: the air/sea rescue service (Ger.)

sitzkrieg: a "sitting"/trench war (British slang)

sous-officier: noncommissioned officer (Fr.)

Staffeln: squadrons (Ger.)

Technisches Amt: technical directorate (T-Amt) (Ger.)

Wehrmacht: army (1933–1945) (Ger.)

Zeugamt: stores depot (Ger.)

BIBLIOGRAPHY

Addison, Paul, and Jeremy A. Craig, eds., *The Burning Blue: A New History of the Battle of Britain*. London: Pimlico, 2000.

After the Battle. *The Battle of Britain (Mark II)*. London: Battle of Britain Printing International. 2nd ed. 1982.

"Air of Authority—A History of RAF Organisation." www.rafweb.org/Biographies.Sorley .htm.

Alexander, Martin S. "The Fall of France, 1940." *Journal of Strategic Studies* 13, no. 1 (Mar. 1990): 10–44.

———. *The Republic in Danger: General Maurice Gamelin and the Politics of French Defence, 1933–1940*. London: Cambridge University Press, 1992.

Allen, S/Ldr H. R. "Dizzy." *Battle for Britain: Recollections of H. R. "Dizzy" Allen*. London: Arthur Barker, 1973.

———. *Who Won the Battle of Britain?* London: Arthur Barker, 1974.

Andrews, Major William F. "The Luftwaffe and the Battle for Air Superiority: Blueprint or Warning?." *Air Power Journal* (Fall 1995); see www.airpower.au.af.mil/ airchronicles/apj/apj95/fal95_files/andrews.pdf.

Angot, E., and R. de Lavergne. *Un figure legendaire de l'aviation française de 1914 à 1940 le General Vuillemin: la combatant, le pioneer de Sahar, le chef*. Paris: Palatine, 1965.

Ashmore, Major General E. B. *Air Defence*. London: Longmans, Green, 1929.

Atkin, Ronald. *Pillar of Fire: Dunkirk 1940*. Edinburgh, Scotland: Birlinn Ltd., 2001.

Azéma, Jean-Pierre. *From Munich to the Liberation, 1938-1944*. The Cambridge History of Modern France 6 (1984).

Baker, David. *Adolph Galland—The Authorized Biography*. London: Windrow and Greene, 1996.

Balke, Ulf. *Der Luftkrieg in Europa: Die Operativen Einsatze des Kampfgeschwaders 2 im Zweiten Weltkrieg*. Koblenz, Germany: Bernard & Graefe, 1989.

———. *Kampfgeschwader 100 Wiking: Eine Geschichte aus Kriegstagebuchern, Dokumenten und Berichten 1934-1945*. Stuttgart, Germany: Motorbuch Verlag, 1981.

———. *Zusammengestellt nach unterlagen aus RL 2 III/707/einstaz-bereitschaft der fliegenden verbände*, archival file from Horst Boog, Freiburg, Germany.

Batchelor, John, and Ian Hogg. *Artillery*. New York: Charles Scribner's Sons, 1972.

Battleground: The Battle of Britain. DVD BGRD440. United States: PBS, 2008.

Beamont, Roland. *My Part of the Sky*. Wellingborough, UK: Patrick Stephens Ltd., 1989.

Beaumont, Roger. *Right Backed by Might: The International Air Force Concept*. Westport, CT: Praeger, 2001.

Beedle, J. *43 Squadron, Royal Flying Corps—Royal Air Force: The History of the Fighting Cocks, 1916–66.* London: Beaumont Aviation Literature, 1966.

Bekker, Cajus. *The Luftwaffe War Diaries.* New York: Doubleday, 1968.

Best, Geoffrey. *Churchill and War.* London: Hambledon Continuum, 2005.

Bickers, Richard Townshend, et al. *The Battle of Britain: The Greatest Battle in the History of Air Warfare.* New York: Prentice Hall, 1990; London: Salamander, 1999.

Blatt, Joel, ed. *The French Defeat of 1940: Reassessments.* Providence, RI: Berghahn Books, 1998.

Bloch, Marc. *Strange Defeat: A Statement of Evidence Written in 1940.* Translated by Gerard Hopkins. New York: Octagon Books, 1968.

Bodleian Library, ed. *German Invasion Plan for the British Isles, 1940.* Oxford: University of Oxford, 2008.

Boillot, Pierre. "Premièrs vols et premièrs batailles d'un jeune chasseur en 1939–1940." *Icare* 145, no. 16 (1993), "La Chasse, 3e partie," 28–34.

Boog, Horst, ed. *The Conduct of the Air War in the Second World War: An International Comparison.* Oxford: Berg, 1988, 1992.

———. *Das Deutsche reich und der Zweite Weltkrieg,* in Militargeschichliches Forschungsamt (Research Institute for Military History, Potsdam, Germany), editor. Stuttgart, 1979.

———. *Die deutsche Luftwaffenfuhrung: 1939–1945.* Vol. 2, in Militargeschichliches Forschungsamt (Research Institute for Military History, Potsdam, Germany), editor. Stuttgart: Deutsche Verlags-Anstalt, 1982.

———. "*Luftwaffe* and Logistics in the Second World War." *Aerospace Historian* (June 1988): 103–110.

———. "The Policy, Command and Direction of the *Luftwaffe* in World War II." *RAF Historical Society Journal* 41 (2008): 67–85.

Botts, Colonel Ferruccio. "Amadeo Mecozzi." *Actes de Colloque International.* Paris (8 Oct. 1990): 131–150.

Bouchier, AVM Sir Cecil. *Spitfires in Japan.* Folkestone, UK: Global Oriental, 2005.

Bowers, Peter M. *Curtiss Aircraft 1907–1947.* London: Putnam 1979.

———. *The Curtiss Hawk 75. Aircraft in Profile* No. 80. London: Profile Publications, 1966.

Bowyer, Michael J. F. *The Boulton-Paul Defiant.* Vol. 5. *Aircraft in Profile* No. 117. Leatherhead, Surrey, UK: Profile Publications, 1966.

———. *No. 2 Group RAF: A Complete History, 1936–1945.* London: Faber & Faber, 1974.

Boyle, Andrew. *Trenchard: Man of Vision.* London: Cassell, 1956.

Breffort, Dominique, and André Joineau. *French Aircraft from 1939 to 1942—Fighters, Bombers, and Observation Types.* 2 vols. Paris: Histoire et Collections, 2004.

"Le Brewster Buffalo." *Aero Journal* 7 (May 2004): 4–39.

Brown, Alan. *Airmen in Exile: The Allied Air Forces in the Second World War.* Stroud, Gloucestershire: UK: Sutton, 2000.

Brown, Eric. *Testing for Combat.* Shrewsbury, UK: Airlife, 1994.

Brown, S/Ldr Peter. *Honour Restored: The Battle of Britain, Dowding, and the Fight for Freedom.* Staplehurst, UK: Spellmount, 2005.

Browne, AVM John. "Airfield Construction by the Royal Air Force, 1939–1966." *Royal Air Force Historical Society Journal* 51 (2011): 8–31.

Bruce, Jim. *The Hawker Audax and Hardy. Aircraft in Profile* No. 140. Leatherhead, Surrey, UK: Profile Publications, 1966.

Buffotot, Patrice, and J. Ogier. "L'armée de l'air français pendant la bataille de France du 10 mai 1940 à l'armistice: Essai de bilan numerique d'une bataille aérienne." *Revue Historique des Armées* 3 (1975): 88–117; reprinted in *Recueil d'Articles et Études, 1974–1975.* Vincennes: SHAA, 1977: 197–226.

Bungay, Stephen. *The Most Dangerous Enemy: An Illustrated History of the Battle of Britain.* Minneapolis, MN: Zenith Press, 2010.

Byford, G/Cpt. Alistair. "The Battle of France, May 1940: Enduring, Combined, and Joint Lessons." *Royal Air Force Air Power Review* 11, no. 2 (Summer 2008): 60–73.

———. "Fair Stood the Wind for France: The Royal Air Force Experience in the 1940s as a Case Study of the Relationship Between Policy, Strategy, and Doctrine." *Royal Air Force Air Power Review* 14, no. 3 (Autumn/Winter 2011): 35–60.

Cain, Anthony C. "L'Armée de l'Air, 1933–1940: Drifting Toward Defeat." In *Why Air Forces Fail: The Anatomy of Defeat,* edited by Robin Higham and Stephen B. Harris, 41–70. Lexington: University Press of Kentucky, 2006.

———. *The Forgotten Air Force: French Air Doctrine in the 1930s.* Washington, DC: Smithsonian Institution Press, 2002.

Caldwell, Donald, and Richard Muller. *The Luftwaffe over Germany: Defense of the Reich.* London: Greenhill Books, 2007.

Catherwood, Christopher. *Winston Churchill: The Flawed Genius of World War II.* New York: Berkley, 2009.

Chadeau, Emmanuel. "Government, Industry and Nation: The Growth of Aeronautical Technology in France (1900–1950)." *Aerospace Historian* (Mar. 1988): 26–44.

———. *L'industrie aéronautique en France, 1900–1950.* Paris: Fayard, 1987.

Christienne, General Charles. "La RAF dans la Bataille de France au travers des raports de Vuillemin de Juillet 1940." *Recueil d'Articles et Études (1981–1983).* Vincennes: SHAA, 1987: 315–333.

———. "L'industrie aéronautique française de Septembre 1939 à Juin 1940." *Recueil d'Articles et Études (1974–1975).* Vincennes: SHAA, 1977: 142–163.

Christienne, Charles, and Pierre Lissarrague et al. *Histoire de l'aviation militaire française.* Paris: Charles-Lavauzelle, 1980); English edition, *A History of French Military Aviation.* Washington, DC: Smithsonian Institution Press, 1986.

Citino, Robert M. *The German Way of War: From the Thirty Years' War to the Third Reich.* Lawrence: University Press of Kansas, 2005.

———. *The Path to Blitzkrieg: Doctrine and Training in the German Army, 1920–1939.* Mechanicsburg, PA: Stackpole, 1999, 2008.

Clark, Ronald W. *Rise of the Boffins.* London: Phoenix House, 1962.

———. *Tizard.* London: Methuen, 1965.

Collier, Basil. *The Defence of the United Kingdom.* London: HMSO, 1957.

———. *Leader of the Few.* London: Jarrolds, 1957.

Colloque Internationale Histoire de la Guerre Aérienne. Paris, SHAA, 10–11 Sept. 1987.

Cooling, B. F., ed. *Case Studies in the Achievement of Air Superiority.* Washington, DC: Center for Air Force History, 1994.

Cooper, Matthew. *The German Air Force, 1933–1945: The Anatomy of Failure*. New York: Jane's, 1981.

———. *The German Army, 1933–1945*. New York: Stein and Day, 1978.

Cornwell, Peter D. *The Battle of France Then and Now*. Old Harlow, Essex, UK: After the Battle, 2008.

Corum, James S. *The Luftwaffe: Creating the Operational Air War, 1918–1940*. Lawrence: University Press of Kansas, 1997.

———. "The Spanish Civil War: Lessons Learned and Not Learned by the Great Powers." *Journal of Military History* 62 (1998): 313–334.

———. *Wolfram von Richthofen: Master of the German Air War*. Lawrence: University Press of Kansas, 2008.

Cot, Pierre. "En 1940, ou étaient nos avions? Le preparation, la doctrine, l'emploi de l'Armée de l'Air avant et pendant la Bataille de France." *Icare* 57 (1991): 36–57.

Cox, Sebastian. "The Air/Land Relationship—An Historical Perspective, 1918–1991." *Royal Air Force Air Power Review* 11, no. 2 (Summer 2008): 1–11.

———. "A Comparative Analysis of RAF and *Luftwaffe* Intelligence in the Battle of Britain, 1940." In *Intelligence and Military Operations*, edited by Michael I. Handel, 427–435. London: Cass, 1990.

———. "An Overview of Airfield Construction Prior to and During WWII." *Royal Air Force Historical Society Journal* 51 (2011): 142–151.

———. "The Sources and Organization of RAF Intelligence and Its Influence on Operations." In *The Conduct of the Air War in the Second World War*, edited by Horst Boog, 553–579. Oxford, UK: Berg, 1992.

Cox, Sebastian, and Peter Gray, eds. *Air Power History: Turning Points from Kitty Hawk to Kosovo*. London: Cass, 2002.

Crabtree, James D. *On Air Defense*. Westport, CT: Praeger, 1994.

Creek, Eddie. "Battle of Britain." *Flight Journal* (Oct. 2010): 60–61.

Cull, Brian, Brice Lauder, and Heinrich Weiss. *Twelve Days in May*. London: Grub Street, 1995.

Cull, Brian, and Roland Symons. *One-Armed Mac: The Story of Squadron Leader James MacLachlan, DSO, DFC and 2 Bars, Czech War Cross*. London: Grub Street, 2003.

Cumming, Anthony J., and Christina Goulter. "Ready or Not? The RAF in the Battle of Britain." *BBC History Magazine* 8, no. 11 (Nov. 2007): 22–23.

d'Abzac-Epézy, Claude. *L'Armée de l'Air de Vichy, 1940–1944*. Vincennes: SHAA, 1997.

Danel, Raymond. *The Lioré et Olivier LeO 45 Series*. Aircraft in Profile No. 173. Leatherhead, Surrey, UK: Profile Publications, 1967.

Davies, R. E. G. *Lufthansa: An Airline and Its Aircraft*. Shrewsbury, UK: Airlife, 1991.

de Cossé-Brissac, LTC. "Combien d'avions Allemands contre combien d'avions français le 10 Mai 1940?." *Revue de Défense Nationale* 4 (1948): 741–759.

de Gaulle, Charles. *L'armée de métier (The Army of the Future)*. Paris: 1934; New York: Lippincott, 1940.

de la Madariaga, Salvador. *Englishmen, Frenchmen, Spaniards*. New York: Hill and Wang, 1969 [1928].

de Lorris, Roland Maurice. "La politique economique et industrielle du Ministre de l'Air." In *Quinze ans d'Aéronautique Français (1922–1937)*, 497–516. Paris: Chambre Syndicale des Industries Aéronautique, 1949.

De Seversky, Alexander P. *Victory Through Air Power*. New York: Simon & Schuster, 1942.

Delve, Ken. *The Story of the Spitfire: An Operational and Combat History*. London: Greenhill Books, 2007.

Diamond, Hanna. *Fleeing Hitler: France 1940*. London: Oxford University Press, 2007.

Diamond, Jared. *Collapse—How Societies Choose to Fail or Succeed*. New York: Viking, 2005.

Donnelly, G. L. *A Quest for Wings: From Tail-gunner to Pilot*. Stroud, Gloucestershire, UK: Tempus, 2000.

Dornberger, General Walter. *V-2*. New York: Ballantine, 1954.

Douglas, W. A. B. *The Official History of the Royal Canadian Air Force*. Vol. 2, *The Creation of a National Air Force*. Toronto: University of Toronto Press, 1986.

Douglas of Kirtleside, MRAF Lord [William Sholto]. *Combat and Command*. New York: Simon and Schuster, 1966.

Dowding Papers. London: RAF Museum, London.

Drake, G/Cpt. Billy. "From Fury Biplanes to Hurricanes." *Flight Journal* (Dec. 2007): 22–30.

Dunlap, Maj. Gen. Charles J., Jr. "Roles, Missions, and Equipment: Military Lessons from Experience in This Decade." *Army History* (Winter 2009): 17–21.

Dunn, Michael M. "Helicopter Losses in Vietnam." http://airforceassociation.blogspot .com/2010/12/helicopter-losses-in-viet-nam.html.

Dye, AVM Peter J. "The Aviator as Super Hero: The Individual and the First War in the Air." *Royal Air Force Air Power Review* 7, no. 3 (Autumn 2004): 65–76.

——. "France and the Development of British Military Aviation." *Royal Air Force Air Power Review* 12, no. 1 (Spring 2009): 1–13.

——. "Logistics and Airpower—A Failure in Doctrine?" *[U.S.] Air Force Journal of Logistics* 23, no. 3 (Fall 1999): 28–30, 43.

——. "Logistics and the Battle of Britain: Fighting Wastage in the RAF and the Luftwaffe." *[U.S.] Air Force Journal of Logistics* 24, no. 4 (Winter 2000): 1, 31–40; *Royal Air Force Air Power Review* 3, no. 4 (Winter 2000): 15–37.

——. "RFC Bombs and Bombing, 1912–1918." *Royal Air Force Historical Society Journal* 45 (2009): 8–14.

——. "Royal Air Force Repair and Salvage 1939–1945." *Royal Air Force Historical Society Journal* 51 (2011): 111–123, 139–141.

——. "Royal Flying Corps Logistic Organisation." *[U.S.] Air Force Journal of Logistics* 22, no. 1 (2008): 30–38.

——. "Royal Flying Corps Logistic Organization, 1914–1918." *[U.S.] Air Force Journal of Logistics* (Winter 2000): 60–73; *Royal Air Force Air Power Review* 1 (2000): 42–59.

——. "Sustaining Air Power: The Influence of Logistics on Royal Air Force Doctrine." *Royal Air Force Air Power Review* 9, no. 2 (Autumn 2006): 41–51.

Ebert, Hans. *Willy Messerschmitt—Pioneer of Aviation Design*. The History of German Aviation Series. Atglen, PA: Schiffer Publishing, 1999.

Edgerton, David. "A Collossus at War." *BBC History Magazine*, April 2011, 42–47.

Ehrengardt, Christian-Jacques. "Les Avions français au combat—le Dewoitine D-520." *Aero Journal* (Paris) 35 (May 2003): 68–71.

——. *Les avions français au combat: le Dewoitine D.520*. Paris: Aéro-Editions, 2004.

———. "La chasse française, 1939–1945 Le GC I/8." *Aero Journal* 34 (Dec. 2003–Jan. 2004): 68–71.

———. "La chasse français 1939–1945 Le GC II/8." *Aero Journal* 35 (Feb.–Mar. 2004).

———. La chasse français 1939–1945 Le GC I/10." *Aero Journal* 41 (Feb.–Mar. 2005).

———. "Le chasseur à la française: la famille Dewoitine D.500–D.510." *Aero Journal* 40 (Dec. 2004–Jan. 2005): 8–37.

———. "Les unités: La couronne t'attend . . . Les écoles de l'Armée de l'Air, 1939–40." *Aero Journal* 37 (June–July 2004): 40–46.

Ellis, John. *Brute Force: Allied Strategy and Tactics in the Second World War.* New York: Viking, 1990, vii–6.

Ellis, L. F. *The War in France and Flanders, 1939–1940.* London: HMSO, 1954.

Ethell, Jeffrey L. *The Luftwaffe at War: Blitzkrieg in the West, 1939–1942.* Mechanicsburg, PA: Stackpole, 1997.

Evans, Richard J. *The Third Reich at War.* New York: Penguin Press, 2009.

"External Ballistics." *Wikipedia.org* (24 Apr. 2008).

Facon, Patrick. "Aperçus sur la doctrine d'emploi de l'aeronautiques de militaire français, 1914–1918." *Recueil d'Articles et Études (1984–1985).* Vincennes: SHAA, 1991: 125–131.

———. "C'était hier—logistique—un impératif? Approvisionner l'Armée de l'Air." *Air ACTU*, 534 (Aug.–Sept. 2000): 44–45.

———. "The High Command of the French Air Force and the Problem of Rearmament, 1938–1939—A Technical and Industrial Approach." In *The Conduct of the Air War in the Second World War: An International Comparison*, edited by Horst Boog, 146–168. Oxford: Berg, 1988, 1992.

———. *L'Armée de l'Air dans la Tourmente: La Bataille de france, 1939–1940.* Paris: SHAA, 1998.

———. "Les milles victoires de l'Armée de l'Air en 1939–1940: Autopsie d'une mythe." *Revue Historique des Armées* 4 (Nov. 1997): 79–97.

———. "Le Plan V (1938–1939)." In *Recueil d'Articles et Études (1979–1981).* Vincennes: SHAA, 1986: 31–80.

———. "La visite du Général Vuillemin en Allemagne." In *Service Historique l'Armée de l'Air, Recueil de'Articles et Études (1981–1983).* Vincennes: SHAA, 1984: 221–226.

Fenby, Jonathan. *The Sinking of the* Lancastrian. New York: Carroll & Graff, 2005.

Ferris, John. "Fighter Defense Before Fighter Command: The Rise of Strategic Air Defence in Great Britain, 1917–1934." *Journal of Military History* (Oct. 1999): 845–884.

Fiedler, Arkady. *303 Squadron: The Legendary Battle of Britain Fighter Squadron.* Los Angeles, CA: Aquila Polonica, 2010. [Orig. published in French, 1942.]

Flying the Secret Sky. DVD, WG42679. United States: PBS, 2008.

Fopp, Michael. "The Battle of Britain—70 Years On." *Royal Air Force Historical Society Journal* 50 (2010): 6–30.

Foreman, John. *Battle of Britain: The Forgotten Months.* New Malden Surrey, UK: Air Research Publications, 1988.

Fozard, John W., ed. *Sydney Camm and the Hurricane.* Washington, DC: Smithsonian Institution Press, 1991.

France. SHAA. *Bulletin de renseignment de 'l'aviation de chasse,* 20 July 1940. Chateau Vincennes: SHAA.

Francis, Martin. *The Flyer: British Culture and the Royal Air Force, 1939–1945.* London: Oxford University Press, 2009.

Franks, Norman L. R. *Valiant Wings: Battle and Blenheim Squadrons over France 1940.* London: Crécy Books, 1994, 1998.

Fraser, David. "Les transmissions de 1919 à 1959." *Revue Historique de l'Armée* 23, no.1 (1967): 51–56.

Fredette, Raymond H. *The Sky on Fire: The First Battle of Britain, 1917–1918.* Smithsonian History of Aviation and Spacecraft Series. Washington, DC: Smithsonian Insitution Press, 1966, 1991; Tuscaloosa: University of Alabama Press, 2006.

Gallagher, Gary W., ed. *Lee, the Soldier.* Lincoln: University of Nebraska Press, 1996.

Galland, Adolf. *The First and the Last.* New York: Henry Holt, 1984.

Gann, Harry. *The Douglas A-20 (7A to Boston III). Aircraft in Profile* No. 202. London: Profile Publications, 1971.

Garrison, Peter. "Hypoxia at Your Fingertips." *Flying Magazine* (July 2011): 88–91.

Geer, Louise, and Anthony Harold. *Flying Clothing: The Story of Its Development.* Shrewsbury, UK: Airlife, 1979.

Gibler, Douglas. *International Military Alliances.* Washington, DC: CQ Press, 2008.

Gibson, Air Cdre. T. M. "The Genesis of Medical Selection Tests for Air Crew in the United Kingdom." *RAFHS Journal* 43 (2008): 8–17.

Gilbert, André. "Robert Gouby." *Aero Journal* 34 (Dec. 2003–Jan. 2004): 45–46.

Gille, Henri. "A un contra cinq au GCII/10." *Icare* 145, no. 2 (1993): 75–79.

Glancey, Jonathan. *Spitfire: The Illustrated Biography.* London: Atlantic, 2006.

Gleed, W/Cdr Ian R. *Arise to Conquer.* London: Victor Gollancz, 1942.

Golley, John. *Aircrew Unlimited: The Commonwealth Air Training Plan During World War II.* Sparkford, UK: Patrick Stephens, 1993.

Goss, Chris. *It's Suicide But It's Fun: The Story of No. 102 (Ceylon) Squadron, RAF, 1917–56.* Bristol, UK: Crecy Books, 1995.

Green, William. *The Warplanes of the Third Reich.* New York: Doubleday, 1970.

Griehl, Manfred, and Joachim Dressel. *Luftwaffe Combat Aircraft: Development, Production, Operations, 1935–1945.* Atglen, PA: Schiffer Publishing, 2004.

Griess, Thomas E., et al. *The Second World War: Europe and the Mediterranean.* The West Point Military History Series. Garden City Park, NY: Square One Publishers, 2002.

Gropman, A. L. "The Battle of Britain and the Principles of War." *Aerospace Historian* (Sept. 1971): 138–144.

Gunsberg, Jeffrey A. "*Armée de l'Air* vs. *The Luftwaffe*—1940." *Defence Update International* (1984): 44–53.

———. *Divided and Conquered: the French High Command and the Defeat of the West, 1940.* Westport, CT: Greenwood Press, 1979.

Haight, James McVicar. *American Aid to France, 1938–1940.* New York: Athenaeum, 1970.

Haining, Peter. *The Chianti Raiders: The Extraordinary Story of the Italian Air Force in the Battle of Britain.* London: Robson Books, 2005.

Hall, David Ian. *Strategy for Victory: The Development of British Tactical Air Power, 1919–1943*. Westport, CT: Praeger, 2008.

Hancock, Peter A., and James L. Szalma, *Performance Under Stress*. Aldershot, UK: Ashgate, 2008.

Hart, Russell A. *Guderian: Panzer Pioneer or Myth Maker?* Washington, DC: Potomac Books, 2006.

Haslam, E. B. "How Lord Dowding Came to Leave Fighter Command." *Journal of Strategic Studies* 4, no. 2 (1981): 175–186.

Hastings, Max. *Winston's War: Churchill 1940–1945*. New York: Knopf, 2010.

Hathaway, Stuart. "The Development of RAF Bombs, 1919–1939." *Royal Air Force Historical Society Journal* 45 (2009): 15–24.

Hayward, Joel. "The Lutwaffe's Agility: An Assessment of the Relevant Concepts and Practices." Presented at Air Power Conference, Hendon, London, 19-20 July 2006.

Heaton, Colin D., and Anne-Marie Lewis. *The German Aces Speak: World War II Through the Eyes of Four of the Luftwaffe's Most Important Commanders*. Minneapolis, MN: Zenith Press, 2011.

Heffernan, John B. "The Blockade of the Southern Confederacy, 1861–1865." *Smithsonian Journal of History* 12, no. 4 (Winter 1967–1968): 23–44.

Higham, Robin. *Armed Forces in Peacetime: Britain 1918–1940*. London: Foulis, 1962.

———. *The Bases of Air Strategy: Building Airfields for the RAF, 1915–1945*. Shrewsbury, UK: Airlife, 1998.

———. "British Air Exercises of the 1930s." 1998 National Aerospace Conference—The Meaning of Flight in the 20th Century, Proceedings. Dayton, OH: Wright State University, 1998, 1999: 303–312.

———. *Diary of a Disaster: British Aid to Greece, 1940–1941*. Lexington: University Press of Kentucky, 1986.

———. *A Handbook on Air Ministry Organization*. London: Air Historical Branch; and Manhattan, KS: Sunflower University Press, 1998.

———. *The Military Intellectuals in Britain, 1918–1940*. New Brunswick, NJ: Rutgers University Press, 1966.

———. *100 Years of Air Power and Aviation*. College Station, TX: Texas A&M University Press, 2004.

———. "The RAF and the Battle of Britain." In *Case Studies in the Achievement of Air Superiority*, edited by B. F. Cooling, 115–178. Washington, DC: Center for Air Force History, 1994.

———. *Two Roads to War: The French and British Air Arms from Versailles to Dunkirk*. Annapolis, MD: Naval Institute Press, 2012.

———. "The Worst Possible Cases." *Australian Defence Journal* 100 (May–June 1993): 63–65.

Higham, Robin, and Charles D. Bright. "Failure of Defensive Imagination." *Australian Defence Force Journal* 117 (Mar.–Apr. 1996): 49–55.

Higham, Robin, and Stephen J. Harris, eds. *Why Air Forces Fail: The Anatomy of Defeat*. Lexington: University Press of Kentucky, 2006.

Higham, Robin, John T. Greenwood, and Von Hardesty. *Russian Aviation and Air Power in the Twentieth Century*. London: Cass, 1998.

Hinchcliffe, Mark. "Commanding Air Power: Some Contemporary Thoughts." Air Power Development Centre Working Paper No. 30. Tuggeranong, ACT, Australia: Air Power Development Centre, 2010, 18–19.

Hinsley, F. H., E. E. Thomas, C. F. G. Ransom, and R. C. Knight. *British Intelligence in the Second World War.* Vol. 1, *Its Influence on Strategy and Operations.* London: HMSO, 1979.

Hoffman, Stanley. *In Search of France.* . . . New York: Harper & Row, 1965.

Hogg, O. F. G. *The Royal Arsenal Woolwich: The Background Origin and Subsequent History.* 2 vols. London: Oxford University Press, 1963.

Holland, James. *The Battle of Britain: Five Months That Changed History, May–October 1940.* London: Bantam Press, 2010.

Holley, I. B. *Buying Aircraft: Matériel Procurement for the Army Air Forces.* In The U.S. Army in World War II Series, Center for Military History Publication, 11–2. Washington, DC: 1964, 1989.

Homze, Edward L. *Arming the Luftwaffe: The Reich Air Ministry and the German Aircraft Industry 1919–1939.* Lincoln: University of Nebraska Press, 1976.

Hooten, E. R. *Luftwaffe at War: The Gathering Storm, 1933–1939.* Horsham, Surrey, UK: Classic, 2007.

——. *Phoenix Triumphant: The Rise and Rise of the Luftwaffe.* London: Arms & Armour, 1994.

Humbert, Agnes. *Resistance: Memoirs of Occupied France.* New York: Bloomsbury, 2008.

Icare. Nos. 57, 59, 80, 91, 92, 94, 112, 113, 116, 121, 123, 131, 143, 145, 150, 156, 159, 189, 202 (1971–1996, 2005, 2007).

Imlay, Talbot C., and Monica Duffy Toft, eds., *The Fog of Peace and War Planning: Military and Strategic Planning Under Uncertainty.* London: Routledge, 2006.

Irving, David. *Göring—A Biography.* New York: Morrow, 1989.

——. *The Rise and Fall of the Luftwaffe: The Life of Field Marshal Erich Milch.* Boston: Little, Brown, 1973.

Jabs, Hans Joachim. "De la 'guerre assise' à la 'guerre éclair' sur Messerschmitt 110." *Icare* vol. 2, no. 14 (Jan. 1986), *La Bataille de France 1939/40: Luftwaffe*: 67–73.

Jackson, A. J. *The de Havilland Tiger Moth. Aircraft in Profile* No. 132. Leatherhead, Surrey, UK: Profile Publications, 1966.

Jackson, Julian. *The Fall of France: The Nazi Invasion of 1940.* New York: Oxford, 2003.

Jackson, Robert. *The Air War over France, May–June 1940.* London: Ian Allan, 1974.

James, Derek N. *Schneider Trophy Aircraft, 1913–1931.* London: Putnam, 1981.

James, Lawrence. *Aristocrats: Power, Grace, and Decadence: Britain's Great Ruling Classes from 1066 to the Present.* New York: St. Martin's Press, 2010.

James, T. C. G. *Air Defence of Great Britain.* Vol. 2, *The Battle of Britain.* Edited with introduction by Sebastian Cox. London: Frank Cass, 2000.

——. *Air Defence of Great Britain.* Vol. 1, *The Growth of the Fighter Command, 1936–1940.* Edited with introduction by Sebastian Cox. London: Whitehall History Publishing/Frank Cass, 2002.

Jarrett, Philip, ed. *Biplane to Monoplane—Aircraft Development, 1919–1939.* Putnam's History of Aircraft. London: Putnam, 1997.

Jefford, W/Cdr. C. G. *RAF Squadrons: A Comprehensive Record of the Movement and Equipment of All RAF Squadrons and Their Antecedents Since 1912.* Shrewsbury, UK: Airlife, 1988.

Jones, Kevin. "From the Horse's Mouth: Luftwaffe POWs as Sources for Air Ministry Intelligence During the Battle of Britain." *Intelligence and National Security* 15, no. 4 (Winter 2000): 60–80.

Kahn, David. "How the Allies Suppressed the Second Greatest Secret of World War II." *Journal of Military History* 74 (Oct. 2010): 1229–1241.

Kainikara, Sanu, and W/Cdr. Bob Richardson. *Air Bases: The Foundation of Versatile Air Power.* Chief of the Air Force Occasional Papers No. 3. Canberra, Australia: Air Power Development Center, Aug. 2008.

Keith, C. H. *I Hold My Aim: The Story of How the Royal Air Force Was Armed for War.* London: Allen & Unwin, 1946.

Kesselring, Field Marshal. *Memoirs.* London: Greenhill, 2007.

King, H. F. *Armament of British Aircraft, 1909–1939.* London: Putnam, 1971.

Kirby, M., and R. Capey. "The Area of Germany in World War II: An Operational Research Perspective." *Journal of the Operational Research Society* 48, no. 7 (July 1997): 661–677.

Kirkland, Colonel Faris R. "Anti-military Group-Fantasies and the Destruction of the French Air Force, 1928–1940." *Journal of Psychohistory* 14, no. 1 (Summer 1986): 25–42.

———. "The Aristocratic Tradition and Adaptation to Change in the French Cavalry, 1920–1940." *European Studies Journal* 4, no. 2 (Fall 1987): 1–17.

———. "The French Air Force in 1940: Was It Defeated by the *Luftwaffe* or by Politics?" *Air University Review* (Sept.–Oct. 1985): 101–118; reprinted at http://www.airpower.maxwell.af.mil/airchronicles/aureview/1985/sep-oct/kirkland.html.

———. "Military Technology in Republican France: The Evolution of the French Armored Force 1917–1940." PhD diss., Duke University, Durham, NC, 1968.

———. "Planes, Pilots and Politics: French Military Aviation, 1919–1940." *1998 National Aerospace Conference . . . Proceedings.* Dayton, OH: Wright State University, 1999, 285–291.

"La Coupe Schneider, 1913–1931." *Icare* 189 (2004) [entire issue].

La Forte, Air Cdre. Russ. "The Strategic, Moral and Conceptual Significance of Victory in the Battle of Britain." *Royal Air Force Air Power Review* 13, no. 2 (Summer 2010): 55–66.

La France des années noires. Vol. 1. *De la defence à Vichy.* Edited by Jean-Pierre Azema, François Bédarida et al. Paris: Seuil, 1993.

Lane, Brian. *Spitfire! The Experiences of a Fighter Pilot.* London: John Murray, 1942.

Langer, Rovika. *The Mermaid and the Messerschmitt: War Through a Woman's Eye, 1939–1940.* Los Angeles, CA: Aquila Polonika Publishing, 2009.

Langer, William L., ed., *An Encyclopedia of World History,* 5th rev. ed. Boston: Houghton Mifflin, 1972, 1138.

Larnder, Harold. "The Origin of Operational Research." *Operations Research* 32, no. 2 (Mar.–Apr. 1984): 465–475.

Lecreox, Capitaine de Frégale. "Leçons Méconnues [Lessons Unknown], 1918–1940." *Revue Historique de l'Armée* 2 (1961): 65–74.

Lee, W/Cdr. Asher. *The German Air Force*. London: Duckwall, 1946.

Leipzig (Germany) State Archives, Annual Reports of *Erle Maschinenfabrik* GmbH for 1940–1944.

Lemay, Benoit. *Erich von Manstein: Hitler's Master Strategist*. Havertown, PA: Casemate Publishers, 2010.

Liflander, Pamela. *Measurements and Conversions*. London: Running Press, 2002.

Lloyd, Ian. *Rolls-Royce*. 3 vols. including *Rolls-Royce*: vol. 1, *The Growth of a Firm*; vol. 2, *Rolls-Royce: The Years of Endeavor*; vol. 3, *Rolls-Royce: The Merlin at War*. London: Macmillan, 1978.

Longden, Sean. *Dunkirk: The Men They Left Behind*. London: Constable, 2008.

Lottman, Herbert. R. *The Fall of Paris: June 1940*. London: Sinclair-Stevenson, 1992.

Lukacs, John. *The Duel: The Eighty-Day Struggle Between Churchill and Hitler*. New Haven, CT: Yale University Press, 2001 [1990].

Lunde, Henrik O. *Hitler's Pre-Emptive War. The Battle for Norway, 1940*. Philadelphia: Casemate, 2005.

Lyall, Sarah. *The Anglo Files: A Field Guide to the British*. New York: Norton, 2008.

Lynn, John A. II. *Battle: A History of Conflict and Culture, From Ancient Greece to Modern America*. Boulder, CO: Westview Press, 2003.

Macksey, Kenneth. *Guderian: Panzer General*. Rev. ed. Barnsley, South Yorkshire, UK: Greenhill Publishing, 2006.

———. *Kesselring: The Making of the Luftwaffe*. New York: McKay, 1978.

Macmillan, Alastair J. F. "The Development of Breathing Systems: Contributions of Flight Research and Flight Trials." *RAFHS Journal* 43 (2008): 54 ff.

Maiolo, Joseph. *Cry Havoc: How the Arms Race Drove the World to War, 1931–1941*. New York: Basic Books, Perseus Books Group, 2010.

Marrett, George. "Don't Kill Yourself: F-4 Testing over the Mojave." *Flight Journal* (June 2008): 62–67.

Marshall-Cornwall, General Sir James. *War and Rumors of War*. London: Leo Cooper, 1984.

Martin, Paul. *Invisibles Vainqueurs: Exploits et sacrifices de l'Armée de l'Air en 1939–1940*. Paris: Yves Michelet, 1990.

Mason, Francis K. *Battle over Britain: A History of the German Air Assaults on Great Britain,1917–18 and July–December 1940, and the Development of Britain's Air Defenses between the World Wars*. New York: Doubleday, 1969.

———. *The Gloster Gladiator. Aircraft in Profile* No. 98. Windsor, Berkshire, UK: Profile Publications, 1966.

———. *The Hawker Hurricane*. London: Macdonald, 1962.

———. *The Hawker Hurricane Mk. I. Aircraft in Profile* No. 111. Leatherhead, Surrey, UK: Profile Publications, 1966.

McNab, Chris. *Hitler's Armies: A History of the German War Machine 1939–45*. New York: Random House, 2011.

———. *Order of Battle: German Luftwaffe in World War II*. London: Amber Books, 2009.

———. *The Third Reich, 1933–1945. World War II Databook.* London: Amber Books, 2009.

Meyer, Corky. "The Best World War II Fighter." *Flight Journal* (Aug. 2003): 30.

———. "Elliptical Elegance: Flying and Evaluating the Seafire Mk III." *Flight Journal* (Oct. 2010): 38–43.

Michel, Henri. *Le Procès de Riom.* Paris: Albin Michel, 1979.

Mierzejewski, Alfred C. *The Most Valuable Asset of the Reich: A History of the German National Railway* vol. 2, *1933–1945.* Chapel Hill: University of North Carolina Press, 2000.

Miller, Donald L. *Masters of the Air.* New York: Simon and Schuster, 2006.

Molina, Lucas, and José Ma Manrique Garcia. *Flak Artillery of the Legion Condor: Flak Abteilung (mot.) F/88 in the Spanish Civil War 1936–1939.* Atglen, PA: Schiffer Publishing, 2009.

Mortimer, Gavin. *The Blitz—An Illustrated History.* New York: Osprey Publishing, 2010.

Moyes, Philip, J. R. *The Bristol Blenheim I. Aircraft in Profile* No. 93. Leatherhead, Surrey, UK: Profile Publications Ltd., 1966.

———. *The Fairey Battle. Aircraft in Profile* No. 34 [Vol. 2, Nos. 25–48]. Windsor, Berkshire, UK: Profile Publications, 1971.

———. *The Handley Page Hampden. Aircraft in Profile* No. 58. Leatherhead, Surrey, UK: Profile Publications, 1965.

———. *The Handley Page Heyford. Aircraft in Profile* No. 182. Leatherhead, Surrey, UK: Profile Publications, 1967.

Muller, Richard R. "Close Air Support: The German, British, and American Experiences, 1918–1941." In *Military Innovation in the Interwar Period,* edited by Williamson Murray and Allan R. Millett, 144–190. Cambridge: Cambridge University Press, 1996.

Murray, Williamson. "The German Response to Victory in Poland." *Armed Forces and Society* 7, no. 2 (Winter 1980): 285–298.

———. "Strategic Bombing: The British, American, and German Experiences." In *Military Innovation in the Interwar Period,* edited by Williamson Murray and Allan R. Millett, 96–143. Cambridge, UK: Cambridge University Press, 1996.

———. *Strategy for Defeat: The Luftwaffe, 1933–1945.* Maxwell AFB, AL: Air University Press, 1983; Baltimore: Nautical and Aviation Press, 1990.

Murray, Williamson, and Allan R. Millett, eds. *Military Innovation in the Interwar Period.* Cambridge: Cambridge University Press, 1996.

Myer, Michael, and Paul Stiodonk, *The Luftwaffe: From Training School to the Front—An Illustrated Study, 1933–1945.* Atglen, PA: Schiffer Publishing, 2004.

Mysyrowicz, Ladislas. *Autopsie d'une Défaite: Origines de l'effondrement militaire français de 1940.* Lausanne: Editions l'Age d'Homme, 1973.

Nelson, Robert I. "Review Article: The Germans and the German Way at War." *International History Review* 31, no. 1 (Mar. 2009): 85–91.

Neumann, Franz, *Behemoth: The Structure and Practice of National Socialism, 1933–1944.* London: Oxford University Press, 1942; 2009.

Nielsen, Generalleutenent Andreas. *The German Air Force General Staff.* USAF Historical Studies No. 173. Translated by Patricia Klamerth. Introduction by Telford Taylor. Maxwell AFB, AL, 1959; New York: Arno Press, 1968.

"Notes and Comments. The Air War over Germany: Claims and Counter-Claims." *Journal of Military History* 72 (July 2009): 925–932.

Nowarra, Heinz. *Heinkel He 111: A Documentary History.* London: Jane's, 1980.

"Oral History Spotlight, Museum Interviews Adversaries Turned Lifelong Friends." *V-Mail, News from the National WWII Museum* 10, no. 3 (Fall 2009): 14–15.

Orange, Vincent. *Dowding of Fighter Command: Victor of the Battle of Britain.* London: Grub Street, 2008.

———. *Sir Keith Park.* London: Methuen, 1984.

———. *Slessor: Bomber Champion. The Life of Marshal of the RAF Sir John Slessor, GCB, DSO, MC.* London: Grub Street, 2006.

Osborne, Eric W. *The Battle of Heligoland Bight.* Bloomington: Indiana University Press, 2006.

Overy, Richard J. "Air Power, Armies, and the War in the West, 1940." *The Harmon Memorial Lectures in Military History,* 32. Colorado Springs, CO: USAF Academy, 1989.

———. *The Air War, 1939–1945.* New York: Stein and Day, 1980.

———. *The Battle of Britain.* London: Penguin, 2001.

———. *Bomber Command, 1939–45.* London: Harper Collins, 1997.

———. "The German Prewar Aircraft Production Plans, November 1936–April 1939." *English Historical Review* 90, no. 357 (Oct. 1975): 778–797.

———. *Goering: The Iron Man.* London: Routledge and Kegan Paul Books, 1984, 1987.

———. *1939. Countdown to War.* New York: Penguin Group Inc., 2009.

———. *The Twilight Years: The Paradox of Britain Between the Wars.* New York: Viking, 2009.

Pakenham-Walsh, Maj. Gen. R. B. *History of the Corps of Royal Engineers.* Vol. 8, *1938– 1945—Campaigns in France and Belgium, 1939–40, Norway, Middle East, East Africa, Western Desert, North West Africa, and Activities in the U.K.* Chatham, UK: Institution of Royal Engineers, 1958.

Parton, Air Commodore Neville. "The Development of Early RAF Doctrine." *Journal of Military History* 72 (Oct. 2008): 1155–1177.

———. "Historic Book Review: *Air Power in War,* by [MRAF] Lord Tedder." *Royal Air Force Air Power Review* 12, no. 1 (Spring 2009): 124–132.

Patterson, Ian. *Guernica and Total War.* Cambridge, MA, and London: Harvard University Press, 2007.

Payne, Stanley. G. *Franco and Hitler: Spain, Germany, and World War II.* New Haven, CT: Yale University Press, 2008.

Peach, Stuart W. "A Neglected Turning Point in Air Power History: Air Power and the Fall of France." In *Air Power History: Turning Points from Kitty Hawk to Kosovo,* edited by Sebastian Cox and Peter Gray, 147–172. London: Cass, 2002.

Peszke, Michael A. "The Polish Air Force in the United Kingdom, 1939–1946." *Royal Air Force Historical Society Review* 11, no. 3 (Winter 2008): 54–74.

Pile, General Sir Frederick. *Ack-Ack: Britain's Defence Against Air Attack During the Second World War.* London: Harrap, 1949.

Pois, Robert, and Philip Langer. *Command Failure in War: Psychology and Leadership.* Bloomington: Indiana University Press, 2004.

Porret, Daniel. *Les As français de la Grande Guerre.* 2 vols. Vincennes: SHAA, 1983.

Porret, Daniel, and Frank Thevenet, *Les As de la guerre 1939-1945.* 2 vols. Vincennes: SHAA, 1991.

Powaski, Ronald. *Lightning War: Blitzkrieg in the West, 1940.* New York: Book Sales Inc., 2008.

Price, Alfred. *Blitz on Britain: The Bomber Attacks on the United Kingdom, 1939-1945.* London: Ian Allan, 1977.

———. *The Luftwaffe Data Book.* London: Greenhill Books, 1997.

Pugh, Peter. *The Magic of a Name: The Rolls Royce Story, The First 40 Years.* Cambridge, Icon Books, 2000.

Quill, Jeffrey. *Spitfire—A Test Pilot's Story.* London: Arrow Books, 1983; Manchester, UK: Crecy Publishing, 1998.

Ramsey, Winston G., ed. *The Battle of Britain: Then and Now.* Rev. ed. London: Battle of Britain Prints International Ltd., 1982 [1980].

Ray, John. *The Battle of Britain: Dowding and the First Victory, 1940.* London: Cassell, 1994, 2000.

———. *The Battle of Britain: New Perspectives—Behind the Scenes of the Great Air War.* London: Arms and Armour Press, 1994.

Revue Historique des Armées. (Nov. 1997): 27.

Revue d'Histoire de la Deuxieme Guerre Mondiale 19, no. 73 (Jan. 1969).

Rexford-Welch, S/Ldr S. C., ed. *The Royal Air Force Medical Services.* Vol. 1, *Administration* (1954); Vol. 2, *Commands* (1955); Vol. 3, *Campaigns* (1958). History of the Second World War, United Kingdom Medical Series. London: HMSO, 1954-1958.

Reynolds, David. "1940: Fulcrum of the Twentieth Century?" *International Affairs* 66, no. 2 (April 1990): 325-350.

Ringlstetter, Herbert. *Helmut Wick: An Illustrated Biography of the Luftwaffe Ace and Commander of Jagdgeschwader 2 During the Battle of Britain.* Atglen, PA: Schiffer Publishing, 2005.

Ritchie, Sebastian. *Industry and Air Power: The Expansion of British Aircraft Production, 1935-1941.* London: Cass, 1997.

Robineau, General Lucien. "French Air Policy in the Interwar Period and the Conduct of the Air War Against Germany from September 1939 to June 1940." In *The Conduct of the Air War in the Second World War: An International Comparison,* edited by Horst Boog, 627-657. Oxford: Berg, 1988, 1992, 627-657.

———. "L'Armée de l'Air dans la bataille de France." *Recueil d'Articles et d'Études, 1984-1985.* Vincennes, SHAA, 1991, 183-200.

———. "L'Armée de l'Air dans la Guerre 1939-1945." *Carnet de la sabretache: Revue militaire rétrospective* 142, no. 4 (1999).

———. "The French Air Force in the War, 1939-1940." *La Lettre* [Newsletter], *Académie Nationale de l'Air et de l'Espace* [ANAE, National Air and Space Academy]. Paris, June 2004: 2-3.

Robineau, General Lucien, ed. *Les français de ciel: dictionnaire historique.* Paris: *Académie Nationale de l'Air et de l'Espace* [ANAE, National Air and Space Academy], 2005.

Robinson, Clark Shore. *The Thermodynamics of Firearms.* New York: McGraw-Hill, 1943.

Robinson, Derek. *Piece of Cake.* London: H. Hamilton; New York: Knopf, 1984.

Robinson, Frank, comp. *The British Flight Battalion at Pensacola and Afterwards.* Manhattan, KS: Sunflower University Press, 1984.

Roos, Joseph. "L'Effort de l'industrie aeronautique français de 1938–1940: La Bataille de la production aérienne." *Icare* 59 (1971): 44–53.

Ross, David. *"The Greatest Squadron of Them All": The Definitive History of 603 (City of Edinburgh) Squadron RAUXAF.* Vol. 1, *Formation to the End of 1940.* With Bruce Blanche and William Simpson. London: Grub Street, 2003.

Sarkar, Dilip. *Spitfire Manual 1940.* Stroud, UK: Amberley, 2010.

Sarkees, Meredith Reid, and Frank Wayman. *Resort to War, 1816–2007.* Washington, DC: CQ Press, 2009.

Saunders, Andy. *Finding the Few: Some Outstanding Mysteries of the Battle of Britain Investigated and Solved.* London: Grub Street, 2009.

Schivelbusch, Wolfgang. *The Culture of Defeat: On National Trauma, Mourning, and Recovery.* New York: Metropolitan/Henry Holt and Co., 2001.

Schlaiffer, Robert, and W. D. Heron, *The Development of Aircraft Engines and Fuels.* Boston: Harvard Graduate School of Business Administration, 1950.

Schliephake, Hanfried. *Flugzeugbewaffnung: Die Bordwaffen der Luftwaffe von den Anfängen bis zur Gegenwart.* Stuttgart, Germany: Motorbuch Verlag Stuttgart, 1977.

Sganga, Rodolfo, Paulo G. Tripodi, and Wray W. Johnson. "Douhet's Antagonist: Amadeo Mecozzi's Alternative Vision of Air Power." *Air Power History* (Summer 2011): 4–15.

Shirer, William L. *The Collapse of the Third Republic: An Inquiry into the Fall of France, 1940.* New York: Simon and Schuster, 1969.

Simpson, Geoff, comp. *Mortal Danger: A Collection of Nicknames, Anecdotes, and Quotations from the Battle of Britain.* West Malling, UK: Battle of Britain Memorial Trust, 2003.

Sinnott, Colin. *The Royal Air Force and Aircraft Design 1923–1939.* London: Cass, 2001.

Smith, Herschel. *A History of Aircraft Piston Engines.* Manhattan, KS: Sunflower University Press, 1981.

Smith, J. R., and Antony Kay. *German Aircraft of the Second World War.* New York: Putnam, 1972.

Smith, Peter C. *Impact! The Dive Bomber Pilots Speak.* London: Kimber, 1981.

———. *Stuka Squadron: Stukagruppe 77—The Luftwaffe's Fire Brigade.* Wellingborough, Nottingham, UK: Patrick Stephens, 1990.

Smith, W. H. B, and Joseph E. Smith, *Small Arms of the World.* Harrisburg, PA: Stackpole, 1962.

Snow, C. P. *Science and Government.* Rev. ed. London: Oxford, 1961.

Spears, Sir Edward. *Assignment to Catastrophe.* 2 vols. London: Heinemann, 1954.

The Spies Who Lost the Battle of Britain. DVD. 2010. www.boffinstv.co.uk.

Staerck, Christopher, and Paul Sinnott. *Luftwaffe: The Allied Intelligence Files*. Washington, DC: Potomac Books, Inc., 2002.

Suleiman, Susan Rubin. *Crises of Memory and the Second World War*. Cambridge, MA, and London: Harvard University Press, 2008.

Sullivan, Brian R. "Downfall of the Regia Aeronautica, 1933–1943." In *Why Air Forces Fail: The Anatomy of Defeat*, edited by Robin Higham and Stephen J. Harris, 135–176. Lexington: University Press of Kentucky, 2006.

Sweeting, C. G. "How the *Luftwaffe* Kept 'Em Flying." *Aviation History* (Sept. 2011): 36–41.

Tanner, John, ed. *British Aircraft Guns of World War Two: The Official Air Publications for the Lewis, Vickers and Browning Machine-Guns and the Hispano 20mm Cannon*. RAF Museum Series. vol. 9. London: Arms and Armour Press, 1979.

Taylor, Frederick. *Dresden, Tuesday 13 February 1945*. London: Bloomsbury Publishing, 2004.

Tegler, Jan. "From Fury Biplanes to Hurricanes: Group Captain Billy Drake's Adventures in Hawkers." *[U.S.] Flight Journal* (Dec. 2007): 23–30.

Teyssier, Arnaud. "L'appui aux forces de surface: L'Armée de l'Air et la recherche d'une doctrine (1933–1939)." *Colloque Internationale—Histoire de la Guerre Aérienne* (Paris: SHAA, 10–11 Sept. 1987): 248–277.

Thetford, Owen. *Aircraft of the Royal Air Force Since 1918*. 8th ed. London: Putnam, 1988.

Tillman, Barrett. "Spitfire and Hurricane vs Bf.109." *Flight Journal* (Oct. 2010): 44–48.

———. "Their Finest Hour." *Flight Journal* (Sept.–Oct. 2001): 16–34.

Tolliver, Col. Raymond, and Trevor J. Constable. *Fighter General: The Life of Adolf Galland*. Zephyr Cove, NV: AmPress, 1990.

Trenchard, CAS Hugh. *Memorandum, Command Paper Cmd. 467*, "An Outline of the Scheme for the Permanent Organisation of the Royal Air Force." 25 Nov. 1919.

Tucker-Jones, Anthony. *Hitler's Great Panzer Heist: Germany's Foreign Armour in Action, 1939–1945*. London: Pen & Sword Military, 2007.

United Kingdom (Great Britain). Air Ministry. *The Rise and Fall of the German Air Force, 1933–1945*. London. HMSO, 1948; New York: St. Martin's Press, 2000.

———. Cabinet [CAB]. CAB 106/282, *Abteilung* [Department] VI [Intelligence] summary of Luftwaffe states during 1939–1945, Luftwaffe QMG figures, and see also translation of the *Abteilung VIII, The Luftwaffe in Poland* (11 July 1944).

———. CAB 102/355, *Cabinet History of .303 Ammunition*, 1 April 1939.

———. Disarmament Branch, British Air Division, *The Supply Organization of the German Air Force, 1935–1945*. London, 1946. Reprint, Uckfield, East Sussex, UK: Naval and Military Press, n.d.

———. General Staff. War Office. *Fighting in the Air, April 1918*. Reprint, Uckfield, UK: Naval and Military Press, n.d. [ca. 2009].

———. *Handbook of Foreign Aircraft Guns*, A.I.2 [G]. London, Nov. 1942 [typewritten material with tabulated information], 123–128, 140, 151, 154, 157, 159.

———. M.I. 14. *Notes on the German Preparations for the Invasion of the United Kingdom*. 2nd ed. Jan. 1942. Uckfield, UK: Naval and Military Press, 2004.

———. Ministry of Aircraft Production, AVIA 46/288, "Ministry of Aircraft Production through AVIA," 1940–1945.

———. National Archives [formerly Public Record Office (PRO)], Air Historical Branch (AHB), AIR 5/299, AP 882, *CD* [Confidential Document] *22, Operations Manual for the Royal Air Force* (July 1922); AIR 2/5205; AIR 2/5246; AIR 8/287; AIR 10/1593 (2nd ed., *SD* [Secret Document] *78,* Nov. 1934), and 10/1594 and 10/1595 (3rd ed., *SD 98,* Sept. 1936), *Air Staff Memorandum No. 50, Data for Calculating Consumption and Wastage in War,* tables 1, 8, 16, 17; AIR 10/1644, *SD 128,* July 1939, *Air Ministry Handbook on the German Air Force,* 56; AIR 10/1648, *SD 132, Handbook of the French Air Forces.* London: Air Ministry, Jan. 1939; AIR 10/5551, AP [Air Publication] 3233, *Second World War 1939–1945: RAF Flying Training,* Vol. 1, *Policy and Planning.* London: Air Ministry, AHB, 1952, 48–107, 272–273, 529–561; AIR 10/5552, *CD 1131, Maintenance.* London: Air Ministry, AHB, 1951, 6–54; AIR 10/5570, *CD 1116, Signals,* vol. 5, *Fighter, Control and Interception.* London: Air Ministry, 1952, 43–50; Air 16/940–946, October 1939–December 1940; AIR 16/1023 (July 1940); AIR 20/1835 (11 June 1945); AIR 20/4174; AIR 20/6208 (1942), Air Intelligence Joint Committee; AIR 27/703, ORB [Operations Record Book] No. 85 Squadron, ORB No. 1 Salvage and Repair Unit; AIR 29/802; AIR 33, *Reports of the Inspector-General;* AIR 35/120; AIR 41/2, App. 13–14; AIR 41/14; AIR 41/21, *The Campaign in France 10 May–18 June 1940,* 273–285, 425; AIR 41/22, 12–28 and App. E, App. 13–14; AIR 41/65, RAF Monograph, *Manning: Plans and Policy,* n.d.; AP [Air Publication], AIR 41/59, *History of Flying Training in the RAF.* London, 1952; AIR 43/21.

———. *Psychological Disorders in Flying Personnel of the Royal Air Force Investigated During the War, 1939–1945.* Air Publication (AP) 3139. London: HMSO, 1947.

Vajda, Ferenc A., and Peter Dancey, *German Aircraft Industry and Production, 1933–1945.* Shrewsbury, UK: Airlife, 1998.

van Creveld, Martin. *Fighting Power: German and U.S. Army Performance, 1939–1945.* Westport, CT: Greenwood Press, 1982.

———. *Supplying War: Logistics from Wallenstein to Patton.* London: Cambridge University Press, 1979.

Vann, Frank. *Willy Messerschmitt: The First Full Biography of an Aeronautical Genius.* Sparkford, UK: Patrick Stephens, 1993.

Vasco, John J., and Peter D. Cornwell. *Zerstörer: The Messerschmitt 110 and Its Units in 1940.* Drayton, Norwich, UK: JAC Publications, 1995.

Vinen, Richard. *The Politics of French Business 1936–1945.* New York: Cambridge University Press, 1991.

Vivier, Thierry. "La commission G entre la défaite et l'Armée de l'Air future, 1941–1942." *Revue Historique de l'Armée* 176, no. 3 (1989): 113–121.

———. *La politique aéronautique militaire de la France: Janvier 1933–Septembre 1939.* Paris: Editions Harmattan, 1996.

von Ishoven, Armand. *Messerschmitt Bf-109 at War.* London: Ian Allen, 1977.

Wallace, G. F. *The Guns of the Royal Air Force, 1939–1945.* London: Kimber, 1972.

Wark, Wesley K. "The Air Defence Gap: British Air Doctrine and Intelligence Warnings in the 1930s." In *The Conduct of the Air War in the Second World War: An International Comparison,* edited by Horst Boog, 511–526. Oxford: Berg, 1988, 1992.

Warmbrunn, Werner. *The German Occupation of Belgium, 1940–1944*. New York: Peter Lang, 1993.

Watkins, Geoff. "Review Article: Recent Work on France and the Second World War." *Journal of Contemporary History* (2002): 637–647.

Weal, John. *Bf 109D/E Aces, 1939–41*. Oxford, UK: Osprey, 1996; Madrid, 1999.

Webster, Sir Charles, and Noble Frankland. *The Strategic Air Offensive Against Germany, 1939–1945*. Vol. 1 of The History of the Second World War Series. London: HMSO, 1961.

Werth, Alexander. *The Twilight of France 1933–1940*. New York: Harper 1942, 1966.

Westermann, Edward B. *Flak: German Anti-Aircraft Defenses, 1914–1945*. Lawrence: University Press of Kansas, 2005.

Whaley, Bart. "Conditions Making for Success and Failure of Denial and Deception: Authoritarian and Transition Regimes." In *Strategic Denial and Deception: The Twenty-First Century Challenge*, edited by Roy Godson and James J. Wirtz, 50–51. Edison, NJ: Transaction Publishers, 2002.

Wheeler, Air Commodore Allan. *That Nothing Failed Them: Testing Aeroplanes in War*. London: Foulis, 1963.

Williams, Anthony G. *Rapid Fire: The Development of Aeronautic Cannon, Heavy Machine Guns and Their Ammunition*. Shrewsbury, UK: Airlife, 2000.

Williamson, Gordon. *The Luftwaffe Handbook 1939–1945*. Charleston, SC: The History Press, 2006.

Witherow, Air Cdre. Mickey. "RAF Regiment Anti-Aircraft (AA) Defence WWII to Belize." *Royal Air Force Historical Society Journal* 51 (2011): 78–82.

Wood, Anthony Terry, and Bill Gunston. *Hitler's Luftwaffe: A Pictorial and Technical Encyclopedia of Hitler's Air Power in World War II*. London: Salamander, 1977.

Wood, Derek. *Attack Warning Red: The Royal Observer Corps and the Defence of Britain, 1925–1975*. London: Macdonald's and Jane's, 1976.

Wylie, Neville. "Loot, Gold, and Tradition in the United Kingdom's Financial Warfare Strategy, 1939–1945." *International History Review* 31, no. 2 (June 2009): 299–328.

Zimmerman, David. *Britain's Shield: Radar and the Defeat of the Luftwaffe*. Stroud, Gloucestershire, UK: Sutton Publishing, 2001.

INDEX